Verses against
the Darkness

Verses against the Darkness

Pablo Neruda's Poetry and Politics

Greg Dawes

Lewisburg
Bucknell University Press

© 2006 by Rosemont Publishing & Printing Corp.

All rights reserved. Authorization to photocopy items for internal or personal use, or the internal or personal use of specific clients, is granted by the copyright owner, provided that a base fee of $10.00, plus eight cents per page, per copy is paid directly to the Copyright Clearance Center, 222 Rosewood Drive, Danvers, Massachusetts 01923. [0-8387-5643-3/06 $10.00 + 8¢ pp, pc.]

Associated University Presses
2010 Eastpark Boulevard
Cranbury, NJ 08512

The paper used in this publication meets the requirements of the American National Standard for Permanence of Paper for Printed Library Materials Z39.48-1984.

Library of Congress Cataloging-in-Publication Data

Dawes, Greg.
   Verses against the darkness : Pablo Neruda's poetry and politics / Greg Dawes.
     p. cm.
   Includes bibliographical references and index.
   ISBN-10: 0-8387-5643-3 (alk. paper)
   ISBN-13: 978-0-8387-5643-0 (alk. paper)
   1. Neruda, Pablo, 1904–1973—Political and social views. 2. Neruda, Pablo, 1904–1973—Criticism and interpretation. 3. Moral realms. I. Title.
PQ8097.N4Z6158   2006
861'.62—dc22
                                                  2006012995

PRINTED IN THE UNITED STATES OF AMERICA

a nuestras hijas:
Amanda y Giuliana

Contents

Acknowledgments	9
Introduction: Light against the Darkness	13
1: Criticism and Ideology: Neruda and the Cold War	22
2: Realism, Surrealism, Socialist Realism, and Neruda's "Guided Spontaneity"	65
3: Realism and the Battle with Language in the *Residencias*	104
4: The Struggle against Alienation in *Tercera residencia*	148
5: Neruda's Moral Realism in *España en el corazón*	182
6: Blood and Letters: Neruda and Antifascism	228
Conclusion: Neruda's Work During the Cold War	266
Notes	291
Bibliography	313
Index	320

Acknowledgments

I began researching and writing this book in the summer of 1993 in Chile, thanks to a travel grant and later a research leave from the College of Humanities and Social Sciences at North Carolina State University. Over the course of this long journey I have relied on many people, most of whom are thanked below. I am very fortunate to have a core of dear friends in North Carolina who have always exchanged ideas with me, suggested readings, put my arguments to the test, and been an indispensable base of support over the years. These friends are: Jim Neilson, Greg Meyerson, Vladimir Bilenkin and Héctor Jaimes. Greg was most responsible for getting me interested in moral realism, which is the philosophical foundation of this book, for reading chapter 2, and for giving me feedback. Jim read the manuscript copiously and perceptively, suggested editorial changes, and recommended adding and deleting parts of the argument. Other friends also contributed greatly to the writing of this book in many ways: Neil Larsen, Misha Kokotovic, Roger Zapata, Gene Bell-Villada, Jaime Concha, and John Mertz. This book project began and has continued because of the many conversations I've had with Neil over the years. His advice has always been on the mark. Jaime, the great Neruda critic, has been an unofficial mentor for many years and an inspiration. Other people also helped this project along: In France, Alain Sicard, another magnificent Neruda scholar; in Chile, Federico Schopf, Soledad Bianchi, and Grinor Rojo. I would also like to thank those who helped me at the Fundación Pablo Neruda and the special collections director at the Universidad de Chile, Gladys Sanhueza and its director, Darío Oses. My gratitude also is due to Hernán Loyola for his indipensable work. Although our interpretations of Neruda's work differ at times, I appreciate the contributions made to Neruda scholarship by René de Costa, Emir Rodriguez Monegal, Enrico Mario Santi, Magery Safir, Manuel Durán and Saúl Yurkievich. I thank the two anonymous readers with Bucknell University Press who aided me in tightening up my manuscript and bolstering my arguments. And I owe deep gratitude to Greg Clingham, Director of Bucknell University Press for his friendly encouragement. Cecilia Hanan's and Billy Acree's help with the final preparation was absolutely vital. Finally, my wife Marcia, who by giving me peace after some restless years and by inspiring me, allowed me to finish this book. I dedicate it to our daughters, Amanda and Giuliana.

Different versions of chapter 2 were published in *Cultura de Guatemala* and *Cultural Logic.* An earlier form of chapter 3 also appeared in *Mester.* In the *Encyclopedia of Latin American Literature,* I published a condensed reading of "Alturas de Macchu Picchu," which has evolved and is now part of chapter 3. Unless otherwise indicated, all translations in the text are mine.

I would like to acknowledge the following permissions granted for the reproduction of texts: New Directions Publishing, for allowing me to reproduce the poems I analyze from *Residence on Earth;* the University of California Press for letting me reprint the poems from *Canto general* that appear in my text; Time Warner Books for the reprinting of "Ode to the Onion"; and La Agencia Literaria Carmen Balcells for consenting to my use of all the Neruda poems in Spanish studied in my book.

Verses against
the Darkness

Introduction:
Light against the Darkness

"La luz vendrá a pesar de los puñales"
—Pablo Neruda

ANY CRITIC WHO STUDIES THE WORK OF A TITANIC LITERARY FIGURE LIKE Pablo Neruda inevitably faces the quixotic mission of reading his work, memoirs, interviews, and letters, as well as the criticism. It is a challenging task that raises an important question: why write another book about Neruda? In part the answer is the surprising paucity of publications on the Chilean Nobel Laureate since the 1980s. Whereas excellent new and revised translations of his poetry continue to appear in print, criticism on Neruda's work has declined precipitously. For many a reader of poetry, including this writer, that is a welcome trend: Neruda the extraordinary verse maker has survived and the critical production has not overshadowed him. Even so, why did the criticism influenced by the Cold War disappear circa 1991?

To some readers the answer is obvious: because of the fall of Soviet Union and the Eastern Bloc socialist countries and the alleged lack of relevancy of Neruda's left-wing politics. According to this commonly held opinion in the Anglo-American world, Neruda's communist worldview, and that of Marxist critics who wrote on him, are hopelessly outdated, but Neruda the lyrical virtuoso, "the greatest poet of the twentieth century in any language," in Gabriel García Márquez's words, stands forever as a classic poet.[1] García Márquez, a Communist fellow traveler, would be the first to note that Neruda's virtues lie not only in his mastery of poetic style, but in his profound rendering of the range of human emotions, the complexity of sociopolitical struggles, the terrible plight of the working class, the great efforts involved in gaining class consciousness and committing oneself to egalitarianism, the horrors and benefits of capitalist "progress," and more. In short, Neruda's work merits recognition and praise for his prodigious talent as a crafter of verses and for his ability to make concrete in his poetry the sociohistorical, political circumstances and ethos of his day.

In large part my book avows for this integral portrayal of Neruda and thereby contests the liberal canonization of him during the Cold War and even today as a brilliant lyricist who had some extreme and mistaken political ideas. The fall of what Michael Parenti calls "seige socialism" in the

USSR and Eastern Europe was due to internal problems, but also and more importantly to the "wars, invasions and an arms race that exhausted their productive capacities and retarded their development."[2] For our purposes what matters is that the collapse of the socialist countries purportedly gave more academic legitimacy to the liberal and left-liberal criticism on Neruda and relegated the Marxist criticism to an interesting but flawed minority opinion. Consequently, the origins, development, and rationale of Neruda's Marxism could summarily be dismissed as passé.

Indeed, from the 1940s to the 1980s, liberal critics established the dominant view of Neruda's poetry in the Anglo-American world and in Latin America and helped create a Neruda who was undeniably and astonishingly talented and yet, after 1936, prone to the distortions of Marxism. For these critics, content matters, but only on condition that it be limited to individual vicissitudes of emotions, unconscious desires, and the poet's unique struggle with the poetic tradition. As regards Neruda's commitment to Communist politics and espousal of Marxism, liberal critics either refuse to delve into the complexities of the poet's worldview, or they denounce his political beliefs with scant or debatable evidence. While several of these liberal studies of Neruda provide enlightening information as regards interviews, correspondence, and analyses of his work, in paying so much attention to form, in the main they miss the evolution of the poet's politics, poetic theory, and poetry. Their Neruda is a visionary in the tradition of William Blake or Arthur Rimbaud with exceptional and innate verbal skill, a dramatic ability to channel his unconscious, a neoromantic impetus to absorb the world subjectively, and a propensity to be melancholic, nostalgic, intuitive, and anti-intellectual. And yet, in the Anglo-American and to some degree in the Spanish-speaking worlds, these aestheticist analyses have exercised considerable influence and have canonized a nonpolitical Neruda. Further, since the 1980s a handful of books have been published on Neruda and none has gained the renown of the earlier studies, thereby reinforcing the authority of studies by Amado Alonso, Emir Rodríguez, Enrico Mario Santí, René de Costa, Saúl Yurkievich, Manuel Durán, and Margery Safir (see chapter 1).

Thus, the liberal critics create two Nerudas: One rejects literary realism, is eclectic, and is a rebellious individual; the other adheres too closely to realism and falls into contradictions, simplifies historical moments, and misconstrues the main sociohistorical forces in Latin America from the pre-conquest to 1950. As these critics see it, the moment Neruda "politicizes" his poetry, its quality diminishes and his critical eye blurs. In the final analysis, this stance ignores his poetic method and socio-historical and geographical factors even in his great love poems (*Veinte poemas de amor y una canción desesperada, Los versos del capitán* and *Cien sonetos de amor*) [Twenty Love Poems and a Desparate Song, The Captain's Verses and One Hundred Love Sonnets]. But even if we entertained the idea of purportedly apolitical poems, we would have to place these in the context of Neruda's complete works. As Hugo Achugar has argued, "the book of poems, because it is in a dialogic relation with other books of poems or even groups of books of poems, becomes an element of what we call a poetic system."[3]

In arguing for the inherent unity of Neruda's work, my study follows critics who have not often been heard in Anglo-American cultures. Marxists critics Alain Sicard, Jaime Concha, and Hernán Loyola have convincingly shown that the *Residencia en la tierra* phase is dialectically related to the rest of Neruda's poetry and that even in his early years the poet was a realist. Concha, covering Neruda's poetic production from the earliest poems to 1936, demonstrates that the poet's world is a microcosm of the socio-historical reality he experienced in Chile and later in the Orient. Concha considers Neruda to be an exceptional poet who is nonetheless rooted in a given class, geographical, political, and historical reality and who is carried along and convinced by the prevailing radical political events of his day.

While both Sicard and Concha rely on sociohistorical and philosophical analyses, Sicard manages to cover all of Neruda's poetic work and presents perhaps the most impressive study written on Neruda both for its philosophical range and its depth of coverage. Sicard combines this philosophical analysis with close readings of representative poems that are grouped around different stages in his poetry or around thematic nodes (death, love, and so on). As the title indicates, *El pensamiento poético de Pablo Neruda* (The Poetic Thought of Pablo Neruda) is an elaboration of the poet's method and Marxist thought via insightful readings of his verses.

For the most part, I find Concha's and Sicard's studies to be indispensable. No serious reader of Neruda's work should forgo reading them. Indeed, to a large degree, my argument depends on the groundwork they established. There are, however, some weaknesses in these volumes. For instance, both Sicard and Concha rely on socio-historical factors and philosophical objectivity to such a degree that they underestimate the role of individual idiosyncrasies in Neruda's work. Also, as Sicard himself confessed to me in 1994, the Neruda he portrayed is too theoretical, too much of a philosopher of historical materialism. Sicard acknowledges Neruda was not an academic type nor was he attracted to theory per se. Indeed, he abandoned the Instituto Pedagógico in Santiago before graduating when he began to gain recognition as a poet. He was then primarily a rebellious poet who was an autodidact, who read voraciously, but who spent time conversing with friends, throwing parties, engaging in political campaigning and agitation, observing nature, and collecting all sorts of objects, including, most notoriously, sea shells. In sum, despite their invaluable contributions,

Sicard and Concha have a tendency to overestimate Neruda's intellectual interests and to underestimate the importance of Neruda's eccentricities and unique individuality.

My study engages with and contests liberal studies and yet it incorporates their insights as well, relies on the Marxist criticism on Neruda, and recovers the historical, political, and biographical context, showing continuities in his work from 1925 to 1954 and, by implication, to his death in 1973. At the center of my analysis is *Tercera residencia*. Neruda created this anthology to demonstrate the different stages he went through poetically and politically from 1935 to 1945. Readers of this text can compare and contrast the gradations and progression in his poetry, poetic method, and political consciousness. An uneven yet steady line can then be traced from the young Neruda affected by anarchist politics in southern Chile, to the poet who defended the Spanish Republic during the civil war, to the Communist who ran for the senate and later the presidency. Likewise, links exist between the vanguardist/realist verses of *Residencia en la tierra*, the openly political, epical, and critical realist verses written in support of the Republic and against the Falangists and Nationalists, and, finally, the incendiary yet accessible poems defending the Soviet Union and the antifascist cause during World War II.

By comparing the *Tercera residencia* poems to others published prior to, during, and after the appearance of this book (1947) (in such works as *Veinte poemas de amor y una canción desesperada* [Twenty Love Poems and a Desperate Song 1924], *Residencia en la tierra* [Residence on Earth 1925–35], *Canto general* (1950), *Los versos del capitán* [The Captain's Verses 1953] and *Odas elementales* [Ode to Common Things 1954]), I argue for an interconnection and progression in Neruda's poetic method and political understanding over the years and suggest that a dialectical relationship exists between the different phases of his poetic corpus in general and *Tercera residencia* in particular. While bearing intertextuality in mind and analyzing the texts closely, my argument also relies on an examination of the historical, political, social, and personal contexts that led Neruda to elaborate his poetic theory and write avant-gardist or socially committed verses.

Thus, in chapter 2, I weigh his poetry and poetic method against his left-wing contemporaries, particularly against Louis Aragon and Octavio Paz. Aragon, one of the main proponents of surrealism in France in the 1930s, later strengthened his ties to the French Communist Party and the Soviet Union and became an advocate for socialist realism. Chapters 2 and 5 attempt to demonstrate that Paz remained close to the Communist parties in Spain and Mexico and associated himself with avant-gardist movements, particularly with late surrealism. Indeed, eventually his aesthetic commitment won out over his radical political convictions: he remained in the artistic vanguard, but, after a sojourn through Trotskyism, he broke his direct links to Marxism.

Though Neruda shared many affinities with Aragon and the younger Paz and was affected by surrealism and socialist realism, these literary movements never fully took root in Neruda's work. It bears mentioning that he never took part in surrealist activities, never helped write a manifesto or signed his name to one, never was openly antagonistic toward the common man and certainly never considered himself an aristocrat of poetry (though he did, at times, play the role of bohemian rebel).[4] Unlike Aragon, he never wrote polemical essays defending socialist realism or overtly advocated it. In charting an independent course, Neruda developed his "dialectical realism" as he became more and more dedicated to the political demands of the Communist Party. As such, Neruda's aesthetic position is most clearly articulated by the aesthetic theory of Georg Lukács, although the Chilean did not seem to be consciously aware that that was the case. Neruda, then, evolved toward realism in both the aesthetic and political realms and held to his theory of "guided spontaneity" (*espontaneidad dirigida*). He was an eclectic, independent thinker who espoused many Marxist ideas and believed strongly enough in those ideas to commit himself to the ideals of the Communist Party from at least 1945 to 1973. In other words, although Neruda accepted many of the Party's ideas regarding international and national politics and engaged in practical political work (such as campaigning) he did voice his criticism of Party policy, particularly as it pertained to aesthetic matters.

In chapters 2 and 3, I argue that during the *Residencia en la tierra* years (1925–35) Neruda did not wallow sorrowfully in his alienation nor did he champion solitude. Though Neruda's *Residencias* are consciously autobiographical and subjectively inclined, they never celebrate his solitude nor make melodramatic claims for the individual. His economic status as a poorly paid bureaucrat in Chile and the Orient, in addition to his childhood experiences as the son of a railroad worker, constantly militated against the neoromantic and solipsistic foundations of bourgeois individualism.

Neruda had a nascent sense of sociopolitical and historical phenomena at this stage, allowing him to describe the social ramifications of his isolation. He understood that the suffering he was undergoing was not a natural or healthy condition: it was a social "illness" (alienation). Neruda's poetry, then, became a diary in which he documented subjectively the effects of this solitude on his life. The torrent of anguish Neruda felt was not a blanket commentary about human nature per se, rather, it was a temporary, alienating circumstance that afflicted him and from which he learned. Neruda used the suffering to create a better life for himself in particular and humanity in general. So the *Residencias* period must fit into the larger context of Neruda's life and work for us to better understand its place in *Tercera residencia* and in the different poetic and political stages through which he passed.

As in other works, in *Residencia en la tierra* Neruda shows a "passionate commitment" and a love of life that are the necessary driving forces of any great realist writer, as Georg Lukács has insightfully noted.[5] However, while this partisanship with and thirst for portraying reality is present in the Neruda of the 1920s, he was not able to do more than represent the alienating circumstances in which he was caught. At that stage he could only combat his solitude and estrangement with his poetry and his erotic encounters with Josie Bliss. He could expel the burning pain momentarily and could only express himself cathartically in somber and, many times, violent images. In other words, Neruda attempted to note excruciatingly his own active misery, and, in rendering this alienation, negate it. In so doing, he left the door open for an eventual escape from his social conditions, hence the tumultuous undercurrent in his relationship with Josie Bliss, present in such poems as "Juntos nosotros" and "Tango del viudo."

However, not even profoundly erotic affairs, whose effects did not begin to wear off until perhaps 1939, could save him from his estrangement from the Spanish-speaking world, his tedious bureaucratic post, and the arrogance of the English colonizers. Aware of his own alienation, Neruda created a realist portrait of his surroundings and his own anguish. His biographer and friend Volodia Teitelboim put it this way: "En un viaje al Oriente, en diciembre de 1976, tuvimos la comprobación física y ambiental del sólido realismo recreado que contienen las 'residencias' asiáticas de Neruda. Nos sobrecogió por la exactitud casi matemática con que se reproduce un espíritu y una atmósfera tan sutilmente captados" (In a trip to the Orient, in December of 1976, we got physical and social proof of the solid realism Neruda recreated in his Asiatic "residences." The almost mathematical precision with which he reproduced and captured the spirit and atmosphere subtly amazed us).[6] This realist depiction of his environment and the grave predicament in which he found himself allowed Neruda, in mid-1930s Spain, to transcend his own limitations and the alienating social relations that afflicted him in Asia.

Beginning with *España en el corazón,* the poet's political stances are more clearly associated with key moral or ethical concepts. Critics have commonly considered Neruda's ostensibly rash value judgments about the atrocities committed by the Nationalists during the Spanish civil war as signs of his biased politics. Though these critics also agree with Neruda's opposition to the Nationalists, they object to his expressionistic language and description of these Spanish fascists. And they charge that his "conversion" to Marxism impairs his critical acumen and blinds him to socialism's many faults. According to this view, once Neruda becomes a Communist he adheres more closely to Marxism and therefore portrays a subjectively distorted sociohistorical reality. For these liberal critics, from the 1930s on Neruda falls prey to political extremism and subjectivism. Nevertheless, as I maintain in chapter 4, these critics commonly misinterpret the poet's ethical stances and thus ignore the connection between his morality and the historical moment and the rationale behind Neruda's populist and Marxist ideas, or they disagree so adamantly with Neruda's political stances that they cannot represent them without distorting them. Critics, leftist and liberal alike, seem to regard Neruda's notions of justice and injustice, for instance, in either a reductionist or relativist way. Leftist critics recognize the socioeconomic factors that contributed to Neruda's political enlightenment and poetic evolution, but they commonly disregard his ethical vocabulary or take it for granted. Liberal critics charge Marxism with economic reductionism and then rely on biographical and formalist approaches to Neruda's poetry while linking his moral stances to a "dogmatic" Marxism.

By contrast, chapters 5 and 6 present Neruda's ethical stances as intricately intertwined with and dependent upon historical, political, and socioeconomic events. Thus, we can say that Neruda's thought and poetic method were informed by moral realism. The passionate opinions he expressed from the late 1930s on were strengthened by his knowledge and use of history and politics. In another context political scientist Alan Gilbert describes moral realism as the recognition of "progress in morality and advance in moral theory through successive approximations to the truth about human potentials for cooperation and freedom. Further, progress in moral theory rests heavily on progress in social theory."[7] Naturally, it would be wrongheaded to suggest that Neruda's worldview neatly fits this description. However, these descriptions of moral realism resemble very closely the type of poetic method and way of thinking that characterized Neruda's work. From 1936 onward, Neruda's poetry illustrated the intricate moral positions he developed and refined in the heat of historical class struggles during the Spanish civil war and the fight against fascism.

Neruda learned from the alienated moral and political consciousness that engulfed him in Asia, came to a more advanced awareness of ethical issues, and became more class-conscious as he was caught up in the horrors of the Spanish Civil War. The moral stances he took after 1936, naturally, were more objective or fallible to the degree to which they approximated the truth via the unity of human inquiry. In other words, Neruda's ethics inserted itself into a competing field of morality and demanded a rigorous defense backed by sociohistorical and economic events. In essence, he rejected capitalism on moral grounds as he perceived the destruction, economic despair, and alienation it wrought. As Neruda became infuriated by real socioeconomic inequalities and injustices, he searched for pragmatic, humane, and radical solutions gaining a better understanding of, say, the socioeconomic and cultural conditions in the USSR, the counter-revolution in

Spain or the struggle against fascism. Humanity can experience moral progress and gain better insights into "human capacities for moral personality" in struggles for classless societies.[8] As a communist Neruda clearly believed that the socialist mode of production was superior because of its egalitarian promise. However, he was concerned with the redistribution of wealth and with providing "the good life," a concept dating back to Aristotle that involves high moral understanding and development. So, for instance, in referring to the Soviet Union in his memoirs Neruda says:

> Amé a primera vista la tierra soviética y comprendí que de ella salía no sólo una lección moral para todos los rincones de la existencia humana, una equiparación de las posibilidades y un avance creciente en el hacer y el repartir, sino que también interpreté que desde aquel continente estepario, con tanta pureza natural, iba a producirse un gran vuelo.[9]

> [At first sight I loved the Soviet land and I understood that from it came not only a moral lesson for all corners of human existence, an equality of possibilities and a growing advancement in doing and sharing, but also I grasped that from that continental steppe, with so much natural purity, a great flight was going to be launched.]

In this context, the USSR sets a "moral lesson" by distributing wealth equally and by addressing basic human needs. For Neruda, then, the objectives of socialism have to do not merely with the development of the economic base, but also with political consciousness raising and, more poignantly, the evolution of morality. In other words, Neruda associates egalitarianism with sophisticated moral understanding.

Neruda uses a similar type of reasoning when recalling the forces that led him to become a fellow traveler of the Communist Party during the Spanish civil war:

> Mientras esas bandas [anarquistas] pululaban por la noche ciega de Madrid, los comunistas eran la única fuerza organizada que creaba un ejército para enfrentarlo a los italianos, a los alemanes, a los moros y a los falangistas. Y eran, al mismo tiempo, la fuerza moral que mantenía la resistencia y la lucha antifascista.[10]

> [While those bands [of anarchists] swarmed the blind night in Madrid, the Communists were the only organized force that created an army to confront the Italians, the Germans, the Moors and the Falangists. And they were, at the same time, the moral force maintaining the anti-fascist resistance and struggle.]

Here the Spanish Communist Party (PCE) spearheads the antifascist cause with its "moral force." In this context morality seems affiliated with the integrity, courage, determination, and vision needed to confront and defeat the fascists, with the destiny of humanity at stake. Thus, Neruda's radical political positions stem from his moral positions. They do not mirror existing socioeconomic conditions, but they describe them and call for the transformation of those very circumstances, taking core human equality as their final objective. Neruda's moral realism takes into account self-critical moral learning based on social struggles and aims practically at attaining "universal human flourishing."[11]

This political and moral philosophy is clearly illustrated in the last section of *Tercera residencia,* written in the early 1940s. At that historical moment, Neruda joined the antifascist cause and penned epic poetry depicting the Popular Front's battle with fascism. By this stage of his life, Neruda had a much more sophisticated understanding of capitalism, fascism, imperialism, and socialism and his poetry is consonant with historical accounts of events during World War II. Chapter 6 highlights Neruda's moral and political positions and shows that although at times hyperbolic, his positions are given a logic and defense by his verse. Neruda's *moral* outrage at, say, the Nazi invasion of the Soviet Union was rooted in and defended by *socio-historical* analyses. The light Neruda sheds on those bleak times has the real promise of illuminating a more just path for humanity despite the dark horror created by reactionary forces in the 1930s and 1940s.

The argument put forth in these pages revisits Neruda's poetry from a different angle than the one offered by liberal critics, although I too rely on detailed and close readings of his poems and books of poetry. However, like Concha and Sicard, I add emphasis to the sociohistorical context to show the matrix in which these poems emerge, the individual (or biographical) events that chart the course of Neruda's progression, aesthetically from alienated realism to dialectical realism and politically from anarchism to communism. By interpreting *Tercera residencia,* along with representative and complementary poems from *Residencia en la tierra, Canto general,* and *Odas elementales,* I reveal a dialectical progression and continuity in Neruda's work from 1925 to 1954. The more committed Neruda becomes to left-wing politics, the more realist his poetry becomes; the more insightful his grasp of the social totality and nature, the more extraordinary his ability to communicate that complexity to the reader.

1
Criticism and Ideology: Neruda and the Cold War

VERY FEW POETS HAVE HAD BOTH THE TALENT OF NERUDA AND A COMmitment to radical politics. Because of his unique ability to write verses, particulary love poems, and his unswerving dedication to Communist politics, he became an unrivaled celebrity. In *The Cultural Cold War: The CIA and the World of Arts and Letters,* Frances Stonor Saunders recounts that the Congress for Cultural Freedom, a U.S.-based, cultural front organization financed by the CIA, sent Robert Lowell to Argentina "as an outstanding American to counteract... Communist people like Neruda." Cultural Freedom member René Tavernier warned that Neruda "used his poetry as 'an instrument' of political engagement which was 'total and totalitarian'; this was the art of a man who was a 'militant and disciplined' Stalinist." Because he had won the Stalin Prize in 1953, Cultural Freedom members feared Neruda might win the Nobel Prize in 1964. As it turned out, Lowell went to Argentina, went on a drinking binge, declared himself the Caesar of that country, and made flattering remarks about Hitler.[1]

In the 1995 Italian film "Il postino" (The Postman), based roughly on Antonio Skármeta's novel on the friendship between Neruda and a young postman, the Nobel Laureate is at once lauded as a great love poet and criticized for his communist politics. The film suggests that he had a natural and marvelous ability to write love poems, but that, since becoming a Communist he was more aloof and unconcerned about his fellow human beings. Massimo, the protagonist, seeks Neruda's tutelage to express his overwhelming feelings of love for his muse. But only after Massimo's insistent pleas does Neruda give in begrudgingly to the humanisitic impulses of helping the young man. The Chilean poet is thus portrayed as a somewhat arrogant recluse who enjoys hiding in his small house overlooking the Caprian sea with Matilde Urrutia, while at the time seeking greater recognition. As a person, the film indicates, Neruda cannot be totally trusted because he has given in to communism. Massimo becomes a member of the Italian Communist Party but then loses contact with Neruda, who selfindulgently busies himself with poetry recitals and political commitments.

Toward the end of the film Massimo is trampled symbolically during a party demonstration in the streets of Rome. So, the protagonist is rendered as Neruda's innocent victim and the poet himself as a kind-hearted yet reckless man driven by political convictions.

More recently, in a two-tome biography of Neruda, *Las furias y las penas: Pablo Neruda y su tiempo* (Furies and Sorrows: Pablo Neruda and His Times) (2003), David Schidlowsky presents a well-documented yet partisan view of the poet. The title of his biography in itself indicates that, against Schidlowsky's own wishes, this is more than just a "scientific" or objective study of the Chilean poet.[2] He chooses an isolated poem from *Tercera residencia* as the title of his biography and suggests in doing so that this represents the "essence" (lo esencial) of Neruda's life.[3] Thus, from the outset Neruda is judged according to a desolate period in his life that the poet himself claimed to have surpassed—his desperate isolation in the 1920s and 1930s. A more fair-minded biographer might have considered that "Las furias y las penas" is placed in *Tercera residencia* as a stage that was later overcome as the poet become more politicized and his work became more accessible. But for Schidlowsky Neruda is rather that anguished individual portrayed in "Las furias y las penas" and in *Residencia en la tierra* and a calculating opportunist. So, for instance, the biographer alleges that Neruda's fame as a poet grew due to his ability to cultivate the right kinds of friendships.[4] If not an opportunist then he is described as lamentable. Schidlowsky attempts to prove that Neruda was ruthlessly impersonal and cruel in the 1940s, particularly with regards to his wife, Maruca Reyes (María Antonieta Haagenar). While it is true that Neruda was never deeply in love with Maruca and that he abandoned her for Delia del Carril, he did not leave "a su mujer Maruca Reyes y su hija enferma en una Holanda ocupada por la Alemania nazi" (his wife Maruca Reyes and his daughter sick in Holland occupied by Nazi Germany) as the biographer maintains, but rather she left Spain when Delia (La Hormiga) made her feelings for Neruda known to his wife and, outlandishly, moved in with the poet.[5] Neruda's and Delia's callousness creates a negative image of the poet that should be taken into account when assessing the poet's life and work but should be judged in concert with his attributes. But Schidlowsky clearly wants to lower the poet several notches: ever the opportunist, Neruda ostensibly abandons his child and wife and, moreover, does so during the fascist occupation. Thus, in one fell swoop Neruda's political and personal credibility is questioned, leading readers to believe that he was a cold-hearted egotist and nothing more. By the 1960s, according to Schidlowsky, Neruda had become, in the words of the great Peruvian novelist and anti-communist, Mario Vargas Llosa, a "soberano absoluto" (absolute sovereign) who nonetheless was jockeying for position to receive the Nobel Prize, inviting criticism from his adversaries and writing criticism of "Stalinism" following the Communist Party's line after the XXth Congress in the USSR.[6] In sum, then, Neruda is depicted as reckless, inhumane, insensitive, selfish, and unsympathetic. To be sure, his biography also highlights many of Neruda's accomplishments and positive characteristics, but in the end it is the troubled poet driven by his furies and pains that emerges in Schidlowsky's representation of Neruda.

These portrayals and countless more in popular culture and in literary criticism show how Neruda was both reviled and loved for his political stances and his poetic work. Liberal critics and public alike during the Cold War generally agree that he was an extraordinarily gifted poet, but they commonly consider him terribly misguided in his politics and personal life.

The most renowned liberal critics of Pablo Neruda's poetry—Amado Alonso, René de Costa, Manuel Durán and Margery Safir, Emir Rodríguez Monegal and Enrico Mario Santí—have produced thorough formalist studies with an aestheticist bent. While variations exist between those dedicated to poststructuralist (and especially deconstructive) readings, those who interpret Neruda's work from a psychoanalytic framework, and those who carry out close readings, these critics share a liberal worldview and a penchant for viewing poetry through the eyes of aestheticism. In other words, as Gene Bell-Villada writes in his splendid study on art for art's sake, "it is the idea that verse and fiction are without any moral, social, cognitive, or other extraliterary purposes."[7] And as Bell-Villada, Aijaz Ahmad, and Terry Eagleton have noted, this formalist tendency in literary theory in the U.S. extended from New Criticism up through various forms of poststructuralism, especially deconstruction.[8] Thus, unsurprisingly, several of the critical works mentioned above deal, in particular, with the *Residencia en la tierra* stage from this vantage point, whereas the sociopolitical content—that is, the driving political and historical ideas that shaped Neruda's consciousness during these years—is considered to be secondary. Consequently, in these books, Neruda's political stance and the historical context that shaped a text like *Tercera residencia* remain understudied. Admirers of Neruda's poetry to 1936, they either seem unable to explain why he evolved into a socially committed poet and accepted many of Marxism's principal ideas, or they consider this evolution merely a hiatus marked by political dogmatism. In the main, these critics deny, misread, or denounce to explain away troubling questions concerning Neruda's acceptance of leftist ideas. Most of these hypotheses have little to do with Neruda's knowledge of socialism, his commitment to the Communist Party, or the relations between his poetic method and his politics; rather, they are attempts to construe his life and work from an overarching liberal and aestheticist point of view. Since poetry is considered the quintessential genre which shows the greatest cultivation of form in a dense format, clear political views not coinciding with a liberal worldview are considered extraneous and excessive. Consequently, the liberal critics grant the impact of Marxism on Neruda but consider that its influence encumbered the talent of the poet and, therefore, they avoid exploring the intricacy of his political beliefs.

These canonical critics often fail to notice the rivalry between different political and philosophical currents within Marxism and the artistic movements that were inspired by it. In the 1930s there were philosophical positions as divergent as Georg Lukács', Walter Benjamin's, Theodore Adorno's, Karl Korsch's, José Carlos Mariátegui's, and aesthetic projects as diverse as socialist realism, constructivism, surrealism, and photomontage within Marxism. One thinks also of the great number of writers who were won over to Marxism at one time or another in Latin America during this period: Nicolás Guillén, Octavio Paz, Alejo Carpentier, Vicente Huidobro, César Vallejo, Miguel Angel Asturias, and others. Neruda, like many of his contemporaries, was drawn to the Marxism embodied in the Soviet Union for a variety of reasons, such as the social reconstruction and five-year plans which demonstrated in practice the national independence vis-à-vis imperialist countries, its anti-imperialism, and its social equality. Canonical criticism on Neruda has tended to underemphasize or omit reference to the practical and theoretical role Marxism played in his thought. So the nature of Neruda's engagement with and belief in Marxism needs to be uncovered.

While these are the dominant positions on Neruda's work, there is, however, a less recognized yet more persuasive critical trend stemming from the Marxist tradition in literary criticism. These critics do close, formal readings of the poetry and rely on biographical, historical, and philosophical information to explain Neruda's political stances from his earliest to his last works. Unlike the other critics, Jaime Concha and Alain Sicard put greater emphasis on sociohistorical and philosophical factors, and this approach gives their studies— especially *El pensamiento poético de Pablo Neruda* (The Poetic Thought of Pablo Neruda) and *Neruda 1904–1936*— a tremendous breadth especially when compared to the work of other critics, including the research of an essential Neruda scholar like Hernán Loyola. In their work a poem is located in and enriched by the interstices of philosophical, historical, and political issues. Concha and Sicard see poetry as a means of understanding the world that complements the social sciences and the sciences, rather than remaining a necessary antagonist to the same. Their methods are convincing because they generally mirror Neruda's own: examined in this multifaceted way, poetry more accurately acknowledges its debt to the heterogeneous synthesis of human knowledge. As Neruda put it in the context of his *Canto general:* "No hay material antipoético si se trata de nuestras realidades" (There is no anti-poetic material having to do with our reality).[9] While their work provides a solid foundation for further Nerudian criticism, it tends to undervalue the mediating role of Neruda's subjectivity in the transformation of objective reality into poetic representation. Sicard and Concha tend to overemphasize the role of objective factors and to underestimate the subjective impact of Neruda's political and poetic consciousness especially as regards the vital moral questions and positions which continually crop up in Neruda's books.

Two very different groups of critics wrote on Neruda's work from the 1940s to the 1980s. The first group concentrated primarily on poetic form and either ignored Neruda's politics or did not consider the well-known attraction to Marxism among the intellectuals and artists of Neruda's generation. The second group came from the Marxist tradition and relied on biographical, historical, political, and philosophical sources to analyze Neruda's poetry and less so on the form. In what follows I analyze different canonical studies on Neruda from both the liberal and the Marxist tendencies in the criticism.

Liberal Critics, or the Content of Form

The Inspired Poet Shackled

The Uruguayan critic Emir Rodríguez Monegal was arguably one of the most influential in Latin America and the United States (where he held prestigious university posts). He was also one of the most ardent liberal cold warriors in the cultural realm during the 1960s, 1970s, and 1980s. A former editor of the renowned Uruguayan journal, *Marcha,* he became the chief editor of the *Mundo Nuevo,* funded by the CIA-sponsored Congress for Cultural Freedom. As Jean Franco has noted, *Mundo Nuevo* "was intended as a response to the Cuban revolution's hold on the imagination of younger writers and to the influence of the Cuban journal *Casa de las Américas,* which was widely distributed in defiance of the censorship that prevailed in many Latin American countries."[10] The name of the journal itself suggests the creation of a new world and a "new man," but certainly not a socialist world. And yet, even after the revelations of CIA funding became public knowledge, Rodríguez Monegal alleged that he was an "independent intellectual" and, as such, that he maintained "aesthetic and political objectivity."[11]

Nonetheless, Rodríguez Monegal's partisanship is self-evident in his approving analysis of Borges and with his sympathetic and critical assessment of Neruda. From Rodríguez Monegal's liberal point of view—which embraces literary pluralism, and which anchors itself in a relativist, antirealist position—Borges becomes the exemplary writer incarnating the best of liberal values. By contrast, Neruda is lauded for his talent as a poet as long as his poetry is apolitical. But once he becomes a Communist his work is tarnished with extremism. Rodríguez Monegal's liberalism depends on skepticism regarding representation and realism. For Rodríguez Monegal reality is always already an on-going chaos and absurdity, so any attempt to make sense of it is futile. In a poststructuralist turn, then, literature can never overcome the gaps and insufficiencies in language itself, nor can it satisfactorily approximate reality. Seemingly, the great writers, like Borges, always highlight the problem of mediation self-referentially by underscoring the ambiguities and undecidibility involved in writing. In sum, Rodríguez Monegal favorably contrasts the complex self-referentiality of Borges with the simplicity of the realists. In upholding a nonrealist philosophical position like this, Rodríguez Monegal also attempts to discredit Marxism per se by associating it with the Stalin years in the USSR and by associating literary realism with reflectionism—an unsophisticated empirical understanding of reality—and the optimism of socialist realism. Thus, he suggests that anyone who is convinced by literary and philosophical realism and is a Marxist must also defend a rigid and dogmatic position as regards literary and political representation. That is why Rodríguez Monegal exalts a (sometimes) liberal writer like Borges and then, as we will see below, focuses on an unquestionably talented but purportedly misguided Communist poet like Neruda.

In Rodríguez Monegal's view, Borges is a "true cosmopolitan," who, by taking up the banner of philosophical skepticism and idealism, is defending himself against the short-sighted realists. In *Borges por él mismo* (1980; Borges by Himself), Rodríguez Monegal argues that Borges sets out to transcend the traditional realism of the regionalist novelists in Latin America.[12] Borges, he claims, invents an "imaginary world," a world that purportedly does not have a direct correspondence with objective physical and social reality (10–11). The Argentine writer "no depende ni de la geografía ni de la historia sino de las palabras" (does not depend on either geography or history but rather on words) (15). Through his dreamy world, limited only by the constraints an individual author imposes upon himself, Borges "marca el final del realismo" (marks the end of realism) (13). For Borges, then, literature becomes a game and the world a text to be deciphered. Thus, Rodríguez Monegal argues, Borges teases out the ambivalences in reality in a way that realists are incapable of. Borges' worldview, Rodríguez Monegal openly admits, is solipcistic and similar to Berkeley's idealism (49), yet this skeptical worldview seems at least tacitly approved by Rodríguez Monegal.

In creating his renowned "fantastic" literature, Borges intends to challenge realism and realist representation deliberately and overtly. Indeed, in a twist of logic, Rodríguez Monegal alleges that Borges "al elegir como forma predilecta de la novela, la lucidez de la magia, Borges está denunciando precisamente la irracionalidad de la pretendida novela realista" (in selecting the preferred novelistic form, the lucidity of magic, Borges is denouncing precisely the irrationality of the so-called realist novel) (62). So, here it is realism, not antirealism, which clinches to and promotes irrationalism. Magical or fantastic literature provides insights into human nature and life which realist literature could never hope to give because it rejects the idea that the world is "an absurdity, an imperfection, senseless" as Rodríguez Monegal puts it elsewhere (80). According to his own logic neither he nor Borges can claim to know what reality is. To sum up Rodríguez Monegal's point then, since Borges considers reality to be chaos and life directionless and senseless, and since he attempts to portray this in his short stories, his work transcends that of the realist authors who believe that is not so. Borges, he explains, is not trying to evade reality in fantastic literature; rather, he is attempting to express "lo que la literatura realista no alcanza a mostrar" (what realist literature is unable to show). Ironically, it is through Borges' allegories of reality that he is able to represent the world in a much more complex way than the realists (69).

Rodríguez Monegal's stance regarding realism is clearly meant as a critique of the cultural politics promoted by the USSR. In fact, Rodríguez Monegal appears to uphold Borges as the archetypal antirealist in order to argue against socialist realism in the Soviet Union. The critic never engages in a sustained rebuttal of the socialist realist or realist positions; but rather lets his portrait of Borges, the antirealist, and side commentaries about the USSR make his case. For instance, in defending Borges' fantastic literature he makes the following generalizations:

> la literatura realista es tan "convencional," tan "artificial," tan "arbitraria" como la fantástica. Ambas son formas de la ficción literaria. Hoy que se ha vuelto a estudiar el formalismo (obliterado por varias décadas en la Unión Soviética y en la colonizada intelligentsia occidental), que el estructuralismo y el posestructuralismo han enterrado para siempre una lectura puramente temática del texto literario, estas palabras de Borges no parecen asombrosas. Lo fueron en 1948, y lo siguen siendo en ciertas provincias culturales del mundo hispánico en que todavía se lee a Lukács con veneración. Hoy es posible leer estos textos de Borges sin asombro pero con alivio de saber que por lo menos alguien, en los años oscuros del stalinismo, era capaz de pensar por cuenta propia en nuestra América. (70)

> [Realist literature is as "conventional," "artificial," "arbitrary" as fantastic literature. Both of them are fictional forms. Today, now that we once again study formalism (obliterated for several decades in the Soviet Union and by the colonized intelligentsia in the West), that structuralism and post-structuralism have buried forever purely thematic readings of literary texts, Borges' words do not seem surprising. They were in 1948, and continue to be in certain cultural provinces of the Hispanic world in which Lukács is still read with veneration. Today it is possible to read these texts by Borges without amazement but rather with the relief of knowing that at least somebody, during the dark years of Stalinism, was able to think on his own in our America.]

Rodríguez Monegal argues for his relativist stance as regards literature against the rigid defenders of realism and he does not engage with or even make any real attempt to understand the subtleties of Lukács' theory of realism; rather, readers of Lukács are summarily dismissed as hopelessly behind the times. Rodríguez Monegal confidently rejects Lukács' theory without acknowledging that the latter's work was dedicated to the dialectic of form and content, and that Lukács, living in the USSR, opposed socialist realism as it was being developed there. Here, as elsewhere, Rodríguez Monegal's liberal ideas regarding literature and politics might prove convincing because he does not address the realist alternative.

So what is Rodríguez Monegal's overall intent? What message is he communicating to his readers regarding Borges? Rodríguez Monegal's objective is to portray Borges as a great imaginative writer who has no need to cower to the "dictates" of realism because his liberalism allows him to follow his own "individual freedom" to do whatever he pleases in the literary realm. From this mainstream vantage point, then, there is no direct acknowledgment of a correspondence theory with reality; literature becomes the domain in which reality can be played with and confounded. Borges can then be praised as the apolitical and eclectic liberal humanist, as the "true cosmopolitan," as Rodríguez Monegal puts it. This stance is close to that of the liberal humanists as Terry Eagleton has described them:

> [S]eeking to understand everybody's point of view quite often suggests that you yourself are disinterestedly up on high or in the middle, and trying to resolve conflicting viewpoints into a consensus implies a refusal of the truth that some conflicts can be resolved on one side alone.[13]

However, while Rodríguez Monegal considers Borges and, by implication, himself, as "disinterestedly up on high or in the middle," he is all too willing to dismiss Marxist positions which might prove threatening to his liberalism. The result is that he, the critic, and Borges, the writer, can appear detached, impartial with regards to politics, and can focus on the literary tradition and Borges's relationship to it, all the while remaining skeptical regarding questions of reference and truth. In that sense, Rodríguez Monegal's study finds its kinship in poststructuralism which, as Aijaz Ahmad has eloquently argued, is virtually indistinguishable from liberalism.[14]

Rodríguez Monegal's liberal position, expressed in his study on Borges, carries over to his analysis of Neruda. Although he makes available essential biographical material and often offers penetrating commentaries on Neruda's work, Rodríguez Monegal's own, centrist, and anticommunist mindset overwhelms his putative objectivity.

In *El viajero inmóvil* (The Immobile Traveler) (1966) Rodríguez Monegal provides invaluable biographical information on Neruda from interviews and unpublished letters, and the first half of his book largely depends on these sources.[15] He coordinates the events chronologically and links the different stages of Neruda's life and work together. He thus manages to play the role of neutral observer who attempts to understand the poet's itinerary from Neruda's point of view. However, from this first section of the book on, where Rodríguez Monegal briefly analyzes Neruda's poetic output while still conveying germaine biographical information, the critic begins making more partisan interventions. Rodríguez Monegal's subtle reading of Neruda suggests that there is a divide between lived experience and political consciousness, and that the latter obfuscates poetic vision. Rodríguez Monegal thus establishes a dichotomy between the "poeta profundo" (the profound poet) and the poet's own seemingly limiting and unnatural leftist politics. Neruda, he declares, "escribe lo que su conciencia política le dicta, no lo que su vivencia creadora le habría inspirado" (writes what his political conscience dictates to him, not what his creative life would have inspired in him) (259). Neruda's essential poetic self, so to speak, does not change even though he might be under the sway of Marxism because the Communist ideas to which Neruda adheres are at one and the same time understandable and objectionable (foreign). This explains why Rodríguez Monegal describes Neruda's life and poetry so favorably for most of *Viajero inmóvil* but then charges the Neruda of *Canto general* with dogmatism and demagoguery. From Rodríguez Monegal's point of view, the poet's "profound" self surrenders to political passion and rigidity. At heart, for the Uruguayan critic, Neruda dedicates himself to the exploration of the self and humanity, but recognizes that life is chaotic and irrational, and believes that any attempt to build a better world is futile.

Rodríguez Monegal arrives at these conclusions because he considers that Neruda's poetic self was already established by *Residencia en la tierra* and that, fundamentally, his mission did not change from that point on. He agrees with the Spanish poet Juan Ramón Jiménez that *Residencia en la tierra* is above all a chaotic and unconscious world where the irrational takes center stage (87). It is a well-founded argument based on Neruda's letters from the late 1920s, when he was swallowed by his isolation in Asia. Neruda sees his task as writing about his suffering and the mysteries of life and therefore becomes something of a "prophetic" figure: "el poeta debe ser una superstición, un ser mítico" (poets should be a superstition, mythic beings) (67). The poet's profound self, following in the tracks of the great visionaries (Blake, Rimbaud, Perse), attempts to absorb the world as a mystical but secular experience. Rodríguez Monegal argues that Neruda is ravaged by his exploration of reality and his search for the mystical, magical, and mysterious. In this regard, Neruda differs little if at all from the Borges portrayed above: he is a visionary who looks beyond immediate reality to seize the deeper, ephemeral reality that escapes the eye of the observer; he is a secular prophet who, like the early Rubén Darío or Blake, makes a religion out of literature.

This might explain how Neruda arrived at his poetic theory, but it leaves one wondering how he became a political radical. Rodríguez Monegal is well aware of this objection, but he is not willing to fully concede that Neruda is a Marxist who lived and breathed the dialectic and whose conscious acceptance of Marxist ideas emerged from his experience. In the following passage he returns to a subtle division between the poet's emotional self and political beliefs:

> Neruda llega a estas convicciones (el materialismo dialéctico) por el camino de una experiencia existencial muy honda, ayudado por su capacidad de visionario, adherido a la realidad más concreta y en medio de una lucha terrible. No llega por el camino de la especulación intelectual ni por la lectura de los especialistas filosóficos. De ahí que en su vocabulario, como en su poesía, sea imprescindible encontrar siempre el tono afectivo, la intuición central, la iluminación poética. (212)

> [Neruda arrives at these convictions (dialectical materialism) via a deep existencial experience, helped along by his talent as visionary, adhering to a most concrete reality and amidst a terrible struggle. He does not arrive via the road of intellectual speculation nor via readings of expert philosophers. So it is that in his vocabulary, as in his poetry, the affective tone, key intuitions and poetic illumination are ever-present.]

Rodríguez Monegal is undoubtedly right that Neruda came to dialectical materialism through his lived experience and not through intellectual or academic speculation. Being the autodidact he was, with an immense personal library, Neruda borrowed from various intellectual channels, but not from the traditional, academic avenues. As E. P. Thompson demonstrates in the case of Blake, Neruda's learning was also likely "eccentric" and "eclectic." As in Blake's case, Neruda was also very critical of, if not hostile to academicism, but this was the case for many Latin American poets. It is more the norm than the exception.[16] The poet is a rebel who rejects traditionalism and bourgeois society as such, but this does not make him anti-intellectual or fundamentally driven only by emotions. Rather Neruda's emotions feed off of his intellect and vice versa.

Since Rodríguez Monegal concentrates on the emotional fountain of inspiration, it often leads him to discard the poignant and complex ideas in Neruda's poetry. As he does so, and as the content becomes more political, Rodríguez Monegal's own analysis becomes much more subjective, especially when he turns to *Canto general* (1950). He considers that since this book was "fomentado por un partido político" (fomented by a political party), namely the Chilean Communist Party, that it is "una pieza de propaganda" (a piece of propaganda) (236) because it portrays history in a one-sided way. Rodríguez Monegal claims *Canto general* is "esencialmente periodística y tiene el vigor, la parcialidad, la demagogia y hasta el terrorismo de los titulares de periódicos" (essentially journalistic and it has the vigor, the partiality, the demogoguery and even the terrorism of newspaper headlines) (238). By siding with the oppressed and marginalized throughout *Canto general*, Rodríguez Monegal asserts, Neruda ignores the significant contributions Spain made and has made to Latin America, and he foments anti-Spanish sentiments. Neruda's emotions blur his vision of the conquest as well as the colonial and modern periods of Latin American history.

To demonstrate the anti-Spanish tendency in this work, Rodríguez Monegal turns to Neruda's portrayal of the conquistadors, who are ostensibly represented as evil men. But what about the complex portrait of—to name one instance—Balboa, who is vehemently condemned in one poem as a human being who has allowed the lowest of instincts to govern him, and, in the following poem, is honored for his discovery of the Pacific Ocean and for his curiosity? In the second of these poems, Neruda attempts to understand the social context that led the Spanish explorer to devalue himself. At the very beginning of the conquistadors section, Neruda discusses the sociohistorical circumstances that weighed upon these Spaniards and recognizes that "el hambre echa los dados" (hunger throws the dice).[17] Economic hardship and necessity go a long way to limiting the conquistadors' freedom, and, as such submit them to a desperate and alienating life. Yet their class position does not condone the horrible acts that they committed; in spite of their class they became pawns in the Spanish conquest and colonization.

Neruda does not refrain from denouncing the conquistadors while attempting to grasp their own historical reality. At the end of this section of the book Neruda shows how well he has understood the dialectical method as an approximation of a contradictory objective reality: "La luz"—the Spanish "*civilizing mission*"—"vino a pesar de los puñales" (Light came despite the daggers) (77). In one verse Neruda manages to communicate the complexity and conflict involved in the betterment of humanity as a whole. Measured by more egalitarian social relations, progress (la luz) comes about despite the horror of the conquest ("los puñales"). Here, as in many other passages, Rodríguez Monegal assumes that Neruda's Marxism is dogmatic and artificial, "primitivo y esquemático" as he puts in this context, and therefore woefully misguided and alien to the profound poet himself (238). According to the Uruguayan critic, the poet's thought is driven by a "dialéctica soviética," which simply does not prove to be convincing. In referring to the "Soviet dialectic," I assume Rodríguez Monegal means to underscore the artificiality of Neruda's Marxism: it is a foreign body that has infected the poet. This guides Rodríguez Monegal to a well-anticipated conclusion: that *Canto general* presents a history of Latin America that is "simplificadora" (simplifying) but impressive from an emotional point of view (238–39).

Rodríguez Monegal's portrait of Neruda as an emotional individual who came to politics in a similarly expressive and subjective way could more accurately be seen as a description of Rubén Darío. In the case of the latter, one could legitimately argue that Darío is drawn to a type of mysticism from *Cantos de vida y esperanza* (Songs of Life and Hope) (1905) on. The Nicaraguan poet makes this abundantly clear in his famous poem, "Yo soy aquel" (It is I). In this self-defense Darío takes on his critics and charges them with misreading his early work (*Azul* [Blue; 1888] and *Prosas profanas* [Profane Prose; 1896]). He alleges that his early poetry, which appeared to be under the influence of Verlaine and thus was perceived as a beautiful marble statue, was really grounded in tumultuous life experiences that marked his soul, which was "Sentimental, sensible, sensitiva" (sentimental, sensitive, sensory).[18] In this autobiographical retort, Darío states that his work was driven by passion and not by the finesse of artificiality:

> todo ansia, todo ardor, sensación pura,
> y vigor natural; y sin falsía,
> y sin comedia y sin literatura...
> si hay un alma sincera, ésa es la mía (341).
>
> [all was anxiety, all was fervor, pure sensations,
> and natural vigor; and without duplicity,
> and without comedy and without literature...
> if there is an honest soul, it is mine.]

In stanzas reminiscent of Neruda's life in Asia, Darío goes on to describe his Dantean descent during which he was tempted by the ivory tower and his heart became filled with bitterness toward the world. Darío finds the strength to summon the emotional courage to carry on when he turns to religion and recognizes the fundamental importance of faith's "fuego interior" (interior fire) as the answer to the solitude that plagues him (343). Here, then, we have a classic Romantic case of the importance of the inner life in literature: a raging inspiration consumes his life and allows him to triumph over his own misery. The final solution is divine inspiration and cultivation of the inner life. As Octavio Paz puts it in his brilliant chapter on Darío, for the Nicaraguan, as well as his contemporaries (the *modernistas*), art is passion.[19] It is an inner passion that derives from pantheistic ideas in the early years, and later from Darío's faith in the "armonía del gran Todo" (harmony with the great Totality) as he comments in "Yo soy aquel"(342).

While there is a parallel between Darío and Neruda—evident particularly in "Yo soy aquel" and "Alturas de Macchu Picchu"—as regards eroticism and passion as the very motorforce of poetry and the desire to absorb the world, they differ significantly in terms of the complexity of their ideas. Neruda was much more involved politically and aware of the Marxist ideas of his times than Darío was connected to panamericanism. Neruda was a nontraditional intellectual who became involved in the struggle for social justice in Latin America and throughout the world; whereas Darío was a great poet who, from the early 1900s on, took occasional political stances. Darío's own political lucidity and naïveté are evident in poems like "Oda a Roosevelt" (Ode to Roosevelt). In that poem, he denounces U.S. imperialism and praises its economic development; then he rejoins with a defense of Latin America as a whole by invoking its mestizaje, deep-seated faith, and ancient cultural history. By contrast, Neruda's works display a concerted effort to follow and reflect upon Marxism and to highlight the class struggle as the driving force of history.

I hope this digression about Darío helps to clarify Rodríguez Monegal's position on Neruda: the Uruguayan critic ends up describing a Darioesque Neruda who relied consistently, brilliantly, and dangerously on emotions as the source of his creativity, casting aside the arduous task of intellectual work. However, for the most part, Rodríguez Monegal's biographical section in *El viajero inmóvil* belies that conclusion. It suggests that Neruda was overtaken by passionate commitment that guided his intellectual and creative inquiries, that dominated his insatiable desire, as Brecht remarked, to portray and learn lessons from reality in order to "teach us to transform reality."[20]

In the end, Rodríguez Monegal sees virtues in Neruda's and Borges's work and he deems both to be great Latin American writers. However, his liberalism, which I have linked to antirealism, pushes him to criticize Neruda's Marxism as extreme and as un-naturally associated with this renowned poet, whereas Borges best represents Rodríguez Monegal's own aesthetic and political positions.

Neruda as Prophet

We can observe a similar contrast between Enrico Mario Santí's superb study of Octavio Paz's work and his book on Neruda. Santí is Rodríguez Monegal's former student and collaborator who shares many of his mentor's ideas on literature. In his book on Paz, *El acto de palabras: estudios y diálogos con Octavio Paz* (1997) (The Act of Words: Studies and Dialogues with Octavio Paz), Santí's own aesthetic and political stance is largely consonant with Paz's own views on art and politics. Focusing on the evolution of his political and artistic ideas throughout Paz's life, Santí dedicates himself to developing an intellectual biography of the Mexican essayist and poet. More importantly, his study follows in the tracks of Paz's thought, filling in the details with indispensible unpublished letters, personal interviews, and thorough archival research. There is no question that this study does Paz justice, in part because Santí and Paz have the same point of view. By contrast, in *Pablo Neruda: The Poetics of Prophecy* (1982), Santí finds it difficult if not impossible to repeat the method, owing to his political differences with Neruda. Therefore, Santí creates a Neruda who is a neo-Romantic prophet-poet grappling with the poetic tradition. Neruda's Marxism, the source of his intellectual formation and his political commitment, is consistently passed over. As in the case of Rodríguez Monegal's book, Neruda is considered to be a great poet who went astray politically, but who redeemed himself in his work from *Estravagario* on because he ostensibly became skeptical regarding socialism and thus returned to his private life as the source of inspiration.

Santí's rendering of Paz is favorable because it dovetails with the critic's own political and aesthetic stances, in which the latter takes precedence over the former. The absolute independence or right of the writer to select his own form becomes the primary consideration, and content depends on that choice. In fact, Paz and Santí perceive the political and aesthetic as realms that affect each other but, ultimately, the individual artist chooses his literary form on his own accord without any imposition from left-wing politics. Even during the Spanish civil war, Santí asserts correctly, Paz defended the republic but, as regards aesthetics, "seguía defendiendo el derecho del artista a crear más allá de toda restricción ideológica" (he continued defending the right of artists to create beyond the restraints of ideology).[21] While Paz committed himself to antifascism individually, he did not feel a need to change his poetic form and content to meet political ends. As Santí puts it, "los tiempos eran revolucionarios, no su poesía" (the times were revolutionary, not his poetry). Poetry demands a commanding presence and influence, whereas politics seems secondary.

Thus, Santí commends Paz's intellectual and creative versatility because of his conviction to remain independent and thus avoid "political" poetry. In the end, the Nobel Laureate's passage through intimate (personal) oeuvre, a very brief period of political verse (during the Spanish civil war), late surrealism, and structuralism, marks him as "el poeta más elocuente de nuestra historia literaria" (the most eloquent poet of our literary history) (257). This conclusion is anticipated in Santí's introduction, where he asks the reader, "¿Qué escritor o intelectual, hoy por hoy, se puede comparar con Paz en excelencia, variedad y abundancia de obra?" (What writer or intellectual, today, can compare himself with Paz as regards excellence, variety and abundance of works?) (18). Santí argues that Paz has been more influential than Neruda because of his "poética universalista" (universalist poetics), his concern with the human condition per se, and the eternal issues that haunt and delight homo sapiens (19). For Paz poetry is, above all, a way to discover oneself and to search for one's "Other" via the sacred and erotic. Santí observes that this aesthetic position is not a political position. However, it would be more accurate to say it is a political stance with which Santí agrees. Since he concurs with Paz's politics, like Rodríguez Monegal, he considers that he is being "objective" and, consequently, has taken a nonpartisan point of view. However, if we turn to Santí's discussion of the political and philosophical influences on Paz, the critic's cultural stance becomes quite clearly a political position.

In Santí's view, Paz finds his own poetic voice once he abandons his political illusions after the Spanish civil war (53). Having essentially been a fellow traveler of the Communist Party in both Spain and Mexico, from 1940 to 1942 Paz began distancing himself from the party after the Nazi-Soviet Pact of 1939, the assassination of Trotsky, and his strong disagreements with his friend Neruda. From that moment on, Paz considered himself a leftist who was critical of the USSR and was loosely associated with the Trotskyist "Left Opposition." Santí argues that from this period on, Paz moved in the direction of a "postura mucho más realista ante la historia" (a much more realistic stance regarding history) (44). At that moment Paz stopped deceiving himself politically and became more of a critical thinker (44–45).

But what does this mean? Santí never offers an explanation explicitly, but if we follow Paz's political itinerary the answer becomes apparent. After 1942, disillusioned with the Communist Party, Paz turned much less to Marxism in his intellectual endeavors and much more to schools of thought which, in my view at least, have had an unhappy coexistence with Marxism: namely, existentialism, psychoanalysis, late surrealism, and phenomenology. Although the presence of Marxism can be discerned in his classic study, *El laberinto de la soledad* (The Labyrinth of Solitude, 1950), it fades in comparison to phenomenology, existentialism, and psychoanalysis. Santí is thus absolutely on the mark when, in his long and very thorough analysis of *El laberinto,* he describes it as an "interpretación mítico-psicoanalítica de la Historia" (mythical-psychoanalytic interpretation of history) (203). The unconscious, myth, and solitude become the dominant themes in this essay on Mexican culture, and they overshadow Paz's observations on ideology and class struggle, save perhaps the chapter "De la independencia a la revolución" (From Independence to the Revolution).[22] From Santí's perspective Paz became more open-minded by following the pluralist path of liberal humanism. Therefore, Santí does not see any inherent incompatibility between Marxism and other schools of thought. It is quite the reverse: phenomenology, psychoanalysis, and existentialism give Paz's analysis in *El laberinto* a depth that would not have been possible if he had relied mostly on Marxism.

Consequently, Santí approves of the Paz who lived in France after World

War II. Having become convinced of the importance of psychoanalytic, existentialist, and phenomenological ideas during his nine years there, Paz became ever more skeptical about the possibilities of socialism, the power of language (always subject to the "arbitrariedad del signo" [arbitrariness of the sign], the word's "presencia falsa" [false presence]), and changes in human nature. At that stage, Paz became a "humanista existencial" (existentialist humanist) (241–44). As a result, Paz turned more pessimistic and settled into a rebellious defense of liberalism. Paz himself commented significantly, "Estoy más cerca de Nietzsche y de Freud que de Marx y Rousseau" (I am closer to Nietzsche and Freud than Marx and Rousseau) (184). This position is remarkably similar to Santí's political and aesthetic stance and quite distant from Neruda's Marxism. As we will see below, that is why Santí finds it so difficult to explain, without misinterpretating them, Neruda's aesthetic and political positions.

In *Pablo Neruda: The Poetics of Prophecy,* Santí argues, as he did in his study on Paz, for the separation between the aesthetic and the political. However, this book on Neruda is not nearly as sympathetic as his "collaboration" with Paz in *El acto de palabras* (the subtitle is *Estudios y diálogos* con *Octavio Paz*).[23] Indeed, Santí seems to consciously attack Neruda's poetic and left-wing ideas in order to advocate the same aesthetic and political positions espoused in his book on Paz. In this case, however, his aim is to deconstruct Neruda's work by following the tradition of Paul de Man and Harold Bloom. He emphasizes rhetoric per se and the virtual impossibility of linguistic reference, poetics as the "space *in between* intention and fulfillment," Neruda's relationship with the poetic tradition, the poet's neo-Romantic inclinations, and his role as a "prophet" who seeks absolute knowledge. Santí also contends that the trope of discourse that prevails in Neruda's poetry is allegory. While there are some valuable insights in this book, overall Santí's method misreads Neruda's work, revealing more about his own ideology than about Neruda's work. Santí admits as much when he states that he may "seem to be arguing for a Borgesian Neruda . . . for a prophet lost in a labyrinth who remained blind to the 'real' issues of human history" (17).

The key to unlocking Santí's stance on Neruda can be found in his skepticism regarding language and referentiality, a skepticism, it should be noted, that Neruda did not share. Before homing in on this question, Santí isolates the author from the text and then focuses solely on rhetoric and the question of prophecy in Neruda's works. He states that the "principal subject of this book . . . is neither religion nor politics but rhetoric" (14). By isolating the text and studying its inner workings and intertextual struggles, Neruda ostensibly has engaged—in Harold Bloom's terminology—with his precursors and his rivals in an endless jostling among stronger and weaker poets in their search for immortality.[24] Santí's analyses deviate little from

Bloom's; the former considers Neruda a Romantic poet who, following the Freudian Oedipal complex, rewrites, misreads, or swerves when faced with his poetic father. Thus, as Aijaz Ahmad has poignantly noted, for Bloom (as well as for Santí I would add) the Romantic becomes the modern, extending itself in time as an on-going textual struggle.[25] Furthermore, Santí argues that these texts can gain no approximately true purchase on reality because poetics is not "simply the answer to the question that the poem poses, but the space where the poet's desire plays itself out—the trace of the origin whose loss the poem dramatizes." A poetics "can be 'known' only in the mode of error" (19). Neruda is then thrust into the role of deconstructionist: he "dramatizes a radical linguistic distrust by showing the gap that exists between word and thing" (35). This is the result of Neruda's alleged struggle with language and the poetic tradition, not with sociohistorical, political, and economic factors. Thus, Santí overlooks most of the events that shaped *Residencia en la tierra:* Neruda's social alienation in Asia, the tedium of his diplomatic jobs, his own economic hardships, his distaste for the English colonizers in India, his love affair with Josie Bliss, and so on.

Like Rodríguez Monegal, Santí suggests that Neruda's natural self is invested in a metatextual *Residencia en la tierra.* His poems contend with others and show the futility of representing the world via the mediation of language. Neruda's political writing can then be seen as an aberration, as a period in which the poet was led astray in a deluded moment when he actually believed in the power of language to anchor itself in epistemic access.[26] Santí claims that after *Canto general* "any political content was put at the service of a poetry of introspection." Neruda's later books—his "apocalyptic" works as Santí calls them—mark "the beginning of an introspective pattern, a shift from external revolution to internal regeneration" which culminates in *La espada encendida* (The Burning Sword, 1970) (207). Neruda is thus cast as a poet who, during one period of his life synthesizes poetry and politics, but later abandons that course to return to the "self's idolatrous fictions" (206). At that point Neruda once again returns to his neo-Romantic roots, to the solitary poet who recreates the world for himself and invents a new language to incarnate it (17). Poetry becomes a narcissistic exercise and politics the reflection of the poet's battle with the poetic tradition and with the elusiveness of language.

In this regard, Santí's method gives primacy to formal and metatextual issues and relegates Neruda's political thought in books like *Canto general* to allegory. By doing so he can claim that Neruda was not a realist at all; rather, he opted for broad brushstrokes of reality and manipulated his representations for his own political purposes. "An allegory," alleges Santí, "makes no pretense of direct observation. Figurative language excludes the possibility of direct perception or even of a dialectic of subject and object." Rather than providing evidence of an "external referent that would provide an unequivocal principle of explanation," the "allusive language" in Neruda's "Alturas de Macchu Picchu" purportedly "maneuvers an enigmatic play among signs or texts." The critic's theoretical objective and Neruda's poetics seem to cross paths at deconstruction: "the poem deconstructs itself in the acknowledgment of its own temporal/historical predicament" (170). Thus, a poem that is considered one of the greatest sociopolitical and realist representations of the exaltation of Incan laborers and, by extension, the modern proletariat, and a denunciation of the exploitation of indigenous peoples and, by extension, the working class in Latin America at the hands of the Spanish conquistadors and the new conquistadors (the U.S. corporations), is judged as an impotent allegory. In fact it is an ideological manuever on Santí's part. For if there is no epistemological or ontological foundation to Neruda's Marxism, then it can be depicted as a system of thought that is ideological, in Marx's sense of the term, that is a moral philosophy and nothing more, with no more purchase on reality than, say, phenomenology.

Santí can then ignore Neruda's Marxism because it is perceived as a period of momentary misunderstanding and worship of the prophet Karl Marx. Santí maintains that Marxism is, in the end, a "modern, secular prophetic movement" (179). In two pages the critic manages to sum up his argument to this effect. Marxism should be considered a "prophetic mythology that stakes scientific and historical claims." Marx's belief in a proletarian revolution against the bourgeoisie as the road to a classless society, Santí says, forms an "apocalyptic paradigm of biblical ancestry which Marx, as the imaginative writer he was, skillfully manipulated for rhetorical purposes" (180). For Santí, then, Marx, like Neruda, becomes a writer who cunningly uses rhetoric as a weapon in order to win converts to the proletarian revolution. Suffice it to say that Santí never cites from Marx's works, but rather, significantly, relies on secondary mainstream sources for his Marxism. Nor does he think this topic merits any rigorous argument or discussion. Having associated Marxism with a mythic apocalypse and having dismissed its economic foundation, Santí can then suggest that Neruda internalizes this type of Marxism and works it into his prophetic form (181).

Santi's quick dismissal of Marxism's economic validity leads him to misinterpret Neruda's *Canto general,* and, of course, Marx's own work. A close reading of *Canto general* makes it clear that Neruda's Marxism was much more sophisticated than Santí imagines it to be. I could give several examples, but let us turn to "El oro." In this poem Neruda traces gold from its status as a natural mineral in the earth to its commodification via the exploitation of labor:

> Tuvo el oro ese día de pureza.
> Antes de hundir de nuevo su estructura

en la sucia salida que lo aguarda,
recién llegado, recién desprendido
de la solemne estatua de la tierra,
fue depurado por el fuego, envuelto
por el sudor y las manos del hombre.

[Gold had that day of purity.
Before plunging its structure again
into the dirty debut that awaits it,
recently arrived, recently extracted
from the solemn statue of the earth,
it was purged by fire, enveloped
in man's sweat and hands.][27]

This first stanza shows the natural relationship that develops between gold and the laborer, a relationship which is then radically altered with the advent of capitalism and the reign of the commodity, a period when "se despidió el pueblo del oro" (There the gold's people said good-bye). Neruda considers the nonalienating relationship between the laborer and the gold as something pure, as yet free from exploitation:

Allí se despidió el pueblo del oro.
Y era terrestre su contacto, puro
como la madre gris de la esmeralda.
Igual era la mano sudorosa
que recogió el lingote enmarañado,
a la cepa de tierra reducida
por la infinita dimensión del tiempo,
al color terrenal de las semillas,
al suelo poderoso de secretos,
a la tierra que labra los racimos.

[There the gold's people said good-bye.
And their contact was earthy, pure
as the gray mother of emerald.
The sweating hand that scoured
the snarled ingot was like,
the stock of soil reduced
by the infinite dimension of time,
the earthy color of seeds,
the ground charged with secrets,
the earth that fashions clusters.]

In this second stanza, significantly, the earth is personified as a laborer who fertilizes and cultivates the land and thus provides fruits of that labor. Neruda conceives the farmer as having a harmonious and reciprocal relationship with the land. At this stage in history gold is not yet a commodity; rather, it is judged to be a natural, communal entity:

> Tierras del oro sin manchar, humanos
> materiales, metal inmaculado
> del pueblo, virginales minerías,
> que se tocan sin verse en la implacable
> encrucijadad de sus dos caminos:
>
> [Lands of unsustained gold, human
> stock, immaculate metal
> of the people, virginal veinstones
> that touch without seeing one another in
> the implacable junction of their two roads]

However, in a dramatic and realistic conclusion, Neruda then compares the relationship between the worker and gold ("*humanos* materiales") outside of capitalism to the brutal dialectic between the commodity and the proletariat:

> el hombre seguirá mordiendo el polvo,
> seguirá siendo tierra pedregosa,
> y el oro subirá sobre su sangre
> hasta herir y reinar sobre el herido.[28]
>
> [man will keep biting the dust,
> he'll keep being flinty soil,
> and gold will rise above his blood
> until it wounds and rules over the wounded.]

In these brilliant verses, undoubtedly inspired by his life experiences and by Marx's own work, Neruda sums up the essence of capitalism. The worker offers his labor power, is exploited (he eats dust), and allows the commodity, the product of his labor, to rule over him. The object of his hours and hours of work becomes something alien and even hostile to him once it gains exchange value for the capitalist and circulates as a commodity. Once it has an exchange value Neruda says "el oro subirá sobre su sangre / hasta herir y reinar sobre el herido" (gold will rise above his blood / until it wounds and rules over the wounded).[29]

This powerful poem is much indebted to Neruda's experience and to Marx's *1844 Manuscripts* and *Capital*. In the latter, Marx states that the laborer "confronts the materials of nature as a force of nature;" nature in this case is not something alien to him.[30] Under capitalism the natural element is converted into a commodity via congealed human labor; "human labour," says Marx, "is accumulated in [commodities]."[31] And gold, of course, is both the raw material for commodities and "a universal measure of value, [for] only through performing this function does gold, the specific equivalent commodity, become money."[32] The capitalist's drive for surplus value can be attained only by exploiting the worker ever more. In Neruda's dramatic final verses, workers get driven into the ground and eat dust, whereas the commodity rises above and rules over the workers.

In the case of "El oro" and even the magisterial "Alturas de Machu Picchu," Santí misses the socioeconomic grounding to these poems, which makes them so much more than rhetorical exercises by a "strong" poet who needs to fend off his competitors. In his analyses of those poems it is clear that Santí is not as fair minded in his study of Neruda as he was in his study of Paz. Where Santí's own ideological and aesthetic beliefs mirror Paz's, his own liberal positions are irreconcilable with Neruda's Marxism. Consequently, he attempts to undermine Neruda's Marxism by making it ideological and alien. But Santí succeeds only in proving that liberalism cannot carry out a full-fledged criticism of Marxism, and as he advocates the dominant ideology, he sees no reason to do so.

Santí's rendering of Neruda has clearly left a lasting and debatable impression, one that can be seen as the dominant canonical interpretation. A number of other major liberal critics have followed suit, and, in so doing, have advocated in one form or another philosophical and literary irrealism.

The Master of Form

Like Santí and Rodríguez Monegal, Costa wrote a sympathetic book on the avant-gardist Chilean writer Vicente Huidobro, dealing quite reasonably and well with the father of "el creacionismo." Nonetheless, Costa's intentions to be "nonpartisan" fall by the wayside when he examines Neruda's work, showing his liberal antipathy for Marxism.[33] How can we explain this paradox? The case of Costa is not as clear as it was for Rodríguez Monegal or Santí. After all, Huidobro was at least a Communist sympathizer for approximately thirteen years. The answer, I believe, may once again lie with the critic's own political and artistic proclivities. Unlike Neruda, Huidobro remained an avant-gardist and a champion of "the new" throughout his life. Even during his years of Communist militancy, Huidobro, like Octavio Paz, never broke his ties to the avant-garde and formal experimentation. Furthermore, in contrast to Neruda, he broke off his ties to the Communist Party in 1947 and turned full circle to become an anti-Communist.[34] It is perhaps this combination of "freedom and heresy," as the poet Gonzalo Rojas put it, in both the political and artistic realms that made more of an impression on Costa than Neruda's firm commitment to Communist politics and to a more accessible poetic work.[35] Costa summarizes the situation this way:

At first [Huidobro] was content to push for a change in aesthetic sensibility; later he became more militant, and as a Communist he agitated for social and political revolution as well. Eventually, disappointed with mass movements, he came to espouse a total revolution of the individual. Naturally, he was considered to be something of a traitor: first to his class; then to the party; and finally, even to his poetry. From the beginning he was a figure of controversy.[36]

Like Santí's emphasis on Neruda's "shift from external revolution to internal regeneration," Costa is not as interested in the intricacies of Huidobro's political militancy as he is in Huidobro's "revolution of the individual." In comparing his books on Huidobro and Neruda the former is a more appealing figure because of his strong adherence to the avant-garde. Whereas his study on Huidobro is vital because Costa includes unpublished poetry, commentary on the poet's early works, analysis of his role in literary magazines, and detailed observations about Huidobro's relationship to modernism, cubism, and surrealism, *The Poetry of Pablo Neruda* covers a great deal of the poet's production but largely from a formalist position. Like T. S. Eliot's criticism, as Terry Eagleton poignantly notes, it "displays an extraordinary lack of interest in what literary works actually have to say: its attention is almost entirely confined to qualities of language, styles of feeling, the relations of image and experience."[37] As regards form, Costa, like Amado Alonso, is one of the most astute critics of Neruda's work, but he does not devote the same attention to theme. When Costa does engage Neruda's Marxist ideas, he does so, in contrast to his careful analysis of the same in his Huidobro book, without lengthy discussions and attempts to explain Neruda's radicalism from the poet's own vantage point.

For the most part, then, Costa's own hermeticist/formalist approach to literature in *The Poetry of Pablo Neruda* seals the poems or books of poems off from their external (and thus internal) references. Neruda's poems are envisaged as intertextually related at least as regards form, or the content of form. Costa judges Neruda's *Residencia en la tierra* as a hermetic work where poetics takes center stage. Thus, for instance, "Galope muerto" (Dead Gallop)—from *Residencia en la tierra* (vol. 2)—"is not based on external correspondences; it relates inward upon itself." Costa says that this poem does not refer to "something definite"; rather, it is a "poetization of undefined experience."[38] In the critic's view this "inwardness" is due to the poet's relationship with language; Neruda's struggle to establish himself as renowned poet. Like Santí, Costa concentrates on formal issues and Neruda's struggle to become, in Harold Bloom's words, a "strong poet." Costa too argues that as Neruda battles with language and his predecessors to become recognized as a poet, he also becomes a prophetic figure who seeks to represent the absolute (66).

While Costa puts emphasis on intertextuality and the internal relations of Neruda's poetry, he nonetheless feels impelled to comment on "extra-poetic" factors which visibly affect the form. As suggested above, Costa is generous in his assessment of Huidobro's political positions, perhaps because the poet was a Communist fellow traveler who became an anti-Communist, or perhaps because Costa himself softened his stance. By contrast, he is less tolerant and understanding of Neruda perhaps because the Chilean remained a Communist to the end of his life. Neruda's Marxist political stance is described in religious terms and thus not judged to be a serious intellectual commitment, but a subjective weakness. In a familiar move, reminiscent of *The God that Failed,* Costa reduces Marxism to the irrational and thereby sidesteps its fundamental arguments. Thus, in the context of *Tercera residencia,* Costa alleges that the poems are more like "pamphlets" written with a "missionary zeal" (90). Sensing perhaps that he might be perceived as too harsh and not objective enough, Costa adds that, although the poems are "propagandistic," they "make use of traditional literary form to achieve a certain effect: to persuade" (90–91). Yet all poems attempt to question or disturb the reader's received wisdom or conventional way of interpreting the world and attempt to persuade in way or another.[39] In truth, Costa is not making this benign argument but is using "propaganda" in its traditional sense as an attempt to persuade the reader that Neruda's politics is irrational. Thus, Costa shortly thereafter refers to Neruda's "new faith" and avoids any forays into the complex historical debates on Marxism. As in the examples of Rodríguez Monegal and Santí, Costa alleges that once Neruda commits himself to communism his poetic work becomes tarnished: "[Neruda] begins to voice societal concerns with the vigor of a pamphleteer and the conviction of a missionary. His new faith is in man" (92). But this point of view conflicts with Costa's acknowledgment of Neruda's naturally slow and contradictory *progression* toward a greater understanding of history and politics.[40] In the instance of religious conversion one expects a sudden, illuminating "awakening" by the convert, not a gradual consciousness raising that makes him more aware and hungry for reality. Unfortunately, Costa's intent, like Rodríguez Monegal's and Santí's, is to associate Neruda's Marxism with religion and thus to discredit the former and prove that his political beliefs are unreliable and, more importantly, a momentary lapse of reason.

This approach can also be discerned in Costa's critical assessment of the content of *Tercera residencia.* He comments, for instance, that in "Canto a los ríos de Alemania" (Songs to the Rivers of Germany) the "message is simple, even simplistic," yet Costa then states that this poem is "powerful and persuasive due to the literary form" (101). Once again, literary form, in Costa's view, takes precedence over content. By dissecting Neruda's poetry in this manner, Costa manages to appear unbiased because he focuses his analytical attention on the mechanics of form. This move sidesteps the need for a sophisticated study of content. Of course, the question remains whether one can indeed mark a divide between form and content in Neruda's or any poet's work. Despite his effort to briefly situate Neruda's various works historically and to comment in passing on the content, Costa fails to analyze the relationship between form and content, and so overlooks the inner workings of Neruda's Marxism.

In the case of *Canto general* Costa claims the middle ground by alleging that he conducts an "unbiased" account of the work. Critics, he notes:

> split into two camps over the contents of this text: those who opposed Neruda's militant politics and those who shared them. For each of these views there arose two Nerudas, one good, one bad. Depending on the critic's political persuasion, the early poetry was either decadent or artistic, the later poetry ennobling or propagandistic. There was no middle ground; both sides forgot that there is an art even to propaganda, especially if it is to be effective. (106)

But by opting for a study of the art (form) of propaganda (content), does Costa take the "middle ground" or does he not view content (specifically a Marxist view of history) as a static phenomenon? In his analysis of *Canto general,* Costa answers this question by maintaining that Neruda contributes to a "mythification of America." This move is possible if Costa's preconceived acceptance of the mythification of history and the emphasis on formal issues emerge from his own theoretical evaluation of the role of aesthetics in society. That is, Costa analyzes Neruda's work from the vantage point that is most familiar to him (his own formalist inclinations) and searches out what he already knows he will find in content (history as myth). But this method only reveals the weakness of his own aesthetic theory, where content is subordinated to form. So Costa reads Neruda as attempting to "convert" the reader to his "ecumenically mythifying" portrait of American continental history (108). Continuing with the religious motif, Costa says that at the beginning of *Canto general* the reader encounters an "authoritative biblical tone of prophecy" (112). Costa, then, dedicates little time to Neruda's Marxism and its ostensible links to Catholicism, and focuses instead on stylistic analysis.

In his interpretation of Neruda's work after *Canto general* Costa marks a divide between form and content, contending that *Odas elementales* (Elementary Odes), for instance, is "deliberately naïve" but not "without a certain sophistication" (145). But in making these observations, Costa refers to the sophistication of the poetic form; with regards to the content, Neruda's political optimism "weighs the text down" (153). Even if the former were true, this critique of poetic form would require a more lengthy defense. Thus, in my view the most interesting questions vis-à-vis form are never posed: What effect does this formal shift in Neruda's work have on the content? Why did Neruda bother "simplifying" his poetic form? Did this change allow for a more profound development of content? If so, how does it contrast with and complement the thematic concerns in his previous books? While Costa's commentary on form in the *Odas* is interesting, the absence of a sustained analysis of theme creates an undialectical divide between form and content (158–60). Consequently, the content suffers from an underdeveloped notion of poetry as "total imaginative construct" that is distorted whenever it is tied to a Marxist view of sociohistorical events (187).

As a case in point, Costa devotes little space to *Las uvas y el viento* (Grapes and Wind) because "the effort was totally unconvincing (except in the Soviet Union which, in 1953, had awarded him the Stalin Peace Prize)" (144). Yet, like Rodríguez Monegal and Santí, Costa considers *Estravagario* (1958), written after the XXth Party Congress in the Soviet Union in which the Stalin regime was denounced—a fact curiously absent from his study—as the book that freed Neruda from "his own literary tradition, at the same time that he managed to free his person from his social, political and literary past" (199). Consequently, Costa highlights Neruda's formal achievements and avoids the historical and political context that is so crucial to understanding this book. He finds that "*Estravagario* is important not so much for its political or personal revision of the past as for its successful adaptation of the tone and style of what has come to be called antipoetry" (180). If Costa were able to argue compellingly that this poetry is antipoetry and that in it, as Mike González and David Treece put it, "conjunctions are accidental, disconnected and thus purposeless" coming to "no conclusion" and producing "only an attitude of fatalism" then Neruda could be seen as turning his back on the dialectical realism of *Canto general* and *Odas elementales*.[41] By extension and more importantly, Neruda would be giving up on his Communist ideals. However, by referring to antipoetry Costa suggests that it contradicts Neruda's Marxist politics and then turns to praising form over content.

But *Estravagario,* not coincidentally, was written after 1954 by a Communist who, toward the end of his memoirs—*Confieso que he vivido* (I Confess I have Lived)—declared that after forty years of militancy he was content to be a Communist.[42] When Neruda sought out silence in *Estravagario* he was not looking for a refuge from the world. As is the case with *Tercera residencia,* it was a moment in the dialectic when negation had to be absorbed in order for it, in turn, to be negated. In other words, Neruda "asks for silence" ("Pido silencio") because the weight of the sociopolitical tragedy in the Soviet Union in the aftermath of the XXth Party Congress is overwhelming. However, it is clear from the context of this and other poems in *Estravagario* that he will come out of this silence and will continue his political militancy as a Communist who has learned from the errors of the Stalin era. Consequently, Neruda ends the poem with this line: "Pido permiso para nacer" (I ask for permission to be born). This moment is analogous to the one we find in "Naciendo en los bosques" (Emerging from the Woods) in *Tercera residencia,* where, after the poet portrays his own desolation and suffering he declares: "Para nacer he nacido" (I was born to be born).[43]

In his book on Neruda, then, Costa, like Rodríguez Monegal and Santí, claims to be balanced in his analysis of the Chilean poet's work, but Neruda's own artistic and political positions force Costa to take a clear stance: either he shares many of Neruda's ideas or he opposes them and retreats to his liberal principles. As we have seen, Costa chooses the latter.

The Revolt of the Unconscious

Saúl Yurkievich shares many of Rodríguez Monegal's and Costa's aesthetic principles and liberal beliefs; however, he claims to uncover the mystical and psychoanalytic origins of Neruda's writing. For Yurkievich the poet's genius lies in his explorations of the inexpressible:

> reveladora de los abismos de la conciencia, una poesía rapsódica, cuyo movimiento predominante es el descendimiento hacia lo oscuro, hacia lo extrañable, hacia lo preformal, hacia lo preverbal o por lo menos preoral, tal como lo expresa Neruda en múltiples textos.[44]

> [revealing of the abyss of consciousness, a rhapsodic poetry, whose dominant movement is to descend toward the dark side, the missing, the pre-formal, the preverbal or at least pre-oral, as Neruda expresses it in his many texts.]

Yurkievich maintains that Neruda's texts primarily deal with exploring the inner, deeper recesses of the unconscious and have less to do with rational intention. For instance, Yurkievich insists that *Canto general* attempts to reconcile an "ensoñación cosmogónica" (cosmogonic dreaming) and "realismo historicista" (historicist realism), but that this relation is really an irreconcilable antagonism (200–201). Following this neo-Freudian line of reasoning, Yurkievich argues that *Canto general* displays this diametrical binarism between the purely instinctive and biological on the one hand (the Id), and on the other, the rational forces (the Superego) that attempt to "harness" this chaotic, natural power. In Yurkievich's view, the attempt to arrest these natural, biological desires can never be fully accomplished, as is evidenced when he characterizes rational thought processes in poetry as:

> discurso político, prosario, de máxima determinación semántica, unívoco, la poética de denuncia, explicitud y aplanamiento, simplificación, despojamiento,

retórica de lo directo para corresponder a las urgencias de la historia inmediata, para extraer fogosidad del presente candente. (202)

[political, prosaic discourse, with a maximum semantic determination, unambiguous, a poetics of accusation, explicitness and shallowness, simplification, depossessed, direct rhetoric to respond to the urgencies of the immediacy of history, to extract fire from the incandescent present.]

As the previous quote indicates, Yurkievich considers that Neruda does avail himself of a conscious, historical poetics in *Canto general*. However, rational explanation necessarily involves some sort of "simplificación" (simplification) and "aplanamiento" (flattening) and, more importantly, it responds to immediate political and historical events in a spontaneous manner. The unconscious, then, subjugates consciousness. By representing rational faculties this way, Yurkievich can then declare that a poem like "La lámpara en la tierra, 'Amor América" (Lantern in the Earth, America Love) is *not* "trabajosa producción, forjadura de una voluntad consciente" (laborious production, a forging of a conscious will) (203). Yurkievich alleges that Neruda's creative power resides in his unconscious; so the moment he attempts to rely on a conscious method he succumbs to simplification. Given the ostensible defeat of rationalism at the hands of biological forces, the Argentine critic claims that Neruda's "afán naturalizante" (naturalizing desire) shows:

[una] suspensión de la conciencia reflexiva, una actitud anti-intelectual, un ahínco espontáneo, lo instintivo, lo prerracional, una obstinación en la iluminación intuitiva, y por ende el menosprecio de la intelección, del pensamiento abstracto, de la crítica y la teoría literaria. (206)

[a suspension of reflexive consciousness, an anti-intellectual attitude, a spontaneous enthusiasm, the instinctive, the pre-rational, an obstinant tendency toward intuitive illumination and therefore the devaluing of intellectual thinking, abstract thought, criticism and literary theory.]

Once again, if Neruda is portrayed as anti-intellectual and intuitive, then his political ideas become secondary or are not examined at all. Yurkievich's method, like Costa's, effectively erases the need for any deep exploration of Neruda's poetic theory and, especially, of his philosophy of life (a species of Marxism). Once the content has been classified as "instinctive," "prerational," "spontaneous," or "anti-intellectual," the critic's own posture can be justified—it is then only a matter of searching for the various static properties or ossified ideas which presumably occupy Neruda's poetic discourse.

The reader presumably is confronted by poetry per se, isolated in "pure production," which allows Yurkievich to import a theory into his study of Neruda's poetry. Rejecting the legitimacy of Marxism as a system of thought, Yurkievich supplements the apparent lack of a cohesive theoretical apparatus in Neruda's work with psychoanalysis. Neruda's Marxism, in other words, is deemed foreign to the body of his work, artificially constructed and placed over the "aura" of his oeuvre. Concisely put, Marxism is not perceived as something organically produced in Neruda's poetic method or poetry.

Yurkievich perceives psychoanalysis in a Bloomian way as the poet's struggle with language, the poetic tradition, and the poet's precursors. Psychoanalysis then establishes a grounding for the poet's "anxiety of influence." Hence, in his criticism of *Canto general* he alleges that Neruda "no tolera una literatura autónoma, una poesía que se autobastezca cortando sus contactos con la realidad colectiva" (does not tolerate an autonomous literature, a poetry that relies on cutting its ties to collective reality). In times of "pure poetry," Neruda purportedly subordinated the poetic to the social (213). Even though Neruda was committed to a critical realism that attempted to condense, via mediation, the numerous sociohistorical events in Latin America and in the world into his poetry, Yurkievich criticizes Neruda's intent and argues for the autonomy of literature. Rather than attempt to explain Neruda's position and then state his disagreements, Yurkievich ends up criticizing it much as Rodríguez Monegal, Santí, and Costa do. In commenting on *Canto general,* for instance, he decries the Chilean poet's "militant poetics" as "rotund and simple, compulsive" (214). Yurkievich maintains that Neruda has given in to distortion and realism by cutting off the flows of his unconscious and attempting to write a conscious verse (217). Like Rodríguez Monegal, Santí, and Costa, he charges that Neruda attempts to harness the multiplicity of reality by relying on Marxism and thus provides schematic views of Latin American history:

> Se puede criticar en Neruda su exceso de determinación ideológica, porque sustituye la realidad con su movilidad, su inagotable y heterogénea simultaneidad, su ambigüedad, su inestabilidad, su mutabilidad, por un realismo estrecho, dual, maniqueo, por un determinismo mecánico, dogmático, que nunca encontraremos en su correligionario y contemporáneo César Vallejo. (217)

> [One can criticize in Neruda the excess of his ideological determination, because he substitutes reality for its mobility, its insatiable and heterogeneous simultaneity, its ambiguity, its instability, its mutability, for a narrow realism, dual, manichean, for a mechanical, dogmatic determinism, that we will never find in his fellow convert and contemporary César Vallejo.]

Yurkievich is half right in this assertion. There is no denying that Neruda did at times succumb to mechanical realism and, consequently, his texts and worldview suffered from distortions. But it is disingenious to suggest that that was always the case. As I show in later chapters, in the great majority of his works Neruda's poetic method and theory are far more complex and heterogeneous than Yurkievich imagines them to be. For the most part, the dialectic acts as the motor force of his poetic method, and, as such, as the very vehicle Neruda uses to analyze society. The poet's method can be likened to Bertell Ollman's definition of the dialectic: "change, all change, and interaction, all kinds and degrees of interaction."[45] "[T]he laws of the dialectic," Ollman argues, "do not in themselves explain or prove, or predict anything, or cause anything to happen. Rather, they are ways of organizing the most common forms of change and interaction that exist on any level of generality for purposes of study and intervention into the world of which they are a part."[46]

In the following chapters and in this one, I have contended that the dialectic is a crucial part of Neruda's way of thinking and poetic method. We can appreciate how the dialectic works in Neruda's poetry in books dating from at least *Veinte poemas de amor y una canción desesperada* to his posthumous verses. Yurkievich chooses to bypass this Neruda and, instead, highlights a partial truth: that the unconscious and spontaneous had some impact on Neruda's work. Literary (and therefore, epistemological) realism is Yurkievich's target: it can never hope to approximate in thought or writing the complexity of reality. So, like Rodríguez Monegal, Santí, and Costa, Yurkievich is a skeptic when it comes to questions of literary representation, epistemology, and ontology. However, as I show in chapter 2, Neruda conceived of his method as "espontaneidad dirigida" (guided spontaneity), an approach which finds its strength in the momentary flashes of imagination but also in the sustained elaboration of ideas based on the dialectical method.

Circling the Wagons Around Form

A final type of criticism that does not exactly follow the formalist studies of Neruda is Manuel Durán and Margery Safir's *Earth Tones: The Poetry of Pablo Neruda*. In this case, the ideological oscillations are more pronounced. On the one hand, Durán and Safir stress Neruda's intellectual background, making it clear that he was not only a talented poet as regards form but also learned in his understanding of content. These critics too attempt to be objective and so they take stock of Neruda's theoretical and practical relationship to nature. On the other hand, Durán and Safir wind up repeating many of the charges laid against Neruda by Rodríguez Monegal, Santí, Costa, and Yurkievich. Like these previous critics, when it comes to the politically charged poetry, they praise the form and decry the content. In the end Durán and Safir are unable to stand back from Neruda's political positions and assess them from anything other than a critical, liberal outlook.

On several occasions, however, Durán and Safir consider Neruda to be a materialist thinker who communicates complex philosophical ideas through his work. They explain his method at least in part in their comments on *Odas elementales:*

> Each poem also examines the object as if it were under a microscope, with loving attention, turning it around and exploring its facets, its uses, its power. Perhaps this very detailed approach, so particular to Neruda, is explained by the fact that Neruda was an accomplished naturalist, a specialist in marine life, and an avid collector of shells.[47]

And they go so far as to state that "Neruda believes in the external world of Nature, in the objective facts and commonsense definitions of our surroundings. As a 'materialist philosopher' he could do no less" (48).

Not only do Durán and Safir acknowledge that Neruda was a philosopher, but they also declare that the Chilean poet was not "converted" to Marxism. His politics, they say, "had been in fact leftist and radical for many years. A young intellectual could hardly have reacted otherwise to the socially stratified world of Chilean society" (75). It was a *logical progression* for Neruda to follow, especially surrounded as he was in Spain during the civil war by three friends who were involved in leftwing politics: Rafael Alberti, whom Neruda describes as his political instructor, Federico García Lorca, and Miguel Hernández.[48] Neruda, then, is portrayed as an intelligent and extraordinarily creative poet whose ideas need to be grappled with.

However, when referring to his 'political' poetry, especially *Canto general,* Durán and Safir generally agree with Yurkievich, Rodríguez Monegal, and Costa that Neruda's books are "more often personal than objective" and that the "vision *is* simplistic on the historical level," citing for example his representation of the United States in Latin American affairs. Durán and Safir contend that the "historical vision of *Canto general* has often been criticized on these grounds, especially for its simplistic division into black and white, good and evil, hero and villain" (83). They charge Neruda with considering only the negative aspects of imperialism. Although capitalism as a system is thoroughly destructive of the environment, extremely unjust in its distribution of wealth, brutally violent as a way of maintaining the status quo, and so on, it is true that it provides human beings with a glimpse—despite this drastic class stratification world wide—of what levels of, say, technological, creative, and scientific development can be attained by human beings. But this is readily recognized in Neruda's work. How else can we explain his homage to Abraham Lincoln, or his praise for Franklin Delanor Roosevelt in *Canto general?* In fact, some Marxists would argue that

Neruda holds reformist capitalism in too high a regard. Yet if critics are not willing to consider the history of Marxism, the major debates, stances, and political conflicts, the different forms of Marxism will go unnoticed. Furthermore, if that is the case, the historical depictions in a book like *Canto general will* seem "simplistic" because the critics have disregarded its explanatory power for their own ideological reasons.

Why, then, does Neruda's work merit close scrutiny and deserve to be regarded as "great" poetry? Like Costa, Durán and Safir argue that, although Neruda adheres to a "strict Soviet-style" communism, his work can be rescued and lauded for its perfection of form. "Neruda's often one-sided ideological vision may fail as history, but once again, it does not fail as epic poetry" (83–84). In their case, too, form can be salvaged even though content is marred. In commenting on *España en el corazón,* for example, they remark, as Costa did, that it is an "exceptional blend of political and lyrical poetry, for if the subject is ideological, the tone and passion are lyrical" (79). For Durán and Safir too the "ideological," that is, Neruda's Marxism, is too extreme and, as such, hinders the appreciation of poetic form. Thus, as in the cases of Rodríguez Monegal and Costa, analyzing form takes full precedent over content. In their study of "Alturas de Machu Picchu" Durán and Safir put it this way: "The dialogue between a poet and the world of matter, space, time cannot be defined except on terms established *in the poem itself*" (91; my emphasis). In the final analysis, they also return to New Critical close readings and leave the commentary on content undeveloped.

This, then, completes a representative survey of the mainstream studies on Neruda. All are skeptical about the poet's capacity to portray the world through the mediation of language. Likewise they all criticize literary and philosophical realism as a way of finally discrediting Neruda's Marxism and his dialectical realism. Lastly, they all conclude that Neruda was a master of poetic form and a great poet as long as he was not persuaded by the virtues of Marxism, but once he became a Communist his work suffered from simplifications and distortions. The views these critics espouse have gained a canonical status in the field of Latin American studies in general, and the study of Neruda's work in particular. However, a minority group of Marxist critics has made, I believe, the most substantial progress in understanding Neruda's work.

Marxist Critics, or the Form of Content

The Return to History

In contrast to the studies above, Jaime Concha's *Neruda: 1904–1936* is the first ambitious and insightful critical study of Neruda.[49] Separating it from the rest of the criticism up to 1972 and from studies to this date is Concha's ability to interweave geography, history, economics, politics, philosophy, and poetry. Furthermore, unlike previous scholars, Concha has a firm grasp of continental philosophy, particularly of Hegel and Marx. This allows him to comprehend the dialectical method not only in the abstract, but also in its fleshing out in history and verse. By identifying Neruda's dialectic and employing one himself, Concha avoids the pitfalls of the formalism we observed in the critics above. This critic assumes and proves that what is imagined by formalists to be the 'extra-aesthetic' is really an integral and dialectially related part of the text itself: "la estetización constata, en su mismo proceder, el dominio de lo extraestético" (aesthetization confirms, in its very procedure, the mastery of the extra-aesthetic) (82). Concha's reading of Neruda's early work, then, depends on geographical, historical, and political factors in Chile at large, and on the poet's own experiences in this social matrix. These circumstances, Concha argues, as well as the poet's own individuality, explain the development of a great poet like Neruda. From the vantage point of the poet's personal situation, the decisive questions are his ties to the laboring classes in the rural south and his subsequent encounter with the urban working class in Santiago, and Neruda's decision to commit himself to a future with the proletariat, guided by the sociohistorical and political factors of his day.

Unlike the critics above, Concha maintains that Neruda's relationship with nature is realist, not Romantic. For the poet nature never "cumplirá el servicio de refugio lírico que cumple la naturaleza románticamente concebida" (will serve the purpose of a lyrical refuge that nature, romantically conceived, does). Concha's Neruda perceives nature as immersed in history and geography, that is, as tied to everyday life: "[La naturaleza] es primero geografía, con lo cual deja de ser inmediatamente figuración sensible del alma, al modo romántico. Y en cuanto a geografía particular, el núcleo histórico de la naturaleza contrastará con la esterilidad de la ciudad, con su subdesarrollo" (Nature is above all geography, as such it immediately stops being a sensitive formation of the soul, in the romantic way. And as regards the specific geography, the historical nucleus of nature contrasts with the sterility of the city, with its underdevelopment) (36). On the one hand, in an underdeveloped country like Chile at the beginning of the twentieth century, the countryside signals the failing efforts to modernize and develop in contrast to the economic booms and inevitable exploitation in the city. As Concha asserts, Santiago at this stage shows the vital signs of the fight to modernize. On the other hand, in the 1920s and 1930s the countryside faced an encroaching modernization. Growing up in rural Temuco in general, and around the railroad in particular, Neruda was privy to the economic development of the once rural provinces.

Indeed, according to Concha, in the south Neruda came in direct contact with the rural working class, and thus acquired a grounded and practical dialectical understanding. He believes Neruda became a dialectical thinker thanks to the sociohistorical and geographical context (39). Instilled at an early age, social consciousness left its imprint on Neruda's poetic imagination. His creative and political evolution emerged from an environment that taught him to appreciate the ingenuity of common laborers and artisans in their marginal employment. In this context, Neruda's father and his work on the railroad stand out clearly. Through his father's job Neruda witnessed first hand the industrialization of the Chilean countryside: "De todos estos hechos se puede concluir que, mediante el trabajo ferroviario de su padre, el niño Neruda enlaza con uno de los aspectos más dinámicos de la base material del país a comienzos del siglo" (46–47) [From all these facts one can conclude, through the railroad work his father did, that Neruda the child hooks up with one of the most dynamic aspects of the material base of our country at the beginning of the century]. As an eyewitness to this social transformation Neruda came to see manual labor as the driving force of society as "trabajo que modifica y transfigura la naturaleza" (49) [work that modifies and transforms nature]. This registers itself in his early poetry with the constant references to hands and eyes and to the human relationship to nature. Even Neruda's early poetry grounded itself in geographical and historical realism, anchoring itself in the Temuco region: the ports, the rain, the railroad, the forests, the arduous work, and more.

And yet, since his father was a railroad foreman and not a worker per se, the young Neruda lived a middle-class existence which allowed him to go to the university in Santiago. Concha argues convincingly that the fact that Neruda's father was part of the small managerial class, but still was generally regarded as a worker, had a profound effect on the young poet. Indeed, this contradiction eventually pushed Neruda to ally himself with the proletariat (221). He was influenced by and joined the anarchists, who were a very active force among workers in the 1920s and 1930s and portrayed the environment and the lives of the working class. By so doing Neruda inserted himself in a national movement (the anarchists) and thus had an experience which is representative of many members of the middle class. As a student in Santiago Neruda realized how unproductive his life was but how intellectually engaging his life became considering his relationship with the working class (221–23). The anarchists, Concha states:

> representan las primeras manifestaciones de la conciencia de clase de los trabajadores. Al mismo tiempo, en el plano político propiamente tal, contribuyen en gran medida a provocar la escisión del Partido Demócrata de las filas radicales. Por otra parte hay que tener en cuenta que grandes dirigentes del Partido Comunista pasarán por una etapa de influencia anarquista (171).

[represent the first manifestations of class consciousness among workers. At the same time, on the political plane as such, they contribute a great deal to provoke the schism with the Democratic Party among the radicals. On the other hand it should be kept in mind that great leaders of the Communist Party went through a stage in which they were influenced by the anarchists.]

Neruda too went through a stage of anarchism before undergoing a new radicalization, which led him to join the Communist Party in 1945. By aligning himself first with anarchists and then with the Communists, Neruda came in direct contact with the class conscious working class and, at that point, became convinced in his Marxism and focused his energies on the struggle of the working class.

Literary realism, then, comes in tandem with his radicalism: as Neruda became more politicized, his texts reflected the social relations and conflicts under capitalism with a clearer and sharper focus. Concha maintains correctly, in my view, that this realism is central to *Residencia en la tierra:* "Desde el origen memorable de la subjetividad hasta la memoria colectiva que aportan las *Residencias,* el sonido del fuego con los armónicos (chispas, cenizas, vientos, humo etc.) crece por una suerte de introspección, devorando la eternidad del alma en el tiempo quemante de la materia" (201) [From the memorable origin of subjectivity to the historical memory that the *Residencias* provide, the sound of fire with the harmonious (sparks, ash, winds, smoke etc.) grows through a type of introspection, devouring the eternity of the soul in the burning time of matter]. Neruda suffered from estrangement that, in its dialectical process, he transcended to achieve solidarity and political commitment (204). As a result there is "ningún tiempo menos metafísico que el de *Residencia en la tierra,* por cuanto crece, justamente, en la fricción dialéctica donde se separan la experiencia natural del devenir y el ritmo laboral impuesto a los hombres con rigurosa uniformidad" (220) [no time less metaphysical than the one in *Residencia en la tierra,* in as much as it grows in the dialectical friction in which the natural experience of transformation is separated from the routine of work imposed on men with rigorous uniformity].

In contrast to the work of Amado Alonso or Rodríguez Monegal, Concha maintains that the *Residencias* period in Neruda's life that appeared to be so destructive and melancholic was actually an alliance of "sufrimiento y de trabajo, el deseo es sufrimiento sin pasividad, sufrimiento activo y es trabajo sin materia física sobre la cual ejercerse, trabajo inmaterial" (204) [suffering and work, desire is suffering without being passive, active suffering and it is work without any material substance on which to act, immaterial work]. From 1925 to 1936 Neruda was living in reckless abandon while writing his *Residencias.* Nonetheless, following Concha, these years were a mediated reflection in which Neruda truly realized the need for solidarity because he was on the margins of society and needed to sell his labor power. The poet attempted to identify with ordinary working people, but this proved to be a "false mimesis" due to his actual working conditions—as an intellectual. Although Concha does not deal with this topic, from 1936 on, Neruda came into alliance politically with the working class. As Alain Sicard has shown, even though a sense of insufficiency and guilt always seemed to haunt Neruda vis-à-vis manual labor, he looked for ways to portray and praise manual labor in his poetry.[50]

Concha stresses that Neruda's poetic method sets him apart from most of his contemporaries because his senses act as the governing body of his poetry in an insatiable attempt to approximate objective reality. In practice, the poet's subjectivity "ha convertido determinadas experiencias de su vida cotidiana en instrumento de conocimiento histórico-social" (has converted certain experiences of his daily life into an instrument of sociohistorical knowledge) (259). Here Concha brings subjectivity to bear upon objective reality, instead of subordinating subjectivity to objectivity. This analysis of the subjective factors proves to be the major weakness of Concha's work because he downplays the importance of Neruda's "moral indignation" in fighting to change the apparent objectivity of socioeconomic injustice in Chilean society at this time (57–58). Instead of contending that Neruda's moral and political positions develop necessarily from specific socioeconomic and political circumstances, Concha could have focused on the ways in which Neruda's radicalization departed from the dominant ideology. Likewise, in the literary realm, the flights from realism are, at times, as interesting as Neruda's vivid portrayals of the social environment in *Residencia en la tierra*. In addition, Concha has a tendency to believe in stagism—the belief in an inexorable sense of progress that will lead from feudalism to emergent capitalism to socialism. And yet his own analysis quite frequently contradicts that intent when, for instance, he notes that Neruda, a dialectical thinker and poet, emerged from the rural south. And this tension between stagism and the exceptional circumstances in Chile may be very close to the political position that Neruda himself held.

All told, Concha's work adds immeasurably to a deeper understanding of Neruda's poetry in the sociohistorical context in which it was written and to the poet's political evolution from anarchist to Communist. It lays an indispensable foundation for further studies.

Neruda as Poet and Philosopher

Concha's work is taken up and elaborated by another landmark in Nerudian criticism: Alain Sicard's *El pensamiento poético de Pablo Neruda.*[51] Building on the work of Hernán Loyola and Jaime Concha, Sicard undertakes an in-depth investigation into Neruda's poetic method and, remarkably, manages to cover all of the poet's work.

As the title of his book intimates, Sicard expresses no reservations about the poet's status as philosopher; indeed, Neruda's poetry would have been inconceivable without a very solid grasp of many important philosophical issues. Like Concha, this critic's background in philosophy and the social sciences allows him to frame the study of Neruda's poetics in a unique way, and then to carry through with an extensive meditation on the very propositions he has elaborated. Sicard also has a firm grasp of the dialectical method, not as some formula to be applied mechanically to social phenomena, but rather as a theoretical instrument that can potentially lead to heretofore unknown historical, political, or social insights. His own dialectical approach allows him to appreciate the nuances in Neruda's poetry and political thought. Having examined Neruda's Marxism and poetic theory in depth, Sicard comments on Neruda's "asombrosa capacidad de abstracción que le permite traducir la unidad profunda del movimiento material, a través de la multiplicidad de esas manifestaciones" (186) [amazing ability to abstract which allows him to translate the profound unity of material movement through the multiplicity of these manifestations].

In the spirit of Loyola's and Concha's research, Sicard seeks out the objective basis of Neruda's writing and succeeds in demonstrating that Neruda's embryonic materialism is present already in the *Residencias*. Living in Asia, in his verses Neruda began yielding to the objectivity of time and space as they in turn collapsed on the subject or engulfed him completely. The more he reflected on his anguishing isolation, the more the world around him started to invade his subjectivity—although it was technically already a part of himself that he had not yet acknowledged. Sicard feels that the experience in India for Neruda was comparable to the life of an exile. At this moment of acute solitude the "objectification of time is equal to the exclusion of the subject" observes Sicard (111). Neruda's inward march and self-deprecating activities led him, once he reached rock bottom, to notice what surrounded him and, more importantly, to recognize that nature and society can appear to have an almost autonomous existence outside the individual (131). Neruda, Sicard suggests, came to terms with and comprehended the objectivity of nature and society through self-negation. Consequently, even though he appeared to be lost in this negation, out of it came a positive, creative force:

> De movimiento material no conserva Neruda más que una dimensión: la acumulación de lo negado y destruido. Pero es una acumulación que está como marcada por la esterilidad: no es generadora de vida. La explicación es sencilla: concebir la discontinuidad como la modalidad del ser continuo. (133)

[From material movement Neruda saves one dimension: the accumulation of all that has been negated and destroyed. But it is an accumulation that is almost marked by sterility: it does not generate life. The explanation is simple: to conceive of discontinuity as the reason for being continuous.]

Objectivity is a source of anguish then, but it is also the seed of a future Neruda who generally overcame this estrangement and then became more authentically *social* or fulfilled. As Volodia Teitelboim has shown, in the *Residencias* Neruda was able, despite himself, to depict the social milieu—the people, the colors, the open markets, the temples and so on—in a realist manner.[52] As Sicard makes clear toward the end of his magnificent study, this realism is in itself a critique of realism:

> se critica más profundamente un realismo que se limite a reflejar pasivamente—estáticamente por lo tanto—lo real, en vez de proponerse aprehender su movimiento, un realismo, dicho con otras palabras, cuyas consecuencias sean el empobrecimiento de lo real y la reducción del campo de la praxis humana" (590)

> [he criticizes more deeply a realism that limits itself to reflecting passively—statically therefore—reality, instead of proposing to aprehend its movement, a realism, in other words, whose consequences would be the impoverishment of reality and the minimizing of human praxis.]

In other words, Neruda did not merely record the objectivity of space and time via the mediation of his verses, but rather vividly externalized the anguish, disaffection, and solitude during the *Residencias* stage. So the alienation that dominates the poet during the 1920s and early 1930s is, as Sicard perceptively notes, a moment in dialectical movement.

> Esa soledad es lo más opuesto a un aislamiento. No es el término contrario antinómico de la Historia: al igual que esta última, tiene como resultado una negación momentánea del individuo dentro de la realidad objetiva que lo supera en todas partes.

> [That solitude is completely opposed to isolation. It is not the antinomian contrary of History: like it, its immediate result is to negate the individual within the objective reality that surrounds him everywhere.]

For Neruda, solitude was a "momento del proceso dialéctico, aquel en que la historia rompe con su propia negatividad, aquel en que la niega al sumergirse en el mundo natural y hallar en él una confirmación de sus orígenes materiales" (moment in the dialectical process, in which history breaks with its own negativity, in which it negates itself by immersing itself in the natural world and finds in it the confirmation of its material origins) (329–30).

Sicard shows how Neruda's poetry evolved as it became embedded in socio-historical circumstances. He proves textually that discontinuity is an integral part of continuity in Neruda's work and that the poet was conscious of this process. A line can be traced from Neruda's early work as regards content and form through his last books of poetry despite the variation present during the different stages of Neruda's oeuvre. By comparison, Amado Alonso tends to let his own criticism reflect the distancing extant in the *Residencias* because he can perceive no way out of bourgeois thought.[53] In the end, the individual is all, and since the subject is drowning in his insignificance, so life itself must be chaos, futile. The dialectic pushes Sicard further: Neruda's experience in India and the poetry written there can be seen as the "no-ser del ser de toda cosa" (the non-being of being of everything) (118). Sicard says that while the poet grounds his work in a Marxist understanding of history, Neruda was not a historian. Neruda's poetry "no niega que haya vías científicas para el conocimiento de la realidad histórica, pero que se propone establecer con esta realidad relaciones no de carácter opuesto, sino diferente" (does not deny that there are scientific ways of knowing historical reality, but it proposes to establish different not opposed relations with this reality). Some critics, argues Sicard, "fingen confundir a Neruda con el historiador marxista que no es, para desacreditar al poeta materialista que es. Desde 1936, Neruda escribe según una concepción materialista de la Historia" (234) [confuse Neruda with a Marxist historian that he is not, in order to discredit the materialist poet he is. From 1936 on, Neruda writes according to a materialist conception of history].

Through careful textual analysis Sicard demonstrates that Neruda was not converted politically or artistically, but rather became convinced gradually of Marxism's analysis of capitalism and socialism. Contrary to assertions about Neruda's rapid acceptance of Marxism, Sicard maintains, as I do, that the poet was progressively won over to Marxism because of its explanatory potential and its political promise. Likewise, Neruda broke with the literary form in the *Residencias* once he recognized it as the result of his disaffection (in Chile and Asia).

Neruda, then, furnishes the reader with a type of photo negative of the social relations in the English colonies where he served as a Chilean low-level bureaucrat. While he was dehumanized because he suffered from alienation, Neruda revealed or objectified his own estrangement in a lucid and persuasive way. By the time he accepted a diplomatic post in Spain and lived through the horrors of the civil war, he became more fully conscious of his emptiness in Asia and found a way out of that abyss.

Neruda not only recognized the objectivity of nature and the "otherness" of society, but also worked out a consistent and flexible poetic method for abstracting those phenomena. Sicard states that Neruda's poetry attains objectivity "en el sentido de que plantea la unidad de lo real como cualidad intrínseca a su multiplicidad" (146) [in the sense that he posits the unity of reality as an intrinsic quality of its multiplicity]. Within this totality, dialectical tensions, like immobility/dynamism and concentration/dispersion, are principal actors giving Neruda's poetry its vitality. This view stands in contradistinction to the cyclical movement that Rodríguez Monegal, Costa, and Santí all claim to find in Neruda's works. Sicard contends that movement or dynamism comes to represent life, while immobility signals the onset of death. To reach a mobile state of being Neruda had to get tired of his own immobility, "hastiarse de no viajar" (161) [get fed up with not traveling]. Indeed, says Sicard, that immobility "no es la muerte sino la búsqueda de la unanimidad por medio de un necesario reajuste del ritmo humano al ritmo material" (169) [is not death but rather the search for unanimity through the necessary adjustment of human rhythm to material rhythm]. It was an attempt to ground his writings in everyday life.

As an example of this dialectic, Sicard focuses on light, a symbol of time, space, energy, and movement, which modifies things and beings (174). This concept of light, though, does not begin to attain a high degree of complexity until the first volume of *Odas elementales,* when Neruda writes a more reflective, philosophical poetry concentrating on the material essence of things more than on the description of socio-historical events. Moreover, it appears that movement and light too, from the *Odas* on, become emblematic of labor. Labor, then, is the intensification of and dominion over bodily movement. In "Oda a la lavandera nocturna" we can see these concepts at work:

> los brazos en la ropa,
> el movimiento,
> la incansable energía:
> va y viene
> el movimiento,
> cayendo y levantándose
> con precisión celeste[54]
>
> [her arms in the clothes
> the movement,
> the tireless energy:
> the movement
> goes and comes
> falling and rising
> with celestial precision.]

In this context, energy is harnessed and congealed in this woman's labor in a precise and magnificent way. To understand the revolutionary nature of the verses in the *Odas,* this connection needs to be identified. Neruda's portrayal of the woman washing clothes is a homage to the ongoing movement embodied in her labor. As the following verses indicate, her position is more complex than it seems, for she is washing workers' clothes:

> van y vienen
> las manos sumergidas,
> las manos, viejas manos
> que lavan en la noche,
> hasta tarde en la noche,
> que lavan
> ropa ajena,
> que sacan en el agua
> la huella
> del trabajo,
> la mancha
> de los cuerpos,
> el recuerdo impregnado
> de los pies que anduvieron,
> las camisas
> cansadas,
> los calzones
> marchitos,
> lava
> y lava,
> de noche.[55]
>
> [the submerged hands,
> come and go
> her hands, old hands
> that wash this evening,
> until late, in the evening,
> that wash
> unfamiliar clothes,
> that in the water take out
> the imprints
> of work,
> the bodies'
> stains,
> impregnated memory
> of feet that walked about,
> tired
> shirts,
> worn
> underwear,
> she washes,
> and washes
> at night.]

This woman who washes the workers' clothes is later fused with stars illuminating the dark skies because, by washing these garments, she seems to be purifying them. By cleansing them she appears to erase the physical manifestations (the stains and the wrinkles) of these laborers' exploitation. She, in turn, is working and being exploited. After all, she is washing "ropa ajena" (unfamiliar clothes). And yet, as I mentioned above, she is then associated with the heavens, held in the highest regard, because she too is working as she washes the clothes of toilers who have left their congealed labor in their pants, shirts, underwear, and socks. Neruda, of course, considers her labor laudable and also recognizes her own exploitation when he refers to her "viejas manos" (old hands) and to the woman herself as "la pobre / lavandera" (the poor washwoman). Sicard concentrates above all on the harnessed energy: her labor reaffirms her unity with the material world. In moving her hands and arms the worker incarnates the energy of the universe; with her work she brings life and light to a still, dark night. Her movement, Sicard observes, is connected with transparency. Transparency, the "hombre transparente" (transparent man) of whom Neruda speaks in the first volume of the *Odas:*

> radicaliza lo que, en la luz, afirmaba una autonomía del movimiento. Con ella, la luz deja de ser iluminación exterior y divana del propio objeto o, si se prefiere, sustituye al objeto y no permite percibir de él más que lo esencial: el movimiento. (177–78)
>
> [radicalizes what, in light, the autonomy of movement was affirmed. With her, light stops being an exterior light and it eminates from the object itself or, if you will, it substitutes for the object and allows us to see only what is essential: the movement.]

According to Sicard, transparency refers to the dialectical relation between subject and object, the latter taking precedence over the former. Human beings play the role of responding to and changing material reality. If movement is labor, and light points to the universe's incessant work (time) as Sicard affirms, then the "transparent man" is a person who has become conscious of his social nature and, from a Marxian vantage point, of the accumulation of social value that occurs through labor. In brief, the poet (the transparent man) reaches such a high level of social awareness that he affirms his own dependency—and the capitalist system's dependency—on the labor of workers (see especially "El hombre invisible" [The Invisible Man]). In *Odas elementales,* in particular, the poet becomes the ally of workers, the observer who glorifies their labor and denounces exploitation.

Sicard declares that when human beings become conscious of objectivity and history or "direction," they become social beings, and, as such, become free and instruments of change (183). Neruda became a conscious instrument of history when he raised his consciousness to a collective level and attempted to magnify his connection with nature and society. As several critics have commented, the impact of the Spanish Civil War initiated a period of personal-political transformation, leading to a lifetime commitment to social justice and the Chilean Communist Party. A parallel shift erupted in his poetry and poetic theory. In this respect, he altered his poetic method after 1947, when his work became more systematized and cohesive. From the fragmented subject in *Residencias* we move to the poems included in *Tercera residencia,* dominated by a less alienated and morally indignant subject, to the dispersed collective subject of *Canto general.* As Neruda became increasingly engaged in political activity, his poetry started to encompass the grand sweep of social relations and forces of production from ancient American civilizations to 1949. Sicard closes his book with the following summary of Neruda's relationship with nature and history:

> La naturaleza en medio de la que se regenera entonces la conciencia no es lo contrario de la historia: es una historia en la que el hombre, al retirarse, parecería haber devuelto a su transparencia. Así, pues, una ficción y no otra cosa es lo deshabitado: no tiene sentido sino por su propia negación. No existe más que como momento de un proceso, al final del cual se revela su misión, la de restaurar—y éste es el papel encomendado al amor—la permanencia de la historia. (629–30)

> [Nature in which consciousness is regenerated is not the opposite of history: it is a history in which man, by removing himself, would seem to have become transparent. So it is that the uninhabited is a fiction and nothing more: it makes no sense unless it is understood as its own negation. It does not exist except as a moment in the process, at the end of which its mission is revealed, that of restoring—and this is the role given to love—the permanence of history.]

While I agree with most all of Sicard's analyses of Neruda's work and am amazed at his ability to cover all the poet's work in such detail and profundity, I disagree regarding two issues: the relationship between objectivity and subjectivity, and the degree to which Neruda himself understood the theoretical matters Sicard brings to the fore. In trying to evade voluntarism (understandably) Sicard sometimes passes over an analysis of individual factors in the determination of the events' outcomes. If matter becomes conscious of itself through human beings, as Sicard argues, then it cannot, one would assume, gain that level of understanding without human beings. Sicard's own objectivism, expressed in the "génesis de la materia a partir de sí misma" (genesis of matter from matter itself) (220) carries with it the pitfalls of structuralism: it de-emphasizes the question of human agency. Matter can, of course, affirm itself independently of human thought. A central intellectual struggle of human beings has been to attain a higher level of understanding of the laws of the universe, of how the universe (matter) displays its own relatively independent existence. But by following Sicard's position there is a danger of collapsing the subject into the object. In other words, in his analysis human beings appear to relinquish their relative autonomy (via consciousness) from the laws of the universe.

I also now agree with Sicard's self-criticism that he had overestimated Neruda's grasp of the theoretical issues in his book.[56] *El pensamiento poético de Pablo Neruda* is a great classical Marxist analysis of Neruda's work, has very insightful readings of many poems and books, and is chock full of brilliant ideas, but it also says a lot more about Sicard's critical acumen than Neruda's. This is not to say that Neruda was not an intellectual; but that he was not an academic and did not want to be. He arrived at his version of Marxism through suffering and experience, and later had his political and moral positions more or less confirmed in his many political readings. Practical, political involvement, great friends, and history changed Neruda and made him the Communist he was. In other words, Neruda was not won over to Marxism through theory; he was convinced because he was *morally* incensed by the social injustice he himself witnessed. As Sicard says, *that* Neruda was a poet who relied on history but was not a historian. Likewise, Neruda was a poet but not a Marxist theorist. Nonetheless, his positions remain intricate and complex, as any reading of his works plainly indicates.

Conclusion

My intent in this chapter has been to analyze the most representative literary criticism on Neruda and to show the virtues and drawbacks of both liberal and Marxist approaches to the poet's work. If I have dedicated more time to demonstrating the ideological inconsistencies of liberal criticism during the Cold War and have been less critical of the Marxist critics it is because I find the latter to be more in keeping with Neruda's own political and aesthetic convictions. This does not mean, of course, that the liberal critics have not made significant contributions to the study of Neruda's texts—in many cases I have tried to single out these important insights—but, because of an ideological impasse, they have not been as convincing in arguing their cases about Neruda's work. As is obvious by now, my study generally follows the great Marxist critics on Neruda (Hernán Loyola, Jaime Concha and Alain Sicard). They have offered compelling close readings of Neruda's poems; have shown the continuity in his work; have placed his poetry in its proper biographical, historical, and political context and, therefore, have provided the most comprehensive and convincing analyses of Neruda's work.

2
Realism, Surrealism, Socialist Realism, and Neruda's "Guided Spontaneity"

FROM THE 1920S TO THE 1950S SOCIALIST REALISM AND LATE SURREALism were two influential political and aesthetic positions for leftist Latin American and Spanish writers. For several eminent poets the literary avant-garde's light went out once the civil war erupted in Spain in 1936. One need only think of some of the most renowned poets, among them Rafael Alberti, Luis Cernuda, César Vallejo, and Pablo Neruda who dedicated themselves to writing quasi-avant-gardist works before the civil war and later, in the throes of the war, committed themselves to the Republican cause by writing verses accessible to the general public. However, others, such as Vicente Huidobro or Octavio Paz, held fast to avant-gardist theory or style. As is well known, Paz became an unofficial member of the second generation of surrealists, and Huidobro invented his own avant-gardist theory, "creacionismo.' And in spite of their political commitment to the Spanish Republic, their leftist commitments were short lived.

At first glance Federico García Lorca also seems to belong to this last group of poets because of his volcanic verses in *Poeta en Nueva York* (Poet in New York). Nonetheless, García Lorca does not fit for two main reasons. First, *Poeta en Nueva York* is a contemporary of *Sobre los ángeles* (About Angels) by Alberti, *Un río, un amor* (A River, A Love) by Cernuda, and *Espadas como labios* (Swords like Lips) by Aleixandre, meaning that it is not affected by the tumultuous events of the civil war (it is, as we know, a posthumous book).[1] Second, while it is avant-gardist poetry, it is also a politically committed poetry that vividly portrays racism, poverty, the ostentatious wealth of the capitalists, and the desperate alienation during the Great Depression in the United States.

As noted, the first group of poets—among them Neruda—established ties, sometimes tenuous, with the avant-garde and, in particular, with surrealism, ties later severed with the advent of the civil war. (Although not entirely convincing, Merlin H. Forster at least shows that Neruda wrote for avant-gardist publications, maintained dialogues with avant-gardists like Vicente Huidobro, and employed some techniques in *Residencia en la tierra* that are characteristic of those movements.)[2] While the winds of avant-gardism died down by 1939 according to the most liberal periodizing, socialist realism had just emerged as a literary alternative.[3] Many poets rejected socialist realism and some, like Paz, for example, criticized it openly as a byproduct of Stalinism. But others, like Alberti and Neruda, accepted some of its premises.

In Neruda's case we can appreciate his navigation between these two literary currents and his choice to chart an independent course. In spite of his work's evolution toward realism during the civil war, Neruda never gave up his literary autonomy or his creative independence. Even in *Canto general* and *Las uvas y el viento* (Grapes and Wind), books that have often been charged with being socialist realist,[4] there is ample evidence of the founding principal of Neruda's poetry: "espontaneidad dirigida" (guided spontaneity).[5] If we turn to Neruda's commentaries in his memoirs we encounter astute, but sometimes contradictory, observations about his ties to the Communist Party and the Soviet Union during this time which the poet considered to be "diabolically confusing," about the Stalin years, and about his own contradictory stance regarding literary realism.[6] Although Neruda was affected by late surrealism and socialist realism and established his independence from both of them, his poetry showed signs of being more swayed by realism, or what I would call his "dialectical realism," driven by his guided spontaneity. In time, in other words, Neruda perceived natural and social phenomena through the lens of the dialectical method, though not programmatically so.[7] This enabled him to think about change and natural and social interactions in more complex ways and to portray that intricacy in his poetic work via his guided spontaneity, that is in an organized and systematic yet free-flowing manner. While Jaime Concha and Alain Sicard have both written on Neruda's poetic method and politics, here I explore it in its historical and cultural contexts and come to a similar yet new consideration of his aesthetic theory.[8] In what follows I maintain that Neruda's poetics is intimately tied to his politics. During the 1930s he showed a growing distaste for surrealism because of its perceived irrationalism and its criticism of the USSR. Likewise, despite his support of the USSR, Neruda never declared himself a follower of socialist realism. However, from the Spanish civil war onward Neruda turned increasingly to realism in order to portray the complexity of the class struggle during these years. Compared to the *Residencia en la tierra* poems his poetic form became more accessible because of the shifting emphasis on sociopolitical content. His deepening political commitment, first to the Spanish Republic, then to antifascism and later to socialism gave him the opportunity to become more politically conscious, and this made its way into the poetry that he wrote during these years, precisely the years that *Tercera Residencia* spans (1925–45).

The Impact of Socialist Realism

Socialist realism became one of the dominant aesthetic currents in the 1930s because it associated itself with the USSR's destiny. This official literary position borrowed from the past—the October revolution—and from oft-made exaggerated claims about the national achievements after the death of Lenin. So, in 1934, in the First Soviet Writers Congress, some four years before the Great Purges, Zhdanov openly declared that the Congress was convening in a historical moment in which "under the leadership of the Communist Party, under the guiding genius of our great leader and master, Comrade Stalin, the socialist system has triumphed irrecoverably and finally in our country." According to Zhdanov, Soviet culture was "growing and developing in exuberant splendour."[9]

As Zhdanov saw it, the challenge for art during this period consisted of overcoming the barriers of underdevelopment in the industrial sector and in the countryside, and, above all, "the vestiges of bourgeois influence in the proletariat, laziness, vagrancy, waste, individualism and the immoral behavior of the petit bourgeoisie" (17). To become the "engineers of the soul" that Stalin imagined artists to be, they should combine "truth and historical specificity in their artistic portrayals" with the "education and shape of the working class in the spirit of socialism" (21).

If socialist realism would have based itself on Zhdanov's stance and the prestige of the USSR as its shining inspiration, then it would have proved convincing to many writers, but probably not to the majority of them. Government officials in the USSR could talk of the "triumph" of socialism in one country, the collectivization of agriculture and the road to industrialization by relying on the main arguments of the 1930s, but they could only do so with some success. Nevertheless, the German, Karl Radek, was the writer who gave the most persuasive speech about socialist realism at the Congress. In Radek's view "proletarian art cannot only be content with the class struggle. It should also describe the processes through which those same social classes pass—their lifestyle, their psychology, their development and their aspirations" (136). So working class culture was conceived as the culture of the future, as an indication of psychological and social struggles that were gestating in the heart of socialism. In sum, Radek believed that proletarian or socialist realism more accurately represented socioeconomic and psychological conditions than its avant-gardist counterpart and that socialist realism was closely tied to the destiny of socialism, that is, to the leading example of the USSR, and, as such, was a mechanism to raise political consciousness among artists around the world. According to Radek, as "worker[s] of consciousness" writers should overcome individualism by becoming "soldiers of the revolution" and abandon their desire for absolute freedom, which, after all, was the product of bourgeois ideology (142, 157).

It would not be surprising if many writers on the left, like Neruda, after hearing the speech by Radek concluded that accepting a socialist realist method, while not required, would allow them to surpass petit bourgeois consciousness and to commit themselves to socialism, incarnated in the Soviet Union. After all, the 1917 revolution was the first socialist revolution in the world, and the hopes for socialism on an international scale, until the purges of the 1930s at least, were to be found in the USSR.

Among the more or less official opinions on aesthetic matters during the 1930s in the Soviet Union, in my judgment, Radek's would have been most convincing to fellow travelers and party members like Neruda or Louis Aragon. On the one hand committing oneself to socialist realism meant that the writer was dedicating himself to the socialist struggle, and, as such, supporting the Soviet Union. On the other hand, it provided the writer with certain artistic freedoms. It was expected that the writer who wanted to ally himself with socialism recognize the economic, social, and cultural achievements in the USSR. Naturally, this expectation grew as fascism raised its head in Italy, Germany, and Spain.[10] Antifascism came to be associated with the defense of the Soviet Union and garnered the support of a great deal of progressive and leftist poets, among them Neruda, Alberti, Miguel Hernández, César Vallejo, García Lorca, Aragon, and Paul Eluard.[11] It is not surprising then that as World War II approached, Neruda, the avant-gardist, should write more realist verses describing the war time conditions, become an antifascist, and openly support the Soviet Union. If there were any doubts they were dispelled in 1942 when Neruda wrote and read in public his "Canto a Stalingrado" (Song to Stalingrad), and, a year later, "Nuevo canto de amor a Stalingrado" (New Song of Love to Stalingrad).[12]

SURREALISM AND TROTSKYISM

For progressive or left-wing writers the most palpable alternative to socialist realism was late surrealism. By the 1930s, the most eminent defender of the Trotskyist critique of the Soviet Union in the cultural realm was André Breton. According to biographer Mark Polizzotti, already by the 1920s Breton considered that "social revolution by the Communists reflected perfectly the aesthetic and moral revolution that surrealism had set out as its goal."[13] As Breton's political position drifted toward Trotsky's, surrealism began to abandon its formerly anarchist views and find closer affinities with communism. In the long run this radicalization of surrealism led to the break up of its founders: Breton, Eluard, and Aragon. The latter two would then become members of the French Communist Party, while Breton would associate himself more with the Left Opposition (Trotsky).

In 1938 Breton visited Trotsky in Mexico and they agreed to write a "Manifesto for Independent Revolutionary Art." In this manifesto they propose a socialist alternative to socialist realism: the freedom of art.[14] Aware of the implications of this position they made it clear that they "defended freedom of creation" and at no time did they intend to "defend political indifference," nor did they want to support "pure art," which commonly serves the more than impure actions of reactionary forces" (31). Having criticized art for art's sake for being potentially reactionary, they then focus on the counterproposal they offer to socialist realism and Stalinism:

> We believe that the major job of art today and this period is to participate assiduously in preparing the revolution. Nevertheless, artists cannot participate in the struggle for emancipation unless they have absorbed its social and individual content, unless they feel its meaning and drama in their nerves and unless they express and incarnate their life experiences freely. (my translation; 33)

In that way Breton and Trotsky put the legitimacy of Stalin's regime in the USSR and socialist realism to the test. They reject "all solidarity with the caste that currently rules in the USSR . . . because . . . it does not represent communism but rather its most dangerous and treacherous enemy" (30). It is worth mentioning in passing that in spite of the crimes committed by Stalin's regime, which are not few nor possible to pardon, it is assumed that the main enemy of socialism is capitalism and not the bureaucracy in the Soviet Union, so Breton and Trotsky's position here is misleading. It is easy to see how Communists who supported the USSR and considered that it was under constant attack by capitalist countries would denounce Trotsky's position and contend that it, in fact, could be used for reactionary purposes. After rejecting the USSR's claim to socialism, Trotsky and Breton concentrate on what the Soviet Union can provide to left-wing writers as far as resources are concerned and they urge artists to break with Stalinism:

> At the present moment, characterized by the slow death of capitalism—democratic as well as fascist—artists, even though they may not protest socially, are threatened with loss of the right to earn a living and to continue their work because they are denied all means to promote creative works. It is natural for them to turn to Stalinist organizations that allow them to escape their isolation. But, in exchange for those resources, the artists are asked to renounce all that could be considered their own message and to show terribly degrading subservience. Therefore, artists have no alternative but to withdraw from these organizations, as long as demoralization has not taken over their characters. (33)

Lukács' Marxist Aesthetic Theory

If left-wing writers did not feel drawn to either socialist realism or surrealism, Georg Lukács' position would have persuaded the dissenters. This stance had the advantage of allowing Communist writers to support the socialist cause, incarnated in the Soviet Union, while still maintaining their independence. As I argue below, this is the theoretical position that comes closest to mirroring Neruda's own beliefs regarding realism, surrealism, and socialist realism. While Neruda rejects all three literary movements, he develops a poetic theory that comes closest to Lukács' theory of realism.

As the title of his 1938 essay "Realism in the Balance" indicates, Lukács argues for realism and against antirealist and avant-gardist literary currents such as surrealism. He maintains that avant-gardist literature that aspires to startle bourgeois consciousness and, ultimately, transform society falls victim to the representation of immediacy. Avant-gardists' artistic creations revolve around the importance of experimentalism and spontaneous expression and, as such, they are only able to capture a fragmented, and thus temporary, purchase on the sociopolitical reality. In Lukács' view:

> both emotionally and intellectually they all remain frozen in their own immediacy; they fail to pierce the surface to discover the underlying essence, i.e. the real factors that relate their experiences to the hidden social forces that produce them. On the contrary, they all develop their own artistic style—more or less consciously—as a spontaneous expression of their immediate experience. (37)

In reproducing the immediate social relations and conflicts through their mediated art forms the avant-gardists end up portraying these phenomena in a naive way. Consequently, while they appear to achieve critical distance in their representations of the sociopolitical reality and the life of the individual, they really do not incisively and comprehensively criticize that reality. Therefore, their writing becomes abstract and lacks concrete and complex depth. As such these avant-gardist representations become one-dimensional and thus succumb, as we now know, to commodification. The avant-gardist shock effect serves a momentary purpose which then vanishes into thin air as its oppositional intent is absorbed by the capitalist system.

As is well known, Lukács then makes a case for realism, arguing that the dialectical method is crucial to any convincing portrayal of reality. Realism thus conceived shares in the unity of human inquiry and attempts to approximate social and physical reality in a mediated, literary form, and then suggests how this reality will be transformed. Lukács cites the poignant words of Lenin on this matter: "In order to know an object thoroughly, it is essential to discover and comprehend all of its aspects, its relationships and its 'mediations'. We shall never achieve this fully, but insistence on all-around knowledge will protect us from errors and inflexibility" (33). So it is paramount that writers aspire to understand the general dynamics of the social totality: the individual thoughts and feelings, the social relations, the class struggle, the drive for profit, and more. In this way the author's consciousness and creation is consistently contrasted with the complexity of social consciousness and reality (35). Lukács sums up this critique of the avant-garde and avowal for critical realism this way:

> For as capitalism develops, the continuous production and reproduction of these reactionary prejudices is intensified and accelerated, not to say consciously promoted by the imperialist bourgeoisie. So if we are ever going to be able to understand the way in which reactionary ideas infiltrate our minds, and if we are ever going to achieve a critical distance from such prejudices, this can only be accomplished by hard work, by abandoning and transcending the limits of immediacy, by scrutinizing all subjective experiences and measuring them against social reality. In short it can only be achieved by a deeper probing of the real world. (37)

Here and elsewhere in this essay Lukács argues that the dialectical method is pivotal for Marxism and a more complete view of reality. Without it distortions, isolations and fragmentations of thought and analysis will occur. The dialectic is just as crucial to literature as it is to any field of knowledge. If it is not an integral part of literature then it cannot be literature that seeks to be Marxist. For all its good intentions, then, surrealism does not follow in the footsteps of Marxism because it never overcomes the level of immediacy.

Lukács' stance on socialist realism during the 1930s is expressed in a more veiled way since he was living in the Soviet Union at the time. In referring to proletarian literature in his essay "Tendency or Partisanship," he scrutinizes the idea of tendentious literature. Lukács says that its proponents disregard literary form, regarding it as bourgeois and calling attention to the immediate sociopolitical situation. Thus tendentious literature becomes mere literature of agitation that lacks the depth and subtlety of even the great works of bourgeois realists. Tendency, as it is conceived by its advocates, is posited as an "ought" in opposition to reality (the "is") and, consequently, makes subjective demands on writers and readers alike within an idealist framework. In spite of its proletarian provenance, tendency fails to grasp its connection to material production, human activity, and the class struggle.[15] In Lukács' words "it is not a tendency of social development itself, which is simply made conscious by the poet (in Marx's sense), but rather a (subjectively devised) commandment, which reality is requested to fulfill" (37). The central vantage point of the proletariat does not, in and of itself, grant it any particular privilege as regards society or literature. Painstaking work is required for the writer to see the class relations, the progression of class struggle, the fetishism of commodities under capitalism, and the seductive dance of the dominant ideology. The process of understanding these laws of capitalism and the accompanying evolution of feelings, thoughts, and experiences in this context is a very difficult one that the tendency writers cannot reach because they hold to mechanistic and idealist thought:

> This knowledge is in no way a mechanical and immediate product of social being. It has rather to be produced. The process of its production, however, is both a product of the internal (material and ideological) disposition of the proletariat, as well as a factor promoting the development of the proletariat from a "class in itself" to a "class for itself." (41)

The demands of social reality are already a natural part of the writing process for those writers who strive to portray reality in this way. This partisanship entails "knowledge and portrayal of the overall process as a synthetically, grasped totality of its true driving forces, as the constant and heightened reproduction of the dialectical contradictions that underlie it" (42). Lukács then proceeds to criticize the proletarian literature of his day for its tendentiousness and, in so doing, carries out a critique that likens itself to his critical assessment of socialist realism:

> Our literature, even in its best products, is still full of "tendency." For it does not always succeed, by a long chalk, in portraying what the class-conscious section of the proletariat wants and does, from an understanding of the driving forces of the overall process, and as representative of the great world-historical interests of the working class, portraying this as a will and a deed that themselves arise dialectically from the same overall process and are indispensable moments of this objective process of reality. (43)

Lukács' commentary on proletarian tendency acts as a prelude to the critical analysis he does of socialist realism. In "Tribune or Bureaucrat?" Lukács addresses the status of socialist realism and the left-wing writer's political and aesthetic commitment more openly than any other essay during these years. In this context he maintains that spontaneity, be it in its avant-gardist or socialist realist variants, is consciousness in its embryonic form, so it is necessarily a partial view of the social totality limited by the recording of immediacy (219). This is the position of the bureaucrat. By contrast, the member of the revolutionary tribunal has passed from the realm of spontaneity to conscious political thought or artistic work. The artist who is able to overcome the spontaneity of thought and to perceive the dialectical complexity of life moves beyond the estrangement and mystery involved in the capitalist system and writes singular, and more complete works of art. Lukács argues that:

Only the love of life gives the artist his unreserved truthfulness towards everything that he perceives and reproduces, his breadth, scope and depth of vision. If a social condition arises in which the artist is forced to hate life, to have contempt for it, and he even begins to develop an attitude of indifference, then the truth of even his best observations is constricted. The surface and the essence of human life grow apart, the former becoming empty and vacuous, requiring invigoration by trimmings that are foreign to the material itself, while the latter becomes alien to life, trivial, or full of simply subjective and false profundities. (218)

The idea behind the revolutionary tribune, in contrast to the bureaucrat, is to return to the roots of the Russian revolutionary experience in order to critique the development of socialism in the 1930s. For someone living in the Soviet Union at the time, this was a delicate matter. Lukács manages to isolate and critique what he considers to be vestiges of capitalism in the USSR at this point in history and to anchor his analysis in classical Marxism. Thus he makes bureaucracy the target of his analysis in the political and cultural spheres and implies that that is what is preventing the dialectical flourishing of socialism in the USSR. In doing so Lukács quotes Lenin's reflections on the eventual withering away of the state as a coercive apparatus in order to implicitly denounce, I assume, the purges taking place internally. He also cites Stalin's own remarks about classless society:

> a classless society cannot come of its own accord, as it were. It has to be achieved and built by the efforts of all the working people, by strengthening the organs of the dictatorship of the proletariat, by intensifying the class struggle, by abolishing classes, by eliminating the remnants of the capitalist classes, and in battles with enemies, both internal and external. (230–31)

For Lukács the blame is laid at the doorstep of the bureaucracy, which has taken things into its own hands and gone against the very founding principles of the Russian revolution.

From there Lukács moves to a critical analysis of socialist realism as the result of bureaucratic thinking in the cultural realm. It is worth remembering though, as his later writings make clear, that his aim is not to declare socialist realism bankrupt, but rather to criticize its development at this moment in history and under these particular social circumstances.[16] By criticizing socialist realism Lukács is indirectly holding the Soviet bureaucracy responsible for the travesties and errors committed.[17] So, for instance, Lukács charges socialist realism with "formal, empty, bureaucratic 'optimism' expressed in certain works that appear at first sight to be socialist, but are in actual fact dead, devoid of ideas, and useless and ineffectual both from the standpoint of aesthetics and from that of propaganda" (235). He also contrasts Gorky's great literary work with socialist realism. The latter is full of bureaucratic optimism and it makes,

[T]he process with its contradictions and difficulties simply vanish. For this school, the only events that exist are victories won without struggle or effort: the resistance of the external enemy, and internal resistance within men themselves, hindering the birth of socialist man and in individual cases frustrating this, does not exist for them. (235–36)

Lukács concludes by declaring that struggle must be waged against this bureaucratization of art, which he judges to be a remnant of capitalist cultural development.

In terms of method (the dialectic), and literature's capacity to represent the complexity of natural and social phenomena as accurately as possible via mediation, Lukács' theory comes remarkably close to Neruda's, particularly after 1936. My analysis of "Alturas de Macchu Picchu" (Heights of Macchu Picchu) and "El hombre invisible" (The Invisible Man) later in this chapter provides an example of how Lukács' theory dovetails with Neruda's poetic method. However, given Neruda's antipathy for any literary schools and any established systems of thought and given his contradictory statements in his memoirs regarding realism, socialist realism, and surrealism (examined below), suggesting that Neruda accepted Lukács' ideas wholesale would be carrying things too far.

Neruda's Contemporaries

The three options that carried more weight for left-wing poets during this period, such as Neruda, are Karl Radek's position on socialist realism, André Breton's left opposition alternative in surrealism, and Lukács' critique of both tendencies and advocacy of a more sophisticated critical realism. Two of his friends, Louis Aragon and Octavio Paz, faced similar choices. Aragon broke ties with Breton and became one of the main defenders of socialist realism; Paz solidified his ties with surrealism in particular and the avant-garde in general. Neruda's course lay somewhere between Aragon's and Paz's stances or, perhaps more accurately, came close to resembling Lukács' critical position.

Neruda's good friend, Aragon, wrote several justifications for his break with surrealism and his defense of the virtues of socialist realism. In his essays "In Moscow there are Sculptors" and "Parenthesis about the Stalin Prizes" he tries to refute Breton's arguments by claiming his role as an insider in the USSR and by suggesting that Breton's view is limited because he can only judge socialist realism from outside the Soviet Union. So, for example, Aragon alleges that critics in France misunderstand socialist realism because they rely on the aesthetic laws, criteria, and taste found in France and they attempt to then apply them to the Soviet case.[18] That is why socialist realism offends so many artists and critics in the West, as any new artistic movement provokes the ire of established artists (54). Aragon maintains that the theme of Soviet art is its point of departure and arrival; whereas in the case of surrealism anarchist tendencies can be discerned that distance it from reality and liken it to art for art's sake (59–60, 63–64). In sum, then, he alleges that the form of surrealist art practically becomes the content, whereas with socialist realism form yields to and deepens content. In echoing Radek, Aragon concludes that there is a great deal of freedom of expression under socialist realism, but he ends the second essay with a definition of socialist realism that is very similar to Zhdanov's (64, 74). So it is that Aragon oscillates between Radek's and Zhdanov's stances.

Although Aragon and Neruda were members of the Communist Party during some very complex, trying, and brutal years—the Stalin period—they took on semiautonomous positions in the political and artistic realms. In interviews and later in his memoirs, Neruda soundly denied that the party interfered in the creation and context of *Canto general* and thus answered some critics' charges that he wrote that great work under the auspices of the party.[19] Neruda insisted that he had always followed his own artistic road. Likewise, according to Ariane Chebel d'Appollonia, the French Communist Party gave Aragon a quasi-independent role allowing him to defend his orthodox aesthetic positions in unorthodox ways.[20] However, as in the case of many of the most salient Communist writers during the Stalin years, Neruda and Aragon also benefited from their advantageous statuses: they were well treated and awarded prizes in the Soviet Union after they joined the party; they had their books published there; they served on the Stalin Prize committee; and they relied on their close ties with USSR to be more persuasive in discussions on artistic matters (although this can be seen more clearly with Aragon). Nevertheless, Mary Ann Caws has demonstrated that even an ardent defender of the USSR and socialist realism like Aragon was able to distance himself from that artistic school and maintain his autonomy.[21]

Surrealism won over the young Aragon, but once he strengthened his ties to the French Communist Party and to the Soviet Union, its influence waned and he became more convinced of the importance of socialist realism. Octavio Paz, on the other hand, drifted, more or less, in the opposite direction. During the Spanish civil war he wrote socially committed and erotic poetry, collected in *Bajo tu sombra clara y otros poemas sobre España* (Beneath your Clear Shadow and Other Poems about Spain) (1937). In writing for the journal *Hora de España* (Spain's Hour) Paz steered a course which showed his artistic independence without breaking with Spanish Communists.[22] In principle, then, Paz's initial position differs little from Neruda's: he aligns himself with the Republican cause and yet, like most poets, searches for his own autonomous space. In fact Paz's poetic theory comes very close to Neruda's "guided spontaneity": "Nunca he creído que la poesía nazca de la mera espontaneidad o del sueño; tampoco es hijo de la conciencia lúcida sino de la lucha—que es también, a veces, abrazo— entre ambos" (I have never believed that poetry is born of mere spontaneity or of dreams; neither is it the offspring of conscious lucididy but rather a struggle—which is also, at times, an embrace—between both).[23] Although Paz's political stance mirrored Neruda's at this stage of their lives, Paz was accused of being a Trotskyist because he refused to believe that Trotsky was an agent of fascism, despite Paz's firm conviction that the main enemy at hand was fascism. Unlike the POUM (Partido Obrero de Unificación Marxista [Workers Party for Marxist Unification]) Paz did not support a revolution above all else in Spain, he was primarily concerned about the defeat of fascism.[24] While Paz's commitment to the Republican cause was unswerving, his association with the Spanish Communist Party was tenuous. In the last years of his life Paz described his oscillation between "adhesión ferviente y una reserva invencible" (fervent adherence and an invencible reserve). Much of his opposition to the PCE at this stage had to do with its intervention as regards cultural matters and the Party's aesthetic stance.[25]

After the Spanish civil war Paz returned to Mexico and published in *El Popular* until shortly after the 1939 nonaggression pact between Germany and the USSR and the assassination of Trotsky, at which point, Paz broke with Neruda and also with the Mexican Communist Party.[26] By 1941 Paz began to chart his own course politically and aesthetically. From this moment on, he was more persuaded by Trotskyist political positions even though he did level criticism at Trotsky. He criticized "Stalinism" along the same lines as Trotsky did and did not reject Marxism per se.[27] By the 1950s Paz turned more and more to existentialist, anarchist, and libertarian ideas even though socialism still held its appeal, but not following the tradition of the USSR and the Eastern Bloc.[28]

Always a critic of the "barbaric partisans of Socialist realism," from this point on Paz sided unequivocally with the avant-garde in the aesthetic realm.[29] He contributed to *Taller,* a surrealist-inspired literary journal, and he refused to write political verse. A turning point thematically in his work is the poem "Himno entre ruinas" (Hymn among Ruins)—far different from the Nerudian equivalent written during the Spanish civil war. In contrast to the social reality, the hymn stands in for the existential and momentary reality because, as Enrico Mario Santí puts it, it is "la eternidad a que puede aspirar el ser humano" (eternity to which human beings can aspire).[30] Paz's political disillusionment creates an independent and even alienated space from which the poet attempted to make sense of life, and he found it in the spontaneous notion of carpe diem. As his later work indicates, Paz's aesthetic preference adheres more to simultaneism and surrealism. His years in Paris after World War II were decisive: they brought him closer than he had ever been to surrealism, and they left the mark of Reverdy's, Breton's, and Camus' influence. From surrealism he clearly inherited his rebellious individualism, the concept of the "other voice" than runs through his poetry, the "subversive" potential of desire and the "revolutionary" character of eroticism; from simultaneism he borrowed the idea of disparate verses linked by metaphors, the conviction that metaphors are intimately connected with analogy and rhythm, the focus on the basic interpoetic elements—vision, sound, and rhythm—and also the insistence on language as the poet's destiny.[31]

As Paz views it in *Los Hijos del limo* (Children of the Mire), the two dominant literary trends in Latin America by 1945 were socialist realism and the social poetry of former avant-gardists. In this context the neo-avant-garde—the works of such poets as José Lezama Lima, Roberto Juarroz, Enrique Molina, Nicanor Parra, Jaime Sabines, and Paz himself—held in common their emphasis on solitary rebellion, language as an expression of the self, reflecting and making fun of oneself, late surrealism, and an oscillation between Trotskyism and anarchism.[32] The neo-avant-garde became the dominant current in Latin American poetry and remains so today, whereas politically committed verse and realism can claim only a minority of representatives, such as Ernesto Cardenal, Juan Gelman, and Mario Benedetti. Paz's own poetic work and theory, up to the end of his life, then, finds its source, generally speaking, in the position carved out by Breton and Trotsky and fully opposes itself to socialist realism and to the Lukácsian theory of realism.

Dialectical Realism or "Guided Spontaneity"

In reading Neruda's comments on realism, surrealism, and socialist realism in his memoirs and in *Para nacer he nacido* (I have been Born to be Born), it is easy to arrive at the conclusion that he searches for a middle road in the debate between these aesthetic schools. Indeed, his opinions about them are often contradictory and confirm that while all three movements influenced his writing, he rejected them as artificial literary models lacking in dynamism and in "guided spontaneity." This explains a commentary like the following:

> En cuanto al realismo debo decir, porque no me conviene hacerlo, que detesto el realismo cuando se trata de poesía. Es más, la poesía no tiene por qué ser sobrerealista o subrealista, pero puede ser antirealista. Esto último con toda la razón, con toda la sinrazón, es decir, con toda la poesía. Me place el libro, la densa materia del trabajo poético, el bosque de la literatura, me place todo, hasta

los lomos de los libros, pero no las etiquetas de las escuelas. Quiero libros sin escuelas y sin clasificar, como la vida.[33]

[As far as realism is concerned I should say, because it isn't in my best interest to do so, that I detest realism when it comes to poetry. Moreover, poetry doesn't have to be overrealist or subrealist, but it can be antirealist. The latter (being) absolutely right, absolutely irrational, absolute poetry. I enjoy a book, the dense matter of poetic work, the woods of literature, I enjoy everything, even the spines of books, but not the labeling of schools. I want books without schools and without classifications, like life itself.]

Here Neruda refuses to associate himself with surrealism and realism. However, he is reacting to a näive realist attempt to "reflect" reality, not, as I will show below, a deeper dialectical reality. Likewise he appears to be rejecting socialist realism by declaring that poetry can be antirealist. And yet we know that once his avant-gardist stage reached its saturation point with *Residencia en la tierra,* with the advent of the Spanish civil war, Neruda began writing poetry that could be called critical realist. From *España en el corazón* (Spain in the Heart) onwards he wrote in a realist yet experimental style, and thus did not abandon his formal innovation or his creative spontaneity. However, the content in his work did change. While Neruda's avant-gardist poetry tends to be self-reflexive and represents a personal crisis in the poet's life, his oeuvre from 1937 to his death was influenced by political matters.[34] As Neruda's political and moral consciousness grew so did his ability to represent the social forces at work in capitalism in a way that Neruda the would-be-avant-gardist did not. Far from impinging on or distorting his poetry and worldview, Neruda's increasing political awareness allowed him to see beyond his own estrangement and that of his fellow human beings in Asia.

The source that leads him to realism can be appreciated in his memoirs. In his poetry prior to 1937 Neruda says that he "[había] explorado con crueldad y agonía el corazón del hombre; sin pensar en los hombres había visto ciudades, pero ciudades vacías" (had explored with cruelty and agony the heart of man; without thinking about human beings I had seen cities, but empty cities.)[35] In "Alturas de Macchu Picchu" he says a similar thing: "poco a poco el hombre fue negándome" (little by little man was being denied to me). And, a few verses later, he echoes the desperate Neruda of "Walking Around" in *Residencia en la tierra:* "rodé muriéndome de mi propia muerte" (I rolled dying from my own death).[36] After 1937, Neruda's books began to reach a wider readership and they served as an exploratory instrument of nature and history. In point of fact Neruda's case is rather unique as far as the readership is concerned: *Veinte poemas de amor y una canción desesperada* has sold more than a million copies and, according to his memoirs and his biographers, his poetry in the 1940s and 1950s was read before thousands of people.[37]

Neruda became so popular due to the quality and intelligibility of his poetry, and because of his ties to the political left. So it would not be an exaggeration to say that Neruda appears to be a "dialectical realist" poet who employs accessible vocabulary and narrations in an oral form with surprising metaphors produced by his "guided spontaneity." I say "dialectical realist" because Neruda's work attempts to express the thoughts and feelings involved in the class struggle of society as a whole while granting an exceptional vantage point to the class-conscious proletariat. Therefore, his poetry does not only aim at representing social relations as they are (through the mediation of language), but also those social relations that are distorted and alienated under capitalism. Moreover, based on actual sociohistorical experience his writing, beginning particularly with *España en el corazón,* tries to capture collective and individual aspirations that portray more humane social relations that could lead to the creation of socialism. As the following chapters prove, this socialist future does not include an unfounded, utopian view or the "bureaucratic optimism" with which Lukács charges socialist realism.

This explains why Neruda gives the following humorous account of realism:

> [el poeta] que no sea realista va muerto. Pero el poeta que sea sólo realista va muerto también. El poeta que sea sólo irracional será entendido sólo por su persona y por su amada, y esto es bastante triste. El poeta que sea sólo un racionalista, será entendido hasta por los asnos, y esto es también sumamente triste.[38]

> [Poets who are not realist are dead. But poets who are only realist are dead also. Poets who are only irrational will be understood by themselves and their lovers, and that is pretty sad. Poets who are only rationalist, will be understood even by donkies, and that too is very sad.]

And yet he praises his friend Paul Eluard because he did not lose himself "en el irracionalismo surrealista porque no fue un imitador sino un creador y como tal descargó sobre el cadáver del surrealismo disparos de claridad e inteligencia" (in Surrealist irrationalism because he wasn't an imitator but rather a creator and as such he fired on the cadaver of Surrealism shots of clarity and intelligence).[39] Neruda's attack against both surrealism and realism in this context underscores my contention that he is not focusing on realism per se, but on reflectionism and socialist realism. From Neruda's perspective each provides a static view of emotional life and the social reality under capitalism and socialism, consequently, they are unacceptable as literary models. As Lukács has shown, näive realism can manifest itself under capitalism as a reflection of the primacy of an immediate, fragmented reality, whose isolation is sketched as natural; or it can emerge in the form of socialist realism which is required to serve as agitation and create a schematic sense of optimism about the future of humanity and socialism.[40]

For Neruda socialist realism was not an option because it attempted to limit the creative capacities of the artist too much and often depicted no major social conflicts or tensions. While Neruda objected to the bureaucratic task assigned to literature, he also acknowledged that the Soviet bureaucracy's manufactured role for literature was contested openly. In his memoirs Neruda states that there was some dogmatism in the USSR vis-à-vis the arts, but he also argues that that dogmatism was denounced (even during the Stalin years):

> La existencia de un dogmatismo soviético en las artes durante largos periodos no puede ser negada, pero también debe decirse que este dogmatismo fue siempre tomado como un defecto y combatido cara a cara. El culto a la personalidad produjo, con los ensayos críticos de Zdhanov, brillante dogmatista, un endurecimiento grave en el desarrollo de la cultura soviética. Pero había mucha respuesta en todas partes y ya se sabe que la vida es más fuerte y más porfiada que los preceptos. La revolución es la vida y los preceptos buscan su propio ataúd.[41]

> [The existence of a Soviet dogmatism in the arts during long periods cannot be denied, but it should also be said that this dogmatism was always taken as a defect and battled face to face. The cult of personality produced, with the critical essays of Zdhanov, a brilliant propagandist, a serious hardening of the development of Soviet culture. But there were many responses all over and we all know that life is stronger and more insistent than its precepts. The revolution is life and the precepts search for their own coffin].

Here Neruda makes it clear that he disagrees with Zdhanov's defense of socialist realism because it impaired the development of Soviet literature. He also indicates that there were plenty of opponents to socialist realism within the USSR, including, I would assume, Lukács. Indeed, Neruda's position here is very similar to Lukács': he supports the USSR and yet opposes the official cultural program offered in the form of socialist realism. However, at other moments his thoughts take a Brechtian direction: he feels impelled to defend the USSR and yet is not comfortable with the literary schools which try to represent socialist life. Neruda was clearly torn between his commitment to the Soviet Union and the literary means available to analyze the situation.

> Por una parte, las nuevas formas, la necesaria renovación de cuanto existe, debe traspasar y romper los moldes literarios. Por otra parte, cómo no acompañar los

pasos de una profunda y espaciosa revolución? Cómo alejar de los temas centrales las victorias, conflictos, humanos problemas, fecundidad, movimiento, germinación de un inmenso pueblo que se enfrenta a un cambio total de régimen político, económico, social? Cómo no solidarizarse con ese pueblo atacado por feroces invasiones, cercado por implacables colonialistas, oscurantistas de todos los climas y pelajes? Podrían la literatura o las artes tomar una actitud de aérea independencia junto a acontecimientos tan esenciales?[42]

[On the one hand, the new forms, the necessary renovation of all that exists, must break and overcome literary models. On the other hand, how could one not follow the steps of a deep and spacious revolution? How could one distance oneself from the main issues, the victories, conflicts, human problems, growth, movement, germination of an immense people who confront a radical change in the social, economic and political regime? How could one not commit oneself with this people attacked by ferocious invasions, fenced in by implacable colonialists, obscurantists from all climates and backgrounds? Could literature or the arts take on an air of independence knowing of these essential matters?]

This position is almost an exact rephrasing of Brecht's own stance as regards realism and experimentation: "New problems appear and demand new methods. Reality changes; in order to represent it, modes of representation must also change." But Brecht was quick to add, as Neruda would, that realism as aesthetic method was necessary.[43] Furthermore, any reader of Brecht's poetry knows that it is dialectics at work in a realist setting. Here we come to the crux of the question of the two opposing sides: on the one hand, the belief in a poetic revolution; on the other, the imminent necessity of supporting the Soviet people and of reacting before the major historical events that afflicted them. In the end, in his works and life, Neruda incarnates both tendencies and thus upholds his notion of "guided spontaneity," "spontaneity" reflecting the sometimes sudden flashes of imagination and the fires of inspiration; "guided" indicating that there was an overarching framework, a coherent, systematization in Neruda's method.

Realism and experimentation form an integral whole in Neruda's poetic work. That is why he chose to pay homage to Mayakovsky in Peking in 1957, because, although there were thematic and formal differences between Neruda's work and Mayakovsky's, the Chilean felt a real affinity with the Russian. Neruda lauds him because he was the first poet to incorporate the party and the proletariat in his work, and he compares his impact on contemporary poetry to that of Baudelaire and Whitman. In an obvious criticism of socialist realism he contends that Mayakovsky's work is not dogmatic, it is poetic:

Porque cualquiera innovación de contenido que no sea digerido y llegue a ser parte nutricia del pensamiento, no pasa a ser sino un estimulante exterior del pensamiento. Maiakovski hace circular dentro de la poesía los duros temas de la lucha, los monótonos temas de la reunión, y estos asuntos florecen en su palabra, se convierten en armas prodigiosas, en azucenas rojas.[44]

[Because any innovation in content which is not digested and becomes part of food for thought, cannot be anything but an outside stimulant of thought. Mayakovsky has the hard issues of struggle circulate in his poetry, the monotonous topics of meetings, and these affairs flower in his poetic word, they become prodigious arms, red lilies.]

In other words, Mayakovsky challenges the reader with his complex and contradictory depiction of the social reality in the USSR, with its ebbs and flows, its glories and its tragedies. Neruda also praises Mayakovsky for his satires of the Soviet bureaucracy and attacks on petit bourgeois consciousness.[45] So while Neruda's poetic method and work show the impact of the Lukácsian theory of realism, he does not quite fit the paradigmatic role of realist. Although he lives and breathes as a realist, he nonetheless holds fast to his rebel spirit, at least until the early 1950s, and experiments with formal devices.

To a certain degree the Chilean Communist Party opened doors for Neruda so he could be independent while remaining a party member. He could do this because, on various occasions in the twentieth century, the party in Chile proved to be independent of, or even antagonistic to, the Comintern.[46] So Neruda benefited from the ideological flexibility in the party and carved out his own niche in its midst. And in that situation he developed what we might call his "dialectical realism": a dynamic method for understanding social and natural forces as well as human nature and the possibilities of human emancipation; a method grounded in human labor as its foundation and the party as an imperfect yet effective vehicle for paving the way for socialism.

In his works and life Neruda remains committed to socialism and the USSR, and this affects the direction his literary form and content take. From *Tercera residencia* (1947) on his verse becomes more realist in both its dialectical portrayal of social relations and in the clarity suggested by his style. And yet Neruda is able to maintain critical distance and to cultivate his passionate commitment. From 1937 on, his poetic method becomes more sophisticated in its ability to represent, in abstraction, the sociopolitical, economic, and moral dilemmas of his time. This transformation, I think, can best be appreciated in the poetry itself.

Neruda's Dialectical Realism at Work

In "Alturas de Macchu Picchu" (The Heights of Macchu Picchu) from section 2 of *Canto general* and "El hombre invisible" (The Invisible Man) from *Odas elementales,* Neruda's artistic independence stands out in spite and because of the winds of history which blow and envelop him, moving him to commit himself to the antifascist cause and socialism. In this context poetic form is not as esoteric as it was during *Residencia en la tierra,* but it continues to be demanding for the reader. And even in the realm of content, if Neruda were following in the steps of socialist realism we would expect a realist and perhaps schematic account of sociopolitical and economic matters at the expense of petit bourgeois consciousness, which, during these years, meant autobiographical details. However, this is not the case even at the height of his poetry during the 1940s and 1950s after he joined the party.

While Neruda's artistic independence is worth noting, the most significant question regarding "Alturas de Macchu Picchu" from *Canto general,* and "El hombre invisible" (The Invisible Man) from *Odas elementales,* is that they demonstrate that Neruda enhances and elaborates his poetic method after *Residencia en la tierra,* and even after *Tercera residencia.* His poetry in the 1940s and 1950s developed as regards three principal aspects. First, it is anchored in a more elaborate understanding of sociopolitical, economic, and emotional matters. By this stage Neruda had read enough and gained sufficient experience to comprehend Marxism more completely. Previously, even in a book foregrounding political struggles like *Tercera residencia,* Neruda's pro-Republican and antifascist stances were more second nature: they were his gut reactions to the injustice perpetrated by the Nationalists in Spain or to Germany's invasion of the Soviet Union which the poet experienced in a primary or secondary way. This is not to say that his political ideas did not cohere, but they began to do so as he was taking part politically in the defense of the Republic or participating in the antifascist movement.

By the 1940s and 1950s, however, Neruda's grasp of Marxism is more systematic and intricate even though or, we might say, precisely because he did not come to Marxism through theory or through academic channels. This is evident in the breadth and depth of his thought present in the poetry of these years. In his avant-gardist texts he had a perceptive yet spontaneous understanding of the dialectic, whereas by *Canto general* he developed it into a persistent mode of thought, or a way of thinking about the reality in which he was immersed. Thus, in *Canto general* he makes use of several poetic and class vantage points to attempt to assess and accurately portray the historical events he is recounting; he employs several levels of generality which link concrete historical events with the totality of colonization, imperialism, and class struggle; and he shows how there is a historical continuity and discontinuity in these specific and general social conflicts. Neruda's dialectical way of thinking can be appreciated in the internal structural relations in the poems. Thus, for instance, in a classic and yet subtle way Neruda makes use of negation as a generating principle that leads to its own negation; he cultivates the interpenetration of opposites as a vehicle for describing complex and antagonistic social situations (a model superior to the literary device "antithesis"); and he carefully avails himself of differences in verb tenses to dramatize qualitative and quantitative changes. These are some techniques among others associated with a coherent and complex way of viewing the world that inform his poetry at this juncture and demonstrate that his texts in the 1940s and 1950s gain in depth of understanding over his previous work.

Likewise in the case of form: while it is as complex as the *Residencias* stage, it is enriched by the realist foregrounding of everyday sociopolitical and economic issues. This poetry's formal difficulty can be seen, for example, in the long and majestic "Alturas de Macchu Picchu." As far as stylistic technique is concerned this poem is clearly one of the most elaborate Neruda wrote: readers are asked to decipher the chain of incomparable and provocative metaphors to understand the speaker's odyssey. In the first stanza we read the following famous verses:

> Del aire al aire, como una red vacía,
> iba yo entre las calles y la atmósfera, llegando y despidiendo,
> en el advenimiento del otoño la moneda extendida
> de las hojas, y entre la primavera y las espigas,
> lo que el más grande amor, como dentro de un guante
> que cae, no entrega como una larga luna.[47]

> [From air to air, like an
> empty net,
> I went along between the streets and atmosphere,
>   arriving and departing,
> in the advent of autumn the outstretched coin
> of the leaves, and between springtime and the ears
>   of corn,
> all that the greatest love, as in a falling
> glove, hands us like a long moon.][48]

As readers we are obliged to analyze the function and meaning of "red vacía," "moneda extendida," as well as the last two verses in order to make sense of the stanza. As far as style is concerned, these verses are at least as difficult to entangle as ones in *Residencia en la tierra* even for the avid and sensitive reader; the difference between the latter and the former manifests itself in the content and composition of the poem. Unlike the avant-gardist poems where solitude, alienation, the overwhelming force of nature, and chaos drown the speaker, these verses portray this same autobiographical moment (the 1920s and 1930s) with the critical eye of a mature poet. Readers of *Residencia en la tierra* observe the speaker entrapped in an endless whirlwind. In the second part of that same book the speaker finds his refuge in Josie Bliss and in nature's creativity, but he does so as he drowns in the chaos that surrounds him. As several critics have noted, it is a desperate world that is very similar to T. S. Eliot's *The Waste Land,* though lacking notably the impersonal tone Eliot cultivated.[49] As "Alturas de Macchu Picchu" powerfully shows, Neruda, unlike Eliot, transcended this moment of existential anguish and moved to the left politically; Eliot, perhaps due to the persistence of bourgeois class consciousness, never freed himself from the cage capitalism had placed him in and he became more right wing (a royalist).[50] By contrast, Neruda became a Communist without surrendering the quality of his poetry.

Neruda's youthful years fit in the structure of "Alturas de Macchu Picchu" as a generating negation, that is, as a negating moment, which is also negated by his life's transformations.[51] The mature Neruda learns from these changes in life and raises his sociopolitical consciousness. From the point of view of the narrator the lost soul that inhabits the *Residencia* poems is perceived as a person who suffers from a "soledad más espesa" (the deepest loneliness) and alienation from his fellow human beings from whom he is only able to "asir sino un racimo de rostros o máscaras / precipitadas" (I could grasp nothing but a clump of faces or / precipitous masks).[52] So it is that the poet narrates his epic misery and decline—in Hernán Loyola's words, a period of "autoasesinato" (killing oneself)—which, ironically produces one of his most famous works.[53]

Unlike the mature Neruda, the poet of the *Residencias* stage was incapable of understanding his years in Asia as a negative period leading to its sublation. That young Neruda was only able to describe vividly and painfully the immediate reality that encircled and suffocated him: his isolation and his estrangement from the diplomatic work, his abhorrence of English imperialism, his yearning for the Spanish language, and his lack of friendships. In the final verses of part II Neruda recognizes the severe limitations of his *Residencias* poetry and concludes that he had lost track of humanity.

In the following section, VII, reminiscent of "Walking around" in *Residencia en la tierra,* he depicts the desperate life that accosted human beings who filled their lives with their "corta muerte diaria" (every day a little death) (31). As Part IV bears witness, Neruda suffered a similar fate: "La poderosa muerte me invitó muchas veces" (Mighty death invited me many times) (32). During the 1920s and 1930s he was so dominated by disaffection that suicide tempted him and he isolated himself even more ("poco a poco el hombre fue negándome" (32). The Neruda of the *Residencias* years poured his anguish and solitude into his verses, but his catharsis left him just as spiritually impoverished as before.

Neruda the elder and wiser, on the other hand, who writes this poem as a self-criticism, manages to evaluate his personal life in the context of other social factors (capitalism as such, imperialism, class consciousness, questions of the human species, and so on) and to reconsider his 20s and 30s as marred by estrangement. Passion's dialectical opposite, self-destruction, runs rampant during these years of his life. The mature Neruda, emboldened by his mistakes and experiences, can judge these years more accurately as a negation, a negation that taught him moral and political lessons that have expanded his knowledge and ignited his passion for life.

The mature Neruda continues this poetic narration of his political awakening in part VI. His travels take him to the splendidly imposing Macchu Picchu, surrounded by smoky mountain peaks, where the speaker finds "la cuna del relámpago y del hombre" (the cradle of lightening and man) (33). Having formerly sought out isolation and thus shunned his fellow human beings, now he encounters one of the sites of hope for humankind. In the Andes, a train's ride from the Incan capital, the speaker is re-humanized when he is confronted with the ruins in Macchu Picchu:

> Miro las vestiduras y las manos,
> el vestigio del agua en la oquedad sonora,
> la pared suavizada por el tacto de un rostro
> que miró con mis ojos las lámparas terrestres
> que aceitó con mis manos las desaparecidas
> maderas: porque todo, ropaje, piel, vasijas,
> palabras, vino, panes,
> se fue, cayó a la tierra. (34)
>
> [I behold the vestments and hands,
> the vestige of water in the sonorous void,
> the wall tempered by the touch of a face
> that beheld with my eyes the earthen lamps,
> that oiled with my hands the vanished
> wood: because everything—clothing, skin, vessels,
> words, wine, bread—
> is gone, fallen to earth.][55]

In these verses the speaker confuses himself with the Incas who, with their remarkable workmanship, created the astounding architecture that he finds in ruins. As he unites and confuses himself with the Incan laborers he recognizes and feels a part of these congealed ruins destroyed by the Spanish conquerors. So, violating the grammatical structure, he states that an Incan "miró con mis ojos" and "aceitó con mis manos." The Incan laborer here inhabits the speaker thus allowing the latter to participate in the construction of Macchu Picchu and to become a worker. As Hugo Montes puts it, "[q]uien quiera alcanzar la vida dolorosa de los hombres vencidos por la piedra de su diario vivir deberá luchar con la dureza de los elementos que lo rodean" (whoever wants to attain the painful life of the men defeated by stone due to their daily life needs to fight against the hard elements that surround him).[55] Moreover, only by refusing the division of labor under capitalism and by becoming a laborer himself can Neruda earn the right to tell the story of these ruins built under the coercion of the Incan monarchy. So, there are three vantage points which are incorporated into the poem—that of the monarchy, the workers, and the conquerors—and yet Neruda chooses to privilege the laborers' point of view. All that is left from this class conflict between the Incan working people, the Incan monarchy, and the Spanish conquistadors is the architecture which is the fruit of the Incan people's toil, proving that it is this class that creates all the value in feudalism and capitalism and that all other classes must depend on it and/or usurp its value. The Incans' manual labor leaves traces of their history on the product of their labor. Engraved with the Incan's own social authorship, this architectural structure is the social and sentient result of their work. Thus, in examining this landscape, Neruda pays homage to the Incan laborers (the slave, the serf, the miserable one in section X) and not to the Inca monarchy.

The poet then takes the readers beyond the particular—the *Residencias* period—to the general, that is, to the sociohistorical circumstances and political forces that can potentially minimize the very conditions from which the speaker suffered in the 1920s and 1930s. What follows proves to be the opposite of the avant-gardist position he previously defended (part XI in "Alturas"): "porque el hombre es más ancho que el mar y que sus islas, / y hay que caer en él como en un pozo para salir del fondo / con un ramo de agua secreta y de verdades sumergidas" (because man is greater than the sea and its islands, / and we must fall into him as into a well to / emerge from the bottom / with a bouquet of secret water and sunken truths) (41). In that way Neruda suggests that the dehumanizing and all-absorbing individualism promoted under capitalism can be overcome by working for political and economic change and committing oneself to socialism. By abolishing capitalism we can arrive at a historical moment that, as Marx and Engels put it in "The Communist Manifesto," provides for "the free development of each [as] the condition for the free development of all."[56]

In examining the material basis of the Incan empire erected by the laborers, Neruda starts to track down an alternative history of the Incas and to associate his own writing with the architectual wonders of Macchu Picchu:

> Pero una permanencia de piedra y de palabra:
> la ciudad como un vaso se levantó en las manos
> de todos, vivos, muertos, callados, sostenidos
> de tanta muerte, un muro, de tanta vida un golpe

de pétalos de piedra: la rosa permanente, la morada:
este arrecife andino de colonias glaciales.

[But a permanence of stone and of word:
the citadel was raised like a chalice in the hands
of all, the living, the dead, the silent, sustained
by so much death, a wall, from so much life a
    stroke
of stone petals; the permanent rose, the dwelling:
this Andean reef of glacial colonies.][57]

Neruda allies himself with the working people who created Macchu Picchu with their suffering: "pétalos de piedra: rosa permanente" (35). Archetype of poetry, life and love, the rose is congealed in the ruins in its association with the stones (they are "pétalos de piedra"). From a descriptive, realist point of view the stones serve an instrumental function in the architectural formations in Macchu Picchu, but, from a dialectical critical realist point of view, the identity of stone, as negation of the rose, is interpenetrated in the relationship between the stone and the rose. The negation of the negation—"la rosa de piedra" which appears in section IX—redefines the stone as something congealed with history and aesthetic work. In this context, arduous and exploitative work under capitalism would be conceived as the stone itself and the human creativity (the rose) ignored or under-appreciated. However, Neruda seems to say that under a more just economic system, with less stratification of social classes and a more equitable distribution of resources (in spite of the Inca empire being a monarchy) collective labor can potentially become more humane and creative. Thus, the dialectical image of the rose and stone points to one of the objectives of Neruda's poetry: the historical materialization of work.[58] So poetry itself is a type of work that can be compared to the historical legacy of the architecture at Macchu Picchu. Part IX clearly attempts to imitate Incan structural designs visually in verses, using the repetition of "stone" to reinforce that point. Neruda thus returns to a fundamental argument made by Marxists that all intellectual labor depends on manual labor because the latter serves as the point of departure for the former.

    In part IX the focus is the personified, mural-like poetic construction in which "los dormidos" [(the Incas whose legacy is embodied in the ruins) scarcely make an appearance, except as the magnificent authors of Macchu Picchu. Logically, then, the vantage point shifts from the congealed work, the ruins, to its creators in part X ("Piedra en la piedra, el hombre, dónde estuvo?" (Stone upon stone, and man, where was he?) (39). Here Neruda concentrates on the fundamental antagonism between the laborer and his product (the architecture). Even though the economic system is not capitalist but rather simultaneously feudalist and communitarian, Neruda places the emphasis on this conflict between the working population which constructed the lion's share of Macchu Picchu and the nobility which coerced, exploited, and profited from the laboring people:[59]

> Macchu Picchu, pusiste
> piedra en la piedra, y en la base, harapo?
> Carbón sobre carbón, y en el fondo la lágrima?
> Fuego en el oro, y en él, temblando el rojo
> goterón de la sangre? (40)
>
> [Macchu Picchu, did you put
> stone upon stone and, at the base, tatters?
> Coal upon coal and, at the bottom, tears?
> Fire in the gold and, within it, the trembling
> drop of red blood?]

The construction of the grandiose buildings on the mountaintops is here contrasted with the exploitation and dehumanization of the people responsible for their creation. Even in this pre-capitalist economic setting, Neruda seems to argue, the product is reified at the expense of its producers. As the rest of this part suggests, a similar thing happened during the conquest and colonial period when the Incas were driven to hunger and subjected to degrading labor.

Part XI continues with the speaker's plea that the Incan slaves, serfs, and miserable ones tell him this tragedy as he interrogates them with a passionate interest; however this section represents a significant transformation in "Alturas de Macchu Picchu." The speaker implores them, "que en mí palpite, como un ave mil años prisionera, / el viejo corazón olvidado!" (let the aged heart of the forsaken beat in me / like a bird captive for a thousand years!) Neruda then reverses his avant-gardist position of describing, in a neo-Romantic vein, a menacing nature and his own despair and focuses passionately on humanity: "el hombre es más ancho que el mar y que sus islas, / y hay que caer en él como en un pozo para salir del fondo / con un ramo de agua secreta y de verdades sumergidas" (because man is greater than the sea and its islands, / and we must fall into him as into a well to / emerge from the bottom / with a bouquet of secret water and sunken truths). The poet turns to the laborers as the cornerstone and liberators of humanity. This is underscored by the speaker's focus: he decides to blind his eyes momentarily to the Incan monarchy and also to the conquistadors, "no veo a la bestia veloz, / no veo el ciego ciclo de sus garras" (I do not see the blind cycle of its claws). And he chooses instead another vantage point: "veo el antiguo ser, sevidor, el dormido / en los campos, veo un cuerpo, mil cuerpos, un hombre, mil mujeres, / bajo la racha negra, negros de lluvia y noche" (I see the man of old, the servant, asleep in the / fields, / I see a body, a thousand bodies, a man, a / thousand women, / black with rain and night). The slumbering worker—"yee prisoners of starvation" as "The Internationale" memorably puts it—will arise with the speaker as he tells their story: "Juan Cortapiedras, hijo de Wiracocha, / Juan Comefrío, hijo de estrella verde, / Juan Piesdescalzos, nieto de la turquesa, / sube a nacer conmigo, hermano" (Juan Stonecutter, son of Wiracocha, / Juan Coldeater, son of a green star, / Juan Barefoot, grandson of turquoise, / rise up to be born with me, my brother) (41).[60]

This purview gives way to the following famous section, XII, in which the speaker, taken in by the fury of passion, demands that the Incan workers use him as a vehicle for telling their story. The sleeping (not dead) artisans and laborers narrate their story to the speaker, but they are only able to convey their tragedy through their labors:

> Sube a nacer conmigo, hermano.
> dame la mano desde la profunda
> zona de tu dolor diseminado.
> No volverás del fondo de las rocas.
> No volverás del tiempo subterráneo.
> No volverá tu voz endurecida.
> No volverán tus ojos taladrados.
> Mírame desde el fondo de la tierra,
> labrador, tejedor, pastor callado:
> domador de guanacos tutelares:
> albañil del andamio desafiado:
> aguador de las lágrimas andinas:
> joyero de los dedos machacados:
> agricultor temblando en la semilla:
> alfarero en tu greda derramado:
> traed la copa de esta nueva vida
> vuestros viejos dolores enterrados. (41–42)

> [Rise up and be born with me, my brother.
> Give me your hand from the deep
> zone of your disseminated sorrow.
> You'll not return from the bottom of the rocks.
> You'll not return from subterranean time.
> Your stiff voice will not return.
> Your drilled eyes will not return.
> Behold me from the depths of the earth,
> laborer, weaver, silent herdsman:
> tamer of the tutelary guanacos:
> mason of the defied scaffold:
> bearer of the Andean tears:
> jeweler with your fingers crushed:
> tiller trembling in the seed:

potter spilt in your clay:
bring to the cup of this new life, brothers,
all your timeless buried sorrows.][61]

In a reference to the Last Communion, the Incan laborers' bring their "buried sorrows," like red wine, like blood and martyrdom to fill the cup of life in Latin America in the late 1940s (a contemporary setting for the Neruda writing at that moment). They are unable to return ("No volverán") because they have sacrificed their lives to exploitative labor, to the creation of the Incan empire. There would be no Incan empire if it were not for their labor. It is a situation analogous to the relationship between the proletariat and Capital that Marx describes: "Capital is dead labour which, vampire-like, lives only by sucking living labour, and lives the more, the more labour it sucks."[62] The Incan laborers' own product—the ruins—remains and is valorized while its creators are apparently lost but are really congealed in the ruins. Although the laborers cannot return, they have shaped and erected the stones that form the structure of every village and city in the Incan empire, including Macchu Picchu. But this fact in and of itself, however accurate it may be, cannot elucidate the subjective factor that then dominates the rest of the poem: not paternalistic pity nor sympathy, but a profound empathy and commitment. In other words, there has to be an accompanying moral dimension to the ravaging exploitation and alienation of labor. Otherwise, how are we to explain Neruda's fervent and impassioned commitment to the working class? How to explicate Neruda's famous moral and political stance late in the poem: "Yo vengo a hablar por vuestra boca muerta" (I've come to speak through your dead mouths) (42)? Identifying a reality—the labor theory of value—in the Incan empire alone cannot account for Neruda's radical moral commitment to the working people and not, say, to Incan society as such. Neruda clearly sees the plight of the Incan laborers as inhuman and unjust based on a concept of human nature perceived in glimpses even in exploitative social systems (feudalist or capitalist) and concludes, based on moral and social progress, that the economic and social relations could be transformed into more just and egalitarian ones.[63]

Canonical, liberal interpretations of "Alturas de Macchu Picchu" and *Canto general* argue that the moral dimension in this book leads to an ideological distortion. In this classic book, Neruda purportedly is unable to hold himself back and thus succumbs to the "simplifications" of his Marxist political position. Emir Rodríguez Monegal, for instance, maintains that since *Canto general* was "fomentado por un partido político" (fomented by a political party), namely, the Communist Party, that it is "una pieza de propaganda" (a piece of propaganda) because it portrays history in a one-sided way. In essence, Rodríguez Monegal claims, *Canto general* is "periodística y tiene el vigor, la parcialidad, la demagogia y hasta el terrorismo de los titulares de periódicos (journalistic and it has the vigor, partiality, the demogoguery and even the terrorism of newspaper headlines).[64] He thus criticizes the moral stances Neruda defends in his poetry as though they had no socio-historical and political support and justification. From that point of view Neruda seems to make outlandish claims that just do not jibe with the liberal perception of reality that Rodríguez Monegal upholds. Enrico Mario Santí's focus in *Pablo Neruda: The Poetics of Prophecy* is on rhetoric per se and on the virtual impossibility of linguistic reference. His aim, as noted in chapter 1, is to describe Neruda as "a prophet lost in a labyrinth who remained blind to the 'real' issues of human history."[65] Lost in the wilderness of human history, the poet as prophet relies on allegory in *Canto general* to represent (inaccurately) the conflicts and tragedies in Latin America from the pre-conquest to 1950. In short, the poet-prophet is left to making empty moral declarations in his poetry. Like Rodríguez Monegal, Santí argues that there is no objective foundation on which Neruda's moral positions rest. Consequently, Neruda's moral/political stances are stripped of their substantiation in socio-historical, economic, and political affairs.

Likewise Cedomil Goic alleges that "Alturas de Macchu Picchu" is driven by "ideologismo sectario" (ideological sectarianism), which "despliega ternura fraternal y solidaria o llena el texto de iracundia y de vehemencia sangrienta" (unfolds fraternal tenderness and solidarity or fills the text with ire and bloody vehemence).[66] Yet, like Sául Yurkievich, Goic asserts that Neruda's poetic vision is based on an "experiencia metafísica" (225) (metaphysical experience).[67] Goic's allegation that Neruda falls prey to a metaphysical experience thus clouds the political and economic underpinnings of the poem and his observations about the historical and personal death. This leads him to make more religious references about Neruda's intentions. Hence, Neruda becomes a messianic poet-theologian who wants to describe this Incan citadel magically and, in the final instance, searches for his own immortality (239–42). Thus, given Rodríguez Monegal's, Santí's, and Goic's relativism, their Neruda is a very talented yet unstable figure who denounces social injustices irrationally.[68]

Yet it is only by recognizing this savage socioeconomic injustice and by reliving the experiences the Incan artisans and workers have been through that Neruda can become their spokesperson, a vessel to retell Incan history from the point of view of the vanquished:

> Yo vengo a hablar por vuestra boca muerta.
> A través de la tierra juntad todos
> los silenciosos labios derramados
> y desde el fondo habladme toda esta larga noche
> como si yo estuviera con vosotros anclado,

contadme todo, cadena a cadena,
eslabón a eslabón, y paso a paso,
afilad los cuchillos que guardasteis,
ponedlos en mi pecho y en mi mano,
como un río de rayos amarrillos,
como un río de tigres enterrados,
y dejadme llorar, horas, días, años,
edades ciegas, siglos estelares.[69]

[I've come to speak through your dead mouths,
Throughout the earth join all
the silent scattered lips
and from the depths speak to me all night long,
as if I were anchored with you,
tell me everything, chain by chain,
link by link, and step by step,
sharpen the knives that you've kept,
put them in my breast and in my hand,
like a river of yellow lightening,
like a river of buried jaguars,
and let me weep hours, days, years,
blind ages, stellar centuries.]

Only by becoming an intellectual laborer, an intellectual whose destiny is united with the working class and whose very existence depends on that class, can the speaker be granted the opportunity of representing the Incan laborers. Only by investing himself with a collective purpose is Neruda able to become something other than the solitary individual poet he was during the *Residencias;* only by making the workers' position his own is he capable of letting his individuality flourish.

ODE TO COMMON THINGS: A PASSIONATE DIALECTIC

Neruda's *Odas elementales* shows both continuity and rupture with *Canto general*. While *Canto general* focuses on the historical and geographical panorama in Latin America, *Odas elementales* deals with dialectical meditations on nature and human existence. As is well known, in short verses and long poems Neruda dedicates odes to things that, at first sight, seem common and even insignificant. On closer inspection, these objects of daily life, like the onion or bread, become sources of contemplation and critical observation. Nothing could be further from the truth than Julieta Gómez Paz's contention that Neruda's realism leads him to adopt "la visión burguesa de la realidad" (a bourgeois vision of reality).[70] As a dialectical thinker Neruda manages to unearth the object's social and natural properties and restore their vital importance. In *Canto general* Neruda's intent was to point out that labor is exploited and disregarded as the object itself is reified; the laborer vanishes for all intents and purposes. As a laborer of words the poet identified with workers and attempted to rewrite history from their point of view, thus textually reversing the state of affairs under capitalism. In *Odas elementales* Neruda concentrates on valorizing the object congealed with the laborer's or nature's hours of work. The poems appear, deceptively, as odes dedicated merely to trivial and even humorous affairs, when, actually, odes like "Oda al tiempo" (Ode to Time) and "Oda a la vida" (Ode to Life) deal with profound social and natural issues. As Jaime Concha puts it, the odes concentrate on the "frágil singularidad de las cosas en medio de las leyes generales de la materia y la historia. Las grandes energías de la totalidad pulsan en estos minúsculos granos simbólicos" (fragile singularity of things amidst the general laws of matter and history. The great energies of the totality pulsate in these miniscule and symbolic grains).[71]

While the form in *Odas elementales* is noticeably more accessible than any of his previous poetry and thus appears simple (elementary), the manner in which the object is located in a matrix of social relations makes this verse, ironically, more complex. Thus, it is true and misleading to affirm, as the poet Luis Rosales does, that "el verso corto de estos poemas no es nunca caprichoso. La intención de Neruda al utilizarlo ha sido establecer la relación más natural entre fondo y forma, ya que el mundo de los objetos elementales debe expresarse en la forma más sencilla y elemental" (the short verse of these poems is never capricious. Neruda's intention in using it has been to establish a more natural relationship between content and form, since the world of elementary objects should be expressed in the simplest and most elementary form).[72] In terms of dialectical method, it would be difficult to find more penetrating poems than, say, "Oda al tiempo," "Oda a la intranquilidad," "Oda a la vida," or "Oda a la cebolla" (Ode to Time, Ode to Restlessness, Ode to Life, Ode to the Onion). Far from being a phenomenological intent to privilege an object's fleeting and independent existence, these poems conceive the object as the intersection of natural and social relations, which give it its identity. In his seminal essay on the *Odas,* Robert Pring-Mill has underscored the importance of profound poems like "Oda al hombre sencillo" (Ode to Simple Men) for the complexity of Neruda's poetic method:[73]

> yo borro los colores
> y busco para encontrar
> el tejido profundo,
> así también encuentro
> la unidad de los hombres,
> y en el pan

> busco
> más allá de la forma.⁷⁴
>
> [I erase colors
> and look to find
> the deep fabric,
> so too I find
> the unity of all men,
> and in bread
> I look
> beyond the form.]

In this context, going beyond the form means transcending the notion of bread as commodity and examining the labor that made it possible. However, in a more general sense, it entails seeing beyond poetic form and its own fetishism particularly in avant-gardist poetry. It also denotes more than a transparent realism, which demands that the object itself be reproduced artistically. Neruda's reference to form is evidently meant as a critique of the avant-garde and of näive realism (or mechanical materialism). The apparent transparency of his poetic form in *Odas elementales* leads to a more elaborate display of the content, to a richer consideration of the endless complexity of reality that Neruda attempts to represent in his poetic form.

In his thesis-poem, "El hombre invisible" (The Invisible Man), Neruda defends this poetic method and poetry.⁷⁵ Neruda begins with a self-criticism, a critique of pure poets and of the Neruda of the *Residencias* years. It spite of that he adds that he adores "toda la poesía escrita" (all written poetry), but has to smile when he hears his "antiguo hermano" (his former brother) the hermetic poet who limits himself by describing events in his own life and does not transcend them. The self-absorbed poet loses himself and fails to notice fellow human beings who suffer and love. According to Neruda these hermetic poets have lost sight of reality completely:

> Yo me río,
> me sonrío
> de los viejos poetas,
> yo adoro toda la poesía escrita,
> todo el rocío,
> luna, diamante, gota
> de plata sumergida,
> que fue mi antiguo hermano,
> agregando a la rosa,
> pero me sonrío
> siempre dicen "yo",
> a cada paso
> les sucede algo,

> es siempre "yo",
> por las calles
> sólo ellos andan
> o la dulce que aman,
> nadie más. (59)
>
> [I laugh,
> I smile
> at the old poets,
> I adore all
> written poetry,
> all the dew,
> moon, diamond, drop
> of submerged silver,
> who was my former brother,
> adding to the rose,
> but I smile
> they always say "I,"
> every step of the way
> something happens to them
> it's always "I,"
> along the streets
> only they stroll
> or the sweet one they love,
> no one else.]

By carrying out a self-criticism while still disapproving of the avant-garde and pure poetry's narrow representation of reality, Neruda avoids any suggestion that he is taking the position, as Pring-Mill puts it, of a member of a "Peoples' Tribunal."[76] Neruda places the emphasis rather on the avant-gardist or pure poet's false consciousness. The problem is one of both form and content, of poetic method and political consciousness. For Neruda they are closely intertwined: the less form obstructs, the less poetry becomes an endless exploration of the vicissitudes of language, the more it can be evenly balanced with the development of the content. That is why, in this poem and in countless others, he incorporates a critique of his avant-gardist poetry in the body of his poems. As I contend in chapter 3, Neruda charges that his *Residencia* book was rich in its exploration of language, but that language served as an alienating refuge from his own social disaffection. Moreover, his poetry of the late 1920s and early 1930s suffered from a poverty of method and class-consciousness. In essence, that is what the speaker refers to in "El hombre invisible." The individual poet and his particular tragedies and pleasantries become the sole focus of this hermetic poetry, thus blindly closing off the rest of society (sólo ellos andan / o la dulce que aman, / nadie más). This poet finds himself enclosed in social alienation and unable to overcome the bourgeois notion of poetry as the realm of the inner dramas of the individual in order to see those sentiments as either opposed to or as representative of social consciousness. So, as Lukács duly noted, the artist portrays immediate reality via his spontaneous method and gives the reader, at best, a fractional view of the society as a whole; at worst his texts are a one-dimensional distortion of the social relations.[77]

Commencing with "nadie más" this alienated point of view is negated: the speaker names what the hermetic poet does not perceive in his false consciousness and contrasts this with his myopic and individualist distortion:

>nadie más,
>no pasan pescadores,
>ni libreros,
>no pasan albañiles,
>nadie se cae
>de un andamio,
>nadie sufre,
>nadie ama,
>sólo mi pobre hermano,
>el poeta,
>a él le pasan
>todas las cosas
>y a su dulce querida,
>nadie vive
>sino él solo,
>nadie llora de hambre
>o de ira,
>nadie sufre en sus versos
>porque no puede pagar el alquiler,
>a nadie en poesía
>echan a la calle
>con camas y con sillas
>y en las fábricas
>tampoco pasa nada,
>se hacen paraguas, copas,
>armas, locumotoras,
>se extraen minerales
>rascando el infierno. (59–60)

>[no one else,
>fishermen don't walk along
>nor booksalesmen,
>bricklayers don't go by,
>no one falls
>from scaffolding,

>no one suffers,
>no one loves,
>only my poor brother,
>the poet,
>things happen to him
>everything
>and to his sweet loved one,
>no one lives
>but him alone,
>no one cries from hunger
>or ire,
>no one suffers in his verses
>because he can't
>pay the rent,
>no one in poetry
>is kicked out of his house
>with beds and chairs
>and in the factories
>nothing happens either,
>nothing happens
>umbrellas, wine glasses, arms
>trains are made,
>minerals are extracted
>scraping hell.]

As in the case of "Alturas de Macchu Picchu," Neruda's vantage point is the working class, the creator of value in capitalism who is nonetheless exploited for profit. In "El hombre invisible" all that is negated by the alienated hermetic poet is foregrounded by the speaker. And yet, his criticism of the lost poet who believes that he is an extraordinary visionary is also connected with a self-criticism of Neruda's previous poetry, stretching as far back at least as *Veinte poemas de amor y una canción desesperada* (1924), thus, as Jaime Concha has pointed out, the reference to the poet who "ama los puertos / remotos, por sus nombres, / y escribe sobre océanos / que no conoce" (loves the remote / ports, because of their names, / and writes about oceans / that doesn't know).[78] So too in the case of the poet who goes through life incapable of grasping its most fundamental elements: "junto a la vida, repleta / como el maíz de granos, / él pasa sin saber / desgranarla" (together with life, replete / like corn on the cob, / he passes by without knowing / how to thresh it) (60–61). Neruda charges that, because of the division of labor, the hermetic poet has lost contact with the labor that sustains him, with those who allow him to write poetry. The alienated poet only sees faded images of nature and of human beings, whereas the speaker declares that he does not consider himself to be superior to his fellow poets, but he smiles because only he, the speaker, does not exist (81). "For this the poet as plain-speaker," states René de Costa, "must abandon his claim to uniqueness as an artist and recognize his genuine ordinariness as one man among many; as a modern-day poet of the people he is now to be, in a word, *invisible*."[79] Unlike the isolated poet, Neruda is immersed in what he observes and in what people tell him. "La vida es una lucha" (Life is a struggle), he says:

> como un río avanza
> los hombres
> quieren decirme,
> decirte,
> por qué luchan,
> si mueren,
> por qué mueren,
> y yo paso y no tengo
> tiempo para tantas vidas,
> yo quiero
> que todos vivan
> en mi vida
> y canten en mi canto,
> yo no tengo importancia,
> no tengo tiempo
> para mis asuntos,
> de noche y de día
> debo anotar lo que pasa,
> y no olvidar a nadie. (63)
>
> [like a river it advances
> and men
> want to tell me,
> tell you,
> why they are struggling,
> if they are dying,
> why they are dying,
> and pass by and I don't have
> enough time for so many lives,
> I want
> everybody to live
> in my life
> and sing in my song,
> I am of no importance,
> I don't have time
> for my affairs,
> at night and during the day
> I need to jot down what is happening,
> and not forget anyone.]

So it is that, in an echo of "Naciendo en los bosques" (Emerging in the Woods) in *Tercera residencia* we reread the autobiographical story of Neruda, the former hermetic poet, who got lost in a sea of solitude but who now thirsts for all that nature and society offer him.[80]

Now we come to the crux of "El hombre invisible" in which the very title can be appreciated in its dialectical tension. As in section XII of "Alturas de Macchu Picchu," the speaker needs to earn his right to represent the working class by struggling with it politically and by examining the world realistically and critically. It is true that Neruda is choosing a specific vantage point from which to view social relations under capitalism, but he is giving credence to the proletarian point of view because they are the architects of capitalist society who are exploited and robbed of their humanity. So the speaker states that he is not "superior a mi hermano" (superior to my brother), denoting that he is equal to his fellow workers, and by becoming equal, he is invisible. He becomes invisible due to the clarity of his consciousness and his position. Being transparent means that for him, unlike the old Neruda, "no hay misteriosas sombras, / no hay tinieblas" (there are no mysterious shadows, / there is no darkness) brought on by the convolution of form and the waves of distancing in content. At first sight, the speaker's declarations that he is "el único invisible" (the only invisible one) and unimportant suggest that he subordinates the individual to the goals of socialism; the individual, as such, seems to disappear, his individuality vanish. And yet, ironically, this poem is written in the first person, making this testimony and poetic form more palpable and realistic for a Communist poet than the alienating effects of art for art's sake or the promised illusions of socialist realism. Therefore, to be invisible in this context involves relinquishing the pedestal that bourgeois society has conferred to the poet which allows him to consider himself more valued and interesting than workers and equating himself with the destiny of the class which can potentially put an end to class society. That is why the speaker is so busy trying to record all that he sees and why his own identity is dependent on other human beings ("No puedo sin la vida vivir, / sin el hombre ser hombre" [I can't without life live / without man be a man). In the last verses of "El hombre invisible"—again in an echo of "Alturas de Macchu Picchu"—he underscores this point beautifully:

> dadme
> las luchas
> de cada día
> porque ellas son mi canto,
> y así andaremos juntos,
> codo a codo,
> todos los hombres,
> mi canto los reúne:

> el canto del hombre invisible
> que canta con todos los hombres (65).

> [give me
> the every day
> struggles
> because they are my song,
> and that way we will walk together,
> shoulder to shoulder,
> all of humanity,
> my song unites them:
> the song of the invisible man
> who sings with humanity.]

First he asks for the workers' dramas so he can retell them in his texts, so, as in "Alturas de Macchu Picchu," his poetry can become a vehicle for interpreting reality in a radically different way than the ruling ideologies under capitalism. Only by struggling side by side with the workers can his poetry have any meaning and gain grounding and depth.

In both "Alturas de Macchu Picchu" and "El hombre invisible" Neruda's capacity to portray social relations in pre-capitalist or capitalist settings develops significantly as he throws his lot in with the working class and perceives it as the fundamental creator of value. Although the language that populates "Alturas" is akin to what is present in the avant-gardist *Residencia en la tierra* as regards its intricacy, the content is more complete, more accurate in its portrayal of the social and natural factors that affected the Incan laborers who left their legacy in Macchu Picchu. Neruda's method has evolved and become more elaborate as his understanding of sociopolitical, historical, and moral questions has grown. Neruda does not content himself with describing the vantage point of the Incan laborers; he attempts to show how they built the edifices-become-ruins, invested their livelihood in that work, were exploited as they constructed something that would not be theirs, and communed with nature. He also portrays the interests of the monarchy and the conquerors indirectly as social forces opposed to but dependent on the laborers. Moreover, after criticizing his early oeuvre for its barren isolationism, the speaker attempts to relive the laborers' experience so that he too might become a laborer and thus earn the right to represent them. So, the formal elements in this poem, which hold much in common with Neruda's avant-gardist stage, as demanding as they are, cannot hold back the torrent of ideas that flood the plain of content.

In "El hombre invisible" the method becomes more visible as the language is ostensibly simplified or made more consonant with everyday language. As in "Alturas," his criticism of his former avant-gardist poetry and of his contemporaries who are still enamored of linguistic labyrinths allows him to show the thematic limitations of this literary school. As form becomes a fetish it loses its concreteness and becomes abstract and, in so doing, it yields to the spontaneity of individual motivations. As a prisoner of immediacy, avant-gardist form reveals the poet's inner life in a heavily constrained and distorted content. Isolated, his poetry becomes strongly subjectivized and relativized as it relies more and more on immediate experience and perceives social reality as hostile. By contrast, in the *Odas,* Neruda reaffirms his connection with social reality and endeavors to probe deeper into it by committing himself politically to the cause of the working class and by becoming a laborer of words. By surrendering the exalted position of the poet and becoming "invisible," that is, equal to his fellow human beings and committed to egalitarianism, Neruda is more able to portray the countless varieties of work that the working people do which constitute the backbone of capitalist and socialist societies. He can focus on a product, say, wine ("Oda al vino" [Ode to Wine]) and describe its personified appearance as a loved one, the labor involved in making wine from the grape, the peasant's cultivation of the grape vine, its enhancement of love and friendship, and its relationship to the earth. Thus, as I indicated above, the form appears to dissolve and the content, to fully blossom. But as any reader of the odes can attest, Neruda's incredible use of metaphor, simile, and synecdoche, among other poetic techniques, frequently confronts the reader unprepared, jolted by the sudden flash of creative spontaneity.

In my judgment in both "Alturas" and "El hombre" the presence of Neruda's independent "guided spontaneity" stands out clearly. He employs a well-thought, internalized method while also providing explosions of verbal creativity that are set off by his spontaneity.

Conclusion

There is no question that the political and historical forces had a tremendous impact on Neruda and his work. As I seek to demonstrate in the remaining chapters on *Tercera residencia,* Neruda reacted to the strife of the Spanish civil war and the onslaught of fascism with impassioned commitment that directed the course of his work from 1936 onwards. As he committed himself more forthrightly to the defense of the Spanish Republic and, later, antifascism, what he had learned became an integral, yet mediated, part of the content of his poetic production. In doing so, he emerged from the solitude that inflicted him in Asia, so present in *Residencia en la tierra,* and superseded that distorted state of being, forever changing and deepening his political outlook. He became a Communist and dedicated his entire life to the struggle for socialism.

Contrary to the dominant opinion voiced by liberal critics, I contend that

Neruda's poetic method was, indeed, more sophisticated, more elaborate from *España en el corazón* until his death. From 1937 on Neruda's poetic form began to act in dialectical unity with the content. His poetry gained in its concrete portrayal of reality as a whole, whereas the *Residencia* verses were only able to represent a limited and immediate individual experience which was not inserted in the social totality and did not interrelate with other social factors within that totality. At this stage, the form is underdeveloped in terms of its ability to condense social reality through mediation. Language comes in thundering reverberations of abstraction, which lose themselves in the labyrinth of concrete alienation. *Tercera residencia* has the virtue of including this avant-gardist phase in Neruda's poetry and then showing how Neruda overcomes it; how he turns from the abstract to the dialectic of abstract and concrete; how this then allows him to depict the individual's place in the sociohistorical setting more accurately and to render the contradictions in capitalist society more visibly. In sum, this and subsequent chapters illustrate how Neruda was able to expand and deepen his knowledge and provide formidable literary approximations of the most important political, social, and moral forces of his day.

3
Realism and the Battle with Language in the *Residencias*

As Pierre Bourdieu has shown, "success" in the field of culture is not defined, as in the economic realm, by direct financial advancement, but rather by the symbolic profits derived from the acquisition of cultural capital.[1] While such success is apparent in the case of those who have inherited cultural and economic capital, it is exceedingly difficult for an artist from a working class background, such as Neruda, to collect symbolic profits—to gain recognition and acceptance in the poetic field. Their many disadvantages weigh working class artists down from the very start, and reduce their chances of "success."[2] Consequently, poets with inherited economic and cultural capital, like Vicente Huidobro, deem poetry to be "prophecy and sport simultaneously."[3] To borrow Bourdieu's words, poets like Huidobro, "move like fish in the water," while the more disadvantaged must swim against the current.[4]

So Neruda's avant-gardist stage, consisting primarily of *Residencia en la tierra* and the first section of *Tercera residencia,* is not a game, a moment of position jostling, or a chance to ruffle the feathers of traditionalists, but rather the poetic expression of a serious and suffering moment in Neruda's life, a period of intense emotional and economic crisis. To a large degree, these harsh circumstances, and his stay in Spain during the civil war, explain his shift from avant-gardist to critical realist poetry, whereas for others, like Huidobro, the avant-garde describes their entire poetic trajectory. For the founder of "creacionismo," the search for a new mode of expression was constant and all-consuming. His avant-gardism led him to write the famous long poem, "Altazor," in which he played with the limits of the Spanish language and created a chaotic linguistic world reflective of the spiritual angst prevading Europe after World War I.[5] However, it should be noted that despite those differences, both became affiliated with the Communist Party, and Huidobro did so before Neruda.[6] Indeed, in the first canto of "Altazor" he declares his faith in the class-conscious working class which provides the only hope for humanity. For Neruda this vanguardist stage fits into a larger framework as a dialectically related part of the whole, of a progressing aesthetic trajectory. Neruda launches into language, first and foremost, so that it will register painfully the anguish and isolation he feels, so that it will serve as recognition of his suffering and its negation. His open political positions are printed years later, during the Spanish civil war.

The second and third sections of *Tercera residencia* mark a transitional and confrontational moment in which the *Residencias* poetry has reached its saturation point and the poet a stage of alienation with which he can no longer cope. The language here continues in the *Residencias* tradition—it is densely metaphorical—but the content begins to invade and overwhelm the form. Hence, for example, the internal and almost unbearable contradictions that abound in "Las furias y las penas" (Furies and Sorrows)—where the poet and his writing engage in self-destruction. These unabating conflicts manifest themselves graphically in both form and content. The acute tension characteristic of this poetry is expressed lucidly at the end of "Furies and Sorrows" as "interminablemente exterminados" (interminably exterminated). Whereas, as we will see below, in "Reunión bajo las nuevas banderas" Neruda breaks definitively with the reigning tragic themes in the *Residencias*.

The fourth and longest section of *Tercera residencia* serves as a transition from his avant-gardism to his socially committed verses in "España en el corazón" (Spain in My Heart) (section four), dominated as it is by the antifascist cause in Spain during the civil war. The language here becomes somewhat more accessible and the tone changes to indignation and exultation.

If *Tercera residencia* is read as a unified whole we can better appreciate Neruda's development and transformation as a poet and an individual. As readers we get a good sense first of the estrangement he encountered and battled in Asia, then of the triumph over that unfulfilling life as he made friends and committed himself politically to the Republican cause. We also see the progression from a language-centered avant-gardist poetry to a content-driven testimonial poetry, from texts based on an omnipresent nature to a poetry populated with human beings attempting to correct social injustices. Moreover, we gain insight into the moral and political stances that Neruda takes as the Spanish civil war breaks out. Finally, we are able to understand more fully Neruda's personal qualities, his redeeming values and faults.

During the *Residencias* years Neruda is obsessed by nature's destructive and creative powers as they contrast sharply with the fragility of human beings. Part of his disquiet is due to his own peculiarly alienating circumstances, as well as his own unfamiliarity with Asia. However, toward the end of the *Residencias* he is able largely to overcome nature's pernicious threat to consume him by recognizing his detachment from it, by coming to understand that the world exists outside of himself. By doing so he can begin *approximating* in his verses both the laws of nature and the social world.[7] During this period Neruda saw the social world, like the natural world, as chaos he scarcely understood and thus could not express in his work. Eventually, he began to comprehend both worlds and attempted to explicate them. He was just as alienated from the social world as he was from the natural world, but he overcame that distancing, personally and poetically during the Spanish civil war. The Neruda that triumphed was the one who did not lay claims to being an exceptional visionary poet, but rather a poet/explorer influenced by and fascinated with other cultures. As early as 1929, in an article for "La Nación," Neruda showed a type of scientific interest in life in Asia, a concern that he cultivated in his poetry.

> No tengo apuro por escribir sobre la India y sobre Birmania y Ceilán, porque muchas cosas y orígenes me parecen ocultos y muchos fenómenos aún inexplicables. Todo parece en ruinas y despedazándose, pero en verdad fuertes ligamentos elementales y vivientes unen estas apariencias con vínculos casi secretos y casi imperecederos.[8]

> [I am in no hurry to write about India and about Burma and Ceylon, because many things and origins seem to me to be veiled and many phenomena still unexplainable. Everything appears to be in ruins and tearing itself apart, but the truth is that strong elementary and living ties unite these appearances with almost secret and imperishable links.]

Besides alluding to the natural chaos that encircles him, Neruda makes it clear that he did not feel he had sufficient knowledge of Asia in 1929 to be able to make accurate observations about these different and alien regions and their customs. He could have contented himself with writing a poetic essay, in which generalizations undoubtedly would have appeared, but the scientist in him could not allow it. Indeed, in the beginning of that same article Neruda criticized the poets, dating back to *modernismo,* who cultivated abstract images of Asia and thus practiced a form of what today would be termed orientalism. He emphasized that he thought it strange that "los escritores 'exotistas' hablen en términos ardientes de las regiones tropicales orientales. No hay tierra que se preste menos para las efusiones panegíricas o alegóricas. Estos dominios requieren solamente constante conocimiento e implacable atención" (writers of the "exotic" speak in burning terms of Asian tropical regions. There isn't a region that lends itself less to panegyrical or allegorical effusions. These dominions only require constant knowledge and implacable attention).[9] These early observations about Asia do not agree with the accepted critical opinion on *Residencia en la tierra.* As indicated in chapter 1, most critics consider the *Residencias* to be irrational and metaphysical poetry of a speaker making his way through infernal life circumstances. Amado Alonso, for example, claims that Neruda's poetic world in the 1920s and 1930s is "un desintegrar por despedazamiento y violencia que se hace a la realidad. Con ello se contempla desintegradamente lo real" (a disintegration via shattering and violence that is done to reality. With it one contemplates desintegratedly the real). He concludes that that chaotic portrayal, so typical of the avant-garde, is a unified existentialist *Weltanshaaung*.[10] Many, including Juan Larrea, believe that this poetry is surrealist, unleashing disparate and chaotic images from the unconscious.[11]

Following the groundbreaking research of Hernán Loyola, Jaime Concha, and Alain Sicard, I argue in this chapter on the contrary, that *Residencia en la tierra* is filled with realist details. Hidden within a seemingly surreal universe, Neruda's verses record the deep estrangement that plagued him as well as the socioenvironment that filled him with a sense of powerlessness. At first the tropes he uses throw the reader off because his image metaphors tax our customary expectations. One can easily get lost in many image correspondences in his poems during the *Residencia* years because Neruda attempts to disturb our conventional knowledge of the environment he is in, the isolation he suffers from, his recurring pessimism, his boredom, the natural world, and other such themes. Yet thematic unity underlies these poems as a kind of infrastructure that, in my view, invalidates the claim that this is surrealist poetry. Neruda's metaphorical mapping onto the representation of his life in Asia, which underscores the emotional effect of his verse, makes it appear as though he is creating a chaotic and irrational literary representation.[12] However, the infrastructure guides the reader to the realist portrayal of a confused and lost Neruda in the 1920s and 1930s. Yet, by negating his alienation from nature and the unfamiliar social circumstances in Santiago, Asia, and Buenos Aires, Neruda set the stage for becoming a great critical realist, and later, dialectical realist poet.

Himself a citizen of a developing yet independent country, Neruda sets out to increase his knowledge about colonial India. Neruda works this into an actual poetic system of thought in the last parts of *Tercera residencia,* but especially in his magnum opus, *Canto general.* His experience in Spain allows him to break free from his previous isolation, to live amongst a group of progressive Republican poets and artists, to question the legitimacy of his former views, and, equally or more importantly, to create a new type of poetry that—while still based on his earlier oeuvre—begins to take stock of socio-political and historical events during the civil war from a Marxist point of view. Far from tarnishing the quality of Neruda's poetry, the most politically and morally charged parts of *Tercera residencia* grant us the opportunity to understand the context in which he is writing. These poems, then, gain in *breadth of knowledge* over the *Residencia* poems. Moreover, the language is every bit as intense as it is in the *Residencias* and the first section of *Tercera residencia.* It is the *tone* that changes significantly due to his estrangement in unknown environments (Santiago, Buenos Aires and Asia). Neruda was indignant and outraged at the injustices being committed.

But before arriving at that point in terms of his poetic method and class consciousness Neruda depicts his own alienation in *Residencia en la tierra.*

ALIENATION AND THE STRUGGLE FOR AUTONOMY: 1925 TO 1935

The first section of *Tercera residencia,* then, follows the similar thematic and formal tendencies as the *Residencias.*[13] Although the dates of the first work stretch from 1935 to 1945, it is quite likely that Neruda composed these poems before 1935 during his years in Asia, or possibly as he made his way to Spain, where he would became embroiled in the civil war. Hence the need to analyze the poems of this first section of *Tercera residencia* coterminously with those of the *Residencias.*

Neruda wrote several of his *Residencias* poems in Santiago and Buenos Aires, but the greater portion of them in Asia. He arrived there as a young consul who barely managed to make ends meet economically. Moreover, he was immediately faced with multifaceted social conflicts that pit the interests of the developed, imperialist countries against those of colonial India:

> Todo el esoterismo filosófico de los países orientales, confrontado con la vida real, se revelaba como un subproducto de la inquietud, de la neurosis, de la desorientación y del oportunismo occidentales; es decir, de la crisis de principios del capitalismo. En la India no había por aquellos años muchos sitios para las contemplaciones del ombligo profundo. Una vida de brutales exigencias materiales, una condición colonial cimentada en la más acendrada abyección, miles de muertos cada día de cólera, de viruela, de fiebres y de hambre, organizaciones feudales desequilibradas por su inmensa población y su pobreza industrial, imprimían a la vida una gran ferocidad en la que los reflejos místicos desaparecían.[14]

> [All the philosophical esotercism in oriental countries, confronted with real life, reveals itself as a subproduct of unrest, of neurosis, of disorientation and Western opportunism; that is, of a crisis of principles in capitalism. In India during those years there weren't many places for contemplating your own profound navel. A life of brutal material demands, a colonial condition cemented in the most refined abjection, thousands of deaths a day due to cholera, smallpox, fevers and hunger, feudal organizations destabilized by their immense population and industrial poverty, gave to life a ferocity in which the reflections of mystics disappeared.]

As a foreigner living out an existence as a consul, Neruda had to deal with these brutal contradictions in Indian society on a continual basis. His own social situation was nothing but ironic. He had been given an official post working for the Chilean government abroad, and thus was accepted as a member of the middle class. As a foreign diplomat he was granted a special status that allowed him to associate with other representatives of the British government. But his own real economic status contradicted the political position with which he had been "consecrated." Neruda found himself trapped between two worlds. He felt uncomfortable among the British civil service who were much better off financially and who represented the British empire in India. By the same token, even though his economic status made him a natural ally of the working population in India, he held a special political post which made him a professional. Neruda was keenly aware of these economic and political disparities:

> Las castas tenían clasificadas la población india como en un coliseo paralelepípedo de galerías superpuestas en cuyo tope se sentaban los dioses. Los ingleses mantenían a su vez su escalafón de castas que iba desde el pequeño empleado de tienda, pasaba por los profesionales e intelectuales, seguía con los exportadores, y culminaba con la azotea del aparato en la cual se sentaban cómodamente los aristócratas del Civil Service y los banqueros del *Empire*.[15]

> [Castes had classified the Indian population like a parallelepiped coliseum of superimposed galleries at whose pinnacles sat the gods. The English, for their part, maintained their casts ranks, which included everybody from the small shop owner on the lowest level, to professionals and intellectuals, to exporters, and was finally topped off by the ceiling of the appartus, where the aristocrats of the Civil Service and the bankers of the Empire sat comfortably.]

From his autobiography, letters he wrote during this period, and the work of his biographers, we know that the open social conflicts that beset Indian society had a very profound effect on Neruda, but he did not feel empowered to do something about them. His duty as a bureaucrat, who at times would have to wait for weeks or months before carrying out official duty, also added to the solitude that engulfed him. In 1928, in a letter to the Chilean writer José Santos González Vera, he expressed his desperation:

> Yo sufro, me angustio con hallazgos horribles, me quema el clima, maldigo a mi madre y a mi abuela, converso días enteros con mi cacatúa, pago por mensualidades un elefante. Los días caen en la cabeza como palos, no escribo, no leo, vestido de blanco y con casco de corcho, auténtico fantasma.[16]

> [I suffer, I anguish with horrible discoveries, the climate burns me, I curse the fortune of my mother and grandmother, I talk for days on end with my parrot, and pay monthly installments on an elephant. The days pass like blows on my head, I don't write, I don't read. Dressed in white with a derby hat, (I'm an) authentic phantom.]

In this atmosphere his poetry developed two different general tendencies. Lack of fulfillment drowned him, but he was able to survive because he believed, desperately, that poetry represented an escape and gave him a reason to live. His desire to succeed as a poet and to save himself from the tedium of his life was so strong that he sometimes made great prophetic claims about his writing talents. Perhaps Neruda did so precisely because he was so removed from the Spanish-speaking world and because he had yet to establish his reputation as a poet outside Chile. Enrico Mario Santí's contention that Neruda considers himself prophetic, then, has its merits. At this stage in his life, Neruda does seem somewhat persuaded by the bourgeois canonization of the poet as a "genius" or "prophet." He describes himself as a gifted person of "ambiciones expresivas bastante sobrehumanas" (superhuman ambitions to express himself).[17] However, these prophetic ambitions reflect his uncertain social and personal circumstance in the late 1920s and early 1930s. Neruda's yearning to be recognized as a young visionary poet and not as a regular bureaucrat held true at least until 1933, but it faded away once he managed to escape his uncomfortable situation in Asia. Further, Neruda was still struggling to gain recognition as a poet and dealing with the socioeconomic and alienating impact of life in India.

Surrounded and virtually lost in his social environment, and overcome by the social injustices and his own economic plight, Neruda sought his expression and "revenge" in the density of language. The more ephemeral and esoteric, the more he could champion himself as a survivor of the circumstances. Poetry, then, compensated in part for the social isolation he was suffering. Language, like his erotic encounters with Josie Bliss, were escapes from an unpleasant and, at times, hostile social environment.

Yet Neruda was not drawn into language games or experimentation for experimentation's sake. In many poems in *Residencia en la tierra* the speaker bears witness to the struggle he is waging against the social environment and his own disaffection. The reality he perceives is often chaotic and the speaker's understanding of it confused, but Neruda attempts to portray the complexity of his individual circumstances in a realist manner. In that vein Alain Sicard, Jaime Concha, Volodia Teitelboim, and Hernán Loyola have argued that the *Residencias* are realist.[18] He exposes his own alienation and, indirectly, the brutalities of capitalism and imperialism in the colonies, even though, at this moment of his life, he does not have the experience or knowledge to comprehend them. Nonetheless, his impulse to depict the social world and his solitary existence in a realist fashion later led him to create the elaborate poetic theory found in *Canto general*.

THE REIGN OF ABSENCE: LANGUAGE AND ALIENATION

Residencia en la tierra shows, above all, the separation pains that afflicted Neruda once he left southern Chile. In his native region he witnessed first-hand the influx of modernization. As Jaime Concha asserts, Neruda's father's work as a railroad foreman provided the young poet with a unique chance to witness the entry of modernity into the Temuco area. A product of this rural area, he ventured into Santiago in 1921 and left in 1927. Several poems written between 1925 and 1927 show the effects of his being overpowered by modern city life. Neruda's reaction might have been due to the streams of people moving to the city, to the construction projects, and to the evident class differences. With the nitrate boom in the late nineteenth and early twentieth centuries the population of Santiago, Concepción, and Valparaíso grew at a rapid rate because the "productive mining economy in the north diverted efforts at industrialization and urbanization elsewhere in Chile." By 1920, fourteen percent of the national population was living in the capital.[19] While middle and upper-middle class homes were built in the downtown and the larger aristocratic houses remained intact, workers in Santiago lived in "crowded and sordid conventillos [slums]."[20]

Moreover, Neruda arrived at a volatile political moment. Arturo Alessandri, the presidential candidate backed by the burgeoning yet still not completely viable middle class, was able to garner the votes of the liberal, radical, and democratic parties and win the elections. He advocated greater state control over the economy generally, important labor reforms, and he pushed for a national social security system. However, given the conservative bent of the Congress he was unable to be effective, and he was summarily deposed by the military in 1924 and went into exile. He returned that same year, however, because the dominant faction in the military had Alessandri restored as president. Yet, according to Julio Faúndez, "it proved impossible to form a stable alliance between the progressive groups and the military" that supported the president. In the meantime Carlos Ibáñez "took advantage of his cabinet post in two short-lived administrations to enhance his influence in the armed forces" and then managed to get himself elected when Alessandri resigned in 1927.[21] As a university student first and then as an office worker, Neruda followed his anarchist upbringing during these years and condemned any form of government as oppressive.[22] This reaction together with his witnessing the class divisions, the increasing population, and the controlled nature in such parks as the Parque Forestal or the Parque Cousiño may have added to his frustrations and desperation in the capital. It may have created the "angustia y desintegración" (anguish and disintegration) that Amado Alonso noted permeates *Residencia en la tierra*.[23]

As a whole the poems in *Residencia en la tierra* can be divided into those that decry solitude and existential anguish; those that denounce estrangement in the cities with despair and anger; and those erotic poems that provide a safe haven from that alienation momentarily. It is tempting to then suggest, as Alonso does, that Neruda demonstrates in this work his "extremado ensimismamiento" (extreme self-absorption) and his progressive decline from "la melancolía hasta la angustia" (melancholy to anguish).[24] However, this viewpoint does not fully account for Neruda's depiction of his struggle against isolation. While there are some parallels between Neruda and T. S. Eliot as regards the obssession with time, death and the chronicling of despair, Eliot accepts this as humanity's fate, whereas Neruda refuses such resignation. We can draw comparisons between their poetic works—especially "Walking around" and *The Waste Land*. But whereas Eliot seeks asylum in God from "a world confused and dark and disturbed by potents of fear,"[25] Neruda, as his letter to Héctor Eandi from Rangoon on September 8, 1928, makes clear, does not content himself with a life "de destrucciones, de muertes, de cosas aniquiladas" (of destruction, deaths and annhilated things). Instead he attempts, heroically, to refashion this despair: "yo he decidido formar mi fuerza en este peligro, sacar provecho de esta lucha, utilizar estas debilidades. Sí, ese momento depresivo, funesto para muchos, es una noble materia para mí" (I have decided to strengthen myself in this danger, take advantage of this struggle, use these weaknesses. Yes, that depressing moment, disastrous for many people, is noble material for me).[26]

Struggles of an Alienated Poet

This recording of and learning from his dehumanization is vividly represented in "Galope muerto," written in Chile in 1926.[27] In this poem he renders the destructive natural and social surroundings and creates an oppressive atmosphere where death reigns supreme. Given the density of "Galope muerto" many critics have, understandably, found it inpenetrable and this has led them to consider it hermetic. René de Costa states that it is "not based on external correspondences; it relates inward, upon itself. Not a composition about something definite or even an autonomous invention as in the best of the avant-garde tradition, it is instead a poetization of undefined experience." "Meaning," he says, "is not imposed. The result is a poetry not of immediate insight but of gradual discernment." Actions "rush toward nothingness" in this meaningless recreated poetic world.[28] Marjorie Agosín also affirms that there is vagueness, mystery in the "incoherent and disordered images" in the poem. Therefore, she concludes, "the reader must accept it as a reference to itself, not a composition about a specific theme."[29] In a comparable way, Enrico Mario Santí interprets "Galope muerto" as a poem which provides a "scene for writing—a textual theater where the self dramatizes its relationship with the writing process." He asserts that the title tries to convey an antithetical "dead or silent sound," which also reflects the speaker's "ironic distance" from the subject matter.

Santí's reading makes the case for a Neruda who is a visionary working out his battle with the language in this poem. Thus, an "impossible experience" and "impossible sound" emerge from Neruda's poem and delineate his anguish as he perceives the world around him. Following in the steps of Alonso, at least as far as noting Neruda's pessimistic approach to reality, Santí also contends that, Neruda highlights his "radical linguistic distrust" of the representation of reality. Moreover, in a poststructuralist move, Neruda "is a witness to his own witnessing" in the act of grappling with language's tortuous attempt to communicate effectively.[30]

By contrast, Federico Schopf agrees that in "Galope muerto" Neruda's style is "antítetico, paradójico, intensamente figurado" (antithetical, paradoxical, intensely figurative style), but he emphasizes Neruda's attempts to understand the overwhelming reality surrounding him. According to the Chilean critic and poet, his "detención en lo inmóvil le entrega la experiencia de una totalidad que no puede aprehender y le resulta inabarcable" (stopping in the immobility provides him an experience of a totality he cannot aprehend and is unencompassable). However, the speaker in the poem does not consider himself a complete part of the disintegrating world—the work of time—he observes around him, but rather an outside observer who has, as Schopf accurately notes regarding *Residencia en la tierra* in general, "la voluntad, el deseo, la necesidad . . . de penetrar la oscuridad con que se le aparece la realidad externa y su propia subjetividad" (the will, desire and necessity . . . to penetrate the darkness with which external reality and his own subjectivity appear).[31]

In his work published after his classic essay on *Residencia en la tierra,* Jaime Concha interprets Neruda's work in a less abstract and more historicized way. In that vein he contends that "Galope muerto" is a revisiting of the impact of the conquest and colonization on southern Chile. Thus, the poem shows "la atracción que experimentan los elementos poéticos centrales de esta poesía hacia una determinada zona histórica, la época de la Conquista, en que se enfrentaron justamente, en palabras de *Galope muerto,* 'la espada' y 'los indefensos'" (the attraction that the main poetic elements of this poetry face in a specific historical area, the period of the Conquest, in which, in the words of *Galope muerto,* "the sword" and "the defenseless" confronted each other). Therefore, "las imágenes de caos, de violencia y de pululación que penetran todo *Galope muerto* no son un caos abstracto, una vulgar experiencia metafísica, sino evidencia concreta, singularísima, de la fase más primordial en nuestro desarrollo histórico" (images of chaos, violence and multiplying that penetrate all of *Galope muerto* are not an abstract chaos, a common metaphysical experience, but rather very unique and concrete evidence of the most primordial phase in our historical development). While Concha's reading of the poem proves interesting and the historical angle fundamental, I am not entirely convinced. This point of view tends to downplay the battle between the poet, his work, and his method, even though Concha is eloquent in other parts of the book on Neruda regarding all of those.[32]

My interpretation of "Galope muerto" recognizes the chaotic nature of the world in which the speaker in entrapped, but, following Schopf's line of thought, it underlines Neruda's awareness of that disorder and his attempt to make sense of it. As Hernán Loyola commented in one of his books on Neruda: "La congoja, la angustia, el llanto desolado, sí; pero jamás se abandonará Neruda a la desesperación" (The grief, the anguish, the desolate sobbing, yes; but Neruda never gave into desperation).[33] Quite the contrary: Neruda tries to use his poetic language to capture the image of the natural forces circling him.

> Como cenizas, como mares poblándose,
> en la sumergida lentitud, en lo informe,
> o como se oyen desde el alto de los caminos
> cruzar las campanadas en cruz,
> teniendo ese sonido ya aparte del metal,
> confuso, pesando, haciéndose polvo
> en el mismo molino de la formas demasiado lejos,
> o recordadas o no vistas,
> y el perfume de las ciruelas que rodando a tierra
> se pudren en el tiempo, infinitamente verdes.[34]

> [Like ashes, like seas peopling themselves,
> in the submerged slowness, in the shapelessness,
> or as one hears from the crest of the roads
> the crossed bells crossing,
> having that sound now sundered from the metal,
> confused, ponderous, turning to dust
> in the very milling of the too distant forms,
> either remembered or not seen,
> and the perfume of the plums that rolling on the ground
> rot in time, infinitely green.][35]

From the outset the reader is bombarded with Eliot-like images: "ashes," "confused," "ponderous" (or weighing), "dust," (formas) "either remembered or not seen" and the "plums . . . [that] rot." The social and natural forms (the bell, the road, the earth, the plums) are here detached from their functions and are decaying. The speaker faces the omnipotence of matter and its forms, which, as Neruda puts it, are too far away. Faced with a barrage of chaotic images, the poet feels helpless, incapable of portraying the destructiveness in this milieu. The metal bell's sound is confusing, weighty, and vanishes. Everything seems to decompose or disintegrate: things are "o recordadas o no vistas" (either remembered or not seen). Since time and death consume all natural and social labor, Neruda fears that his texts will meet this fate as well. Even if he is able to begin to capture the decaying world around him in his poetry, he confronts the fact that his verses, too, will succumb to those forces. Nature is productive—the cherries' perfume, the ash, the populating seas, the bell's sound—but it is ephemeral. Moreover, human beings appear only tangentially and impotently in this rendering of the all-consuming natural forces—someone, after all, must smell the plums' "perfume" and ring the bell.

In these beginning verses Neruda shows nature's rampant destructiveness over human beings, so much so that his terrifying representation of nature's dominion seems naturalistic. There seems no escaping it. Neruda has isolated the physical world's objectivity through his poetic sensibility. Yet the remnants of this devastation counteract this entropic process. Granted, this dialectical process and understanding have not reached the heights of *Canto general,* but, as Jaime Concha and Alain Sicard maintain, we can already see them at work in the *Residencias*.[36]

In the following verses the speaker, lost amidst nature, observes it from a distance, as though he were not a part of it:

> Aquello todo tan rápido, tan viviente,
> inmóvil sin embargo, como la polea loca en sí misma,
> esas ruedas de los motores, en fin.
> Existiendo como las puntadas secas en las costuras del árbol,
> callado, por alrededor, de tal modo,
> mezclando todos los limbos sus colas.
> Es que de dónde, por dónde, en qué orilla?
> El rodeo constante, incierto, tan mudo,
> como las lilas alrededor del convento
> o la llegada de la muerte a la lengua del buey
> que cae a tumbos, guardabajo, y cuyos cuernos quieren sonar (9–10).

> [All that so swift, so living,
> yet motionless, like the pulley loose within itself,
> those wheels of the motors, in short.
> Existing like the dry stitches in the tree's seams,
> so silent, all around,
> all the limbs mixing their tails.
> But from where, through where, on what shore?
> The constant, uncertain surrounding, so silent,
> like the lilacs around the convent
> or death's coming to the tongue of the ox
> that stumbles to the ground, guard down, with horns that
> struggle to blow.]

At first glance the first verse appears to contradict the second verse. Things appear static and sluggish yet fast and out of control. And the speaker seems utterly confounded. Neruda observes death's presence in nature and how it defines natural things. Significantly, the gerunds, the only verb form in these verses, demonstrate this struggle between life and death very well because they prolong and therefore underline the process of natural destruction. These lines show that living things are able to sustain themselves despite the onslaught of death.

A key to understanding Neruda's objective in these verses is the pulley metaphor. Though referring to the social world and human beings' transformation of nature, it captures succinctly the idea of life within death. Although the wheel appears, from a distance, to be a still sphere, it is rotating at a rapid rate. But the wheel's shape does not change when it is in motion. The same can be said for the rope attached to the pulley: its geometrical outline—the straight line—seems to be immobile, but the rope too is moving. However, Neruda emphasizes the pulley itself or, as in the following verse, motor wheels to suggest—as he does in "Walking around"—that time is relentless. The wheels in the pulleys are like "dry stitches" in a tree's seams, indicating that the passage of time and life's struggles leave scars on trees and, by extension, on human beings. Objects in the social world or nature—like human beings—often appear to be immobile and dying as the industrialization of modern life consumes them. Life, then, appears to be dispassionate, confusing, and meaningless and human beings, impotent.

Though the speaker is not present at this stage of the poem, Neruda provides an allegorical reference to him. Like the ox who has death come to his tongue and who stumbles to the ground and struggles to blow his horns, the poet too battles with death and barely manages to write his verses in the process. A beast of burden used to furrow underproductive fields in southern Chile, the poet struggles to compose his poetry and find meaning in life.

The speaker as poet emerges in earnest then in the third stanza

> Por eso, en lo inmóvil, deteniéndose, percibir,
> entonces, como aleteo inmenso, encima,
> como abejas muertas o números,
> ay, lo que mi corazón pálido no puede abarcar,
> en multitudes, en lágrimas saliendo apenas,
> y esfuerzos humanos, tormentas,
> acciones negras descubiertas de repente
> como hielos, desorden vasto,
> oceánico, para mí que entro cantando,
> como con una espada entre indefensos. (10)

> [Therefore, in the stillness, stopping, to perceive,
> then, like an immense fluttering, above,
> like dead bees or numbers,

ah, what my pale heart cannot embrace,
in multitudes, in tears scarcely shed,
and human efforts, anguish,
black deeds suddenly discovered
like ice, vast disorder,
oceanic, to me who enters singing,
as if with a sword among the defenseless.]

The speaker who sings "como una espada entre indefensos" (like a sword among the defenseless) contrasts drastically with "desorden vasto" (vast disorder), the "aleteo inmenso" (immense fluttering), "multitudes" (multitudes) and the "abejas muertas o números" (dead bees or numbers). While the speaker appears to despair because he wants to portray his surroundings and cannot as yet ("ay, lo que mi corazón pálido no puede abarcar" [ah, what my pale heart cannot take in]), he does not dwell on his capacity to express that chaos, but rather fights back with his own testimony (his singing and his sword). In declaring war on the "acciones negras" (black deeds) that freeze life (and thus the reference to ice) that encircles him, Neruda surpasses the limits of his "corazón pálido" (pale heart). The poet does not capitulate to the objective forces of nature, but rather attempts now to describe them. In confronting the forces of nature he also ceases to be a static observer and begins to perceive and render the reality that alienates him. Indeed, the thematic tensions in this stanza are reinforced by the formal layout of the poem. The cumbersome syntax that several critics have identified in the poem helps mirror the battle of the speaker with the surrounding disorder.[37]

Armed with a newly found determination, in the fourth and fifth stanzas Neruda returns to the question he posed in the second regarding the effects of time on living beings.

> Ahora bien, de qué está hecho ese surgir de palomas
> que hay entre la noche y el tiempo, como una barranca
> húmeda?
> Ese sonido ya tan largo
> que cae listando de piedras los caminos,
> más bien, cuando solo una hora
> crece de improviso, extendiéndose sin tregua.
> Adentro del anillo del verano
> una vez los grandes zapallos escuchan,
> estirando sus plantas conmovedoras,
> de eso, de lo que solicitándose mucho,
> de lo lleno, oscuros de pesadas gotas. (10)

[Well now, what is it made of, that upsurge of doves
that exists between night and time, like a moist ravine?

> That sound so prolonged now
> that falls lining the roads with stones,
> or rather, when only an hour
> grows suddenly, stretching without pause.
> Within the ring of summer
> the great calabash trees once listen,
> stretching out their pity-laden plants,
> it is made of that, of what with much wooing,
> of the fullness, dark from heavy drops.]

These final stanzas address and clarify the questions raised throughout the poem. If the doves, commonly associated with poets and poetry, fulfill their archetypal role, the connection with the sound ("ese sonido") becomes clearer. Like the sound of the bell or the ox's horns above, poetry is only meaningful when it arms people with time to use against death, when it makes them aware of how they grow suddenly and stretch without pause.

Like several *Residencia* poems, here Neruda is forced to come to grips with time and recognition of his own mortality. This is true also in Chile, before his departure to Asia, where his tenuous economic status seemed to weigh heavily on him. As noted in early chapters, he led a precarious existence as a student and, later, as a functionary in Santiago before his departure to Asia. Significantly, though, in this poem Neruda does not turn away from the pressure of time, but rather launches himself into an exploration of it. In so doing, he begins to discover the limits of his own existence, mutually determined by time and space, as well as by social conditions. The title of the poem itself, "Galope muerto" (Dead Gallop), testifies to this negative dialectic. While "gallop" appears to represent change, motion, entropy, its dialectical opposite, "dead," appears to signal the abrupt end to a life mysteriously granted and then taken away. Based on the synedoche "gallop," Neruda suggests that Time—the objectification of Time as Alain Sicard puts it—represented as a horse, inhabits us and runs its course and then suddenly abandons us.[38]

Neruda describes this stage more visibly in the last stanza of his short poem "Unidad":

> Trabajo sordamente, girando sobre mí mismo,
> como el cuervo sobre la muerte, el cuervo de luto.
> Pienso, aislado en lo extremo de las estaciones,
> central, rodeado de geografía silenciosa:
> una temperatura parcial cae del cielo,
> un extremo imperio de confusas unidades
> se reúne rodeándome.[39]
>
> [I work silently, wheeling over myself,
> like a crow over death, the crow in mourning.

3/REALISM AND THE BATTLE WITH LANGUAGE   119

> I think, isolated in the expanse of the seasons,
> central, surrounded by a silent geography:
> a partial temperature falls from the sky,
> an ultimate empire of confused unities
> gathers surrounding me.][40]

Although he is surrounded by the effects of time, by faded and old things, he attributes unity to death's destruction. Here the poet "trabaj[a] sordamente" (labour[s] silently), as though he were deaf, like a crow preying on death, depending on it for his sustenance. He studies time and death and lets them encircle him so he can write his verses. Jaime Concha perceives correctly that "Unidad" is a step beyond "Galope muerto" because "a Neruda le interesa captar el espesor de la materia, esos fondos de la vida, cuya consistencia todavía era algo borroso en 'Galope muerto'" (Neruda is interested in capturing the thickness of matter, those depths of life, whose substance was somewhat blurred in "Galope muerto"). Observing himself at work, he installs himself "en esa energía que constituye a lo real como un proceso" (in energy that constitutes reality as a process).[41]

This is in fact the thread that the reader can follow throughout the *Residencias* (including the first half of the *Tercera residencia*). Written in 1928 in Rangoon, "Sonata y destrucciones" (Sonata and Destructions) is an intensification of the speaker's search for meaning in an environment which appears bereft of meaning. Enrico Mario Santí considers this poem a manifestation of Neruda's "visionary experience" and method. Writing furnishes Neruda with an "introspection that unveils patterns of selfhood that are structured as those in the object" yet it is also "destined for its own oblivion." However, despite the repetition of motifs and themes in the *Residencias* poems Santí asserts that there is "actual dialectical progress" consisting "mainly of a negative knowledge about the object."[42] This position sums up nicely the difference between this poem and preceding ones: the speaker observes the destruction about him which causes his alienation, but he now confronts those pernicious forces and does not give in to them:

> Después de mucho, después de vagas leguas,
> confuso de dominios, incierto de territorios,
> acompañado de pobres esperanzas
> y compañías infieles y desconfiados sueños,
> amo lo tenaz que aún sobrevive en mis ojos,
> oigo en mi corazón mis pasos de jinete,
> muerdo del fuego dormido y la sal arruinada,
> y de noche, de atmósfera oscura y luto prófugo,
> aquel que vela a la orilla de los campamentos,
> el viajero armado de estériles resistencias,
> detenido entre sombras que crecen y alas que tiemblan,
> me siento ser, y mi brazo de piedra me defiende (43).

> [After a good deal, after vague leagues,
> confused about domains, uncertain about territories,
> accompanied by faint hopes
> and faithless companies and uneasy dreams,
> I love the tenacity that still survives in my eyes,
> I hear in my heart my horseman steps,
> I bite the dormant fire and the ruined salt,
> and at night, dark in atmosphere and fugitive mourning,
> he who keeps vigil at the edge of camps,
> the armed traveler of sterile resistances,
> prisoner amid growing shadows and trembling wings,
> I feel that I am he, and my arm of stone defends me.][43]

In these verses a qualitative leap has taken place as regards his disaffection. In the beginning of *Residencia en la tierra*, void, motion and death dominated the scene and confounded the speaker. This enclosed and yet nebulous atmosphere is captured in the images "vaguas leguas" (vague leagues), "confuso" (confused), "incierto" (uncertain). As in "Galope muerto," the speaker then reverses his direction: rather than fleeing from what apparently threatens him—change in the universe, the finality of the self—he faces the destruction that lies before him. As the title suggests, the very instrument of his liberation ("sonata"—poetry) is dependent on the realm of necessity (the objective forces that exist semi-autonomously from human life). What appears to be a negation becomes the object of affirmation: "Amo lo tenaz que aún sobrevive en mis ojos, / oigo en mi corazón mis pasos de jinete, / muerdo del fuego dormido y la sal arruinada" (I love the tenacity that still survives in my eyes, / I hear in my heart my horseman steps, / I bite the dormant fire and the ruined salt). Rather than seeking a safe haven from nature's destructive forces and Time's all consuming appetite, the speaker likens himself to a horseman who can presumably control time and use it to his advantage. At the very least he can consume Time tenaciously and accept the rule of time, and his own death.

Neruda ingeniously portrays this transition in both form and content. He begins with ambiguous images ("vague," "confused," "uncertain"), then moves in verses three and four to apparent oxymorons (or dialectical relations)—"pobres esperanzas" (faint hopes), "compañías infieles" (unfaithful company) and "desconfiados sueños" (distrustful dreams)—and then to bold affirmations ("amo" [I love], "oigo" [I hear], "muerdo" [I bite]). Consequently, the process Neruda had to go through to come to a clearer comprehension of his life and the world is recaptured in three distinct yet intertwined stages (chaos, antithetical tensions, and then relative certainty). Moreover, Neruda's understanding of this transformation has evidently followed a similar pattern. The images evolve from the abstract to the concrete. In sum, Neruda has become accustomed to the desolation that has

3/REALISM AND THE BATTLE WITH LANGUAGE 121

plagued him and it has become the force against which he can make his life meaningful or at a minimum less alienated.[44]

In this context his verse documents his engagement with objective natural forces. As he defines his own limitations and nature's power and accepts them he becomes more knowledgeable about his own alienation. With passion and persistence he comes to terms with his abandonment and isolation as a moment in the dialectic: "Me siento ser" (I feel myself becoming), or as he announces in the second stanza, "adoro mi propio ser perdido" (I adore my own lost self). Much as in *Estravagario* (1958), specifically in "Pido silencio" (I Ask for Silence), his period of silence and solitude is productive. It is a moment of reflection, remorse, and renewal. In "Pido silencio" he puts it this way: "Pero porque pido silencio / no crean que voy a morirme: / me pasa todo lo contrario: / sucede que voy a vivirme. / Sucede que soy y que sigo" (But because I ask for silence / do not think that I am going to usher death in: / quite the opposite is happening to me: / It happens that I am going to relive / It happens that I am and that I continue).[45] A similar stage is set in this poem in *Residencia en la tierra*. Neruda affirms his alienation in the dialectic's first movement, which, provided the right personal and social circumstances, leads to its negation:

> Hay entre ciencias de llanto un altar confuso,
> y en mi sesión de atardeceres sin perfume,
> en mis abandonados dormitorios donde habita la luna,
> y arañas de mi propiedad, y destrucciones que me son queridas,
> adoro mi propio ser perdido, mi substancia imperfecta,
> mi golpe de plata y mi pérdida eterna.
> Ardió la uva húmeda, y su agua funeral
> aún vacila, aún reside,
> y el patrimonio estéril, y el domicilio traidor.
> Quién hizo ceremonia de cenizas?
> Quién amó lo perdido, quién protegió lo último?
> El hueso del padre, la madera del buque muerto,
> y su propio final, su misma huida,
> su fuerza triste, su dios miserable? (43–44)

> [There is among the sciences of weeping a confused altar,
> and in my session of perfumeless twilights,
> in my abandoned bedrooms where the moon dwells,
> and inherited chandeliers, and destructions that are dear to me,
> I adore my own lost being, my imperfect substance,
> my silver set and my eternal loss.
> The moist grape burned, and its funereal water
> still wavers, still resides,
> and the sterile patrimony, and the treacherous domicile.

> Who made a ceremony of ashes?
> Who loved the lost, who protected the last?
> The bone of the father, the wood of a dead ship,
> and his own ending, his very flight,
> his sad force, its miserable god?]

The speaker lists the estranging conditions and gives them more ominous weight through the repetition of conjunctions and commas. This poetic technique forces the reader to digest the bitterness of these characterizations of his struggling life: "adoro mi propio ser perdido, mi substancia imperfecta" (I adore my own lost self, my imperfect substance). The destruction and change he observed before him in nature has, at this stage, become part of him. In this context a perplexing statement like "destrucciones que me son queridas" (destructions which are dear to me) can be grasped in its dialectical complexity. The suffering he has endured has led to a better understanding of himself.

As half this stanza testifies, and Rodríguez Monegal is correct to point out, family relations cause much of Neruda's suffering. Exile and his economic status do take their toll, but his relations with his father in particular, who never encouraged him as a young poet, crushed his self-confidence. So Neruda needed to face this antagonistic relationship with his father to rehabilitate himself.[46] In this setting too, repetition plays a crucial role. Possessive adjectives pertaining to the first person—the speaker—clash structurally and thematically with those connected to the third person (his father). For example, "mi sesión" (my session), "mis abandonados dormitorios" (my abandoned rooms), and "mi sustancia imperfecta" (my imperfect substance) contrast with "el patrimonio estéril" (the sterile patrimony) and the "domilicio traidor" (treacherous domicile). The tension in this domestic scenario is thereby increased.

Indeed, Neruda's poetry occupies more space in his life as his ties to his father and his family deteriorate. His family is characterized here in unmistakably negative terms as "patrimonio estéril" (sterile patrimony) and "domicilio traidor" (treacherous home). The religious images here recreate the scene of his father's (symbolic?) funeral: "El hueso del padre, la madera del buque muerto / y su propio final, su misma huida" (The bone of the father, the wood of the dead ship, / and his own end, his very flight). His loss is eternal, he perceives "agua funeral" (funereal water), and he witnesses "una ceremonia de cenizas" (a ceremony of ashes). In the absence of strong familial and social ties, the speaker posits poetry as an intimate, cathartic vehicle for expressing his feelings of desolation, his involvement in spontaneous passionate affairs, and his disenchantment with his economic and professional status.

By the last stanza of "Sonata y destrucciones," writing clearly becomes a therapeutic medium for confronting his personal and social estrangement:

Acecho, pues, lo inanimado y lo doliente,
y el testimonio extraño que sostengo,
con eficiencia cruel y escrito en cenizas,
es la forma de olvido que prefiero,
el nombre que doy a la tierra, el valor de mis sueños,
la cantidad interminable que divido
con mis ojos de invierno, durante cada día de este mundo (44).

[I spy, then, on the inanimate and the doleful,
and the strange testimony that I affirm,
with cruel efficiency and written in ashes,
is the form of oblivion that I prefer,
the name that I give to the earth, the value of my dreams,
the interminable quantity that I divide
with my winter eyes, during each day of this world.]

The first verse sums up the essence of his struggle. He lies in wait for the ever mutable natural and social forces that attack him. Oscillating between self-negation and self-transformation, his poetic enterprise, his "strange testimony" (testimonio extraño) is still rooted in the recognition and acceptance of alienation. Indeed, death still weighs heavily on him. Neruda writes verses under death's influence and looks on with death's "winter eyes" (mis ojos de invierno).

However, he finds meaning in documenting his own struggle for survival in an alien environment. Without his dialogic relationship with his own writing as a way of dealing with his lack of knowledge of Hindi-Urdu, the suffocating tropical climate, his monotonous job, his piercing solitude, and the "espantosos ingleses que odio todavía" (terrible English whom I hate still)—as he puts it in "Tango del viudo" (The Widower's Tango)—there would not even be a glimmer of hope in his life and darkness would soon claim him. In Jaime Concha's words, "Su condición de oscuro exiliado, su oscuridad de paria social encuentra en esos otros millones de parias que mueren cada día bajo sus ojos, a orillas del Irrawahdy o en el puerto de Colombo, un ensanchamiento colectivo, horrorosamente tangible, de su propia situación" (His condition as a dark exile, his darkness as a social pariah finds in those other millions of pariahs who die every day under his view, on the shores of the Irrawahdy [river] or at the port in Colombo, a collective and horribly tangible amplifying of his own situation).[47]

"Sweet Matter"

Critics have split into two basic camps regarding the interpretation of Neruda's classic poem, "Entrada a la madera" (Entrance to Wood). One group remains undecided regarding the poet's worldview expressed in the poem. They deem it, in the words of René de Costa, a "mystic poem" exalting a simple object and hence describing the "physical communion with matter" and, simultaneously, "'unpoetic realism'."[48] Emir Rodríguez Monegal is even more ambivalent regarding Neruda's poetic method because he alleges that matter becomes transcendent via the poet's metaphysics, yet he believes that this mysticism leads him to materialism (but not yet dialectical materialism).[49] In an early seminal essay on *Residencia en la tierra* Jaime Concha also writes of Neruda's "metafísica materialista" (materialist metaphysics), although it seems clear from the context that he is referring to a Hegelian metaphysics as an overarching, unified system of thought that nonetheless relies on his "adhesión inquebrantable a la verdad de la Naturaleza" (an unbreakable adhesion to Nature's truth). Neruda's worldview at this stage is "inmensamente físico" (immensely physical) and grounded in nature.[50]

The debate among the second group of critics—Concha, Alain Sicard, and Hernán Loyola—centers on the degree to which Neruda is a dialectical thinker at this stage in his life. In the aforementioned article Concha refers to three different moments in the poem: the speaker's access to a material foundation, the "invocación y visión" (invocation and vision) of the foundation, and the description of the "estado de indeterminación dialéctica de la materia" (the state of dialectical indeterminacy of matter). Further, Concha maintains that Neruda employs the dialectical method even in *Residencia en la tierra*.[51] Similarly, Hernán Loyola writes of Neruda's "intuición dialéctica de la vida."[52] While Sicard generally agrees with Concha and Loyola, he suggests that "Entrada a la madera" is a "búsqueda de una dialéctica" (search for a dialectic). Therefore, "incapaz de hacer dialéctica su relación con la naturaleza, es a través del aniquilamiento como realizará por fin su unión con la madera" (incapable of establishing a dialectical relationship, it is through annihilating himself that he will finally find his unity with the wood). Succinctly put, the speaker disappears and becomes a part of the object he perceives and thus negates a dialectical view of reality. For Sicard, then, "Entrada a la madera" is a step toward dialectical thinking.

Although Neruda employs dialectical images in "Entrada a la madera" and the speaker moves beyond nature's perceived devastation and the fatality of human life, I concur with Sicard that Neruda had not yet become the dialectical thinker he was in *Canto general*. By this stage Neruda begins to open his poetic horizon to the positive elements in nature, returning to some degree to his rendering of it in *Veinte poemas de amor y una canción deseperada* (Twenty Love Poems and a Desperate Song). In that earlier book nature incarnated both his lover and their shared love as well as his melancholy. In "Entrada a la madera" Neruda regards nature as a fascinating and enticing object of poetic investigation that envelops him and not as an exterior menace whose evolutionary laws will devour him.

3/REALISM AND THE BATTLE WITH LANGUAGE

According to Hernán Loyola's estimate, "Entrada a la madera" was published at the end of 1934 or the beginning of 1935 in Madrid.[53] Having spent six months in Buenos Aires working in the Chilean consulate, during which time he met and became friends with Federico García Lorca, Neruda arrived in Barcelona in May 1934, and shortly thereafter, settled in Madrid. Despite its date of publication, "Entrada" does not make even a passing reference to this moment of intense political agitation, indicating that Neruda was still overpowered by alienation.

While "Entrada a la madera" does not explicitly address the sociopolitical issues of the time, it does begin to address Neruda's interior consuming battle. Unlike the previous speaker, this one has a thirst for knowledge about the multifaceted aspects of nature which formerly haunted him. In this context he wants to learn about the diversity of nature to understand its effects on human nature:

> Con mi razón apenas, con mis dedos,
> con lentas aguas lentas inundadas,
> caigo al imperio de los nomeolvides,
> a una tenaz atmósfera de luto,
> a una olvidada sala decaída,
> a un racimo de tréboles amargos.
> Caigo en la sombra, en medio
> de destruidas cosas,
> y miro arañas, y apaciento bosques
> de secretas maderas inconclusas,
> y ando entre húmedas fibras arrancadas
> al vivo ser de substancia y silencio.[54]
>
> [Scarcely with my reason, with my fingers,
> with slow waters slow inundated,
> I fall into the realm of the forget-me-nots,
> into a tenacious atmosphere of mourning,
> into a forgotten, decayed room,
> into a cluster of bitter clover.
> I fall into the shadow, amid
> destroyed things,
> and I look at spiders, and I graze on thickets
> of secret inconclusive woods,
> and I walk among moist fibers torn
> from the living being of substance and silence.][55]

In these first two stanzas the speaker is present as an explorer who moves about and who, with his senses ("with my reason," "with my fingers," "I look at"), searches for the enigmatic connections among natural things. In this context, nature's mysteries are perceived to be knowable, not only as objects of nature, but also as part of what Marx called the "sensuous external world."[56] Neruda's whole battle is to recover the nature that perished in him and emptied him. Coming from southern Chile, with its dramatic mountains, thick pine forests, and cold lakes and with the brutal beauty of its sea, Neruda could not help but feel estranged in industrialized Santiago, and later in Asia. Marx's comments in the *Economic and Philosophical Manuscripts* drive home the point here: "Man lives from nature, i.e. nature is his body, and he must maintain a continuing dialogue with it if he is not to die. To say that man's physical and mental life is linked to nature simply means that nature is linked to itself, for man is part of nature."[57] So, in Dantean fashion the speaker descends—as he does in later works, most notably in *Canto general*—in order to explore nature and thereby associate it with human development. From this moment on, Neruda's poetry works and receives its sustenance from nature's labor:

> Dulce materia, oh rosa de alas secas,
> en mi hundimiento tus pétalos subo
> con mis pies pesados de roja fatiga,
> y en tu catedral dura me arrodillo
> golpeándome los labios con un ángel.
> Es que soy yo ante tu color de mundo,
> ante tus pálidas espadas muertas,
> ante tus corazones reunidos,
> ante tu silenciosa multitud. (109–10)

> [Gentle matter, oh rose of dry wings,
> in my collapse I climb up your petals,
> my feet heavy with red fatigue,
> and in your harsh cathedral I kneel
> beating my lips with an angel.
> I am the one facing your worldly color,
> facing your pale dead swords,
> facing your united hearts,
> facing your silent multitude.]

Here, then, the reader comes upon nature's "sweet matter," metaphorically represented by the red rose—the archetype of poetry, life, love (carpe diem). This is the first real indication in the *Residencias* that nature, in the eyes of the speaker, can be something other than confusing, nebulous, or brutally destructive. Nature can be the source of knowledge and empowerment for the individual who struggles fiercely against his alienation from nature.

Cast in neo-romantic imagery, nature is incarnated in the rose. But what does this "rosa de alas secas" (rose of dry wings) represent? What meaning does Neruda ascribe to it? Given the religious references to the rose and nature in "ángel" (angel) and "catedral" (cathedral) and the semi-erotic attraction (the rose and sweetness as emblems of love and passion), Neruda seems to be praising and seeking beauty. Before nature's beauty, in its "cathedral," he kneels. Others have come before him and have been consumed, but not he. The speaker identifies ("es que soy yo" [I am the one]) and distinguishes himself from those whom nature subsumed ("ante tus pálidas espadas muertas, / ante tus corazones reunidos, / ante tu silenciosa multitud" [facing your pale dead swords, / facing your united hearts, / facing your silent multitude]). He encounters the vestiges of human lives that have joined the driving forces of nature. In recognizing the collective struggle with and against nature, he is a step away from confirmation of the collective history apparent in later works, such as *Canto general*. In "Alturas de Macchu Picchu," for example, the silent multitude is analogous to a deceased people who are now an organic part of nature and who have forged their own history despite the destruction of the Spanish conquistadors. At this point, however, Neruda considers himself to be part of and yet a combatant against this omnipotent nature.

Indeed, the fourth stanza highlights the identity of the speaker amidst the adversity that is facing him ("Soy yo" [I am the one] is repeated three times in eight verses). In the last half of the stanza there is a major change in the speaker's relation with nature. He finds in nature's tragic beauty the essence of his life. Rather than perceiving nature as a pernicious threat that will destroy him, the speaker observes and appreciates nature. In discovering natural phenomena, Neruda ceases to work exclusively on his own "interiority"—as Jaime Concha puts it—and begins to discover nature's sweet and mysterious matter.[58]

> Soy yo ante tu ola de olores muriendo,
> envueltos en otoño y resistencia:
> soy yo emprendiendo un viaje funerario
> entre tus cicatrices amarillas:
> soy yo con mis lamentos sin origen,
> sin alimentos, desvelado, solo,
> entrando oscurecidos corredores,
> llegando a tu materia misteriosa. (110)

> [I am the one facing your wave of dying fragrances,
> wrapped in autumn and resistance:
> I am the one undertaking a funereal voyage
> among your yellow scars:
> I am the one with my sourceless laments,
> foodless, abandoned, alone,
> entering darkened corridors,
> reaching your mysterious substance.]

The speaker affirms his own identity repeatedly in the uneven verses in the face of a personified nature's own death and life. Neruda crystallizes this struggle metaphorically via the image "otoño y resistencia" (autumn and resistance)' with its "ola de olores muriendo" (wave of dying fragrances) and "cicatrices amarillas" (yellow scars). Nature follows its course impervious to the speaker. And yet he repeats "soy yo" insistently to regain his identity, his individuality before Nature's cold objectivity. His "viaje funerario" (funereal voyage) seems to be analogous to the reign of death in nature, but he goes to great pains to show his vitality and determination nonetheless.

Much as in "Alturas de Machu Picchu" (in *Canto general*), where the speaker confuses himself with the Incan laborers and must go through their hell to tell their story, so here Neruda needs to become nature, while never abandoning his own identity in order to recount the death and life in nature:

> Veo moverse tus corrientes secas,
> veo crecer manos interrumpidas,
> oigo tus vegetales oceánicos
> crujir de noche y furia sacudidos,
> y siento morir hojas hacia adentro,
> incorporando materiales verdes
> a tu inmovilidad desamparada. (110)

> [I see your dry currents move,
> I see interrupted hands grow,
> I hear your oceanic vegetation
> rustle shaken my night and fury,
> and I feel leaves dying inward,
> joining green substances
> to your forsaken immobility.]

In these verses, then, the speaker is an active witness and recorder of nature's work. On the surface the references to aborted creativity ("tus corrientes secas" [your dry currents] and "manos interrumpidas" [interrupted hands]) suggest that nature's growth is sterile. But the last three verses in "Sonata y destrucciones" make it clear that this is an optical illusion. For the dying leaves incorporate green—i.e., life sustaining substances—into their apparent immobility. Because of his earlier pessimism, he was overtaken by death's presence in nature and ignored the lifeforce that resists death. Moreover, in his darkest moments in Rangoon around 1928, Neruda was a passive observer unable to contend with nature's active and regenerating forces. In this poem he attempts to understand nature by absorbing it, by imagining it as personified and by acknowledging its power over him. Once he overcame his view of nature as grim reaper, it became a compelling and prevailing force in poetry and his life; it rooted him as he confronted social alienation in the city.

WITH A PEN AND A GREEN KNIFE

After almost six years in Asia, in the second volume of *Residencia en la tierra* Neruda regains nature as an essential weapon with which to attack his estrangement from the urban landscapes of Santiago and Buenos Aires. From being accosted by nature's pernicious forces to accepting its ways, he now seizes it as a weapon to brandish against his dehumanization in the city. In his well-known poem, "Walking around," written in Buenos Aires either in the fall of 1933 or the spring of 1934, the city, not nature, corrupts, dehumanizes, and offers death. Neruda arrived approximately three years after the military coup that deposed Hipólito Yrigoyen and at a time when the negative effects of the Great Depression were still evident. According to historians Thomas E. Skidmore and Peter H. Smith, this led to a sharper divide between the social classes in the Argentine capital:

> In Buenos Aires elegantly attired aristocrats met at their European-style clubs while workers struggled to protect their families from inflation. The Argentine boom, like so many others in capitalist countries at this time, did facilitate considerable upward mobility. But it also fostered huge income discrepancies, which were ultimately bound to create social and political tensions.[59]

With the waves of immigrants coming to the city or moving from the provinces, particularly from 1870 to 1914, by the depression era Charles S. Sargent notes that the greater Buenos Aires' population had ballooned to approximately three million people. And by 1932 the "economy, heavily dependent on the British-shaped economía agroportuaria quickly lost its stability."[60] Le Corbusier, who arrived in Buenos Aires in 1929, considered it "the most inhuman that [he] had ever known." He deemed the Argentine capital a city "without hope." The French architect was particularly concerned that the Avenida de Mayo divided the city into the rich in the north and the poor in the south.[61]

It stands to reason, then, that Neruda, who cherished the wild and lush countryside in southern Chile, would be shocked by this urban environment. This is evident from the very first verses:

> Sucede que me canso de ser hombre.
> Sucede que entro en las sastrerías y en los cines
> marchito, impenetrable, como un cisne de fieltro
> navegando en un agua de origen y ceniza.[62]

> [I happen to be tired of being a man.
> I happen to enter tailorshops and moviehouses
> withered, impenetrable, like a felt swan
> navigating in a water of sources and ashes.][63]

Similar to a prizefighter in the ring, the man appears beaten, "withered" and "impenetrable," a mere semblance of a man on the city streets of Buenos Aires. Like the city dweller Walter Benjamin describes in his commentary on Baudelaire, Neruda demonstrates "what had to become of the *flaneur* once he was deprived of the milieu to which he belonged."[64] Appointed to the diplomatic corps in the Argentine capital until he was reassigned to Barcelona in May 1934, Neruda does not fit the description of a man of leisure or a flaneur. Although his job provides him with free time, he still has duties that occupy stretches of time. Nor, for that reason, is he a typical pedestrian in the crowd merely walking the streets. Neruda is, rather, a bureaucrat who writes poetry and who would like nothing better than to dedicate himself exclusively to writing verses. Consequently, borrowing the maximum symbol of beauty, perfection, and sensibility from the *modernistas* and also the image of the poet per se, in these lines he describes himself as a swan. However, he is a swan contaminated by the city. A "cisne de fieltro" (felt swan) is worse: it is not natural nor is it manufactured with skilled labor. According to *The Oxford American Dictionary* felt is "a kind of cloth made by rolling and pressing wool." Better than any other image in this poem, this antithesis (the felt swan) shows how nature has been denuded in the city and how the poet, consequently, has lost his source of inspiration and has become degraded in this city life. The somber images formerly describing the natural landscape are now imputed to the city and have left the speaker "navegando en un agua de origen y ceniza" (navigating in waters of origin and ash) or life and death.

The only salvation lies in his being able to escape from his suffocating life in the city:

> El olor de las peluquerías me hace llorar a gritos.
> Sólo quiero un descanso de piedras o de lana,
> sólo quiero no ver establecimientos ni jardines,
> ni mercaderías, ni anteojos, ni ascensores. (85)

> [The smell of barbershops makes me wail.
> I want only a respite of stones or wool,
> I want only not to see establishments or gardens,
> or merchandise, or glasses, or elevators.]

His evident desperation and rejection of modernization give way to the possible escape found in the countryside: "un descanso de piedras o de lana" (rest of either stones or of wool)." Only a return to nature can replenish him

3/REALISM AND THE BATTLE WITH LANGUAGE   131

after his battles in Buenos Aires. The urban atmosphere and his tedious job increase his tension and frustration and lead him to reject himself, to feel alienated from himself:

> Sucede que me canso de mis pies y mis uñas
> y mi pelo y mi sombra.
> Sucede que me canso de ser hombre. (85)
>
> [I happen to be tired of my feet and my nails
> and my hair and my shadow.
> I happen to be tired of being a man.]

Neruda underlines his boredom and irritation by employing successive conjunctions (polysyndeton) and possessive adjectives. He deliberately calls attention to himself in Spanish by using the possessive adjectives rather than definite articles and thus emphasizes his extreme degree of isolation in an environment that ignores him.

By the fourth stanza, he directs his anger, however randomly, at institutions that aid in social control, namely, the church and the state:

> Sin embargo sería delicioso
> asustar a un notario con un lirio cortado
> o dar muerte a una monja con un golpe de oreja.
> Sería bello
> ir por las calles con un cuchillo verde
> y dando gritos hasta morir de frío. (85)
>
> [Nevertheless it would be delightful
> to startle a notary with a cut lily
> or slay a nun by striking her with an ear.
> It would be lovely
> to go through the streets with a sexy knife
> and shouting until frozen to death.][65]

Here Neruda takes aim at bureaucratic jobs which are very similar to his own (he was a paper pusher) and approaches the artificiality of that job with nature's authenticity. Likewise, he suggests that the church would do better to listen than to preach (thus the blow to the ear). In the final lines, too, the speaker falls back on nature to attack the inhospitable city.

In the next two stanzas the speaker leads a passive existence in a downward spiral toward death. He considers himself a part of nature in his battle to survive in the city:

> No quiero seguir siendo raíz en las tinieblas,
> vacilante, extendido, tiritando de sueño,
> hacia abajo, en las tripas mojadas de la tierra,

> absorbiendo y pensando, comiendo cada día.
> No quiero para mí tantas desgracias.
> No quiero continuar de raíz y de tumba,
> de subterráneo solo, de bodega con muertos,
> aterido, muriéndome de pena. (86)
>
> [I don't want to go on being a root in the dark,
> vacillating, stretched out, shivering with sleep,
> downward, in the soaked guts of the earth,
> absorbing and thinking, eating every day.
> I do not want for myself so many misfortunes.
> I do not want to continue as root and tomb,
> subterranean only, a vault with corpses,
> stiff with cold, dying of distress.]

Here the speaker has become a sedentary part of nature accosted by the city's dehumanization. The gerunds in the first stanza underscore his scarce survival. In the darkness, he leads an inactive life, for the moment, dedicated to "absorbing and thinking, eating every day" and nothing more. As in "Dead Gallop" and "Sonata and Destructions," he manages to carry on despite the life-threatening environment, yet here he is alienated from his fellow human beings and, seemingly, himself. The speaker's only resistance to death's encirclement is his verbal and emotional rejection of the cityscape ("I do not want" in contrast to "I only want" from the second stanza). It is safe to say that solitude haunts him at this point due to his having recently arrived in Buenos Aires, having been overwhelmed by the hard economic and political times (the depression era and the fall of Yrigoyen), having battled with the tediousness of his job and the impersonal character of a city with which he was not acquainted, and having struggled with his uninspiring marriage to María Antonieta. Overcome by these circumstances, he seems to be dying from misery.

He registers his boredom and anguish on the job in particular in the following stanza:

> Por eso el día lunes arde como el petróleo
> cuando me ve llegar con mi cara de cárcel,
> y aúlla en su transcurso como una rueda herida,
> y da pasos de sangre caliente hacia la noche. (86)
>
> [That is why Monday burns like petroleum
> when it sees me coming with my prison face,
> and it howls in its transit like a wounded wheel,
> and it takes hot-blooded steps toward the night.]

A personified Monday, the first day of the work week, darkens his skies with clouds reminiscent of death and he arrives at his bureaucratic post like a pris-

3/REALISM AND THE BATTLE WITH LANGUAGE

oner. In the third line Neruda captures the impact of the city on his daily life: his day "aúlla... como una rueda herida" (howls... like a wounded wheel) much as the wheels of the trolleys frighten the pedestrians along the city streets. Monday, the first day of the work week and the howling and wounded wheel point to the grim, painful, and tedious mechanization of labor under capitalism. The large sprawling and dominating Buenos Aires and his own bureaucratic routine at the time of the depression sap the speaker of most of his creative energy and he can only fight back with indignant verses.

From alienation in the workplace, in the final stanzas he turns to a description of the horrors of the city:

> Y me empuja a ciertos rincones, a ciertas casas húmedas,
> a hospitales donde los huesos salen por la ventana,
> a ciertas zapaterías con olor a vinagre,
> a calles espantosas como grietas.
>
> Hay pájaros de color de azufre y horribles intestinos
> colgando de las puertas de las casas que odio,
> hay dentaduras olvidadas en una cafetera,
> hay espejos
>
> que debieran haber llorado de vergüenza y espanto,
> hay paraguas en todas partes, y venenos, y ombligo.
> Yo paseo con calma, con ojos, con zapatos,
> con furia, con olvido,
>
> paso, cruzo oficinas y tiendas de ortopedia,
> y patios donde hay ropas colgadas de un alambre:
> calzoncillos, toallas y camisas que lloran
> lentas lágrimas sucias. (86)
>
> [And it pushes me into certain corners, into certain moist houses,
> into hospitals where bones stick out of the windows,
> into certain shoestores with a smell of vinegar,
> into streets as frightening as chasms.
> There are brimstone-colored birds of horrible intestines
> hanging from the doors of houses I hate,
> there are dentures left forgotten in a coffee pot,
> there are mirrors
> that ought to have wept from shame and fright,
> there are umbrellas everywhere, and poisons, and navels.
> I walk along with calm, with eyes, with shoes,
> with fury, with forgetfulness,
> I pass, I cross by offices and orthopedic stores,
> and courtyards where clothes hang from a wire:
> underdrawers, towels and shirts which weep
> slow dirty tears.]

In these stanzas Neruda employs anaphora to underscore the city's monotony and crushing power and its inhabitants' acquiescence to this passive dying lifestyle. The distant and cold city wreaks havoc on its inhabitants: bones come out of the windows of the hospitals, the streets are like huge crevices, horrible intestines hang from doors, and everywhere there are umbrellas, poisons, and navels. From the readers' point of view, these expressionistic images surprise, shock, and seem disjointed. As such, they surely accomplish the task Neruda had set before him: to portray the chaos of this industrial city and its dehumanization as they are "fuertemente anclado en lo real inmediato" (strongly anchored in real immediacy) as Hernán Loyola puts it.[66] The poem is a spontaneous response to his daily alienating conditions and, consequently, does not provide a way out of that labyrinth. The speaker's actions fluctuate according to the urban environment dictating the terms of his existence. His boredom and exasperation at work push him into corners. Even in the final stanza, he walks along but with a torment inside him that, in many ways, mirrors the disarray he sees in Buenos Aires. He is at once calm and furious, attentive ("con ojos" [with eyes]) and forgetful as though he is unable to come to terms with the pervasive estrangement he perceives in the final two lines: "calzoncillos, toallas y camisas que lloran / lentras lágrimas sucias" (underwear, towels and shirts which weep / slow dirty tears). Here Neruda personifies the empty clothes that hang from the line as though that is all that is left of human beings in the city, and he portrays the tragedy of their existence in the "lágrimas sucias" (dirty tears). The (Chilean) Spanish version also uses alliteration of the 'l,' 'll' and 's' to imitate the inhabitants' sobbing and thus to put the final exclamation point on their misery.

Unlike the previous poems in *Residencia en la tierra,* "Walking around" furnishes a social critique of the impact of capitalist modernization and social disaffection in the city. However, Neruda does not react with the "fear, revulsion, and horror" Benjamin perceptively finds in Poe's work on the city and its crowds. Valéry's stance comes close to reflecting Neruda's own: he considered the city to be the cradle of civilization and, simultaneously, the site of "savagery" because it subjugated human beings to isolation. "Any improvement of [the social] mechanism," according to Valéry, "eliminates certain modes of behavior and emotions."[67] Like Neruda, Valéry sensed that the price of unequal socioeconomic "progress" was too high.

Neruda's emotional reaction is recorded in esoteric metaphors that populate the poem, thus achieving a social critique of life under industrial capitalism on the plane of content and also in the very expressionist character of the poetic language. There is then a unity between form and content as they both describe realistically the haunting experiences and state of mind of the speaker and of many residents in Buenos Aires who have been thrust into modernity. Thus, "Walking around" provides a sophisticated *realist—*

not surrealist—portrait of the urban environment and of its effects on the average city dweller.

My interpretation, however, differs from the received readings of "Walking Around," like those of *Residencia en la tierra* as a whole, that contend that it is existentialist and/or prototypically surrealist. In keeping with the theme of his book on Neruda, Enrico Mario Santí sees "Walking around" as a "failed revolt against vision, a failure that exposes the limits of the speaker and his fall into irony." It is the "overwhelming power of vision" that weighs the speaker down, not (necessarily) the modern industrialized city and his concomitant estrangement. In Santí's view the speaker "revolts against his own limits [as a poet] and casts his discontent in the form of ironic language."[68]

While Marjorie Agosín points to the speaker's alienation in an oppressive urban milieu she also observes in *Residencia en la tierra* the "syncopated use of words, the absence of adverbs and adjectives, and the constant use of similes that invoke incongruous images." Agosín remarks that these techniques are not orchestrated, but rather lack "logical connections."[69] She claims that some of the verses have no apparent referents and that the reader is often confronted with "incoherent and disordered images" (41). *Residencia en la tierra* offers a speaker who passively endures alienation in the city and faces the ostensible senselessness of life. The book's inherent unity, she says, is "in the process of disintegration" (45). And it is the combination of the chaos being observed, the jolting metaphors, the nontraditional poetic techniques employed and the dreamy atmosphere that make *Residencia en la tierra* in general and "Walking around" in particular surrealist. Despite reaching this conclusion, Agosín devotes more space to an analysis of the social environment's destructive impact on the speaker than to her argument for surrealism. Indeed, her analysis dovetails well with my own.

Manuel Durán and Margery Safir do dedicate much of their interpretation of *Residencia en la tierra* to making a case for Neruda's surrealism.[70] They caution that to pass over the influence of surrealism in this avantgardist work would be an error, an error encouraged by the poet himself who rejected surrealism on political grounds years after the publication of *Residencia en la tierra:*

> Neruda's rejection of surrealism was largely political, since the Breton group soon evolved toward an independent, semi-anarchist position, later affiliated with Trotskyism. It was also political in that Neruda's Communism later led him to reject all hermetic forms of "elitist" poetry. (38)

Following this reading, they suggest that Neruda's works go through distinct and unconnected phases. In the 1920s and 1930s, despite his denials,

Neruda labors under the influence of surrealism: "Whatever Neruda's animosity toward the surrealists, the fact remains that many of the essential feelings and stylistic manifestations in *Venture* [of the Infinite] and *Residence* [on Earth] coincide powerfully with those of the surrealist movement, and must be looked at within that context." Additionally, Durán and Safir state that "Breton's early writings . . . would have attracted the Neruda of the 1920s" and they enumerate surrealism's political and aesthetic stances (39). In *Residencia en la tierra* they find "unexpected combinations of words and images, the flow of obscure voices from the unconscious mind" and consider it "surrealist poetry" (44). From this point of view, Neruda's delirium and unconscious intuition drive him to portray his personal crisis in poems like "Walking around" as a disjointed and chaotic experience that puts him face to face with death. Durán and Safir draw a parallel between Neruda's *Residencia en la tierra* and Federico García Lorca's *Poeta en Nueva York* (Poet in New York). Both "are permeated with chaotic catalogues and enumerations, startling and disjointed metaphors, reflecting the breakdown of natural boundaries, the natural elements in disarray, images of impending doom, feelings of guilt, premonitions of death and destruction" (46). Nonetheless, it is worth noting though that García Lorca's understanding of the root causes of the chaos is much more developed than Neruda's at this stage. The framework of *Poeta en Nueva York* makes it clear that the Great Depression lays bare the class conflict under capitalism and highlights the drive for profit. In poems like "El rey de Harlem" (The king of Harlem), "Danza de la muerte" (Dance of Death), and "Grito hacia Roma" (Cry to Rome), García Lorca also makes it clear that he understands that racial segregation is intimately tied to class divisions.[71] Neruda does not reach that plateau until *España en el corazón* or *Canto general.*

While Durán and Safir (and Agosín) do come to the conclusion that *Residencia en la tierra* is surrealist and point to specific characteristics of that artistic movement, they nonetheless confess that "Neruda's poetic descriptions in *Residence* in fact reflected accurately his external world" (46). Based on this reading, one would seemingly have to conclude that either the social environment is chaotic and destructive and the poet perceives it realistically as such, or that surrealism and all that it implies renders reality more faithfully than literary realism. In other words, either Neruda possessed a poetic method for expressing the collapsing social world around him (in Chile, Asia, Buenos Aires, or Madrid) and yet was not able to step away from his own alienated immersion in it (this would be the argument for realism), or he absorbed the destruction and chaos in the external world unconsciously and committed it to writing (this would be the case for surrealism). Durán and Safir offer another possible position: that "the crisis, the breakdown of clear boundaries, is also the solution." Neruda's work indicates that "the best way for man to approach this [infinite and chaotic] world, to grasp it, is by erasing his inner boundaries. The human mind has become too tightly compartmentalized; to move closer to the cosmos, it must become as open and vast as the cosmos" (48–49). Although they don't state it outright, these critics suggest that the third option above is correct: Neruda gave in to his intuitive and unconscious impulses in order to consciously portray the disintegration of the urban environment and the devastation of nature. However, as Durán and Safir admit, there is no denying that there is a *realist* intent on Neruda's part and that his descriptions of the social world are generally accurate. And this conclusion contradicts their thesis that Neruda is a surrealist in the 1920s and 1930s. (See chapter 1 for a more detailed discussion of surrealism and realism in Neruda's work.)

"Swimming Against the Cemeteries"

Besides confronting death in nature (particularly in Asia) and in the city and thereby finding a temporary escape from his existential and social disaffection, Neruda also rediscovers his sensuality in the solace and wild passion of his love affairs. Neruda's close friend and biographer Volodia Teitelboim gives contradictory explanations for the poet's erotic exploration. On the one hand, Teitelboim states that Neruda confided to him that he "no podía resistir el amor o la insinuación femenina, sobre todo si esa mujer le gustaba" (couldn't resist feminine flirtation or love especially if he liked the woman). On the other hand, the biographer says that Neruda "(s)e agarra a la vida. Lo atan a ella las mujeres, porque no es todavía la Mujer. Pero esto de ir de cama en cama, de niña en niña, nativa, mulata o inglesa, lo daña por dentro y lo satura de hastío" (latches on to life. Women keep him tied to it, because he has to find the Woman. But this practice of hopping from bed to bed, from woman to woman, native, mulatta, or English, damages him emotionally and wears on him).[72] For Neruda writing was virtually dependent on women, and without them, his verses would have been doomed. His work was always grounded in the profound sensuality and passion he gained from the women in his life.

However, individual women had different levels of importance in his life. Albertina, whom he was prepared to marry until she was unable or unwilling to travel to Asia in 1929, was his muse for many of the love poems in his classic early book, *Veinte poemas de amor y una canción desesperada* (Twenty Love Poems and a Desperate Song; 1924).[73] According to critic Hernán Loyola, she evoked love and intense erotic passion in the young poet.[74] And this sweet and lethal combination led Neruda to pour his soul into writing the famous twenty-one poems. It helped too that he was not apparently marked by estrangement during this period. Add to this

Neruda's knowledge of poetry and his rare talent and a renowned work like *Veinte poemas de amor* emerges. In the first poem of the book Neruda describes the electrical charges between them and the more profound sentiments of love that have overtaken him:

> Cuerpo de mujer, blancas colinas, muslos blancos,
> te pareces al mundo en tu actitud de entrega.
> Mi cuerpo de labriego salvaje te socava
> y hace saltar el hijo del fondo de la tierra.
>
> Fui solo como un túnel. De mí huían los pájaros
> y en mí la noche entraba su invasión poderosa.
> Para sobrevivirme te forjé como un arma,
> como una flecha en mi arco, como una piedra en
> mi honda.
>
> Pero cae la hora de la venganza, y te amo.
> Cuerpo de piel, de musgo, de leche ávida y firme.
> Ah los vasos del pecho! Ah los ojos de ausencia!
> Ah las rosas del pubis! Ah tu voz lenta y triste!
>
> Cuerpo de mujer mía, persistiré en tu gracia.
> Mi sed, mi ansia sin límite, mi camino indeciso!
> Oscuros cauces donde la sed eterna sigue
> y la fatiga sigue, y el dolor infinito.[75]
>
> [Body of a woman, white hills, white thighs,
> you are like a world lying in surrender.
> My rough peasant's body digs in you
> and makes the son leap from the depth of the earth.
> I only was a tunnel. The birds fled from me
> and night swampd me with its crushing invasion.
> To survive myself I forged you like a weapon,
> like an arrow in my bow, like a stone in my sling.
> But the hour of vengeance falls, and I love you.
> Body of skin, of moss, of avid and firm milk.
> Oh the goblets of the breast! Oh the eyes of absence!
> Oh the roses of the pubis! Oh your voice, slow and sad!
> Body of my woman, I will persist in your grace.
> My thirst, my boundless desire, my shifting road!
> Dark river-beds where eternal thirst flows,
> and weariness follows, and infinite ache.][76]

In this case erotic pleasure is intertwined with a deep sense of mutual possession, of love. His relationship with Albertina is not a fleeting affair nor

3/REALISM AND THE BATTLE WITH LANGUAGE 139

an excuse to escape the "invasión poderosa" (powerful invasion) of the night. The desire and awe that fill Neruda as he praises her beauty lead him beyond sexual attraction to a confession of love. True, the wonder she inspires in him is due, in great measure, to her physical splendor ("Cuerpo de mujer, blancas colinas, muslos blancos" [Body of a woman, white hills, white thighs]) and grace (her bodily rhythm), but also to the intangibles that form the nucleus of love: insatiable thirst and desire, and the unique compatibility between these lovers. In the relationship he clearly takes the initiative and she surrenders herself to him. Yet, unlike most of the poems in *Residencia en la tierra,* here the focus shifts continuously from his lover to the speaker and back, thereby showing the spiritual and physical reciprocity between them. This portrayal of their love confers on the poem an inherent thematic and formal unity not found in *Residencia en la tierra.* Moreover, the salient poetic techniques give the poem and such majesterial poems as 6 and 20 a breadth that Neruda is not able to achieve in *Residencias* because of his extreme isolation.

The poems in section III of *Residencia en la tierra* present a radically different view of his relationship with a young woman. Penned around the same time as "Walking around," they are erotic poems but also suffused with death images. Presumably a young woman he met in Buenos Aires while he was married to María Antonieta Hagenaar (whom he called "Maruca"), the anonymous lover gave him carnal pleasure so he could swim "against the cemeteries"—as he puts it in "Oda con un lamento" (Ode with a Lament).[77] As in "Walking Around" the persona observes wild and unconnected scenes about him pointing to the apparent senselessness of life. In "Agua sexual" (Sexual Water), for example, his sexual encounter takes up one of the five stanzas; the rest is dedicated to describing his survival amidst the dehumanization he finds. Indeed, the third stanza bears witness to the social anarchy in depression-era Buenos Aires:

> Veo el verano extenso, y un estertor saliendo de un granero,
> bodegas, cigarras,
> poblaciones, estímulos,
> habitaciones, niñas
> durmiendo con las manos en el corazón,
> soñando con bandidos, con incendios,
> veo barcos,
> veo árboles de médula
> erizados como gatos rabiosos,
> veo sangre, puñales y medias de mujer,
> y pelos de hombre,
> veo camas, veo corredores donde grita una virgen,
> veo frazadas y órganos y hoteles.[78]

> [I see the vast summer, and a death rattle coming from a granary,
> stores, locusts,
> towns, stimuli,
> rooms, girls
> sleeping with their hands folded upon their hearts,
> dreaming of bandits, of fires,
> I see ships,
> I see marrow trees
> bristling like rabid cats,
> I see blood, daggers and women's stockings,
> and men's hair,
> I see beds, I see corridors where a virgin screams,
> I see blankets and organs and hotels.][79]

These random expressionistic impressions of the city graphically document the speaker's isolation and hopelessness. It is collage of Buenos Aires predicated on the free association of an abandoned individual. Certainly, at least two tropes here seem so arbitrary that surrealism could have inspired them: "Veo árboles de médula" (I see trees made of medullas) and "erizados como gatos rabiosos" (erect like rabid cats). And yet they are inserted in a stanza that points up the irrationality of life in the city, which could lead readers to believe that these are simply tropes requiring us to look outside of our conventional conceptual system to uncover a new way of viewing trees in the winter time. However, interpreting these verses does not really entail that much of a leap of imagination. As a prototypical symbol of life, the tree suffers a metamorphosis as it is assailed in the city. He pictures the trees as sentient beings by comparing their trunks to medullas. Devoid of leaves and gray perhaps, the trees' branches and shapes look like cats' heads. The branches protrude beneath the cloudy, wintry skies in Buenos Aires. By employing these tropes Neruda draws a link between the inhabitants of the city and the trees and shows that the speaker and the *porteños* suffer dehumanization. But, like rabid cats, they fight for survival and bring out the worst human characteristics. These images, along with the remaining verses in this stanza, focus on the fragmentation of urban life during a major crisis in the capitalist system and they leave scant room for enriching human relationships. Indeed, summed up in five verses in stanza five, the speaker depicts his affair also in a detached and impersonal way: "Y entonces hay este sonido: / un ruido rojo de huesos, / un pegarse de carne, / y piernas amarillas como espigas juntándose. / Yo escucho entre el disparo de los besos" (And then there is a sound: / a red noise of bones / a gluing of flesh / and yellow legs like joined mastheads. / I listen between the discharges of kisses). The passion and sensibility masterfully orchestrated in *Veinte poemas de amor y una canción desesperada* are nowhere to be found in

Residencia en la tierra. The darkness of the city has also invaded his intimate relations and appears to tear apart the speaker.

"Oda con un lamento" comes closest to the sensuality and completeness of the *Veinte poemas de amor.* However, in this poem as well as in many others, the speaker's own solemnity and solitude dominate:

> Oh niña entre las rosas, oh presión de palomas,
> oh presidio de peces y rosales,
> tu alma es una botella llena de sal sedienta
> y una campana llena de uvas es tu piel.[80]
>
> [Oh girl among the roses, oh crush of doves,
> oh fortress of fishes and rosebushes,
> your soul is a bottle full of thirsty salt
> and your skin, a bell filled with grapes.]

These lines praising his young lover's beauty are followed by a speaker who is still overtaken by the isolation, agony, and death he observes in Buenos Aires. His torment and sorrow come to a head in the third stanza:

> Sólo puedo quererte con besos y amapolas,
> con guirnaldas mojadas por la lluvia,
> mirando cenicientos caballos y perros amarillos.
> Sólo puedo quererte con olas a la esplada,
> entre vagos golpes de azufre y aguas ensimismadas,
> nadando en contra de los cementerios que corren en
> ciertos ríos
> con pasto mojado creciendo sobre las tristes tumbas de yeso,
> nadando a través de corazones sumergidos
> y pálidas planillas de niños insepultos.
>
> [I can love you only with kisses and poppies,
> with garlands wet by the rain,
> looking at ash-gray horses and yellow dogs.
> I can love you only with waves at my back,
> amid vague sulphur blows and booding waters,
> swimming against the cemeteries that run in certain rivers
> with wet fodder growing over the sad plaster tumbs,
> swimming across submerged hearts
> and pale lists of unburied children.][81]

In contrast to the smooth and sensual images in *Veinte poemas de amor,* once again there is an array of bizarre references. Nonetheless, it is clear that death creates the poet's sense of chaos and futility, a depiction consistent with sections one and two. Yet after describing his struggle for survival, in the last two stanzas Neruda returns to his young lover. As the last lines of the poem make clear, she can at least take his mind off the devastation and death that surround him, but cannot save him from his fate:

> Ven a mi alma vestida de blanco, con un ramo
> de ensangrentadas rosas y copas de cenizas,
> ven con una manzana y un caballo,
> porque allí hay una sala oscura y un candelabro roto,
> unas sillas torcidas que esperan el invierno,
> y una paloma muerta, con un número.
>
> [Come to my heart dressed in white, with a bouquet
> of bloody roses and goblets of ash,
> come with an apple and a horse,
> because there there is a dark room and a broken chandelier,
> some twisted chairs waiting for winter,
> and a dead dove, with a number.]

In an echo perhaps of Adolfo Bécquer's lyric poem XI, the speaker awaits the arrival of his lover dressed in white. However, rather than cleanse his soul, she is asked to bring a bouquet of "ensangrentadas rosas y copas de ceniza" (bloody roses and goblets of ash). With her, it would seem, he will be able to face death head on; without her, death could overpower him. By consummating their passion with her tenderness and sweetness ("una manzana" [an apple]) and her voluptuous surrender ("un caballo" [a mare]), he will be able to carry on despite, as he puts it in the fourth stanza, "mucha muerte, muchos acontecimientos funerarios / en mis desamparadas pasiones y desolados besos" (much death, many funereal events / in my homeless passions and desolate kisses). Thus, though this young anonymous lover provides him carnal fire at a moment when Neruda feels lost on the streets of Buenos Aires, she can only momentarily stave off his spiritual crisis.

His last and most significant lover, Josie Bliss, is the inspiration for at least five, perhaps six, poems in *Residencia en la tierra* and, as Hernán Loyola argues, she became Neruda's consummate lover during this period.[82] So powerful was Josie Bliss' effect on Neruda that in his memoirs he notes that had it not been for her terrible jealousy "tal vez yo hubiera continuado indefinidamente junto a ella" (maybe I would have continued indefinitely with her).[83] But she offers more than carnal love to the young poet. In Josie Bliss Neruda finds respite from the torments of his life and fulfillment in his innerlife. With her he discovers the pleasure and, at moments, the disappointments of sharing a life together. Above all they explore each other with ravenous erotic desire nourished by love. In contrast, as noted above, the poems written during his affair in Buenos Aires show that Neruda's sexual encounters with the young woman in "Oda con un lamento" did not help to keep his suffering at bay. At this juncture of his life, then, Josie Bliss is the only woman capable of conquering Neruda both physically and emotionally.

He expresses the depth of his relationship with Josie Bliss in an unparalelled way in *Residencia en la tierra* in "Juntos nosotros" (Together), rivaling some of his best poems in his classic later works: *Los versos del capitán* (The Captain's Verses) and *Cien sonetos de amor* (One Hundred Love Sonnets). Written in Rangoon in 1928, it has few references to the social environment and to mortality. The verses mostly extol Josie's beauty and passionate hunger, his own self-discovery as a lover and man, and their ardent union:

> Qué pura eres de solo de noche caída,
> qué triunfal desmedida tu órbita de blanco,
> y tu pecho de pan, alto de clima,
> tu corona de árboles negros, bienamada,
> y tu nariz de animal solitario, de oveja salvaje
> que huele a sombra y a precipitada fuga tiránica.[84]
>
> [How pure you are as sunlight or fallen night,
> how trimphal and boundless your orbit of white,
> and bosom of bread, high in climate,
> your crown of black trees, beloved,
> and your lone-animal nose, nose of a wild sheep
> that smells the shadow and of precipitous, tyrannical escape.][85]

In this apostrophe dedicated to Josie Bliss, Neruda captures some of the elusive outlines of his lover, of his "pantera birmana" (burmese panther), as he called her in his memoirs.[86] He highlights her curves, skin, wavy hair, breasts, and wild passion.

In section three the poet provides perhaps an analogous description of his lover, but one that is immediately followed by scores of lines decrying the misery of life in the city.

In the second stanza he explores her effects sensually on him as a man. She has allowed him to abandon his solitude and desolation and has awakened his senses and, thus, an appreciation of himself:

> Ahora, qué armas espléndidas mis manos,
> digna su pala de hueso y su lirio de uñas,
> y el puesto de mi rostro, y el arriendo de mi alma
> están situados en lo justo de la fuerza terrestre.
> Qué pura mi mirada de nocturna influencia,
> caída de ojos oscuros y feroz acicate,
> mi simétrica estatua de piernas gemelas
> sube hacia estrellas húmedas cada mañana,

y mi boca de exilio muerde la carne y la uva,
mis brazos de varón, mi pecho tatuado
en que penetra el vello como ala de estaño,
mi cara blanca hecha para la profundidad del sol . . .

[Now, what splendid weapons are my hands
worthy their bone spades and their lily nails,
and the place of my face, and the tie to my soul
are situated in the just earthly force.
How pure is my sight of nocturnal influence,
falling on my dark eyes and ferocious incentive,
my symmetrical statue of twin legs
rises toward humid stars every morning,
and my mouth of exile bites the flesh and the grape,
my manly arms, my tatooed chest
in which my hair like a winged tin,
my white face made for the sun's depth . . .]

And so, in these and the following eleven verses, this twenty-four-year-old young man rediscovers almost every part of his body and thereby regains his sensuality and spiritual life ("el arriendo de mi alma" [the tie to my soul]) thanks to his companion Josie Bliss. Having been fully awakened in this shared pleasure, hence the insistent references to himself, in the final three stanzas he praises his lover once again:

Y tú como un mes de estrella, como un beso fijo,
como estructura de ala, o comienzos de otoño,
niña; mi partidaria, mi amorosa,
la luz hace su lecho bajo tus grandes párpados,
dorados como bueyes, y la paloma redonda
hace sus nidos blancos frecuentemente en ti.
Hecha de ola en lingotes y tenazas blancas,
tu salud de manzana furiosa se estira sin límite,
el tonel temblador en que escucha tu estómago,
tus manos hijas de la harina y del cielo.
Qué parecida eres al más largo beso,
su sacudida fija parece nutrirte,
y su empuje de brasa, de bandera revuelta,
va latiendo en tus dominios y subiendo temblando,
y entonces tu cabeza se adelgaza en cabellos,
y su forma guerrera, su círculo seco,
se desploma de súbito en hilos lineales
como filos de espadas o herencias del humo.

[And you like a star month, like a steady kiss,
like winged structure, or the beginning of the fall,

child; my partisan, my beloved,
light makes its bed beneath your large eyelids,
golden like oxen, and the round dove
makes its white nests frequently in you.
Made of ingots and white pliers,
your vigor like a furious apple stretches beyond bounds,
the trembling barrel in which your stomach hears,
your hands daughters of flour and the heavens.
How similar you are to a long kiss,
its steady shaking seems to nourish you,
and its coal-like push, rebellious flag,
beating in your domains and rising shaken,
and then your head thins into locks,
and its warrior shape, its dry circle,
tumbles suddenly in straight threads
like swords' blades or smoky legacies.]

This penultimate stanza brilliantly combines the different senses associated with Josie Bliss: her undulating and perspiring body ("ola de lingotes" [wave of ignots]), her strong legs ("tenazas blancas" [white pliers]), her sweetness and her loving fury ("manzana furiosa" [furious apple]), her round torso, and her unbearably smooth hands ("hijas de harina y del cielo" [daughters of flour and the heavens]). In the following lines Neruda incarnates her voluptousness with even greater metaphorical precision. The reader can vividly picture her every reaction as they kiss ardently: she shivers, hungers for his warm lips, trembles, and falls forward and then backward as he lays her down. As Jaime Concha observed, in "Galope muerto" and in this and many other poems in *Residencia en la tierra* the speaker plays the role of hero. He frequently portrays himself as a warrior (as in "Junto nosotros") or as a soldier who brandishes a sword, though he need not be the image of the conquistador that Concha claims he is.[87]

It could be argued that "Juntos nosotros" is an erotic poem without the nuisance and torture of the city bearing down on the speaker. However, the Josie Bliss poems contain more than just carnal love. As noted above, the speaker's soul is involved in this rapturous act of making love. Furthermore, in the second stanza his eyes look on with "sal avida" (avid salt) with "matrimonio rápido" (swift matrimony), indicating that he sees Josie Bliss as his companion or as his "partidaria" (partisan) and "amorosa" (beloved). Indeed, in "El joven monarca" (The Young Monarch) he refers to her as his Burmese wife: "Y mi esposa a mi orilla, al lado de mi rumor tan venido / de lejos, mi esposa birmana, hija del rey" (And my wife at my shore, beside my rumor from afar / my Burmese wife, daughter of the king).[88] Josie Bliss, then, provides Neruda with a haven in an environment he considers alien and destructive and inspires him to lose himself in the linguistic world of his poetry. She heals his wounds from the personal and social conflicts in Asia and furnishes him with coherence, with meaning in his life. The imprints of that love stayed with him even as he wrote his memoirs some forty-five years later. Yet from this moment on, Matilde Urrutia would reign supreme over Neruda with her burning love. Nevertheless, during the late 1920s and perhaps years later, Josie Bliss dominated Neruda's life as no other woman had. In his renowned poem, "Tango del viudo" (The Widower's Tango) he puts it this way: "Cuánta sombra de la que hay en mi alma daría por recobrarte" (How many shadows in my soul would I give to have you back).

"A Lesson for a Tortured Lyrical Poet"

In a species of manifesto in the journal *Caballo Verde para la Poesía* (Green Horse for Poetry) (1935), Neruda drew the outlines of the new poetics that would undergird *España en el corazón* and subsequent works:

> Es muy conveniente, en ciertas horas del día o de la noche, observar profundamente los objetos en descanso: Las ruedas que han recorrido largas, polvorientas distancias, soportando grandes cargas vegetales y minerales, los sacos de las carbonerías, los barriles, las cestas, los mangos y asas de los instrumentos del carpintero. De ellos se desprende el contacto del hombre y de la tierra como una lección para el torturado poeta lírico. Las superficies usadas, el gasto que las manos han infligido a las cosas, la atmósfera a menudo trágica y siempre patética de estos objetos, infunde una especie de atracción no despreciable hacia la realidad del mundo.[89]

> [It is worthwhile at certain hours of the day or night, to deeply observe objects at rest: The wheels that have covered long, dusty distances, carrying big loads of vegetables and minerals, the bags in the coalyard, the barrels, the baskets, the handles of the carpenter's tools. From there the contact with man and the earth emanates like a lesson for a tortured lyrical poet. The used surfaces, how the hands have worn things down, the often tragic and always pathetic appearance of these objects, inspires a type of healthy attraction for the reality of the world.]

From this moment on, Neruda's poetic theory and work began to change radically. Like César Vallejo's *España, aparta de mí este cáliz* (Spain, take this chalice from me), Neruda's language ceased to be a refuge for existential anguish and emerged out of its concentrated, self-reflexive stage. From 1935 on, Neruda's poetry became historicized, specified, and concrete without losing its towering ideals and its "espontaneidad dirigida" (guided spontaneity). As Alain Sicard and Jaime Concha have argued, Neruda's texts prior to *España en el corazón* are realist because they depict the multiple alienations that dehumanize the speaker. Yet this realist effort to make the speaker's alienation concrete remains helplessly limited by the speaker's unwillingness to consciously understand the forces that alienate him and his conviction that only hermetic language can qualify as poetic. After drowning in his own estrangement from his fellow human beings, his work, nature, and even himself in Santiago and in Asia, Neruda managed to face his dehumanization and, as such, to portray it imperfectly in his *Residencias* verses. But that was the first step in trying to defeat the social ills that seized him and left him powerless. *Residencia en la tierra* and the first seven poems in *Tercera residencia* show Neruda's mastery of form and his limited yet revealing rendering of the sociohistorical and objective realities of the 1920s and early 1930s. While a study of *Residencia en la tierra* can point up many of the matters outlined above, as, for instance Concha's and Sicard's work does, my intent is to demonstrate that *Tercera residencia* represents one stage in Neruda's poetic and political development which is then reaffirmed and negated in subsequent stages.

4
The Struggle against Alienation in *Tercera residencia*

BOTH IN ANTHOLOGIES AND CRITICAL WORKS ON NERUDA THERE HAS BEEN a tendency to underrate the value of *Tercera residencia* (Third Residence, 1947). Rafael Alberti's popular anthology of Neruda's work includes a wide assortment of poems from *Residencia en la tierra* and only one poem ("Vals") from *Tercera residencia.* Hernán Loyola's classic anthology on Neruda naturally includes poems from *Tercera residencia* that break thematically with *Residencia en la tierra.*[1] Interestingly, bilingual anthologies have been more generous. In consultation with the poet, Ben Belitt provides poems from the three *Residencias* and, like Loyola, incorporates those that mark a major shift in Neruda's political awareness. Nathaniel Tarn's excellent bilingual edition offers the only selection of poems from the different stages in *Tercera residencia,* thereby showing Neruda's political and poetic progression from 1935 to 1945.[2] *Tercera residencia* has been equally neglected by the criticism, which has warranted at most three to four pages in major studies. The book has been passed over despite Neruda's deliberate attempt to show his successive political and poetic periods. As an individual who had dedicated decades of his life to left-wing politics and the Communist Party, Neruda wanted to demonstrate that the alienation that suffuses the *Residencia en la tierra* stage (1925–1935) is unhealthy and can be overcome. He found a strange kind of comfort in his isolation that led him to regard it, years later, as "luminous" (luminosa) and as an opportunity that illuminated his "destino por dentro y por fuera" (destiny from within and without).[3] In sum, thanks to his inner strength and his ability to prevail over dreadful personal and social circumstances, Neruda was able to write most of the poems that appear in *Residencia en la tierra.*

Written during the same period as Neruda's second volume of *Residencias* (1925–35), the first seven poems of *Tercera residencia* have themes and formal features that overlap with the earlier work. These verses may have been conceived in the mid to late 1920s or in the early 1930s and included in this book in 1946 as a way of synthesizing the *Residencia* years. Given the lack of information about the dates and places of publication it is hard to know. In all of them save "Naciendo en los bosques" (Coming to Life in the Woods) the speaker struggles to subsist in and testify to a natural environment that accosts him. In the process he vacillates between bold "prophetic" pronouncements and debilitating insecurity; he feels terrible loneliness and agony as nature's death pursues him and/or he attempts to save himself from the decaying urban surroundings by seeking solace in a woman friend. Indeed, his desire to latch onto the women in his life at this time merits further exegesis because it is tied to the everyday realism that counteracted the linguistic density in which his solitude resided. Neruda's inquisitiveness and passion coexisted in an appreciation of his surroundings and in his love for certain women, and both helped conquer his terrible isolation.

His personal relationships were the mainstay for Neruda, his escape from the drudgeries of life, but also the vital and sensuous connection to the life he led. His appetite for his own type of literary realism arose from those love affairs. Without those deep and fortifying forays into his emotional makeup as a person he probably would not have had the inner strength to pen his verses or to find a way out of the debilitating environment in which he found himself in the Orient. Without that inspiration it is unlikely that he would have been able to embrace the altruism of the republican cause. In the *Prison Notebooks* Antonio Gramsci, the Italian Marxist, wrote regarding the individual and collective nature of love: "How many times have I asked myself whether it was possible to tie oneself to a mass without ever having loved anyone . . . whether one could love a collectivity if one hadn't deeply loved some single human beings."[4] The Neruda of *Residencia en la tierra* and the first poems in *Tercera residencia* desperately needed those amorous relationship to overcome his solitude, to describe his environment in a realist manner, and to pave the way for radical political commitments from 1936 on.

Scarce difference, then, separates this group of poems from the *Residencia en la tierra* verses until "Naciendo en los bosques," which provides a transition for the definitive break with avant-gardist poetry in "Reunión bajo las nuevas banderas." The latter serves as the crucial bridge between this and Neruda's socially committed work because it furnishes a nascent dialectic that lays the foundation for Neruda's more complex and unified understanding of sociopolitical, historical, and individual affairs and the more profound grasp of poetic method found in "España en el corazón" and subsequent works, particularly so in *Canto general*.

A Dance with Death

"Vals" follows in the tracks of the *Residencia* poems by drawing attention to the speaker's separation from nature, his deep feeling of uncertainty and rejection in an alien setting, and his devastating yet pleasing solitude:

Yo toco el odio como pecho diurno,
yo sin cesar, de ropa en ropa vengo
durmiendo lejos.

No soy, no sirvo, no conozco a nadie,
no tengo armas de mar ni de madera,
no vivo en esta casa,

de noche y agua está mi boca llena.
La duradera luna determina
lo que no tengo.

Lo que tengo está en medio de las olas.
Un rayo de agua, un día para mí:
un fondo férreo.
No hay contramar, no hay escudo, no hay traje, no hay especial solución
insondable, ni párpado vicioso.
Vivo de pronto y otras veces sigo.
Toco de pronto un rostro y me asesina.
No tengo tiempo.

No me busquéis entonces descorriendo
el habitual hilo salvaje o la
sangrienta enredadera.

No me llaméis: mi ocupación es ésa.
No preguntéis mi nombre ni mi estado.
Dejadme en medio de mi propia luna,
en mi terreno herido.[5]

[I touch hatred like a daily breast,
I ceaseless, from clothes to clothes, come
sleeping far away.

I am not, I am no good, I don't know anyone,
I have no weapons of sea or wood,
I do not live in this house,

with night and water my mouth is filled.
The durable moon determines
what I do not have.

What I do have is in the midst of waves.
A thunderbolt of water, a day for me:
an iron bottom.
There is no countersea, no shield no suit,

there is no special unfathomable solution,
or vicious eyelid.

I live suddenly and at other times I follow.
I suddenly touch a face and it murders me.
I have no time.

Do not seek me, then, removing
the customary savage thread or the
sanguinary ivy.

Do not call me: that is my occupation.
Do not ask my name or my estate.
Leave me in the midst of my own moon,
in my wounded terrain.][6]

Unlike the *Residencia* poems in which the speaker finds strength and meaning in nature and uses them as weapons against the menaces of the city, here he faces the natural and social worlds although they are drowning him. The first two stanzas indicate that he is most likely in an urban environment facing impersonal social interaction and "hate." He barely lives in his house, sleeps elsewhere continually, does not feel he exists or is worth anything, knows nobody, and is stripped of nature ("no tengo armas de mar ni de madera" [I have no weapons of sea or wood]). His emptiness threatens to drown him in a sea of death ("de noche y agua está mi boca llena" [of night and water my mouth is full]). He has no way of combating his situation; there is, as he remarks, no "contramar" (countersea). Sometimes living and other times surviving, the speaker is caught in a state of limbo.

As readers, too, we get lost in the enigmatic panorama Neruda has sketched. The sentiments of self-degradation, resignation, and simmering anger punctuate the entire poem, but they are not accompanied by details, contexts, and rationales. For example, when he asserts, "No me busquéis entonces descorriendo / el habitual hilo salvaje o la sangrienta enredadera" (Do not seek me, then, removing / the customary wild thread or the sanguiary ivy), does he mean nature can no longer come to his defense? Or does he mean his poetry will, from now on, expose everything, no matter how ugly or tragic? What is the "profession" to which he refers in the final stanza? Given this open reading, we can only venture some interpretations. His occupation must be to record his daily tragedies in his "terreno herido" (wounded terrain) and to document his survival with references to himself (especially in the final stanza). In that regard, "Vals" comes close to replicating the profound and troubling sensations in a poem like "Sonatas and Destructions." Assailed by his loneliness, nature, and society, Neruda latches onto his struggle and bears witness to it in writing.

In the context of the *Residencias,* the reader becomes immune to the speaker's ubiquitous descriptions of his alienation. The frequency of this negativity and isolation weakens its power to shock. Expecting the somber descriptions, we are immediately drawn to any slivers of light. These flashes of hope grab our attention. But there are textual reasons why we read the first section of the *Tercera residencia* that way. "Vals" invites us to feel the speaker's suffering, agony, and solitude as much as it asks us to notice his increasing insistence and tenacity. Throughout his work Neruda described this dire stage of his life again and again to underline the fact that one must not surrender to alienating circumstances but must overcome them. As attentive readers can attest, almost any book of his poetry narrates this tragic episode in his life. In "Alturas de Macchu Picchu" (Heights of Macchu Picchu) in *Canto general* (1950) he declares that during this period "rodé muriéndome de mi propia muerte" (I tumbled dying from my own death).[7] In "Oda a la vida" (Ode to Life) in *Odas elementales* (Odes to Common Things)(1954), it emerges as a dominant theme: "El que de ti reniega / que espere / un minuto, una noche, / un año corto o largo, / que salga / de su soledad mentirosa, / que indague y luche, junte / sus manos a otras manos" (He who disowns you / let him wait / a minute, a night, / a short or long year, / let him come out / of his false solitude, / let him inquire and struggle, and join his hands with other hands).[8] Once Neruda saw a way out of his anguish and solitude, he returned didactically to the topic to discourage others from following in his footsteps, to remind himself perhaps of the traps of language-centered poetry, and to remember how far he had come personally and politically since the *Residencias* years.

"Nocturnal Sugar"

If "Vals" deals with the dominion of solitude, the race to the grave, and the absence of any panacea in nature, "Alianza (Sonata)" (Alliance [Sonata]), representative of the years spanning from 1925 to 1935, describes his lover's incarnation of nature in an impersonal urban environment. Curiously, Neruda authored an earlier poem with the same title in the first volume of *Residencia en la tierra.* Published in 1926 in Chile, death images in nature permeate the earlier poem, but they are partially redeemed by his lover, who converts the emptiness, death, and ruin in the city into light and love: "pero caen dentro de tu voz de luz. / Oh dueña del amor, en tu descanso / fundé mi sueño, mi actitud callada" (but they fall into your voice of light. / Oh possessor of love, in your repose / I founded my dream, my hushed way). Deterioration and the obsession with time carry the day; however, the speaker is able to live on thanks to her:

Con tu cuerpo de número tímido, extendido de pronto
hasta las cantidades que definen la tierra,
detrás de la pelea de los días blancos de espacio
y fríos de muertes lentas y estímulos marchitos,
siento arder tu regazo y transitar tus besos
haciendo golodrinas frescas en mi sueño.
A veces el destino de tus lágrimas asciende
como la edad hasta mi frente, allí
están golpeando las olas, destruyéndose de muerte:
su movimiento es húmedo, decaído, final.[9]

[With your body timidly number, suddenly extended
to the quantities that define the earth,
behind the struggle of the days white with space
and cold with slow deaths and withered stimuli,
I feel your lap burn and your kisses travel
shaping fresh swallows in my sleep.
At times the destiny of your tears ascends
like age to my forehead, there
the waves are crashing, smashing themselves to death:
their movement is moist, drifting, ultimate.][10]

These final two stanzas return to the familiar somber milieu Neruda created in other early *Residencia* poems. He compares his lover's body to the earth he endlessly explores and contrasts it with the struggles of the white and cold days that hasten withering and death. Their passion brings nature back to the speaker and it inhabits his dreams. However, the last lines of the poem show that that is not enough, for it is only "A veces" (At times") that the lovers are seemingly able to halt death's ferocious stampede. At times with death haunting them, they are able to rob some time, "And tear their pleasures with rough strife / Thorough the iron gates of life," as Andrew Marvell puts it in "To His Coy Mistress."[11]

Enrico Mario Santí offers a complementary yet different reading of "Alianza (Sonata)". For him it is about a "failed vision." The woman in this poem becomes the "foundation" on which the speaker hopes to lay his "visionary structure" but this attempt falls short. The reader discovers it was only a dream and that the speaker's attempt to establish his visionary experience was illusory.[12]

The second "Alianza (Sonata)" in *Tercera residencia* also associates his lover with nature and suggests more emphatically and dramatically that all can be conquered with her. Confronted with the insidious dehumanization of the city, the speaker looks to his lover for salvation.

Ni el corazón cortado por un vidrio
en un erial de espinas,

> ni las aguas atroces vistas en los rincones
> de ciertas casas, aguas como párpados y ojos,
> podrían sujetar tu cintura en mis manos
> cuando mi corazón levanta sus encinas
> hacia tu inquebrantable hilo de nieve.
>
> Nocturno azúcar, espíritu
> de las coronas,
> redimida
> sangre humana, tus besos
> me destierran,
> y un golpe de agua con restos del mar
> golpea los silencios que te esperan
> rodeando las gastadas sillas, gastando puertas.[13]
>
> [Neither the heart cut by a sliver of glass
> in a wasteland of thorns,
> nor the atrocious waters seen in the corners
> of certain houses, waters like eyelids and eyes,
> could hold your waist in my hands
> when my heart lifts its oak trees
> toward your unbreakable thread of snow.
> Night sugar, spirit
> of crowns,
>   redeemed
> human blood, your kisses
> banish me,
> and a surge of water with remnants of the sea,
> strikes on the silences that await you
> surrounding the worn-out chairs, wearing doors away.][14]

In the beginning verses the city controls and misuses nature and dehumanizes the inhabitants (their eyes are atrocious and their hearts lacerated). The description here and elsewhere in the poem is reminiscent of the urbanscape in "Walking around." However, in mid-stanza that mood swings toward their unbound passion and love. Significantly he seizes her by the waist to possess her (in a positive sense) and later kisses her ardently, but he also offers up his heart to her. All his being is moved by his deeply rooted sentiments for her. He lifts his arms, doubtless to seize her thin white waist. An "inquebrantable hilo de nieve" (unbreakable thread of snow), her waist seems to melt in his hands because of their sensuous warmth. Used as metaphor for her waist here and her breast later, the snow describes her white skin and suggests purity.

The snow image then links with the wonderful "nocturnal sugar" in the synesthesia in the following stanza, thereby capturing the enticing tactile sensations and the savoring associated with his lover. In embracing, exploring each other and kissing, they beat back the devastation surrounding them and give humanity redemption. By joining in this spiritual and bodily "alliance," they regain their sensuous humanity and fight the alienation (the "silencios" [silences]) in the nearby "gastadas sillas, gastando puertas" (worn chairs, wearing out doors).

Indeed, the torrent of intensely erotic verses that follow attempt to drown out the destruction in the city. In the next stanza the lovers create their own world separated from the desolation of the city:

> Noches con ejes claros,
> partida, material, únicamente
> voz, únicamente
> desnuda cada día.
> Sobre tus pechos de corriente inmóvil,
> sobre tus piernas de dureza y agua,
> sobre la permanencia y el orgullo
> de tu pelo desnudo,
> quiero estar, amor mío, ya tiradas las lágrimas
> al ronco cesto donde se acumulan,
> quiero estar, amor mío, solo con una sílaba
> de plata destrozada, solo con una punta
> de tu pecho de nieve (10).
>
> [Nights with clear axis,
> departure, matter, uniquely
> voice, uniquely
> naked every day.
> Upon your breasts of still current,
> upon your legs of harshness and water,
> upon the permanence and pride
> of your naked hair,
> I want to lie, my love, the tears now cast
> into the raucous basket where they gather,
> I want to lie, my love, alone with a syllable
> of destroyed silver, alone with a tip
> of your snowy breast.]

As in the Josie Bliss poems, the lovers are the focus of these lines and the urban problems recede into the background, making their passion all the more intense. Neruda captures this fervor with the juxtaposition of the lovers, the use of antitheses, and the repetitions of "quiero estar, amor mío" (I want to be, my love) and "solo con" (alone with). He portrays her enticingly and imagines himself making love to her, then he shuttles back to his deep emotional state ("quiero estar, amor mío" [I want to be, my love]), and finally he focuses on their melting together. The antitheses evoke the fiery physical and affective attributes that draw the speaker powerfully to her. One side of the dialectic signals her as an anchor that stabilizes and nurtures him ("inmóvil," "dureza," and "permanencia" [immobile, hardness, permanence]), while the other side points to her bodily rhythm and beauty ("corriente," "agua," and "orgullo" [current, water, pride]) as he lies over her. Following those images, Neruda encapsulates his passion for her dramatically in the line, "quiero estar, amor mío," by representing verbally his momentary possession of her as they seduce each other. And the stanza ends significantly on that note: he craves desperately melting into "pecho de nieve" (breast of snow).

In verses similar in tone to those in "Walking around," the fourth stanza describes the extreme fragmentation and disintegration of life in the city:

> Ya no es posible, a veces
> ganar sino cayendo,
> ya no es posible, entre dos seres
> temblar, tocar la flor del río:
> hebras de hombres vienen como agujas,
> tramitaciones, trozos,
> familias de coral repulsivo, tormentas
> y pasos duros por alfombras
> de invierno. (11)

> [It is not now possible, at times,
> to win except by falling,
> it is not now possible, between two people,
> to tremble, to touch the river's flower:
> man fibers come like needles,
> transactions, fragments,
> families of repulsive coral, tempests
> and hard passages through carpets
> of winter.]

Whether this is depression era Buenos Aires or pre-civil war Madrid circa 1934 is difficult to discern. However, for readers of *Residencia en la tierra* the speaker's expressionistic emotions are familiar. To borrow Herbert Marcuse's phrase, human beings have become one-dimensional, individualistic, and cold. Thus the references here to the "tramitaciones, trozos," (transactions, fragments) "familias de coral repulsivo" (families of repulsive coral) and the dread of winter. He confesses that a love affair like his seems almost impossible in this impersonal environment.

The last two stanzas continue with the depiction of the confusion and emptiness of city life, but they also intersperse allusions to the lovers and end with the speaker's climactic plea that she rescue him from time's assaults.

4/THE STRUGGLE AGAINST ALIENATION

> Entre labios y labios hay ciudades
> de gran ceniza y húmeda cimera,
> gotas de cuándo y cómo, indefinidas
> circulaciones:
> entre labios y labios como por una costa
> de arena y vidrio, pasa el viento.
>
> Por eso eres sin fin, recógeme como si fueras
> toda solemnidad, toda nocturna
> como una zona, hasta que te confundas
> con las líneas del tiempo.
> Avanza en la dulzura
> ven a mi lado hasta que las digitales
> hojas de los violines
> hayan callado, hasta que los musgos
> arraiguen en el trueno, hasta que del latido
> de mano y mano bajen las raíces. (11)
>
> [Between lips and lips there are cities
> of great ash and moist crest,
> drops of when and how, indefinite
> traffic:
> between lips and lips, like along the coast
> of sand and glass, the wind passes.
> That is why you are endless, welcome me as if you were
> all solemnity, all nocturnal
> like a zone, until you merge
> with the lines of time.
> Advance in sweetness,
> come to my side until the digital
> leaves of the violins
> have become silent, until the moss
> takes root in the thunder, until from the throbbing
> of hand and hand the roots come down.]

Only their physical and spiritual alliance save him from the chaos and senselessness of the city. By prolonging their love and becoming time's nightrider she can save him. Thus, the "digitales / hojas de los violines" (fingery / leaves of the violins) or personal tragedy will subside, thanks to her. An incarnation of nature's splendor, his lover furnishes him with the spiritual fortitude and sustenance to escape estrangement in the city.

Like the earlier version of "Alianza (Sonata)," then, this proposes passion and love as the vehicles by which one may flee from death in the city and in nature. This poem's speaker, however, wraps himself around his lover more completely and profoundly to ward off the spiritual desolation of the city. In sum, he finds in his lover (Josie Bliss? Delia del Carril?) the comfort, vigor, and humanity he needs to carry on with life. We thus see continuity between *Residencia en la tierra* and the first poems in *Tercera residencia* that carries into Neruda's later works.

In his now canonical study on Neruda's oeuvre prior to the poet's open political commitment, Amado Alonso contended that "Pablo Neruda ve como un incesante morir lo que Heráclito vio como el incesante cambiar de las cosas" (Pablo Neruda sees incessant dying where Heraclitus saw the incessant change in things).[15] As I see it, Alonso points to exactly the fundamental difference that separates my discussion from liberal ones. Hernán Loyola, Alain Sicard, Jaime Concha, (and I) argue that in the *Residencia en la tierra* period there is a vivid realism that highlights the speaker's estrangement from himself, his work, and his environment. Morever, we maintain that Neruda's dialectical way of thinking is already present in those books. Far from being a poet who believed in "incessant dying," Neruda, even at this moment in his life, saw things constantly transforming and was already a formidable dialectical thinker. Like Alonso, Emir Rodríguez Monegal declares that with *Residencia en la tierra* Neruda's eloquent prophetic stage comes to a close and it only resurfaces some twenty-five years later in *Estravagario* (1958).[16] By contrast, here I have attempted to show the correspondence between Neruda's way of perceiving the world and his desire to document his alienation realistically in *Residencia en la tierra* and the early part of *Tercera residencia,* a section of the book that provides the indispensable foundation for and simultaneously gives way to his later poetry, a poetry that is both negated and transformed into the raw material of his more mature poetic work.

A Poet "Born to be Born"

"Naciendo en los bosques" (Coming to Life in the Woods) is the first fundamental qualitative leap to take place in *Tercera residencia* with regards to form and content. This poem pushes beyond the constraints of the *Residencias* poetry and develops new verses which equate poetry with nature's work. In doing so Neruda rejects death's "olas del tiempo" (waves of time) present in nature, recovers his sense of wonder regarding the natural world, and begins his life anew:

> Cuando el arroz retira de la tierra
> los granos de su harina,
> cuando el trigo endurece sus pequeñas caderas y levanta su
> rostro de mil manos,
> a la enramada donde la mujer y el hombre se enlazan acudo,
> para tocar el mar innumerable

de lo que continúa.
Yo no soy hermano del utensilio llevado en la marea
como en una cuna de nácar combatido:
no tiemblo en la comarca de los agonizantes despojos,
no despierto en el golpe de las tinieblas asustadas
por el ronco pecíolo de la campana repentina,
no puedo ser, no soy el pasajero
bajo cuyos zapatos los últimos reductos del viento palpitan
y rígidas retornan las olas del tiempo a morir.[17]

[When rice withdraws from earth
the grains of its flour,
when wheat hardens its flanks and lifts up
    its thousand-handed face,
I hasten to the arbor where man and woman are linked,
to touch the innumerable sea
of what endures.
I am not a brother of the tool carried on the tide
as if in a cradle of aggressive pearl:
I do not tremble in the region of dying despoliation,
I do not wake to the thump of darkness frightened,
by the raucous clapper of the sudden bell,
I can not be, I am not the passenger
beneath whose shoes throb the last redoubts of the wind
and the rigid waves of time return to die.][18]

In these verses the ever present confusion and desperation concerning natural forces in *Residencia en la tierra* have evaporated as Neruda uncovers in nature a passion for life. By personifying nature and picturing it as analogous to human relations, the poet creates an erotic natural world in contrast to the dispassionate and imposing nature portrayed in the *Residencias*. In that poetry his amorous encounters were evasions of an impersonal environment and of the absurd breakdown in human relations in the city; here the organic world has become benevolent, has become an integral part of the speaker through the humanizing force of desire, much more akin to the sentient and neoromantic ambiance in *Veinte poemas de amor y una canción desesperada*. The wheat seed, for instance, prepares its hips in the soil and gives birth to shoots of wheat (represented with the synecdoche "manos" [hands]). The speaker also makes his way to the grove where couples make love ("se enlazan" [intertwine]) and thus become part of nature.

Thus, Neruda's stance regarding nature departs considerably from his battle with death in *Residencia en la tierra*. In the second stanza the speaker refuses to identify himself with the agony and fear that prevailed in his previous poetry and he ends with the following negation of his former self: "no puedo ser, no soy el pasajero / bajo cuyos zapatos los últimos reductos del viento palpitan / y rígidas retornan las olas del tiempo a morir" (I cannot be, I am not the traveler / beneath whose shoes the last bastion of the wind throbs / and the rigid waves of time return to die). By criticizing his vanguardist poetry and self, Neruda also rejects the reification of individual mortality as a dominant and tired theme and calls, in the following verses, for a poetry embedded in nature.

> Llevo en mi mano la paloma que duerme reclinada en la semilla
> y en su fermento espeso de cal y sangre
> vive Agosto,
> vive el mes extraído de su copa profunda:
> con mi mano rodeo la nueva sombra del ala que crece:
> la raíz y la pluma que mañana formarán la espesura. (17)

> [I bear in my hand the dove that sleeps reclining on the seed
> and in its thick ferment of lime and blood
> lives August,
> lives the month extracted from its deep goblet:
> with my hand I surround the new shadow of the growing wing:
> the root and the feather that tomorrow will form the thicket].

These lines return to the harvest or procreation alluded to in the first stanza, suggesting an allegorical reading. Having discarded his earlier worldview and work, Neruda yearns to create a renewed verse that will imitate the forces of nature. Like the nature depicted in *Veinte poemas de amor y una canción desesperada* (Twenty Love Poems and a Desperate Song), his new poetry, that is, the dove he holds in his hand, rests on a seed, is later fermented, grows, and then is ready for the harvest (in August). His desire to link his work with nature is summed up in "raíz" (root) and "pluma" (feather). Both are connected to the poet's hand which discovers nature *and* writes his verses. The root looks physically like the hand and it signals the poet's intention of probing deeper into nature. As regards the feather, Neruda manages to take advantage of the double meaning of "pluma" as feather and writing instrument, thereby creating a link with the dove image above (his new poetry).

The following stanza elucidates ever more clearly the objectives of his new poetry:

> Nunca declina, ni junto al balcón de manos de hierro,
> ni en el invierno marítimo de los abandonados, ni en mi paso ardío,
> el crecimiento inmenso de la gota, ni el párpado que quiere ser abierto:
> porque para nacer he nacido, para encerrar el paso
> de cuanto se aproxima, de cuanto a mi pecho golpea como un nuevo
> corazón tembloroso. (18)

4/THE STRUGGLE AGAINST ALIENATION 161

[It never abates, neither next to the iron-handed balcony,
nor in the sea winter of the abandoned ones, nor in
    my slow step,
the immense swelling of the drop, or the eyelid that
    wants to be opened:
because I was born to be born, to cut off the passage
of everything that approaches, of everything that beats
on my breast like a new
trembling heart.]

In contrast to the negations Neruda employs in the second stanza, here he alludes to already having surpassed his solitude and depression of the mid 1920s and early 1930s. While three of the negations point to his former somber life, the two others—"Nunca declina" (It never abates) and "ni el párpado que quiere / ser abierto" (or the eyelid that wants to / to be opened) negate the negations, leading the reader to the famous line, "para nacer he nacido" (I was born to be born), the title given to the poet's published notebooks.[19] What follows is just as significant with reference to poetic method: "para encerrar el paso / de cuanto se aproxima, de cuanto a mi pecho golpea como un / nuevo corazón tembloroso" (to cut off the passage / of everything that approaches, of everything that beats in my breast like a new / trembling heart). In this context Neruda reverses his worldview and poetry. Instead of dwelling existentially on his own fatality and alienation from nature and society, here he rediscovers his astonishment with the natural world and wants to absorb it as part of his poetic corpus. Neruda considered himself a visionary in the romantic tradition who, like William Blake, tried to absorb whatever crossed his path into his "nuevo corazón" (new heart). Led by his heart and mind Neruda looks to describe the natural, social, and moral phenomena in more palpable and accurate ways. This conscience of his new calling, his new approach, is revisited in the following lines:

> Vidas recostadas junto a mi traje como palomas paralelas,
> o contenidas en mi propia existencia y en mi desordenado
> sonido
> para volver a ser, para incautar el aire desnudo de la hoja
> y el nacimiento húmedo de la tierra en la guirnalda: hasta
> cuándo
> debo volver y ser, hasta cuándo el olor
> de las más enterradas flores, de las olas más trituradas
> sobre las altas piedras, guardan en mí su patria
> para volver a ser furia y perfume? (18)
>
> [Lives lying next to my costume like parallel doves,
> or contained in my own existence and in my disordered sound

to be again, to seize the naked air of the leaf
and the moist birth of the earth in the garland:
    how long
must I return and be, how long does the fragrance
of the most buried flowers, of the waves most pounded
on the high rocks, preserve in me its homeland
to be again fury and perfume?]

In the previous lines it seemed that the speaker had triumphed over his own dehumanization and pessimism with his "new heart," but these enigmatic lines indicate that his victory is partial. He has yet to resolve the internal contradictions that, in a Faustian drama, inhabit his soul: "Vidas recostadas junto a mi traje como palomas paralelas, / o contenidas en mi propia existencia" (Lives lying next to my costume like parallel doves, / or contained in my own existence). Like "palomas paralelas" (parallel doves) his different poetic and life periods co-exist dialectically in the poet, one gaining momentary favor over the other. The temporary defeat over the forces that haunted him in *Residencia en la tierra* only permits him to begin again ("volver a ser") and face once more the struggle of describing nature's life cycle. In his poetry he will depict yet again marvels like "el nacimiento húmedo de la tierra en la guirnalda" (the moist birth of the earth in the garland) as well as sobering realities like the presence of death in nature ("flores enterradas" [buried flowers]). Beginning anew leads the speaker to "return and be" (volver y ser) until, thanks to the buried flowers and shivering waves, he will finally return, in an echo of Baudelaire, to "furia y perfume" (fury and perfume). Following both Baudelaire and Neruda's own "Las furias y las penas" (Furies and Sorrows) is the Chilean advocating a return to the beauty and passion he found in Josie Bliss to supersede the misery that still lingers in him?[20] Only those deep waves of sensibility and intimacy, it appears, can stir within him the desire to write inspired poetry and thereby release him from his tragic condemnation.

In the final lines of the poem, that vital desire seems to revisit him as he perceives the fire amidst the smoke, the light filled with petals, the sun in his mouth:

Hasta cuándo la mano del bosque en la lluvia
me avecina con todas sus agujas
para tejer los altos besos del follaje?
Otra vez
escucho aproximarse como el fuego en el humo,
nacer de la ceniza terrestre,
la luz llena de pétalos,
y apartando la tierra

en un río de espigas llega el sol a mi boca
como una vieja lágrima enterrada que vuelve a ser semilla. (18)

[How long does the hand of the woods in the rain
bring me close with all its needles
to weave the lofty kisses of the foliage?
Again
I hear approach like fire in smoke,
spring up from earthly ash,
light filled with petals,
and pushing earth away
in a river of flowerheads the sun reaches my mouth
like an old buried tear that becomes a seed again.]

It appears as though the speaker has been privy to nature's own artistic creation, its weaving of "los altos besos del follaje" (lofty kisses of the foliage), but he has been unable as yet to forge his own creativity into new poetry. However, the last verses suggest that like Phoenix, light (life, creation) arises out of the ashes: poetry comes to his mouth. Born of the "vieja lágrima enterrada" (old buried tear), like the "flores enterradas" (buried flowers), his new expression, bursts forth out of a twofold contradiction. The new poetry negates the old, but a buried tear (like tragedy itself) resides in the previous poetry, serving as the impetus for his poetry's rebirth in the form of a seed. The very source of tragedy and its negation inaugurate a new phase in the speaker's poetry and life.

"Naciendo en los bosques" rounds out the first section of *Tercera residencia* and supplies it with a pivotal link with the only poem of the following section, "Las furias y las penas" (Furies and Sorrows), which also provides a link to Neruda's socially committed poetry. Alain Sicard also considers this the moment in which "el universo residencial se abre a la historia," but he quickly adds that though Neruda rejects his previous agony and solitude it still has not completely vanished.[21] Toward the end of "Naciendo en los bosques," Neruda intimates that he will only be able to overcome his alienation and create new verses if he can burrow his way into nature and the human soul. He recovers that sense of "fury and perfume" in "Las furias y las penas."

From an Indelible Love to a Drop of Blood

Some five years after he escaped the grasp of his lover Josie Bliss, in 1934, Neruda penned "Las furias y las penas." As critic Alain Sicard asserts, it is not easy to determine whether Neruda wrote the poem for Josie Bliss or for another lover and, in the final instance, it does not matter since its significance lies in the poet's portrayal of the woman as the incarnation of time and the cause of his "deseo y la angustia" (desire and anguish).[22] While those are undoubtedly the dominant themes in this poem, ascertaining whether or not he dedicated this poem to Josie Bliss is critical for understanding the deep emotions that carried him along at this time and that encouraged him to include "Las furias y las penas" as a separate section of *Tercera residencia* as late as 1947. Sicard notes that Neruda called Josie Bliss "la furiosa" (the furious one) and, in "Tango del viudo" (The Widower's Tango), he names her "maligna" (pernicious or evil one). The latter refers quite likely to Eulalia, the protagonist of Darío's "Era un aire suave" (It was a Soft Air), who is both "maligna y bella" (pernicious and beautiful), an archetypal *femme fatale*. In "Tango del viudo" Neruda identifies her as evil and exclaims that she has probably already "llorado de furia" (cried in fury). However, he quickly adds that her name is made of "impenetrables substancias divinas" (impenetrable divine substances) and that he "daría este viento de mar gigante por tu brusca respiración / oída en largas noches sin mezcla de olvido, / uniéndose a la atmósfera como el látigo a la piel del caballo" (would give up the wind of this giant sea to hear your hoarse breathing / heard on long nights enmeshed with oblivion, / joining the atmosphere like a whip on a horse's skin).[23] His relationship with Josie Bliss, then, is not a fleeting affair, but rather a profound love that covers the range of his intense sentiments for her.

Neruda's point in isolating this poem about Josie Bliss and yet including it in a book which illustrates the different stages he traverses toward greater political and moral consciousness is to identify a profoundly shared emotional sensitivity vital to his later commitment to socialism. In this relationship—and later with Matilde Urrutia—Neruda learned to act for the good of others, an altruism which emerges out of friendships and intense loving relationships. Personally demanding and reciprocal relationships which are fulfilling provide Neruda with a pattern of unselfishness needed for his political radicalization. At this stage he was thus able to develop what in another context Alan Gilbert calls a "human capacity for moral personality." In short, one could even declare that without these passionate relationships, Neruda would have been much more reticent to get involved in left-wing political causes.[24]

"Las furias y las penas" displays sentimental extremes which divulge his acute feelings toward Josie Bliss at this stage of his life. His feelings for her stretch from fiery instincts to deep, inseparable, and inexplicable love to resentment and hate. In Florence L. Yudin's view, these violent and repetitive furies "personify dehumanization and nihilism: an irrational rejection of the self and others."[25] At first glance it does appear to be a self-destructive relationship that consumes both lovers, but the ties that bind them are so tight that the antipathy and anger must be due to outside factors. The most prob-

4/THE STRUGGLE AGAINST ALIENATION

able of these is their distance and the anguish produced by their separation. Thus the oscillations between stanzas that describe their savage erotic encounters and their shared love and the ostensible hate and animosity.

The first stanza, for instance, begins with their exploration of the flesh and their spiritual union:

> En el fondo del pecho estamos juntos,
> en el cañaveral del pecho recorremos
> un verano de tigres,
> al acecho de un metro de piel fría,
> al acecho de un ramo de inaccesible cutis,
> con la boca olfateando sudor y venas verdes
> nos encontramos en la húmeda sombra que deja caer besos.[26]

> [In the depts of our breasts we are together,
> in the canefield of the heart we cross through
> a summer of tigers,
> watching over a meter of cold flesh,
> watching over a bouquet of inaccessible complexion,
> with our mouths sniffing sweat and green veins
> we find ourselves in the moist shadow that drops kisses.][27]

Analogous to other Josie Bliss poems, and to "El tigre" (The Tiger)—dedicated to the woman of his life, Matilde Urrutia—Neruda depicts the speaker and his lover as tigers lounging about in the shade and then pouncing on one another with insatiable erotic hunger.[28] Neruda expresses their physical love in a masterful way: he contrasts cold with hot and uses synesthesia to show how their senses weave together as they unite. Moreover, their souls appear interlocked, bound by their love ("en el fondo del pecho" [In the depths of our breasts]). At this point in the poem, there is no reason to suspect that there will be any significant transformations—it appears to be merely another erotic poem in the *Residencia en la tierra* mode.

However, a change begins in the second stanza as she comes to represent simultaneously his lost dreams, his lost love:

> Tú mi enemiga de tanto sueño roto de la misma manera
> que erizadas plantas de vidrio, lo mismo que campanas
> deshechas de manera amenazante, tanto como disparos
> de hiedra negra en medio del perfume,
> enemiga de grandes caderas que mi pelo ha tocado
> con un ronco rocío, con una lengua de agua,
> no obstante el mudo frío de los dientes y el odio de los ojos,
> y la batalla de agonizantes bestias que cuidan el olvido,
> en algún sitio del verano estamos juntos
> acechando con labios que la sed ha invadido. (25)

[You, my enemy of so much sleep broken just
like bristled plants of glass, like bells
destroyed menacingly, as much as shots
of black ivy in the midst of perfume,
my enemy with big hips that have touched my hair
with harsh dew, with my tongue of water,
despite the mute coldness of the teeth and the hatred of
    the eyes,
and the battle of dying beasts that watch over oblivion,
in some summer place we are together
watching with lips invaded by thirst.]

Save the references to his "enemigo" (enemy) and "el odio en los ojos" (hate in his eyes), the steamy erotic atmosphere is similar to the first stanza. Neruda characterizes the lovers as "agonizantes bestias" (agonizing beasts) who are on the prowl, "acechando con labios que la sed ha invadido" (hunting with lips that thirst has invaded). They destroy and consume each other in their summer rendezvous, inextricably together. And yet he calls her his enemy and has hatred in his eyes because she has ruined their love and because, as becomes clear later in the poem, the poet senses Josie Bliss is sexually intimate with others. Turning to "Tango del viudo" is illustrative of the oscillations of love. Anger overtakes him apparently because he had to leave her due to her blind jealousy, that "el perro de furia que asilas en el corazón" (furious dog you harbor in your heart). Though she alone seems torn by jealousy and fury, he shares many of the same suspicions and fears, but not the anger. He suspects she will find the knife he hid by a coconut tree "por temor de que me mataras" (for fear you would kill me), showing that he is just as capable as she of displaying his unbridled anger and violence. In other words, he imagines she will react as he himself would to her sudden departure.[29] Hence, in "Las furias y las penas," he hates her in part because he had to make a tragic decision he did not want to make: he had to leave her. And, at the time of writing (1934, in Spain) he misses her as never before, abhors the distance that separates them and regrets more than ever having let her go. Despite everything the speaker firmly believes that "este río / va entre nosotros" (this river / runs through us).

Due to the distance that has put Josie Bliss on one shore of the river and he on the other, he hates her because, like the young Neruda of the famous "Poema 20" (Poem 20), he imagines she has been with other men. In his self-consuming jealousy and remorse, in the earlier poem, he wrote: "De otro. Será de otro. Como antes de mis besos. / Su voz, su cuerpo claro. Sus ojos infinitos" (Another's. She must be another's. As before my kisses. / Her voice, her bright body. Her infinite eyes).[30] Here he imagines the worst scenario: she has given herself, body and soul, to another man. In the second verse of the couplet, he palpably longs for her by employing the uncommonly used possessive adjectives in Spanish, as though he were trying to gain her back through his poetry. In "Las furias y las penas" his sentiments are even stronger; they have evolved into hate:

> Oyes caer la ropa, las llaves, las monedas
> en las espesas casas donde llegas desnuda?
> Mi odio es una sola mano que te indica
> el callado camino, las sábanas en que alguien ha dormido
> con sobresalto: llegas
> y ruedas por el suelo manejada y mordida,
> y el viejo olor del semen como una enredadera
> de cenicienta harina se desliza a tu boca (27).
>
> [Do you hear the clothes, keys and coins
> on the thick houses where you come naked?
> My hatred is a single hand that shows you
> the silent road, the sheets where someone has slept
> in fear, you come
> and roll on the floor handled and bitten,
> and old odor of semen, like a clinging vine
> of ashy flour slips from your mouth.]

In this instance he pictures himself in her presence, against the odds of the detestable distance, accusing her of betrayal. He feels the very jealousy and fury he envisions she felt in "Tango del viudo."

However, as in "Poema 20," in the following stanza he praises her again and relives their tumultuous lovemaking, only to then accuse her of betrayal. He begins by delighting at her "locas copas y pestañas" (mad goblets and eyelashes) and ends the stanza by asking, "Entonces, este río / va entre nosotros, y por una ribera / vas tú mordiendo bocas?" (This river, then, / runs between us, and along one shore / you are biting mouths?). From the feeling of rejection he then swings back emotionally to hate: "Ay cuántas veces eres la que el odio no nombra" (Oh how often you are one hatred does not name) because "tu estatua en mi corazón devora el trébol" (her statue devours the clover in my heart) (28). Persisting "como en un túnel roto" (as if in a ruined tunnel) (29), he then returns to his vivid memories incapable of capturing her, only to then call her his enemy once again because she has let their love slip away:

> Enemiga, enemiga
> es posible que el amor haya caído al polvo
> y no haya sino carne y huesos velozmente adorados

> mientras el fuego que se consume
> y los caballos vestidos de rojo galopan al infierno? (30)
>
> [Enemy, enemy,
> is it possible that our love has fallen to the dust
> and that there is only flesh and bones swiftly adored
> while the fire is consumed
> and red-dressed horses gallop into hell?]

His rage runs through the final stanzas of the poem, but he finds some satisfaction, it would seem, in the apocalyptic ending he imagines. Josie can render her body unto anybody but she is now worn out, destroyed by the love she shared with him, thus, both are "interminablemente exterminados" (interminably exterminated) (31). Florence L. Yudin maintains that there are a plethora of destructive contradictions in the poem but they do not lead to antitheses and therefore to a dialectical process.[31] Alain Sicard takes stock of the destructive images in this poem as well; however, he notes on the contrary that there are at least as many positive images. This shows Neruda's intuition that there is a "reverso dialéctico" (dialectical reversal) of devastation caused by time whose final answer can be found when the poet becomes part of history.[32] By the time he joins history circa 1936, Neruda begins to allow the dialectical method to inform his worldview and his view on poetry (his poetic method). Briefly stated, his dialectical approach consists of different levels of generality (one's individual and unique circumstances, people's behavior and activities under capitalism, capitalism as such, class society, the animal world, and our relationship with nature), the vantage point that Neruda chooses to examine the generality, and the time and space in which something is considered.[33] Neruda combines this understanding of the dialectical method and marxism with the poetic method he had been developing before his commitment to egalitarianism to form a synthetic dialectical realism.

Having summarized the drama in "Las furias y las penas" and referred to the elaboration of Neruda's political thought and poetic process, it is worth asking why he isolated this section before turning to his socially committed poetry. In this poem he recovers his profound sense of "fury and perfume" which was essential to becoming a full human being and poet. In the epigraph to "Las furias y las penas," Neruda provides insight into the poem's subjective importance. Written in 1939, some ten years after the end of his relationship with Josie Bliss, he says: "El mundo ha cambiado y mi poesía ha cambiado. Una gota de sangre caída en estas líneas quedará viviendo sobre ellas, indeleble como el amor" (The world has changed and my poetry has changed. A drop of blood on these lines will remain living within them, indeleble as love). The Spanish civil war erupted and Neruda was caught in its whirlwinds and was as moved morally and emotionally as he was by the torrential love for Josie Bliss. In that sense, "Las furias y las penas" is the necessary bridge between the *Residencia en la tierra* poetry and his poems dedicated to the Spanish Republic.

The Conquest of Autonomy and Social Commitment: Spain, 1934–1937

Anchored in Madrid and in daily contact with the artistic figures of Spain's second "Golden Age"—the 1920s and 1930s—Neruda was welcomed as an unofficial member of this active intelligentsia, which included the likes of Rafael Alberti, Miguel Hernández, Vicente Aleixandre, Federico García Lorca, Luis Cernuda, Manuel Altolaguirre, and José Bergamín.[34] In contrast to Neruda in the Orient, Neruda in Spain was very active socially and literarily during these years. He published translations of William Blake's "Visions of the Daughters of Albion" and "The Mental Traveller," he took charge of editions of Quevedo's and Villamediana's poetry, and he directed the journal *Caballo verde para la poesía*.[35]

Doubtless, the special circumstances in Madrid and his friendship with Rafael Alberti in particular, who seemed to incarnate the type of left-wing intellectual and activist Neruda wanted to become, and his affair with the Communist painter Delia del Carril, had a significant influence on Neruda's political beliefs and poetic theory. "Naciendo en los bosques" and "Tres cantos materiales" (Three Material Songs) in *Residencia en la tierra,* both composed between 1934 and 1935, are fruits of this transitional moment. Hernán Loyola argues that this period was aesthetically and politically decisive because Neruda was morally shaken and moved to take a side by the injustice and horrors of the Spanish civil war. On the aesthetic front, he felt obligated to step out of the solitude, anguish, and linguistic labyrinths that populated *Residencia en la tierra*. On the political front, he witnessed many atrocities or heard news of them, leading him to question himself and his previous anarchist and individualist political stance:

> El proceso que vive Neruda hacia finales de 1934 supone entonces una *elección* entre varias direcciones posibles, elección que el adjetivo *materiales* subraya en cuanto reafirmación explícita del materialismo que es, digamos, con-natural a la vivencia del mundo en Neruda aún antes de las *Residencias;* y en cuanto velada, pero inocente señal de preferencia o simpatía respecto de cierto materialismo ideológico político (que el término *materiales* por aquel tiempo no podía dejar de convocar en alguna medida). Los acontecimientos de Asturias y sus secuelas juegan en este proceso un papel precipitante y reforzador. No faltan la cautela y las dudas iniciales . . . , aunque más bien parecen autodefensa contra la fascinación. Neruda no es hombre de compromisos fáciles, tanto menos en

tan delicado terreno. En efecto, la consolidación del paso inicial—su inequívoca explicitación en la escritura—vendrá sólo con la guerra civil.[36]

[The process that Neruda lives toward the end of 1934 assumes then a *choice* among various possible directions, a choice that the adjective *material* underlines. It is an explicit reaffirmation of materialism that is, let us say, co-natural with the status of the world in Neruda's work even before the *Residencias*. It is a veiled, but innocent signal of preference or sympathy for a certain ideological and political materialism (that the term material, in that period, could not help but evoke in some way). The events in Asturias and sequels play a precipitating and reinforcing role in this process. The initial caution and doubts are not missing . . . , although they appear to be an act of self-defense against his fascination. Neruda is not a man given to easy commitments, less so on such delicate terrain. Indeed, the consolidation of the initial phase—its unequivocal exposition in his writing—only comes about with the civil war.]

Life as a consul in Madrid, his association with progressive and active members of the intelligentsia in Madrid, the close relationships with Alberti and Delia del Carril, the context of the Asturias uprising in 1934, and his daily contact with the Spanish language again all had a decisive impact on Neruda. Nonetheless, as Loyola points out, he *voluntarily* and *consciously* chose to commit himself to the Republican cause and to write social poetry like *España en el corazón* (Spain in My Heart). As he became embroiled in the Spanish civil war, Neruda became more politically conscious and emboldened.[37]

A War of Classes

Neruda arrived in Spain in 1934, a year of worker uprisings and further political polarization. A summary of those events is crucial to understanding more fully how Neruda became more radicalized politically.

In early October 1934, after the collapse of the Republican government, the right-wing political party, CEDA (The Spanish Confederation of Autonomous Rights) formed a coalition government. The membership of the CNT (National Confederation of Work) labor union had abstained from voting in the elections, thereby effectively guaranteeing a right-wing victory. One of the CNT's principal objectives had been to demonstrate that worker's power could not be won at the ballot boxes, but could be achieved only through strikes and armed insurrection:

> Compared to the waves of ultra-leftism which swept the CNT nationally, the Asturian CNT had a long history of revolutionary realism. Perhaps because of its minority position within a strongly proletarian mining region dominated by

the social-democratic Asturian mineworkers' union; perhaps because of its isolation from the extreme southern rural poverty; but certainly because of the presence of one man, Eleuterio Quintanilla, the most formative single influence in Asturian anarcho-syndicalist development, it had always been willing to join in common action with the socialist proletariat in the struggle against the class enemy.[38]

At the beginning of 1934, the UGT and the CNT had signed a pact which stipulated that if the bourgeoisie seized power and betrayed working class interests, they would work together to bring about a social revolution. Led by the unions, the left-wing political parties followed suit and joined the cause, the PCE joining just before the uprising. The PCE, however, had issued a call for a general strike which was summarily rejected by the socialists who called for an armed uprising. Within two days,

> miners and metalworkers had captured nearly seventy guardia civil posts in the mining valleys, won their first pitched battle against the army on the outskirts of Oviedo and were fighting in the city; to the south, they had pinned down army units sent from León. Foreshadowing what would happen in most parts of Popular Front Spain less than two years later, revolutionary committees were set up in the villages and townships. Each set about making the revolution, instituting forms of war communism. For two weeks in the Nalón and Caudal mining valleys the proletariat held power. (554–55)

The CNT, which had originally come to terms with the CGT, decided against joining the Workers' Alliance in Barcelona and the uprising across Spain. Thus, while workers had seized power in many parts of Asturias, they were not supported in kind by similar uprisings throughout the country. Consequently, the social revolution begun in Asturias could not sustain itself. Led by General Francisco Franco, the military crushed the Asturias rebellion. Approximately 3,000 were injured and 1,500 were killed in this suppression of the insurrection.[39]

Needless to say these events had a profound impact on Neruda. Suddenly, he, like many progressive and left-wing writers of his day, felt compelled to side with the Spanish Republic. It is safe to say that Neruda felt as stirred morally and emotionally by these tumultuous events as he did by the "fury and perfume" with Josie Bliss. When the renowned Spanish poet, Rafael Alberti, met him for the first time, Neruda declared, "Yo no entiendo nada de política, soy un poco anarcoide, quiero hacer lo que me plazca" (I don't understand anything about politics, I'm somewhat anarchist, I want to do whatever pleases me).[40] A lifelong Communist, Alberti had a major impact on Neruda's worldview, as did his companion Delia del Carril (also a Communist). During these years he would see that his former political stance was that of a rebellious individualist, and that his anarchism was a very comfortable position, because a real rebellious spirit requires "la organización de las masas y . . . una extensiva conciencia de clase" (the organization of the masses and . . . deep class consciousness). Decades later, in his memoirs, he recognized that in Spain he became class conscious and a fellow traveler of the Communists: "el carnet militante lo recibí mucho más tarde en Chile, cuando ingresé oficialmente al partido, creo haberme definido ante mí mismo como un comunista durante la guerra de España" (Though I received my membership card much later in Chile, when I officially became a member of the Party, I think I acted like a Communist during the war over Spain).[41]

Neruda's radicalization registered itself too in his poetry, leading him to publish *España en el corazón* (Spain in my Heart) in 1937. However, the decisive break with the worldview expressed in *Residencia en la tierra* that steered him toward increasing political awareness is "Reunión bajo las nuevas banderas" (Meeting Under New Flags). Like "Las furias y las penas" it stands as a separate section (III) and represents an important stepping-stone in Neruda's political and poetic awakenings. The loving personal passion surfacing in poems such as "Las furias y las penas" thus lays the groundwork for the altruism that dominated his poetry from 1936 on.

"Beating With Human Dreams"

For a clearer understanding of Neruda's political development and committment in the historical context, it is important to turn to "Reunión bajo las nuevas banderas" (Meeting Under New Flags), because in it Neruda criticizes his vanguardist poetry and nears his Popular Front politics. Unlike the preceding poems, in "Reunión bajo las nuevas banderas" Neruda shows more self-awareness about his alienating life and work in Asia. As Alastair Reid has commented, Neruda "was constantly fingering through his own experience in language, putting himself into words, questioning himself, discovering himself, creating himself."[42] Consequently, as a poet who invested himself fully in his verses and had them act like a diary of the dramas in his life, he could not help but absorb the shock of the civil war and attempt to communicate it in a radically new way. Nor could Neruda help but find his former life and poetic corpus, during *Residencia en la tierra,* to be individualistic and pessimistic. From 1925 to 1935 Neruda had followed his personal whims aesthetically, losing himself in the search for ever more audacious and solemn words to describe the terrible isolation out of which he gained artistic inspiration. In "Reunión bajo las nuevas banderas" he acknowledges that the poetic world he created in *Residencia en la tierra* and the life he led during those years was due to his own distancing from nature and other human beings:

> Quién ha mentido? El pie de la azucena
> roto, insondable, oscurecido, todo
> lleno de herida y resplandor oscuro!
> Todo, la norma de ola en ola en ola,
> el impreciso túmulo del ámbar
> y las ásperas gotas de la espiga!
> Fundé mi pecho en esto, escuché toda
> la sal funesta: de noche
> fui a plantar mis raíces:
> averigüé lo amargo de la tierra:
> todo fue para mí noche o relámpago:
> cera secreta cupo en mi cabeza
> y derramó cenizas en mis huellas.[43]
>
> [Who has lied? The foot of the lily
> broken, inscrutable, darkened, all
> filled with wound and dark splendor!
> All, the norm from wave to wave to wave,
> the imprecise tumulus of the amber
> and harsh drops of the flower!
> I based my heart on this, I listened to all
> the sorrowful salt: by night
> I went to plant my roots.
> I discovered the bitterness of the earth:
> for me everything was night or lightning flash:
> secret wax settled in my head
> and scattered ashes in my tracks.][44]

As a bureaucrat in the Orient isolated by the nature of his work, fascinated by and yet cut off from the native cultures of Ceylon, Java, and Singapore, and equally estranged from the colonialist English, dejected by the economic misery that surrounded him, far removed from his language and his homeland, the Neruda of the 1920s and 1930s sought his salvation, his symbolic compensation, in his poetry. In language reminiscent of *Residencia en la tierra* Neruda recollects the images that haunted him during those years of pain and "resplandor oscuro" (dark splendor). He developed emotionally in that "sal funesta" (sorrowful salt), made a sort of life, discovered "lo amargo de la tierra" (the bitterness of the earth) and, in the excesses of youth, he yearned for the extremes (night or lightning flash). Shackled by his alienation and despair he found a haven in his verses which recorded his struggle and his hope of a way out through his love for Josie Bliss. However, this route led only to death:

> Y para quién busqué este pulso frío
> sino para una muerte?

Y qué instrumento perdí en las tinieblas
desamparadas, donde nadie me oye?
No,
ya era tiempo, huid
sombras de sangre,
hielos de estrella, retroceded al paso de los pasos humanos
y alejad de mis pies la negra sombra! (35)

[And for whom did I seek this cold pulse
if not for death?
And what instrument did I lose in the forsaken
darkness, where no one hears me?
No,
it was high time, flee,
shadows of blood,
starry ice, retreat at the pace of human steps
and remove from my feet the black shadow!]

By becoming engulfed in solitude, he not only negated himself, but also sheltered himself with his painful monologue. And his seclusion took him on the road to death. He concedes that his interior monologue and esoteric, self-consuming language left him without a readership ("nadie me oye" [no one hears me]). In short, the poet furthered his own alienation.

Neruda was keenly aware that his poetry during these years was incapable of saving him from sweet misery. Unable to find a publisher for the first edition of *Residencia en la tierra* until 1933, nearly four years after he had completed the manuscript of nineteen poems, Neruda went through a long period questioning his poetic theory, the poems he had written, and his own ability to write, as is evidenced by "Reunión bajo las nuevas banderas."[45] Moreover, the Chilean Editorial Nascimento agreed to publish only one hundred copies of his book. A second edition, which included the two *Residencias* (1925–1935), appeared in print in Spain in 1935. But again, the manuscript was issued by a new, left-wing publishing house—Cruz y Raya—at which Alberti and Neruda had both worked steadily. Alberti gave this account of the initial reception to Neruda's *Residencias*. "Yo lo llevé a varios sitios. Entonces no entendía nadie este libro y no lo querían publicar. Lo más que logró Pedro Salinas fue que aparecieran unos poemas por vez primera en la "Revista de Occidente" (I took it to several places. Back then no one understood the book and they didn't want to publish it. The most that Pedro Salinas was able to do was to publish some poems for the first time in *Revista de Occidente.*)[46] Significantly, it was reissued in 1938 by Ercilla, a small publishing house in Chile, and, in 1944, by Losada in Buenos Aires.[47] It was only in 1944, after Amado Alonso had published his early classic study on Neruda, *Poesía y estilo de Pablo Neruda: Ensayo de interpretación de una poesía hermética* (Pablo Neruda's Poetry and Style: An Interpretative Essay on a Hermeneutic Poetry) (1940) that the *Residencias* began to circulate among a wider readership. At the time of "Reunión bajo las nuevas banderas," however, *Residencia en la tierra* could not rescue him from his socioeconomic and personal estrangement.

In the second stanza of the poem Neruda disapproves of the alienated poet he was, denounces his own poetry's inaccessibility to lay readers, and criticizes its focus on his solitude, anguish, and erroneous belief in his exceptionality:

> No,
> ya era tiempo, huid
> sombras de sangre,
> hielos de estrella, retroceded al paso de los pasos humanos
> y alejad de mis pies la negra sombra! (35)
>
> [No,
> it was high time, flee,
> shadows of blood,
> starry ice, retreat at the pace of human steps
> and remove from my feet the black shadow!]

The "No" here spatially divides the old poetic theory from the poet's critique of it. Given that Neruda's audience was not very large, it would be safe to say that he aims these verses at other poets and, perhaps more importantly, at himself. He uses the imperative forms ("huid" [flee], "retroceded" [retreat], and "alejad" [remove]) to remind himself and other poets not to be tempted by the cult of the genius and the pain of the past ("sombras de sangre" [shadow of blood]). By undermining his previous poetry, assessed at a distance, Neruda is also taking the bourgeois notion of poetry to task. In Gene Bell-Villada's words, what the avant-gardists or modernists advocated was

> in great measure conditioned by a bourgeois society that on principle placed high value on purely personal enterprise and on across-the-board technical innovation, exploration, and experimentation. It was no fault of the artists if "what they wanted" was a crafted kind of artifact not at that time possessing sufficient exchange value to furnish most of them an adequate livelihood.[48]

At this moment in his life, Neruda could no longer accept modernism's values, alluring as they might have been prior to his years in Spain. In this poem he rejects its ahistoricism, its bent toward subjectivism (individualism and emotivism), its paradoxical degradation of human potential, and its ironic exaltation of solitude. Having renounced these values as dehumanizing, he then adjusts his footsteps so that they will fall in line with other human beings ("los pasos humanos" [in step with other humans]). The former avant-gardist, who once considered himself a type of prophet, now recognizes that he and other vanguardist poets need to take a step back ("retroceded" [retreat]) and join the masses.

> Yo de los hombres tengo la misma mano herida,
> yo sostengo la misma copa roja
> e igual asombro enfurecido:
> un día
> palpitante de sueños
> humanos, un salvaje
> cereal ha llegado
> a mi devoradora noche
> para que junte mis pasos de lobo
> a los pasos del hombre. (35–36)

> [I have the same wounded hand that men have,
> I hold up the same red cup
> and an equally furious amazement:
> one day
> burning with human
> dreams, a wild
> oat reached
> my devouring night
> so that I could join my wolf steps
> to the steps of man.]

Estranged in his poetic labor and his social relations, the other Neruda had become a beast and his former poetry a product of alienation. In escaping from the bourgeois image of the artist's superior and innate insights, which the masses cannot possibly understand, he points up his similarity to and connection with other human beings. Thus he reaffirms his individuality and egalitarianism. This is apparent in the social organization of the discourse: the pronoun "yo" is distinctly placed in the verses even though it need not be in the Spanish language. Indeed, all of the previous verses refer to a first person, but they do so via possessive adjectives or the conjugation of the verbs without the accompanying pronoun. In these verses he abandons the wolves' steps to join the steps of man (and the future of humanity).

> Y así reunido,
> duramente central, no busco asilo
> en los huecos del llanto: muestro
> la cepa de la abeja: pan radiante

para el hijo del hombre: en el misterio el azul se prepara
para mirar un trigo lejano de la sangre (36).

[And thus united,
sternly central, I seek no shelter
in the hollows of weeping: I show
the bee's root: radiant bread
for the son of man: in mystery blue prepares itself
to look at a wheat distant from the blood.]

In clear allusions to Christianity, he now repents and refuses to write recondite verses that "shelter in the hollows of weeping" and intends to write poetry that can be shared among common people like "pan radiante / para el hijo del hombre" (radiant bread / for the son of man). Like bread, this poetry hopes to be a form of subjective nourishment, so to speak, dedicated to the development of humanity as a whole, and avoids the angst ("la sangre" [the blood]) that saturated *Residencia en la tierra*.

In the rest of the poem Neruda questions himself incredulously, lays his old poetry to rest, and then emerges with his "nuevo corazón" (new heart):

Dónde está tu sitio en la rosa?
En dónde está tu párpado de estrella?
Olvidaste esos dedos de sudor que enloquecen
por alcanzar la arena?
Paz para ti, sol sombrío,
paz para ti, frente ciega,
hay un quemante sitio para ti en los caminos,
hay piedras sin misterio que te miran,
hay silencios de cárcel con una estrella loca,
desnuda, desbocada, contemplando el infierno.
Juntos, frente al sollozo!
Es la hora
alta de tierra y de perfume, mirad este rostro
recién salido de la sal terrible,
mirad esta boca amarga que sonríe,
mirad este nuevo corazón que os saluda
con su flor desbordante, determinada y aúrea. (36)

[Where is your place in the rose?
Where is your starry eyelid?
Did you forget those sweaty fingers mad about
to reach the sand?
Peace to you, dark sun,
peace to you, blind brow,
there is a burning place for you in the roads,
there are stones without mystery that look at you,

there are silences of a prison with a mad star,
naked, foulmouthed, contemplating hell.
Together, facing the sobbing!
It is the high
hour of earth and perfume, look at this face
just come from the terrible salt,
look at this bitter mouth that smiles,
look at this new heart that greets you
with its overflowing flower, resolute and golden.]

The perplexed poet wonders how he lost the "párpado de estrella" (starry eyelid), the dramatic and positive insight that motivated him to write ethereal verses like the ones in *Veinte poemas de amor.* He questions himself, his lack of orientation, his poetry ("la rosa" [the rose]), his lack of discernment and perception, and the work and desire needed to give sustenance to his poetry ("Olvidaste esos dedos de sudor que enloquecen / por alcanzar la arena?" [Did you forget those sweaty fingers mad / to reach the sand?]). Neruda finds himself guilty, then, of solipsistically cutting himself off from his fellow human beings by remaining passive in the face of human suffering (in Asia) and by writing abstract, dense, and detached poetry that foregrounded inhumane conditions under capitalism without criticizing them directly. Writing in his memoirs, the mature Neruda asserts that the *Residencia en la tierra* poetry was driven by "melancolía frenética" (frenetic melancholy) and governed by a "estilo amargo que porfió sistematicamente en mi propia destrucción" (bitter style that persisted systematically in my own destruction).[49]

In this poem Neruda seems to consciously recognize his own estrangement and bids farewell to his former poetry. He incarnates the inner conflict that plagued him in the 1920s and 1930s with the antitheses "sol sombrío" (dark sun) and "frente ciega" (blind brow) and puts the former poet to rest ("Paz para ti" [peace for you]). At first negated, the somber side of himself and his poetry is then synthesized with his new, resurrected self. Verses seven through ten characterize his former poetry as a prison cell and a living hell. Thus Neruda uses his own painful experiences to contradict the exalted image of the self-absorbed poet. The former Neruda got lost in a sea of loneliness and self-pity ("sollozo" [sobbing]) and was unable to combat the very forces that were eating away at him. Yet, as the final stanza shows, this blinding experience provided the internal friction he needed to surpass it.

He begins the final stanza with the verse, "Together, facing the sobbing" (Juntos, frente al sollozo!) to state that only by linking arms with others can individuals overcome adversity. It is a plea to his readers, but it also reminds him to avoid the false attraction of "frenetic melancholy." However, the *Residencias* stage in his life also allowed him to survive and prevail over the estrangement that had trapped him. In the final verses such dialectical images as "este rostro / recién salido de la sal terrible" (this face / just come from the terrible salt) and "esta boca amarga que sonríe" (this bitter mouth that smiles) yield a new synthesis ("nuevo corazón" [new heart]) and propose a humanized and collective poetry in place of the self-consuming *Residencia en la tierra*.

"Reunion bajo las nuevas banderas," then, provides a crucial passage from the *Residencias* to the development of a poetry immersed in social and political circumstances and driven by a moral imperative to change the status quo. Whereas in *Residencia en la tierra* Neruda tries, as Mario Rodríguez Fernández comments, to "fundamentar la propiedad de su existencia" (found the property of his existence), and ends up falling short in his attempt to come to a unified understanding of reality, in "Reunión bajo las nuevas banderas" he is able to "aprehender, presentir sobre todo una realidad unitaria en la cual el mundo interior y exterior se fundan en una correspondencia exacta" (apprehend, intuit above all a unified reality in which the interior and exterior worlds are founded on an exact correspondence).[50] Perhaps it is not an exact correspondence, but it would be accurate to say that Neruda's work depended on a correspondence theory of truth consisting of the sociohistorical events in which he became deeply involved. Neruda's "new heart" might not have been possible without his arrival in Spain during the sweeping events of the civil war, but neither would *España en el corazón* have been conceivable without the *Residencias*.

Beyond the Avant-garde

Up to the publication of *España en el corazón,* Neruda, like most every poet, engaged in a battle over autonomy within the social field, which, as Pierre Bourdieu has noted, is a commonplace in artistic production:

> the evolution of the different fields of cultural production toward a greater autonomy is accompanied by a sort of reflective and critical return by the producers upon their own production, a return which leads them to draw from it the field's own proper principle and specific presuppositions. This is firstly because the artist, now in a position to rebuff every external constraint or demand, is able to affirm his mastery over that which defines him and which properly belongs to him, that is, the form, the technique, in a word, the art, thus instituted as the exclusive aim of art.[51]

Like the artisan, the poet must first thoroughly learn the tricks of his trade. Yet in doing so, in becoming increasingly specialized, he risks isolating himself. Avant-gardist work remains at this self-reflective stage in constant need of self-critique yet it seldom surpasses its formalist concerns. But Neruda's *Residencia en la tierra* and the first parts of *Tercera residencia* partook of avant-gardist aesthetics because the poet's own alienation prevented him from letting his realist portrait of Asia, Santiago, Buenos Aires, and Madrid stand out more fully. While his poetic language is often moving, it is also often a dense jungle of images that only the patient and determined reader can begin to understand. However, Neruda's poetry after 1936 broke with this self-reflective stage and consciously incorporated the sociohistorical, geographical, and economic factors that were the source of both his alienation and his freedom.

As chapters 5 and 6 demonstrate, in the long term Neruda challenges the idea of a "lyrical" language and hence reaffirms poetry's place in ordinary language. He also historicizes his "poetic" discourse and thereby undercuts any attempt to delimit the fields of knowledge, he questions the status of the poet as prophet, and he undermines the legitimacy of "metapoetry" by recounting his own journey through this labyrinth and his rejection of its bourgeois precepts. By dialectically negating his *Residencias* poetry, Neruda, in his work commencing with *España en el corazón,* negates avant-gardist aesthetics even as he does participate in it. While Neruda is significantly influenced by literary realism, particularly after the Spanish civil war, he nonetheless maintains his autonomy from it. Thus, Neruda's practice of "espontaneidad dirigida" as a poetic method places him outside the surrealist, realist, and socialist realist camps. Yet his realism becomes even more elaborate as he moves to critical realism in *España en el corazón* and to dialectical realism from *Tercera residencia* on.

In contrast to *Residencia en la tierra* and several of the poems in *Tercera residencia, España en el corazón* is a major, innovative step toward a radical historicist poetry. Yet, while it represents a significant qualitative leap in Neruda's poetics, the ideas and the method he develops only begin to reach maturity in *Canto general.* Indeed, the strength of *España en el corazón,* in contrast to the *Residencias,* is that it presents a poetic chronicle of the Spanish civil war. According to Emir Rodríguez Monegal, Enrico Mario Santí, and Florence Yudin, its chief weakness is that Neruda's account of the civil war in the last half of *Tercera residencia* is too subjective. It is not without reason that they underline the indignation of the speaker and the leftist politics. However, critics such as René de Costa and Emir Rodríguez Monegal level such complaints against this poetry based on their modernist inclinations. In their view, Neruda's search for ever more unique linguist expression, his mastery of poetic techniques, his complicated and sometimes impenetrable poems, as well as his pessimistic conclusions regarding human nature and the future of humanity, mark him as great poet. In short, they consider the self-reflective period of the 1920s and early 1930s as Neruda's defining moment and refuse to take his critique of his earlier poetry seriously because it is tainted with moralistic Marxist "dogma" (see chapter 1). Hence Rodríguez Monegal asserts that Neruda's "vocación profética" (prophetic vocation) and his belief in poetry as "iluminación, como rito y como salvación" (illumination, as rite and as salvation) returns in an eternal return, a "circularidad" (circularity) which only aims at appreciating the "misterio metafísico" (mysterious metaphysics) of the universe.[52] Nevertheless, by latching onto this stage of his poetry and exalting him as the quintessential modernist, these critics ignore Neruda's own dialectical negation of this phase of his work and the complex differences that manifest themselves in the works after 1936.

In departing from his avant-gardist poetry and committing himself to critical realism, Neruda abandoned obscure and abstract poetic language for a more accessible medium and he made the events of the Spanish civil war central to his works. It is true that Neruda's poetry is filled with his emotional and impassioned condemnations of the Spanish Nationalists and of the human tragedy perpetrated by General Franco and his followers, but one cannot simply ignore or condemn these proclamations; one must analyze their signficance in *Tercera residencia.*[53]

But how can we evaluate this subjectivity? How does this subjectivity differ from that of the *Residencias?* In the following chapter I contend that one can judge Neruda's ethical statements in the context of his moral and political development. That, and poetry's connection to social, historical, economic, and psychological factors, are the significant differences between the *Residencias* phase and "España en el corazón." Subjective declarations abound in the *Residencias* as well; however, Neruda's moral and political stances in "España en el corazón" are more advanced than those in his earlier work. As Neruda becomes more class conscious and understands, with obvious limitations factored in, the major forces in the social totality in capitalism and the radical transformations under, for instance, socialism in the USSR, his moral consciousness grows in kind. His ethical stances develop dialectically in response to socioeconomic injustices and inequalities under capitalism and the struggles for a classless society.

5
Neruda's Moral Realism in *España en el corazón*

How are we to interpret Neruda's tone in "España en el corazón"? How should we construe the insults he hurls at the Falangists and the Nationalists in these expressionistic verses?

> vestida de asma y huecos levitones sangrientos,
> y su rostro de ojos profundos detenidos
> eran verdes babosas comiendo tumba,
> y su boca sin muelas mordía cada noche
> la espiga sin nacer, el mineral secreto,
> y pasaba con su corona de cardos verdes
> sembrando vagos huesos de difunto y puñales.[1]
>
> [dressed in asthma and bloody hollow frock coats,
> and its face with sunken staring eyes,
> was green slugs eating graves,
> and its toothless mouth each night bit
> the unborn flower the secret mineral,
> and it passed with its crown of green thistles
> sowing vague deadmen's bones and daggers.][2]

Is Neruda displaying a lack of concern for other human beings—regardless of their political position? Is he driven to excess because of the destruction wrought by the Spanish civil war? Given its political and moral stances and expressionistic descriptions, is this poetry qualitatively inferior to the *Residencias* as Rodríguez Monegal and Costa both suggest?

Any reader of *Tercera residencia* can testify to the profusion of political images in these poems. But the excesses of alienation and violence that ravaged the *Residencias* do not seem to disturb the critics until they read the second half of *Tercera residencia*. Alfred J. McAdam, for example, frames *España en el corazón* in religious and political terms. Neruda ostensibly separates the "rhetoric of poetry and the rhetoric of ideology" and lets himself be carried away by the immediacy of left-wing politics. McAdam claims that "Auden's melancholy voice preaches a lesson about living, while

Neruda's impassioned hymn directs its audience into the jaws of death." Carried along by his putative zeal, Neruda, in McAdam's words, mixes "anything with a call to arms."[3] Robin Warner goes to great lengths to try to prove that *España en el corazón* "embodies a number of ideological formulas which coincide with the Communist [Party's] point of view" and that, consequently, it glosses over contradictions during the civil war and makes a misguided "strong emotional [not rational] appeal to Republican sympathizers."[4] Likewise René de Costa calls *Tercera residencia* "the least studied and most maligned of the *Residencia* volumes" and insists that it "deserves much more careful attention than it has received to date." To begin to rectify that error, Costa dedicates several pages to that neglected book, but he too resorts to religious language when describing Neruda's political stances. In his view the poems in *Tercera residencia* "are like pamphlets written with an almost missionary zeal for causes which, while once perhaps controversial, are now merely a part of contemporary history." Neruda "begins to voice societal concerns with the vigor of a pamphleteer and the conviction of a missionary."[5] In these studies the political framework in "España en el corazón" leads the critics to conclude that Neruda underwent a conversion experience when he became convinced of Marxism's virtues and that that experience distorted his worldview and his outlook on poetry.

The critical views above hold in common a general belief that Neruda's radicalization led him to take extreme ethical positions during the Spanish civil war, yet many of the stances Neruda takes could dovetail with liberal ones. He defends constitutionality, upholds the Republic's right to govern and supports its (social democratic) economic programs, virulently condemns the Nationalists' illegal attempt to seize the government, abhors the devastation and violence caused by the war and started by the Nationalists, considers the feudalist economic and political system prior to the Republic to be an anachronism, and calls for an armed defense of the Republic. In principle, these are political and ethical positions that liberals would espouse as well. In short, liberals and radicals alike share a common moral (and political) belief that this explanation provides a more just and accurate account of the civil war than the Nationalists'. So why do the critics object to Neruda's language in "España en el corazón"?

One possible reply could be that while liberals might favor the Republican government, they likely oppose the Republican methods used to defend it and Neruda's "aggressive" vocabulary (as seen in the lines at the beginning of this chapter). As political scientist Alan Gilbert comments, this position stems from a liberal tendency to uphold equality under the law and yet claim that the state is and should be neutral. Moreover, this liberal stance offers "no positive vision of a noncoercive politics."[6] Thus, while the liberal critics would certainly agree with the positions Neruda and other

Republicans take, they might not condone the methods for defending those stances.

Another possible objection might deal with the critics' views on poetry. According to this view, evident for instance in Alfred McAdam's comments above, Neruda allows ideology (read: politics) to innundate his poems and thus gives in to excesses. The beauty of the poetry is purportedly weighed down by the insistent political references, the speaker's passionate opposition to the Nationalists, and his support for the Republicans. According to this view, if Neruda's moral/political views were not so baldly stated and so pervasive, the writing would be more pleasing.

Both questions lead us into the terrain of moral realism, the political and philosophical underpinnings of Neruda's poetry from 1936 until his death. Moral realism insists that moral opinions have an objectivity and that, as such, they can be true or false (approximately true, predominately false, and so on); that those moral statements are independent of our own theories and opinions (that is, they are shared by others and have to do with the intrinsic value of the poem); that our moral stances, thanks to the unity of human inquiry, constitute, as Richard Boyd puts it, "a reliable method for obtaining and improving (approximate) moral knowledge;" and that "we test general moral principles and moral theories by seeing how their consequences conform or fail to conform to our moral intuitions about particular cases." According to moral realists, there can be a nonlinear, dialectical form of moral progress that is intimately tied to historical, political, economic, and psychological advances for humankind.[7]

From the moral realist vantage point, then, Neruda's evaluative judgments regarding the Nationalist assault on the Spanish Republic and his unwavering support for the values the Republic upholds are bolstered by his complex understanding of historical and political affairs and by his personal experiences. In other words, Neruda's moral positions and his expressive vocabulary are defended by the "logical" chain of ideas in his poems and by the historical and political conditions in which he was immersed. While his stances may make liberal readers or critics uncomfortable, they are, nonetheless, legitimate and rationally founded moral/political ideas.

Moral, Political, and Poetic Progress

I argue for an integral unity in Neruda's work, stretching from *Residencia en la tierra* (1925–35) to *Tercera residencia* and to his later books, based on the evolution of Neruda's political awareness and common thematic principles. In his early twenties Neruda latched onto rebellious ideas and identified with anarchist politics, and this served as a foundation for his political radicalization and his turn toward Marxism in his thirties. Indeed, part IV of *Tercera residencia,* covered in this chapter, shows a pivotal transformation in Neruda's social consciousness that ultimately serves as a stepping stone to his adherence to Marxism. He considered the Spanish civil war a battleground between the rights of political democracy (the Republic) and those reactionary social forces wanting to reclaim the state illegally; the Communists, Socialists, anarchists, and liberals on the one hand and the Falangists and the monarchists on the other hand; the working class, the peasantry, and the intellectuals versus the neo-feudalist landlords, the church, and the weak capitalist class. While his analysis of the civil war is not as sophisticated as his understanding of Latin American history in *Canto general,* there is a significant qualitative leap in his grasp of sociopolitical matters in this section of *Tercera residencia.*

There is continuity and enrichment as regards topics in this section as well. Alienation and violence pervade the atmosphere as they did in *Residencia en la tierra* but these do not encumber the isolated individual, but instead reflect the sociopolitical conflict that made life unliveable in Spain from 1936 to 1939. Neruda is so overwhelmed by the destructiveness and despair of the civil war that he cannot record it in a documentary manner, nor would we expect him to in a poetic text. Neruda's sympathies openly lay with the Republican cause, and he is incensed by the Nationalists' violation of the rights of the Spanish Republic. As a result, the reader here is witness to a battle in language akin to the real battles over the Republic; whereas in the *Residencias*—as observed in chapter 3—the reader encounters the poet's tension-ridden struggle for survival and meaning. The two conflicts are part of one continuous, yet dialectically discontinuous movement. The *Residencias* stage is neither a secondary nor even insignificant period, nor is it the grand apotheosis of Neruda's oeuvre. Instead, it serves as a powerful preamble to all of Neruda's subsequent books.

In his critical appraisal of the surrealist movement and—one could argue—of his own poetry, the Peruvian poet César Vallejo claimed that pessimism and desperation "deben ser siempre etapas y no metas. Para que ellos agiten y fecunden el espíritu, deben desenvolverse hasta transformarse en afirmaciones constructivas. De otra manera, no pasan de gérmenes patológicos, condenados a devorarse a sí mismos"[8] (should be always stages and not goals. To flare up and fecundate the spirit, they should open up until they become constructive affirmations. Otherwise, they are no more than pathological germinations, condemned to devour each other). Vallejo, like many of Neruda's contemporaries, went through a similarly intense yet prolonged phase in his verse and then wrote socially engaged poetry in *España, Aparta de mí este cáliz* (1937) (Spain, Take This Chalice From Me) and his posthumous book *Poemas humanos* (1939) (Human

Poems). Like Neruda and Miguel Hernández—who published his explosive *Viento del pueblo* (Wind of the People) in 1937—Vallejo was given to "excesses" as well.[9]

But how does this immoderation in "España en el corazón" differ in its vigor from the self-reflexive stage Neruda and his contemporaries underwent? What we can observe in Neruda's case is the sheer intensity of his disquieting experience in Asia, the pressure to conquer his own autonomy—in both the cultural and economic realms—and the anxiety about establishing himself as a legitimate poet. Concisely stated, the *Residencias* focus on Neruda's coming to terms with his own mortality through recognition of the regenerative power of nature, and cultural, linguistic, and economic ostracism. *Tercera residencia* shifts and widens this focus, allowing space for the poet's own autobiographical intervention at a time when the complex sociopolitical struggle takes precedence over individual concerns. Since these pressing sociopolitical matters are paramount, they impinge upon the function of poetry. The insularity of the *Residencias* will not do because during these years he confronts the turmoil engulfing the Spanish people during the civil war. Likewise, the intricate poetic language in *Residencia en la tierra,* accessible to a small readership, could not hope to address the tragedy that had overtaken Spain during these years. So, as Neruda was moved by the strife of the civil war, he devised a new poetic method that responded to that moment. However, he did not change his style to be more marketable, but rather because he was convinced that his *Residencias* poems were far too self-reflective, metalinguistic, and narrow to effectively express that historical moment.

The moral-political declarations that one confronts throughout Neruda's account of the civil war are firmly tied to his personal life. Neruda's historical and poetic exposé engraves itself with his own formal and thematic signature. His new living conditions in Spain during these years, despite their severity, proved to be much less alienating, more fulfilling, and more productive. Neruda became an active and notable member of literary circles in Madrid, and once the gaps of economic survival and cultural acceptance were ameliorated, he moved beyond individual concerns to sociopolitical ones.[10] Furthermore, once the demands of financial necessity were met, he developed more complex views of the social world. These more nuanced yet pronounced political and moral views find their concrete elaboration in *Tercera residencia,* from "España en el corazón" to the poems dedicated to the antifascist cause. So behind each moral pronouncement in the fourth and fifth parts of the book lies an inter- and extra-poetic justification based on historical and political struggle. This then is what I have called Neruda's concept of moral realism, without which his work of this period does appear to be out of joint with his previous poetry.[11]

Moral and Political Outrage: The Lyric Poet Amidst the Civil War

Throughout *España en el corazón* the reader encounters innovative poetry which responds to the times. In the first stanza of "Invocación" (Invocation) we find a concise, yet abstract and tentative, testimony to this developing poetry that negates his writing leading up to the *Residencias*.

> Para empezar, para sobre la rosa
> pura y partida, para sobre el origen
> de cielo y aire y tierra, la voluntad de un canto
> con explosiones, el deseo
> de un canto inmenso, de un metal que recoja
> guerra y desnuda sangre,
> España, cristal de copa, no diadema,
> sí machacada piedra, combatida ternura
> de trigo, cuero y animal ardiendo.[12]

> [To begin, pause over the pure
> and cleft rose, pause over the source
> of sky and air and earth, the will of a song
> with explosions, the desire
> of an immense song, of a metal that will gather
> war and naked blood.
> Spain, water glass, not diadem,
> but yes crushed stone, militant tenderness
> of wheat, hide and burning animal.][13]

In contrast to the rose in his earlier poetry, this "rosa pura y partida" (the pure and parted rose), a metaphor for poetry, is also emblematic of the poet's heart (love, life) and his blood, which, a familiar religious symbol, is shed for others. Thus, from the outset, openness ("partida") negates the centripetal tendency of Neruda's earlier books. Nature, however, takes on the status that it achieved in the last poems in the *Residencias* and also in *Tercera residencia:* it is not the menacing and pernicious external force whose constant change horrified the speaker. Here it is a source of curiosity (of knowledge), whose natural elements ("cielo y aire y tierra" [sky and air and earth]) help establish the foundation for his poetry. Negating this fear of the passage of time leads Neruda to substitute it with a desire ("voluntad" [will], "deseo" [desire]) to investigate and give testimony to it. The desire to express various facets of the Spanish civil war contrasts with the limitations of human knowledge and communication. Yet this Neruda affirms his passion for recording the infinite elements that cause so much misery ("guerra y desnuda sangre" [war and naked blood]) and hope ("combatida ternura" [militant tenderness]) at this time in Spain.

The weight of the stanza gravitates toward the only active verb "recoja" (gather), underlining the task of this new poetry. This poetic objective recalls his early manifesto-in-verse: "para nacer he nacido, para encerrar el paso / de cuanto se aproxima" (because I was born to be born, to cut off the passage / of everything that approaches) (18). But significantly, in this context Neruda's realist impulse aims not only to represent the complexity of nature, but also to describe the very nerve center of the civil war. The poet intends to recover history as part of his poetic theory. This is not to suggest that history was ever absent but it was obscure. In "España en el corazón" history comes into focus as does Neruda's own understanding of its driving forces.

Both the representation of historical incidents and Neruda's understanding of its forces are critical, as is the reader's own knowledge of the Spanish civil war. The more familiarity he or she has, the more Neruda's abstract figurative language is grounded and made intelligible. But does this not place most of the burden of interpretation on the reader? Perhaps, but the expectations have shifted significantly. His previous poetry placed heavy demand on the reader because of his startling juxtaposition of images and density of language. Here the reader confronts the weight of historical content. For, on the one hand, if Neruda's goal is to capture—through the mediation of language—the points of tension in the civil war, would this not require a transformation in *form?* As we shall see, by changing the orientation of the content he has already altered the form, moving from generalized abstraction to concrete abstraction.[14] The language is less enigmatic in these poems and the *historical specificity* more salient. As the poetry moves away from self-reflection, it begins to incorporate other facets of reality (in the form of discourse). In "España en el corazón" we observe a progressive movement in that direction, from the general to the particular, the abstract to the concrete, which will be even more evident in their dialectical interplay in *Canto general.*

The weight of history is evident from "Invocation" on in *España en el corazón.* In describing the civil war Neruda chooses a decidedly republican vantage point. The speaker identifies Spain as a nation, in fact, as republican: "cristal de copa" (water glass) points to light or illumination and to the wine (blood of the people) that a crystal glass would hold. Thus, Neruda seems to imply here that republicanism is more naturally Spanish than monarchism ("no diadema"). Representative of the nation, of all that is historically Spanish, the Spanish Republic is being destroyed by the Falangists ("combatida ternura . . . ardiendo" [militant tenderness . . . burning]). This then is the epic introduction to the numerous poems that he defends argumentatively and, of necessity, poetically.

Neruda recounts the military uprising in 1936, headed by General Francisco Franco and begun in Morocco, against the democratically elected republican government in "Bombareo / Maldición":

> Mañana, hoy, por tus pasos
> un silencio, un asombro de esperanzas
> como un aire mayor: una luz, una luna,
> luna gastada, luna de mano en mano,
> de campana en campana!
> Madre natal, puño
> de avena endurecida,
> planeta
> seco y sangriento de los héroes!
> Quién? por caminos, quién,
> quién, quién? en sombra, en sangre, quién?
> en destello, quién,
> quién? Cae
> ceniza, cae
> hierro
> y piedra y muerte y llano y llamas,
> quién, quién, madre mía, quién, adónde?
> Patria surcada, juro que en tus cenizas
> nacerás como flor de agua perpetua,
> juro que de tu boca de sed saldrán al aire
> los pétalos del pan, la derramada
> espiga inaugurada. Malditos sean,
> malditos, malditos los que con hacha y serpiente
> llegaron a tu arena terrenal, malditos los
> que esperaron este día para abrir la puerta
> de la mansión al moro y al bandido:
> qué habéis logrado? Traed, traed la lámpara,
> ved el suelo empapado, ved el huesito negro
> comido por las llamas, la vestidura
> de España fusilada. (39–40)

> [Tomorrow, today, in your steps
> a silence, an astonishment of hopes
> like a major air: a light, a moon,
> a worn-out moon, a moon from hand to hand,
> from bell to bell!
> Natal mother, fist
> of hardened oats,
> dry
> and bloody planet of heroes!
> Who? by roads, who,
> who, who? in shadows, in blood, who?
> in a flash, who,

who? Ashes
fall, fall,
iron
and stone and death and weeping and flames,
who, who, mother, who where?
Furrowed motherland, I swear that in your ashes
you will be born like a flower of eternal water,
I swear that from your mouth of thirst will come to the air
the petals of bread, the split
inaugurated flower will come. Cursed,
cursed, cursed be those who with ax and serpent
came to your earthly arena, cursed those
who waited for this day to open the door
of the dwelling to the Moor and the bandit:
what have you achieved? Bring, bring the lamp,
see the soaked earth, see the blackened little bone
eaten by the flames, the garment
of murdered Spain.][15]

By describing a personified, maternal Spain ("Madre natal") in the first nine verses without employing any verbs, Neruda suggests that the apparently placid communal life of the Spanish people was disrupted by outsiders, by those who let the Moors (the Moroccan troops) and bandits (those who ceased believing in constitutional democracy) carry out the insurrection. By using indefinite articles Neruda also underscores the unity of republican Spain and contrasts it with the chaos in the first nine verses. Thus, the devastation brought about by the war is compared to the solidarity of the Republicans; an opposition Neruda highlights by elucidating it in the disruption and unity of language and in content. The speaker stresses collective human solidarity ("luna de mano en mano" [a moon from hand to hand]) among various towns and regions in the national territory ("de campana en campana" [from bell to bell]: a bell found in the main plaza of every town and used to congregate people).

By posing a series of unanswered questions—beginning with verse ten—that attempt to identify the perpetrator, Neruda focuses the reader's attention on the illegal and pernicious character of the violence and destruction. The reader reacts with indignation and thus identifies later with the speaker when he condemns the insurrectional troops because of their unwarranted and unjust violence. To react this way, the reader has to share several moral and rational judgments about life in modern society. Robin Warner asserts that there simply is no room for rational debate in this context and, consequently, the reader is expected to surrender to his emotions.[16] Warner is correct that Neruda's verse seems to overwhelm rational debate; nonetheless, there is logic behind Neruda's ethical positions. He assumes that most people will accept the fact that democracy is preferable to a military dictatorship because it allows for a greater representation of popular rights. And, in the tradition of the Enlightenment, this affirmation takes into account a general recognition of the fundamental equality of all human beings. In other words, Neruda advocates a core human equality founded on the well-being of all members of the human species.[17] In historical terms he is referring to the fact that the Popular Front was democratically elected by a majority of the Spanish population in 1936 and that this government "derive[d] its just powers from the governed," as the U.S. constitution puts it. In principle this is the view that many sectors of the Popular Front, whether anarchist, liberal, Communist or Socialist shared. Leftists, of course, would argue that class interests affect the outcome of elections so that the financial and political interests of the dominant class (the bourgeoisie) commonly win. But this is not as yet Neruda's position. The point here is that a political, historical, and moral pact—a "social contract" in the words of Rousseau—a product of long struggles and cherished by the majority of people, has been broken. So it is that the speaker in this poem and the reader both can condemn the military uprising and, henceforth, the Falangist movement as illegitimate.

Furthermore, it follows that defending the constitutional government with arms can also be legitimately upheld by the poet and the people (thus Neruda's allusion to the "héroes" [heros], the Republican soldiers). In the context of the poem this is structurally highlighted by the long description of the ruin caused by military insurrection, by five verses identifying the guilty party, and by a plea to the collaborators who permitted the uprising. This last point merits further exegesis. The implication in the last four verses ("qué habéis logrado? Traed, traed la lámpara, / ved el suelo empapado, ved el huesito negro / comido por las llamas, la vestidura / de España fusilada" [what have you achieved? Bring, bring the lamp, / see the soaked earth, see the blackened little bone / eaten by the flames, the garment / of murdered Spain]) could be construed as rather naïve on Neruda's part. However, it is worth noting that his reaction mirrors that of the republican government: "Casares Quiroga and the government of Spain first attempted to crush the revolt against them by constitutional means."[18] The speaker appeals to the same respect for a constitutionally elected government that we underlined above, but the Falangists rejected the legitimacy of the government because it was ostensibly unable to handle the illegal unrest in Madrid.[19] Once the military uprising took place, left-wing, anarchist parties, and workers generally felt that asking for arms from the government to defend themselves and their country was a natural right. But the requests were turned down. Since the national guard ("Guardia Civil") and the army had joined the military rebellion, the republican government believed that giving weapons to the workers would be tantamount to a call for revolution, so they did not give in. By July 19, three days after the uprising, the government did distribute 65,000 rifles; however all but 5,000 were missing cylinder heads. Despite this state of events, the UGT and CNT were able to seize arms in some military barracks across the country.[20]

However, it would be a mistake to claim that Neruda defended constitutionality blindly without seeing the prevailing economic inequalities that were part of the system. Indeed, in "España pobre por culpa de los ricos" (Spain Poor because of the Rich) one sees the resurgence perhaps of the Neruda of old, the (Bakunian?) anarchist. Here he manages not only to "import" history into the poetic discourse, but also to sketch out the major contradictions which are endemic to Spanish capitalism-feudalism:

> Malditos los que un día
> no miraron, malditos ciegos malditos,
> los que no adelantaron a la solemne patria
> el pan sino las lágrimas, malditos
> uniformes manchados y sotanas
> de agrios, hediondos perros de cueva y sepultura. (40)

> [Cursed be those who one day
> did not look, cursed cursed blind,
> those who offered the solemn fatherland
> not bread but tears, cursed
> sullied uniforms and cassocks
> of sour, stinking dogs of cave and grave.][21]

These six verses anticipate more abstractly what will later be specified and defended. Because the extreme right-wing refused to adhere to the constitutional government and sought to impose a reactionary regime anchored in the feudalist past, the speaker considers that they have become alienated, estranged from their fellow human beings and thus from themselves.[22] Plagued by "blindness"—by the unwillingness to respect and honor the flourishing of all— they, like the Neruda of the *Residencias,* have become animals ("agrios, hediondos perros" [sour, stinking dogs]). Isolated and driven by pessimism ("cueva y sepultura"), they seek to protect the socio-economic inequalities dividing society into classes. Rather than providing bread for all, they take up arms and cause further misery for the general population:

> La pobreza era por España
> como caballos llenos de humo,
> como piedras caídas del
> manantial de la desventura,
> tierras cereales sin
> abrir, bodegas secretas

de azul y estaño, ovarios, puertas, arcos
cerrados, profundidades
que querían parir, todo estaba guardado
por triangulares guardias con escopeta,
por curas de color de triste rata,
por lacayos del rey de inmenso culo. (41)

[Poverty was throughout Spain
like horses filled with smoke,
like stones fallen from the
spring of misfortune,
grainlands still
unopened, secret storehouses
of blue and tin, ovaries, doors, closed
arches, depths
that tried to give birth, all was guarded
by triangular guards with guns,
by sad-rat-colored priests,
by lackeys of the huge-rumped king.]

Neruda underscores the static and stagnating nature of the capitalist, yet semifeudalist economic system, which wastes human potential in the majority of the cases ("caballos llenos de humo" [horses filled with smoke]) to benefit a privileged minority of the population: the monarchy, the Church, and the military. The latter two are depicted as deformed or as beasts: the affluence of the king amidst the misery is underlined by his "immense ass" and priests are seen as parasitic rats that presumably feed off the misfortune, economic and otherwise, of the poor. Here, then, Neruda perceives the crux of the economic system: that the dominant social class plunders the working class. Yet the blame is not placed directly on this class conflict, but rather on the feudalist structures that continue to hinder economic development. In the Spain of the 1930s, Neruda maintains, there was not a crisis of overproduction—endemic of the capitalist mode of production—but rather a crisis of underproduction which benefited only the ruling class. The Spanish economy appears to be totally unproductive ("tierras cereales sin abrir" [grainfields still / unopened]) and sterile ("ovarios, puertas, arcos / cerrados" [ovaries, doors, arches / closed]), yet the ruling class can benefit from "bodegas secretas" (secret storehouses). Supported by the Spanish Communist Party, Libertarians, the Spanish Socialist Party, and Republican Liberals (the Popular Front) who lived in urban areas, this argument had a legitimate foundation as Ronald Fraser poignantly notes:

The dominant problem in a dominantly agrarian country like Spain lay in the land. To "modernize" Spain it was necessary to reform agriculture: industrialization could not fully develop unless agricultural productivity increased, creating a home market for consumer goods and transferring an increased surplus from the land into industrial development.

In the southern latifundist region, where a few thousand landowners controlled two thirds of the available land, the exploitation of close to three quarters of a million labourers at subsistence wages, and the estate owners' refusal to invest in their land, impeded this. Instead, low levels of agricultural techniques immobilized half-starving labour on the land, jeopardizing industrial development which could absorb that surplus labour productively in the towns.[23]

The Socialists, Communists, and Liberals all advocated agrarian reform as a precondition for the full development of capitalism and liberal democracy, but the landowners—beneficiaries of the feudal system (the church and the monarchy)—were, for their own "class" interests, firmly opposed to this republican program. It is this dominant sector of the economy that is under scrutiny in Neruda's poem:

> España dura, país manzanar y pino,
> te prohibían tus vagos señores:
> A no sembrar, a no parir las minas,
> a no montar las vacas, al ensimismamiento
> de las tumbas, a visitar cada año
> el monumento de Cristóbal el marinero, a relinchar
> discursos con macacos venidos de América,
> iguales en "posición social" y pobredumbre.
> No levantéis escuelas, no hagáis crujir la cáscara
> terrestre con arados, no llenéis los graneros
> de abundancia trigal: rezad, bestias, rezad,
> que un dios de culo inmenso como el culo del rey
> os espera: "Allí tomaréis sopa, hermanos míos." (41)
>
> [Tough Spain, land of apple orchards and pines,
> your idle lords ordered you:
> Do not sow the land, do not give birth to mines,
> do not breed cows, but contemplate
> the tombs, visit each year
> the monument of Columbus the sailor, neigh
> speeches with monkeys come from America,
> equal in "social position" and in putrefaction.
> Do not build schools, do not break open earth's
> crust with plows, do not fill the granaries
> with abundance of wheat: pray, beasts, pray
> for a god with a rump as huge as the king's rump
> awaits you: "There you will have soup, my brethren.][24]

In these lines, the crisis of underproduction, legislated by the idle royalty and landlords ("vagos señores" [idle lords]), dovetails with the reactionary ideology which maintains it. Thus the emphasis on tradition (Christopher Columbus as representative of the empire), the Latin Americans ("macacos"—degenerates, drunkards) who share the same class values—engage in supporting their social class at the expense of others ("ensimismamiento" [egotism]). Ironically, the various negative statements ("Do not sow," "Do not build," and so on), all tied to this dominant yet unproductive class, have a positive effect, suggesting that the problems that beset Spain can be solved via production, egalitarian distribution, and education.

The final five verses mark a change in the thematic direction of the poem and a return to the beginning. The imperative forms are redirected at the members of the ruling class. Compared to beasts who deny the basic necessities of life, the dominant class will, Neruda seems to declare, be buried with its values.

What is significant here is that Neruda now includes in his work and records in his consciousness the ill effects that capitalism—albeit with feudalist vestiges—can have on human well-being. Neruda's understanding of his unique situation as an individual is thereby woven into the greater social fabric as he begins to comprehend more fully the estrangement that tormented him during the *Residencias* period.

A Type of Realism

In that spirit, "Explico algunas cosas" represents a conclusively different type of poetry, which in an epic-realist tradition explains the genesis of the transformation in his political and poetic consciousness. To explain is to recognize and be concerned about one's audience. And to illustrate something effectively, to reach as broad a readership as possible, one must not only effect changes in content, but also in form.

This brings up a fundamental historical question: why did Neruda—along with a host of other poets, among others, César Vallejo, Nicolás Guillén, Rafael Alberti, Miguel Hernández—radically change his poetic form? There are several dimensions to this question. First of all his petty-bourgeois/working class background could be seen as one of the primary forces economically and socially that casts him in an ambiguous class position. As a fluid class pinned between the bourgeoisie and proletariat, the petty bourgeoisie's ideology tends to oscillate between the interest of the other two classes. Normally its social consciousness derives from the values of the bourgeoisie, yet it is generally aware—even if vaguely—that it, like the working class, must sell its labor power to the dominant class. In capitalism the professionals are also dependent upon the interests of the ruling class. But the acute internal contradictions of this historical period in Spain make a defense of the bourgeoisie or of the monarchy much more difficult, if not ethically impossible. To be sure, siding with the Republicans did not automatically indicate that one identified wholeheartedly with the interests of the working class, for the main governmental posts were held by the petite bourgeoisie. But as supporters of the Popular Front their lot was thrown in with the proletariat. The military uprising is illustrative in this regard. The Republican government attempted to retain its constitutional legitimacy in the face of the military insurrection and, later, the unions' demands for arms. As noted above, seeing that there was no room for negotiation, the government issued arms to the workers and the civil war began in earnest. In the face of this sociohistorical situation and given his own anarchist background, Neruda felt drawn and quickly impelled to support the Republic. This may explain why poets of Neruda's generation felt compelled to write in accessible language and to become deeply committed to the Republican cause.

In altering his poetic form, Neruda saw his readership change as well. Originally printed on the battle front by Republican soldiers, *España en el corazón* was not meant to reach members of the cultural establishment.[25] The clarity in content, the naked depiction of the class struggle in Spain during the civil war from a partisan perspective, made (and makes) this book unacceptable in traditional literary circles. As Neruda's perception of sociopolitical, economic, and historical events is distilled, he modifies his poetic form. The act of drawing the class struggle into focus constitutes the adjustment of form to content, laying bare the socioeconomic conditions as form becomes more transparent. Consequently, Neruda chooses to portray the world the working class inhabits on a daily basis—a world the ruling class chooses to gloss over or consider banal. The form, then, is critical realist, and the audience is the working class and the petite bourgeoisie.

Consequently, while it may be considered a dialectical product of Neruda's earlier work, "Explico algunas cosas" represents a fundamental departure from his former poetry. "La organización del poema" (The organization of the poem), states Jaime Alazraki, "se define así como un diálogo de dos lenguajes: el primero funciona como un interrogante en cuya respuesta se inscribe el segundo. Estos dos lenguajes confrontados dramatizan y 'explican' el salto operado en la poesía de Neruda" (defines itself as a dialogue of two languages: the first operates as an interrogative whose answer is inscribed in the second [language). These two opposing languages dramatize and 'explain' the leap that takes place in Neruda's poetry].[26]

> Preguntaréis: Y dónde están las lilas?
> Y la metafísica cubierta de amapolas?
> Y la lluvia que a menudo golpeaba
> sus palabras llenándolas
> de agujeros y pájaros?

5/NERUDA'S MORAL REALISM IN *ESPAÑA EN EL CORAZÓN* 197

Os voy a contar todo lo que me pasa.
Yo vivía en un barrio
de Madrid, con campanas,
con relojes, con árboles.
Desde allí se veía
el rostro seco de Castilla
como un océano de cuero.
Mi casa era llamada
la casa de las flores, porque por todas partes
estallaban geranios: era
una bella casa
con perros y chiquillos.
Raúl, te acuerdas?
Te acuerdas, Rafael?
Federico, te acuerdas
debajo de la tierra,
te acuerdas de mi casa con balcones en donde
la luz de Junio ahogaba flores en tu boca?
Hermano, hermano!
Todo
eran grandes voces, sal de mercaderías,
aglomeraciones de pan palpitante,
mercados de mi barrio de Argüelles con su estatua
como un tintero pálido entre las merluzas:
el aceite llegaba a las cucharas,
un profundo latido
de pies y manos llenaba las calles,
metros, litros, esencia
aguda de la vida,
pescados hacinados,
contextura de techos con sol frío en el cual
la flecha se fatiga,
delirante marfil fino de las patatas,
tomates repetidos hasta el mar. (43–44)

[You will ask: And where are the lilacs?
And the metaphysical blanket of poppies?
And the rain that often struck
your words filling them
with holes and birds?
I am going to tell you what is happening to me.
I live in a quarter
of Madrid, with bells,
with clocks, with trees.
From there one could see
the lean face of Spain
like an ocean of leather.

> My house was called
> the house of flowers, because it was bursting
> everywhere with geraniums: it was
> a fine house
> with dogs and children.
> Raúl, do you remember?
> Federico, do you remember
> under the ground,
> do you remember my house with balconies where
> June light smothered flowers in your mouth?
> Brother, brother!
> Everything
> was great shouting, salty goods,
> heaps of throbbing bread,
> markets of my Argüelles quarter with its statue
> like a pale inkwell among the haddock:
> the olive oil reached the ladles,
> a deep throbbing
> of feet and hands filled the streets,
> meters, liters, an acute
> essence of life,
> fish piled up,
> pattern of roofs with cold sun on which
> the vane grows weary,
> frenzied fine ivory of the potatoes,
> tomatoes stretching to the sea.][27]

In this first third of the poem, the reader encounters anecdotal poetry, no different from ordinary language. This autobiographical account of his communal life, shared intensely with Federico García Lorca, Rafael Alberti, Miguel Hernández, Raúl González Tuñón, and others, parallels the non-alienated, collective life among towns and citizens that the poet described in "Bombardeo Maldición": it is the silence before the storm. By referring to the physical images where possession cannot be distinguished ("grandes voces," "pies," "manos" [great shouting, feet, hands]), Neruda stresses the communal nature of his life in Madrid. Yet he associates the unity between them with the profound heartbeat and the pulsating bread. Their hearts are metaphors for shared emotions and thoughts. Heart is source, metaphor, and synecdoche of this collective intellectual life. Sharing a meal (the fish, the potatoes, the tomatoes, the cooking oil) becomes an integral part of that communal experience. The poem shifts its attention, formally and thematically, from the autobiographical specificity of Neruda's individual case to the collective nature of the poet's life.[28]

But this somewhat idyllic environment is interrupted:

Y una mañana todo estaba ardiendo
y una mañana las hogueras
salían de la tierra
devorando seres,
y desde entonces fuego,
pólvora desde entonces,
y desde entonces sangre.
Bandidos con aviones y con moros,
bandidos con sortijas y duquesas,
bandidos con frailes negros bendiciendo
venían por el cielo a matar niños,
y por las calles la sangre de los niños
corría simplemente, como sangre de niños.
Chacales que el chacal rechazaría,
piedras que el cardo seco mordería escupiendo,
víboras que las víboras odiaran! (44–45)

[And one morning all was aflame
and one morning the fires
came out of the earth
devouring people,
and from then on fire,
gunpowder from then on,
and from then on blood.
Bandits with airplanes and with Moors,
bandits with rings and duchesses,
bandits with black-robed friars blessing
came through the air to kill children,
and through the streets the blood of the children
ran simply, like children's blood.
Jackals that the jackal would spurn,
stones that the dry thistle would bite spitting,
vipers that vipers would abhor!]

Here too the poet describes the effects before he identifies the agents of the destruction. By employing the repetition of temporal clauses ("y una mañana" [And one morning] and "desde entonces") in the first of these stanzas, and the name for the perpetrator and the victims in the second, he intensifies the conflict. The reader's eyes tend to focus more on the unrepeated words and phrases. Therefore, within the framework of the first stanza itself the indiscriminant violence is highlighted yet the perpetrators are not linguistically identified.

It is all the more dramatic when, in the second stanza, the speaker accusingly names them. Again, the utilization of a term like "bandits"—which serves as a "social" metaphor here—needs to be investigated further. In the first three verses Neruda establishes an equivalence between "bandidos" and each of the different reactionary sectors of society: the Falangists, the military, the monarchy, and the church. They are all "bandidos" because they disregarded the constitutionality of the democratically elected government, and, by extension, stole the government and the people's right to universal suffrage. Neruda suggests here that like professional criminals, they also inflict senseless violence on innocent people (the children). Moreover, from a moral realist point of view—of a liberal or leftist persuasion—children represent the future hopes of the human species. (The Nationalists would also lay claim to this moral stance, but by supporting war against the Republican government they undermined that moral position.) According to Neruda, the Nationalists' position does not advocate human well-being and flourishing, but rather unwanted destructiveness which, as the following stanza makes clear, is founded on the belief that human beings are beasts; they are hordes that need to be guided. According to the third of these stanzas, the Nationalists violate the interests of human society and the animal world. They are worse than "beasts": they are so alienated from their fellow citizens and so much in need of exploiting the rest of the citizenry to maintain their wealth and economic power that they can only cause widespread social misery. From a moral standpoint then, the Nationalist position is inconsistent and therefore flawed, whereas the Republicans espouse a moral stance that is supported (in general) by their political and economic platform.

Having depicted the Falangist bombings, the poem returns to the speaker's point of view:

> Frente a vosotros he visto la sangre
> de España levantarse
> para ahogaros en una sola ola
> de orgullo y de cuchillos!
> Generales
> traidores:
> mirad mi casa muerta,
> mirad España rota:
> pero de cada casa muerta sale metal ardiendo
> en vez de flores,
> pero de cada hueco de España
> sale España,
> pero de cada niño muerto sale un fusil con ojos,
> pero de cada crimen nacen balas
> que os hallarán un día el sitio
> del corazón.
> Preguntaréis por qué su poesía
> no nos habla del suelo, de las hojas,
> de los grandes volcanes de su país natal?

> Venid a ver la sangre por las calles,
> venid a ver
> la sangre por las calles,
> venid a ver la sangre
> por las calles! (45–46)
>
> [Facing you I have seen the blood
> of Spain rise up
> to drown you in a single wave
> of pride and knives!
> Treacherous
> generals:
> look at my dead house,
> look at broken Spain:
> but from each dead house comes burning metal
> instead of flowers,
> but from each hollow in Spain
> Spain comes forth,
> but from each dead child comes a gun with eyes,
> but from each crime are born bullets
> that will one day seek you out
> where the heart lies.
> You ask: why does your poetry
> not speak to us of sleep, of the leaves,
> of the great volcanoes of your native land?
> Come and see the blood in the streets,
> come and see
> the blood in the streets,
> come and see the blood
> in the streets!]

These ardent verses have more of an impact on the reader because Neruda is witnessing and denouncing the atrocities first hand. As René de Costa has pointed out, the speaker here is a chronicler who uses the oral tradition as his vehicle to "persuade the reader of the truth, the factuality of what is being narrated."[29] As he identifies the commonalities between his experiences and those of others, Neruda's own unique experience in Madrid and his understanding about this sociohistorical moment expands and gains force. In the case of resistance against the putschkists, the nation—here associated with the Republic—overcomes the trap of individualism to become "una sola ola" (a single wave) determined to crush the Falangists. The specific historical references to this resistance—the International Brigades, the Republican militias and battalions—made in subsequent poems, are crystallized here in the description of the union of diverse political factions in the fight against fascism.

For Neruda, the Nationalists are not what their name implies; their conception of the nation involves its destruction. Since they began the civil war against the wishes of the populace, their nationalism is a contradiction in terms. Neruda identifies Spain as Republican, an association which is summarily used in the battle against the "Nationalists." Repetition ("pero de cada . . ." [from each]) binds the members of the Republican resistance together linguistically (in the poem's structure) and thematically. The inhuman devastation, which the Falangist bombings inflict upon the population, ironically helps unify the Republicans in their struggle. Significantly Neruda notes that instead of enhancing the creative potential of human beings ("en vez de flores" [instead of flowers]), the Nationalists force the rest of the population to take up arms. From the vantage point of the Republicans, Neruda argues, the war against fascism is—in the words of Aristotle—a "just war": it is ethically defensible because it is for the "good" of the human species to defend itself and the flourishing of all human beings.[30] In Neruda's view, defending the Republic is paramount because it is a political system that provides freedom from necessity—social goods—to its citizens; whereas the alternative, fascism, would wipe out the crucial social and political gains made by the Republic.

A historical materialist position on this matter would build upon and elaborate the liberal argument regarding human equality—derived from the Enlightenment. From this point of view, the Falangists' war on the Spanish population impedes the future development of social and economic conditions based on a core human equality, and their position justifies and imposes social, economic, and political inequalities that reinforce the interests of the ruling class over those of the working class and the petite bourgeoisie. As we confirmed in our reading of "España pobre por culpa de los ricos" (Spain Poor Through the Fault of the Rich), Neruda adhered to a radical and advanced interpretation of the Spanish civil war—he was aware that the struggle among classes was central to this historical event. While the historical, political, and social analysis that informs these ethical judgments is not as sophisticated as that of *Canto general* and his later work, it is nonetheless a much more complex ethical position than we find in the *Residencias*. Neruda's moral indignation is substantiated with his understanding of class conflict as a driving force in capitalism. In his later works, some of which are analyzed in chapter 6, he incorporates a more elaborate understanding of the dialectical method, the labor theory of value, interclass conflict, the crucial role of ideology, and other aspects of Marxism into his work and takes more advanced moral positions based on that knowledge.

A case in point among many would be Neruda's lengthy poem "Que despierte el leñador" (Let the Woodcutter Awaken) in *Canto general* (1950). This poem differs from the verse in *Tercera residencia* in poetic method and understanding of Marxism and, consequently, of the general socioeconomic and historical tendencies in the development of capitalism and socialism. In the first section alone Neruda begins with his love for nature and his identification with the black and white working people in the United States; he then turns to the state of the world and life in the United States when it is not belligerantly and nakedly carrying out imperialist invasions of Latin America and other regions; he refers to the shared aims among American writers (understood as pointing to the continent as a whole) and their commitment to fight injustices; and, finally, he addresses the question of the united triumph over fascism during World War II. In the space of four pages he covers the major social, economic, and historical issues behind his love of the peaceful working people in the U.S. and his repugnance for the Nazis (whom he calls "rats"). Overall, Neruda admires the natural and man-made beauty of the U.S., the work ethic of farmers and of industrial laborers who built Manhattan, the country's humble origins, the politically committed writers, and lastly, the struggle in World War II (which was "verde y amarga la historia" [a green and bitter history]). The information provided in this mural-like rendering of the U.S. as well as on the dehumanizing and alienating social relations and exploitative economic relations in 1948 that are described in section II form the basis of Neruda's moral and political stances.[31] In other words, his ethical positions are backed up by his incisive analysis of the U.S. and of its capitalist economic system as well as by his involvement in left-wing politics.

Neruda's familiarity with and participation in political, historical, and social matters from 1936 altered not only his moral views, but also his poetic theory. Indeed, the events of the civil war, which the poet experienced first hand, provided the impetus for reconsidering his poetic theory and ushering in a stage of critical realism. Neruda the critical realist cannot turn his back on this struggle, cannot declare it all part of the human condition. Without relinquishing awareness of the dialectical and tragic dimensions of human existence, Neruda commits himself to the defense of the Republican cause because it involves him personally and because the Nationalist assault on the Republic offends his ethical sensibilities and political convictions.

Carried along by the current of the civil war, Neruda no longer conceives of himself as an exceptional, "prophetic" poet, but rather as a chronicler of the Republican cause. Thus his interest in recording a humanist and realist version, from a Republican vantage point, of the historical events, the names of towns, and descriptions of each of the contending forces.

Such is the case of "Llegada a Madrid de la Brigada Internacional" (Arrival to Madrid of the International Brigade), written during the winter of 1936 immediately after the arrival of these international Republican forces. Seen by the Comintern as a key way of contributing to the Republican cause and as a way of counteracting the German and Italian military aid to the

Nationalists, approximately 35,000 Communist Party members and progressive antifascists from various nations joined the Republican army.[32] These brigades came at a critical moment in the war when they, and the Spanish Republican troops, were able to ward off the Nationalist offensive on Madrid until the end of the war. One of the most bloody and crucial battles, which Neruda describes in this poem, took place in the university campus area in Madrid where the poet himself lived. By this point in the war, the Largo Caballero (Republican) government had decided to move to Valencia because it was no longer able to carry on administrative duties in Madrid. This battle thwarted the Nationalists' taking the capital and thus winning the war from November 15 to 23. Franco, who had declared his preference for destroying Madrid completely rather than leaving it in the hands of "Marxists," ordered the bombing of the capital until the enemy surrendered. The German "Condor Legion" dropped firebombs on every sector of the city without respite. This only had the effect, as Hugh Thomas observed, of enraging the population.[33]

Neruda's reaction here, then, mirrors that of the majority of the madrileños:

> Una mañana de un mes de frío,
> de un mes agonizante, manchado por el lodo y por el humo,
> un mes sin rodillas, un triste mes de sitio y desventura,
> cuando a través de los cristales mojados de mi casa se oían los chacales africanos
> aullar con los rifles y los dientes llenos de sangre, entonces,
> cuando no teníamos más esperanza que un sueño de pólvora,
> cuando ya creíamos
> que el mundo estaba lleno sólo de monstruos devoradores y de furias
> entonces, quebrando la escarcha del mes de frío de Madrid, en la niebla
> del alba
> he visto con estos ojos que tengo, con este corazón que mira,
> he visto llegar a los claros, a los dominadores combatientes
> de la delgada y dura y madura y ardiente brigada de piedra.[34]
>
> [One morning in a cold month,
> an agonizing month, stained by mud and smoke,
> a month without knees, a sad month of siege and misfortune,
> when through the wet windows of my house
> the African jackals could be heard
> howling with rifles and teeth covered with blood, then,
> when we had no more hope than a dream of powder,
> when we already thought
> that the world was filled only with devouring monsters
> and furies,

then, breaking the frost of the cold Madrid month,
in the fog,
of the dawn
I saw with these eyes that I have, with this heart
that looks,
I saw arrive the clear, the masterful fighters
of the thin and hard and mellow and ardent stone brigade.]35

Repetition plays a key role in the presentation of this historical period. By employing indefinite articles and temporal adverbs ("cuando" [when]; "entonces" [then]) Neruda manages to extend the time period, underscore the duration of the Nationalist advance on Madrid, and focus on the emotional resignation of the madrileños. All this sets the stage formally and thematically for the arrival of the International Brigades. In "Explico algunas cosas" the indefinite articles reflect the destruction of the sense of community among Neruda and his friends, as well as peaceful existence under the Republic for the people as a whole. Here the repetition of the indefinite articles ("un mes" [a month], for instance) induces in the reader an oppressive and impotent feeling toward the war. But this feeling of desperation, in the face of the Moroccan-led attack by the Nationalists, is a collective or socially generalized reaction. The structural layout of these verses reflects the real historical conflict: the Republican position is delineated in the first part of the poem and the onslaught of the Nationalist attacks is depicted in subsequent parts. Set off against the speaker ("mi casa" [my house]) and the rest of the population ("no teníamos más esperanza" [we had no more hope]; "creíamos" [we thought]) one encounters the "chacales africanos" (African jackals) and "monstruos devoradores" (devouring monsters), with the latter dominating the scene. As in the last poem, the Moroccan mercenaries are portrayed as jackals who make war a way of life.

When the reader comes to "en la niebla del alba" (in the fog / of the dawn) he or she senses a change in this desperate state of affairs. Indeed, the invocation of these distant and ambiguous images of hope ("alba"= hope) prefigures the arrival of the International Brigades, or at least of some possible liberating force. Following these verses, the speaker is introduced in order to confirm visually and ethically ("corazón que mira" [heart that looks]) the appearance of the International Brigades. Neruda attributes characteristics to them that remind the reader of the heroic, epic figures depicted on wall posters of the time: the physical strength of the Republican soldier becomes a metaphor for his military prowess and vigilance. Yet, it is noteworthy that unlike the last third of *Tercera residencia,* here the portrayal is abstract and symbolic: The organic complexity and peculiarity of these historical agents cannot be fully appreciated, but the concrete historical conflict can be discerned:

> Era el acongojado tiempo en que las mujeres
> llevaban una ausencia como un carbón terrible,
> y la muerte española, más ácido y aguda que otras muertes
> llenaba los campos hasta entonces honrados por el trigo.
> Por las calles la sangre rota del hombre se juntaba
> con el agua que sale del corazón destruido de las casas:
> los huesos de los niños deshechos, el desgarrador
> enlutado silencio de las madres, los ojos
> cerrados para siempre de los indefensos,
> eran como la tristeza y la pérdida, eran como un jardín escupido,
> eran la fe y la flor asesinadas para siempre. (52)
>
> [It was the anguished time when women
> wore absence like a frightful coal,
> and Spanish death, more acrid and sharper than other deaths,
> filled fields up to then honored by wheat.
> Through the streets the broken blood of man joined
> the water that emerges from the ruined hearts of homes:
> the bones of the shattered children, the heartrending
> black-clad silence of the mothers, the eyes
> forever shut of the defenseless,
> were like sadness and loss, were like a spit-upon garden,
> were faith and flower forever murdered.]

Having introduced the International Brigades, Neruda turns once again to daily life in times of war. Death and grieving, normally regarded as private affairs in bourgeois society, become a public phenomenon. The war creates widows by the thousands ("las mujeres / llevaban una ausencia como un carbón terrible" [women / wore absence like a frightful coal]) and forms a new social stratum. But the driving force in these verses is contradiction: the corpses of soldiers fill the fields once used for the cultivation of wheat. Class conflict carried to this horrendous degree accentuates the internal contradictions that exist in capitalism even under a "peacetime" economy.

The third stanza shows quite clearly that the war kills human beings (perhaps soldiers in this case), destroys the physical environment, and thereby disrupts and harms a social institution: the family ("corazón destruido de las casas" [ruined hearts of homes]). Indeed, during the war, on one particular night between November 19 and 20, 150 innocent people died in the Madrid bombings.[36] As Neruda underlines in the last line of the stanza, the people's hope for vitality and for an end to the disaster of war ("flor" [flower]) has been wiped out. Yet this negation, which seems to be permanent ("para siempre" [forever]), although it is engraved in the memory of the people, confronts its own dialectical negation:

> Camaradas,
> entonces

5/NERUDA'S MORAL REALISM IN *ESPAÑA EN EL CORAZÓN*

os he visto,
y mis ojos están ahora llenos de orgullo
porque os vi a través de la mañana de niebla llegar a la frente
pura de Castilla
silenciosos y firmes
como campanas antes del alba,
llenos de solemnidad y ojos azules venir de lejos y lejos,
venir de vuestros rincones, de vuestras patrias perdidas, de
vuestros sueños
llenos de dulzura quemada y de fusiles
a defender la ciudad española en que la libertad acorralada
pudo caer y morir mordida por las bestias.
Hermanos, que desde ahora
vuestra pureza y vuestra fuerza, vuestra historia solemne
sea conocida del niño y del varón, de la mujer y el viejo,
llegue a todos los seres sin esperanza, baje a las minas corroídas
por el aire sulfúrico,
suba a las escaleras inhumanas del esclavo,
que todas las estrellas, que todas las espigas de Castilla y del
mundo
escriban vuestro nombre y vuestra áspera lucha
y vuestra victoria fuerte y terrestre como una encina roja.
Porque habéis hecho renacer con vuestro sacrificio
la fe perdida, el alma ausente, la confianza en la tierra,
y por vuestra abundancia, por vuestra nobleza, por vuestros
muertos,
como por un valle de duras rocas de sangre
pasa un inmenso río con palomas de acero y de esperanza. (52–53)

[Comrades,
then
I saw you,
and my eyes are even now filled with pride
because through the misty morning I saw you reach
the pure brow of Castile
silent and firm
like bells before dawn,
filled with solemnity and blue-eyed, come from far,
far away,
come from your corners, from your lost fatherlands,
from your dreams,
covered with burning and guns, gentleness
to defend the Spanish city in which besieged liberty
could fall and die bitten by the beasts.
Brothers, from now on
let your pureness and your strength, your solemn story
be known by children and by men, by women and by old men,
let it reach all men without hope, let it go down to the mines

corroded by sulphuric air,
let it climb the inhuman stairways of the slave,
let all the stars, let all the flowers of Castile
and of the world
write your name and your bitter struggle
and your victory strong and earthen as a red oak.
Because you have revived with your sacrifice
lost faith, absent heart, trust in the earth,
and through your abundance, through your nobility, through your dead,
as if through a valley of harsh bloody rocks,
flows an immense river with doves of steel and of hope.]

The poet communicates his hope through visual confirmation ("os he visto" [I have seen you]; "mis ojos" [my eyes]; "os vi" [I saw you]), which counteracts the desolation that reigned before the arrival of the International Brigades. Significantly, Neruda perceives these volunteers as "comrades," which brings to mind the two principal definitions of the word: "friends," "fellow workers" on the one hand, and "fellow socialists or communists." Either definition points to the poet's alliance with the volunteers' political stance. Obfuscation and appearance, often products of bourgeois and petit bourgeois thought, give way to critical mimesis: the poet allies himself with the working class and suggests that only their leadership can rescue the Republic. Indeed, in these verses Neruda rejects the incessantly oscillating values of liberalism and of his class (the petite bourgeoisie)—a mortal sin according to several Neruda scholars—and chooses to ally himself with the interests of the working class at a time when liberal ideology is in crisis.

When Neruda describes the International Brigades, then, he is identifying with the values they uphold and he is calling for a poetry that will be "como campanas antes del alba" (like bells before dawn), that is, that will occupy a public space and issue a clarion call to the Spanish people. If the Republican volunteers are filled with "dulzura quemada" (burning sweetness), the poet after having spent time in the Orient must, like the brigadists, have a hardened good will and political convictions tempered by their benevolence. As we have seen, Neruda also shares many of the Socialist and Communist political convictions. But he is not such an idealist (and elitist) to assume that his verse will also defend Madrid from the Falangists ("las bestias" [beasts] here again). In the tradition of epic poetry, his mission as a poet is to recount the story of the Republican participation in the war, to sing of arms and the men. That is why in the last stanza he declares, "vuestra historia solemne / sea conocida" (your solemn story / be known). The poet sees himself not as an exalted "prophet" but through his familiarity with nature, the Iberian Peninsula, and the struggles of its people, a vessel for "vuestro nombre y vuestra áspera lucha" (your name and your bitter struggle). But even when he writes epic poetry, like Bertolt Brecht, his own individuality is highlighted. Neruda rarely remains in a realm of abstraction; whether manifested in references to his own life or specific battle scenes, the concrete is ever present. Verses four through nine anticipate the attempted synthesis between the historical agents and the poet in *Canto general.* Through Neruda, the Spanish people and humanity itself ("todas las espigas de Castilla y del / mundo") (let all the stems of Castile and the / world) will recognize and write the history of the International Brigades. He ends "Batalla del río Jarama" (Battle of the Jarama River) with the recognition that he is no high priest of culture, but rather a humble artisan: "no es mi boca / suficiente, y es pálida mi mano: / allí quedan tus muertos" (54) [my mouth is not / enough, and my hand, pale: / there are your dead]. To be sure, the poet takes on the role of writing about their struggle; however, given that the speaker's persona does not intervene in this stanza, the poet becomes, by extension, an observer and chronicler of this historical movement. This hesitation and seeming objectivity—the despairing wave to the dead—suggest both the need for realism and Neruda's feeling of insufficiency as a poet given the atrocious events of the war.

Neruda does not represent this struggle along the lines of the traditional epic, with its penchant for hyperbole about the glorious feats of the hero. Rather, he considers this historical moment as a tragedy—an "historia solemne" (solemn story)—which forces the oppressed (miners, slave laborers, and people without hope) to defend themselves against their class enemy: "Porque habéis hecho renacer con vuestro sacrificio / la fe perdida, el alma ausente, la confianza en la tierra" (Because you have revived with your sacrifice / lost faith, absent heart, trust in the earth). These lines are more realist than one might imagine. It is humanly and historically tragic that some 266 Republican volunteers were killed and 6,029 wounded defending Madrid from the Nationalist army.[37] Yet their sacrifice prevented further bloodshed in the Spanish capital and forestalled further exploitation under Franquismo. So, in that sense, the International Brigades did restore confidence and hope in the people on the Republican side of the battle lines. Neruda's view of this particular moment and most moments of the civil war is dialectical: the Republican soldiers' terrible sacrifices stem the Nationalists' advance on Madrid and thus give the people some hope. In "Tierras ofendidas" (Offended Lands) he offers perhaps the most succinct analysis of this tragic period: "Nada, ni la victoria / borrará el agujero terrible de la sangre" (Nothing, not even victory / will erase the terrible hole of blood).[38] Neruda does not turn a deaf ear to the human cost of the war and celebrate the Republican cause optimistically; rather, he recognizes the grievous nature of the conflict.

Contrary to critical observations about the jaded and simplistic nature of Neruda's poetry after the *Residencias,* "Llegada a Madrid de la Brigada

International" (Arrival in Madrid of the International Brigades) indicates that Neruda's radicalization in the political realm permitted him to present as a concrete abstraction different spheres of reality and to delve into the complexity of his historical moment in a way he was unable to do before this period in his texts.[39] While the historical dialectic that operates in his poetry may not have attained the level of refinement one finds in *Canto general,* it is still present, throughout *Tercera residencia,* as the motor force of his worldview.

Toward "Guided Spontaneity" or Dialectical Realism

The most poignant Neruda poem, in which one can observe the high resolution of the dialectical method in *Tercera residencia,* is "Canto sobre unas ruinas" (Song About Some Ruins), probably written in late 1937. These verses, and the poem itself, distinguish themselves from his other reflections on the events and historical figures of the Spanish civil war because he sees these from a different vantage point, from a higher level of understanding. In essence it is a dialectical meditation on ontology, natural laws, history and, a materialist theory of poetry:

> Esto que fue creado y dominado,
> esto que fue humedecido, usado, visto,
> yace—pobre pañuelo—entre las olas
> de tierra y negro azufre.
> Como el botón o el pecho
> se levantan al cielo, como la flor que sube
> desde el hueso destruido, así las formas
> del mundo aparecieron. Oh párpados,
> oh columnas, oh escalas.
> Oh profundas materias
> agregadas y puras: cuánto hasta ser campanas!
> cuánto hasta ser rejoles! Aluminio
> de azules proporciones, cemento
> pegado al sueño de los seres![40]

> [This that was created and tamed,
> this that was moistened, used, seen,
> lies—poor kerchief—among the waves
> of earth and black brimstone.
> Like bud or breast
> they raise themselves to the sky, like the flower that rises
> from the destroyed bone, so the shapes
> of the world appeared. Oh eyelids,
> oh columns, oh ladders.

> Oh deeper substances
> annexed and pure: how long until you are bells!
> how long until you are clocks! Aluminum
> of blue proportions, cement
> stuck to human dreams!]⁴¹

Neruda begins by concentrating on the work of geophysical nature, in which he attempts pointing up distinctions and similarities vis-à-vis human nature. The title of the poem itself, "Canto sobre unas ruinas," encapsulates the relationship as Neruda envisions it. Human creation ("canto" [the song]) depends upon nature, but it is not homologous with natural phenomena. In renovating nature consciously, human beings create something other than themselves that is, simultaneously, part of themselves. As Marx puts it in the *Economic and Philosphical Manuscripts:*

> Nature is man's *inorganic body,* that is to say nature in so far as it is not the human body. Man *lives* from nature, i.e. nature is his *body,* and he must maintain a continuing dialogue with it if he is not to die. To say that man's physical and mental life is linked to nature simply means that nature is linked to itself, for man is a part of nature.⁴²

Even though human beings are fruits of nature, their autonomy is revealed in the way they differ from other biological beings—they utilize their consciousness as a force to change certain aspects of nature or to discover universal laws. "Animals," declares Marx, "produce only according to the standards and needs of the species to which they belong, while man is capable of producing according to the standards of every species."⁴³ Human beings produce above and beyond the level of actual, physical necessity; they engage in aesthetic production as well. What Neruda observes here are the major differences and similarities between nature and human beings. Through the limitations of time and space, nature creates and destroys. (Neruda's example here is: The bud becomes a flower and then it dies.) Likewise human beings are certainly capable, as the Spanish civil war makes patently evident, of destroying and recreating what they have created. Yet, in opposition to nature, the human species is quite able—contra Social Darwinist (or reductionist) arguments—to organize a political and economic system that responds to the general and vital interests of humanity as a whole.

Neruda is not reflecting on the status of nature in the abstract but is choosing to focus on human labor and its transformation of nature. The entity ("Esto" [this]) that was invented and used must have been created by nature itself or by human beings. But in this instance, humans have intervened because of the poet's reference to vision and reflection ("visto" [seen]). So, all that humans have forged has been buried by them. While an analogy is drawn between nature and human beings ("el botón *o* el pecho" [the bud or the breast; my emphasis]) in the second stanza, their difference is brought out in two significant ways. First, human beings can be a source of life in nature when they are deceased; hence the "flor que sube desde el hueso destruido" (the flower that rises / from the destroyed bone). Second, as long as homo sapiens exist, they will forge something out of nature for their immediate physiological needs or pleasure. Thus Neruda's reference to "campanas" (bells), "relojes" (clocks) and natural elements tied to the "sueño de los seres" (human dreams). The "profundas materias" (deep sustances) he is alluding to must pass through human labor in order to become socially valuable and useful. As the line "cuánto hasta ser campanas" (how long until you are bells) attests, Neruda's concern here is with the effort involved in—unforced or creative—labor. These same lines can be read in a negative way as well. The deeper, truer substances are turned into practical material objects that mark time. They show signs of our alienation from nature, as evidenced in the last two lines: "de azules proporciones, cemento / pegado al sueño de los seres" (of blue proportions, cement / stuck to human dreams!).

In contrast, what we observe in the following verses is a symptom of forced labor under a capitalist system in crisis (war):

> El polvo se congrega,
> la goma, el lodo, los objetos crecen
> y las paredes se levantan
> como parras de oscura piel humana.
> Allí dentro en blanco, en cobre,
> en fuego, en abandono, los papeles crecían,
> el llanto abominable, las prescripciones
> llevadas en la noche a la farmacia mientras
> alguien con fiebre,
> la seca sien mental, la puerta
> que el hombre ha construido
> para no abrir jamás.
> Todo ha ido y caído
> brutalmente marchito.
> Utensilios heridos, telas
> nocturnas, espuma sucia, orines justamente
> vertidos, mejillas, vidrio, lana,
> alcanfor, círculos de hilo y cuero, todo,
> todo por una rueda vuelto al polvo,
> al desorganizado sueño de los metales,
> todo el perfume, todo lo fascinado,
> todo reunido en nada, todo caído
> para no nacer nunca. (61)

> [The dust gathers,
> the gum, the mud, the objects grow

and walls rise up
like arbors of dark human flesh.
Inside there in white, in copper,
in fire, in abandonment, the papers grew,
the abominable weeping, the prescriptions
taken at night to the drugstore while
someone with a fever,
the dried temple of the mind, the door
that man has built
never to open it.
Everything has gone and fallen
suddenly withered.
Wounded tools, nocturnal
cloths, dirty foam, urine just then
spilt, cheeks, glass, wool,
camphor, circles of thread and leather, all,
all through a wheel returned to dust,
to the disorganized dream of the metals,
all the perfume, all the fascination,
all united in nothing, all fallen
never to be born.]

The first stanza seems to be a description of the barricades set up by the Republican forces to protect Madrid from the Nationalists' assaults (mud and tires being the primary substances used for these walls). But this undertaking would appear to be in vain: the areas of the capital that are off-limits to ground troops ("Allí dentro" [Inside there]) have been bombarded on a daily basis. The destruction carried out by these bombings has wreaked havoc on the physical environment, which is "en fuego, en abandono" (on fire, abandoned). Neruda presents the reaction of the population in a way that corresponds formally and thematically to the urgency and chaos of wartime conditions. We read about a series of seemingly disparate (yet connected) events: "el llanto abominable" (the abominable weeping), "las prescripciones / llevadas" (the prescriptions / taken); "alguien con fiebre" (someone with a fever), "la puerta / que el hombre ha construido / para no abrir jamás" (the door / that man has built / never to open it).

The last two lines—("Todo ha ido y caído / brutalmente marchito" [Everything has gone and fallen / suddenly withered])—are key because they lend themselves to a figurative interpretation. What has been destroyed in this war—in this class conflict—is the congealed labor of the working class. All that has been constructed, and which could have led to a more promising future, has been obstructed by the onslaught of the war engineered by the ruling class. Indeed, after the establishment of a workers' commune in Asturias in 1934, the continuing demands for higher salaries by the unions under the Republic, and the institutionalization of the Agrarian Reform Program (which led to the widespread outright seizure of the lands by the farmers that worked them), the church—which was a target of anarchist vandalism—the landowning bourgeoisie, and the military were determined to alter the course of Republican government. That is, from 1936 to 1939, the traditional bourgeoisie was willing to carry out an open war on the working class and on any forces that supported working people. So, as these verses by Neruda suggest, under the Second Republic those who constructed the society physically and literally saw their labor and their hopes destroyed by the civil war. It is in this vein that Neruda details the chaos caused by the war: "todo por una rueda vuelto al polvo, / al desorganizado sueño de los metales, / todo el perfume, todo lo fascinado, / todo reunido en nada, todo caído / para no nacer nunca" (all by a wheel returned to dust, / to the disorganized dream of the metals, / all the perfume, all the fascination, / all united in nothing, all fallen / never to be born). A sense of that chaos is captured vividly in Ronald Fraser's account of the attempted seige of Madrid—where Neruda was living in 1937.

> Nationalist artillery continued sporadically to shell the city from Mount Garabitas, in the Casa de Campo, although there were no more direct assaults. In the barrio of Argüelles, facing the University city, few houses remained intact. An area so close to the front was also an area in which it was relatively safe to hide. Standing in the doorway of a house, a man watched three children playing behind a cobble barricade in the sand of the street. Only two families lived in the three still habitable houses; one was a chemist whose children he taught, to earn money because, as a leader of the clandestine Falange, private works was safest. As he watched, spent bullets from the University city splattered against the barricade and the walls of the houses. Three mortar shells suddenly exploded over the roofs.[44]

Historian Helen Graham describes the circumstances in a similar way:

> *Madrileños* had already experienced air raids and were fearful of more. If the rebels broke through, would there be atrocities in Madrid like those in the south reported by the refugees? The mood in the city was tense. Nor were such apprehensions limited to the ordinary population. The nerves of those political cadres who had remained to staff the Council [The Madrid Defence Council] were also taut: the government was gone, they were alone with so much to organise and with so few means. Maybe tomorrow they would wake up to the rebels in the city and their own executions? The sense of living on the edge, of there only being two choices in the fight—survival or obliteration—enveloped the November days, hugely increasing the fear of—and animosity towards—the enemy within.[45]

There is at least one other main reading of this poem which emerges having to do with the omnipresent chaos. Significantly, the disorganization that reigns in the social realm closely reflects entropic processes in nature. In

Neruda's view the fascist war on the Spanish Republic has had the effect of retarding the development of history so that the Republicans must deviate from their peace-time, populist political program ("todo el perfume, todo lo fascinado" [all the perfume, all the fascination]) because they are checkmated into war ("sueño de los metales" [dream of the metals]). Rather than benefiting from nature, the Nationalists carry out unwarranted destruction and cause the breakdown of civil society and thus imitate nature's most pernicious side. In essence, they become defenders of Social Darwinism, preying on the worst tendencies in human nature. This represents a human misfortune of great proportions that—to paraphrase Lenin—forces history to take two steps backward for every step forward.

The tragic consequences of the wartime chaos are apparent in the final verses of the poem:

> Sed celeste, palomas
> con cintura de harina: épocas
> de polen y racimo, ved cómo
> la madera se destroza
> hasta llegar al luto: no hay raíces
> para el hombre: todo descansa apenas
> sobre un temblor de lluvia.
> Ved cómo se ha podrido
> la guitarra en la boca de la fragante novia:
> ved cómo las palabras que tanto construyeron,
> ahora son exterminio: mirad sobre la cal y entre el mármol
> deshecho
> la huella—ya con musgos—del sollozo. (61–62)
>
> [Celestial thirst, doves
> with a waist of wheat [sic]:[46] epochs
> of pollen and branch: see how
> the wood is shattered
> until it reaches mourning: there are no roots
> for man: all scarcely rests
> upon a tremor of rain.
> See how the guitar
> has rotted in the mouth of the fragrant bride:
> see how the words that built so much
> now are extermination: upon the lime and among the shattered
> marble, look
> at the trace—now moss-covered—of the sob.]

Spanish society appears as a tree that destroys itself ("la madera se destroza" [the wood is shattered]); the social relations that once held it together are severed ("no hay raíces / para el hombre" [there are no roots / for man]).

In these circumstances, poetry, linked to the musical instrument associated with Spanish music (the guitar), has no place ("Ved cómo se ha podrido / la guitarra en la boca de la fragante novia" [See how the guitar / has rotted in the mouth of the fragrant bride]). Neruda seems to suggest that Spanish civilization and its grand apotheosis in poetry (and music) from the Golden Age through the generation of 1927 are now in ruins and even aid in the destruction of the Spanish Republic ("la fragante novia" [the fragrant bride]). So too with the Spanish language. *Lingua franca* of the empire, but also source for the work of Cervantes and the poets and playwrights during the Golden Age, Spanish is being used to destroy national unity and the positive humanistic achievements of the culture in the name of nationalism.

Given the profoundly tragic ravages of the civil war, the poet's role comes under much greater pressure as he is being thrust into the midst of this war and asked to commit himself fully to the Republican cause. This, in turn, leads him to reflect on and create anew his poetic method. Neruda veers in the direction of critical realism, the insatiable desire to understand and express the historical moment he is living in as tangible a way as possible. So if Neruda declares that in nature and human society forms may appear from the destruction of contents, the flower from the shattered bone in the earth, he emphasizes the same for his poetry (60). It too must be able to express in the mediation of language the sensuous nature that surrounds the poet. Like a laborer the poet must take nature and transform it. In this poem and in his later works, his texts become social labor. Words, like the marble cited above, must be constructed, refined, and polished. Thus, the interruption and negation of socially necessary and valuable labor during the civil war is, mutatis mutandis, the negation of poetry, of creative labor.

Moreover, if the traditional bourgeoisie is carrying out a war against the laboring classes, it follows that the poet is among those working and is subject to the same aggression. That is why the short poems that follow "Canto sobre unas ruinas" (Song Above Some Ruins) are homages to a Republican victory, the unions on the battlefront, the anti-tank troops, and so on. The poet's task as a critical realist can be summed up in Neruda's plea at the end of "Paisaje después de una batalla" (Landscape After a Battle): "agárrenlo mis párpados hasta nombrar y herir, / guarde mi sangre este sabor de sombra / para que no haya olvido" (may my eyelids grasp it until they can name and wound, / may my brow keep this taste of shadow) (64). Via synesthesia Neruda describes his aesthetic and political process: from vision to comprehension (as memory and understanding) to words to wounding (to using words as weapons in the civil war). The poet's obligation is to rescue the events like a historical chronicler yet he is not mechanically and dutifully recording myriad details without assessing them critically and productively. Neruda implies that there is a much deeper comprehension at issue here having to do with specific human beings, geographical locations, and a neo-feudalist economic system. As a partisan transcriber of these wartime incidents, Neruda attempts to painfully document the immoral atrocities committed by the Nationalists. He elects partisanship then over tendency along the lines described by Lukács in his memorable essay: "'tendency' is a demand, an 'ought', an ideal, which the writer counterposes to reality; it is not a tendency of social development itself, which is simply made conscious by the poet (in Marx's sense), but rather a (subjectively devised) commandment, which reality is requested to fulfill."[47] The pervasive moral accusations and indignation in *Tercera residencia* seem to indicate that Neruda falls prey to "tendency" (to his spontaneous responses) and not to "partisanship" (to the hard work involved in depicting—in the mediation of language—the social totality); however, that is only if we isolate these ethical stances from the sociohistorical conditions that give rise to them. Neruda's moral positions are intimately tied to the historical moment and to his own political rationale, and they become more profound as they are synthesized with his comprehension of such issues as social and productive relations under capitalism, the nature of feudalism in Spain, the way class divisions operate, and the importance of defending parlimentary republicanism in the face of fascism. Overall, though, memories of Chile prior to his departure to the Orient and his sojourn in the East never allow him to neglect the role suffering plays in human growth and understanding. Collective misery magnifies terribly our own individual misfortune and pain, yet collectively we can potentially overcome them.

Unwilling Exile

At the end of 1936 Neruda was discharged from his duty as consul in Madrid. He left the Spanish capital and traveled first to Valencia and then to Paris, where he would remain for approximately a year before returning to Chile in October 1937. In Paris he continued to work in solidarity with the Republican cause, founding with César Vallejo an organization called "Grupo Hispanoamericano de ayuda a España" (Latin American Group for Aid to Spain) and organizing a conference entitled, "Los Poetas del Mundo Defienden al Pueblo Español" (Poets of the World Defend the Spanish People). The Chilean publishing house, Ediciones Ercilla, first published "España en el corazón" on November 13, 1937. Three new editions came out in early 1938, and then, in the midst of the Spanish civil war, Republican soldiers printed an edition.[48] There is little doubt then that the last two poems of *España en el corazón*—included in *Tercera residencia*—were written in Chile.[49] Hence, "Madrid 1937" differs from the previous poems in that its orientation is not based on Neruda's eye witness accounts or second-hand reports while in the midst of the war, but rather is anchored in Neruda's previous experiences and the reports he received from friends still living in Spain. This poem, then, is not an immediate response to the sociohistorical situation in Spain, but a conscious interpretation that benefits from a measured distance from the demands of living wartime conditions:

> En esta hora recuerdo a todo y todos
> fibramente, hundidamente en
> las regiones que—sonido y pluma—
> golpeando un poco, existen
> más allá de la tierra, pero en la tierra. Hoy
> comienza un nuevo invierno.
> No hay en esa ciudad,
> en donde está lo que amo,
> no hay pan ni luz: un cristal frío cae
> sobre secos geranios. De noche sueños negros
> abiertos por obuses, como sangrientos bueyes:
> nadie en el alba de las fortificaciones,
> sino un carro quebrado: ya musgo, ya silencio de edades
> en vez de golodrinas en las casas quemadas,
> desangradas, vacías, con puertas hacia el cielo:
> ya comienza el mercado a abrir sus pobres esmeraldas,
> y las naranjas, el pescado,
> cada día atraídos a través de la sangre,
> se ofrecen a las manos de la hermana y la viuda.
> Ciudad de luto, socavada, herida
> rota, golpeada, agujereada, llena
> de sangre y vidrios rotos, ciudad sin noche, toda
> noche y silencio y estampido y héroes,
> ahora un nuevo invierno más desnudo y más solo,
> ahora sin harina, sin pasos, con tu luna
> de soldados.
> A todo, a todos.[50]

> [At this hour I remember everything and everyone,
> vigorously, sunkenly in
> the regions that—sound and feather—
> striking a little, exist
> beyond the earth, but on the earth. Today
> a new winter begins.
> There is in that city,
> where lies what I love,
> there is no bread, no light: a cold windowpane falls
> upon dry geraniums. By night black dreams
> opened by howitzers, like bloody oxen:
> no one in the dawn of the ramparts

but a broken cart: now moss, now silence of ages,
instead of swallows on the burned houses,
drained of blood, empty, their doors open to the sky:
now the market begins to open its poor emeralds,
and the oranges, the fish,
brought each day across the blood,
offer themselves to the hands of the sister and the widow.
City of mourning, undermined, wounded,
broken, beaten, bullet-riddled, covered
with blood and broken glass, city without night, all
night and silence and explosions and heroes,
now a new winter more naked and more alone,
now without flour, without steps, with your moon
of soldiers.
Everything, everyone.][51]

In the act of remembering and based on news probably communicated to him, what clearly comes to Neruda's mind is the terribly tragic damage of the war, particularly from the point of the view of the Republicans, who, as the poet maintains, are victimized at the expense of the Nationalists' zeal for political power. Neruda describes the empty desolation that invades the city, where all forms of life fight for a glimpse of hope. Deprived of public life, always so lively in Madrid, the city appears abandoned ("nadie en el alba" [no one in the dawn]) to lifeless objects ("secos geranios"; "un carro quebrado"; "casas quemadas, desangradas, vacías" [dry geraniums, a broken cart, burned houses, drained of blood, empty]). The days and nights are filled with destruction, with the negation of human life and livelihood, so that hope too is dried up in the infernal conditions of war. Devastated by hunger and dismal hope, the population appears as an impersonal "ciudad" (city).

This despair due to food shortages and the ruin caused by the war resemble actual historical accounts of this year. The transportation of food items from France was precarious to say the least because the Nationalists had taken over roughly one-third of the Spanish-French border by October 1937.[52] The second half of the line also reflects historical accounts: frequent blackouts due to the continuous bombings of Madrid and, by this stage of the war, little hope even among members of the Republican cabinet. By late autumn of 1937, Hugh Thomas notes, "Azaña, Martínez Barrio, Prieto, perhaps all the ministers, except for Negrín and the communists, believed that the republic could now not win the war militarily, but they realized that they could not abandon those millions of Spaniards, who supported the republic, to their fate."[53]

In the line "no hay pan ni luz" (there is no bread, no light), Neruda appears to refer literally to the lights out during blackouts and, figuratively, to hope. In the thick of the war, the *madrileños* can only have black dreams ("sueños negros") constantly interrupted by exploding artillery shells. By this stage of the war, despite the valient attempts to defend the Spanish capital, hope had dimmed considerably. Neruda describes in these verses the emptiness of the city landscape filled with the destructive consequences of the war. As though he were attempting to help defend the city as a bastion of civilization under seige, he personifies it. Yet the balance of the discourse, like that of this historical moment, underlines the ruin to which Madrid (and Spain itself) has been subjected. The Republican soldiers—the "héroes"—figure here surrounded by the dreary landscape: "Ciudad de luto, socavada, herida, / rota, golpeada, agujereada, llena / de sangre y vidrios rotos, ciudad sin noche, toda / noche y silencio y estampido y héroes" (City of mourning, undermined, wounded, / broken, beaten, bullet-ridden, covered / with blood and broken glass, city without night, all / night and silence and explosions and heroes). Neruda replicates the struggle that the Republicans experience by naming disparate elements—the last verse above—reinforced by the polysyndeton, and, by naming the social ills that eat away at the Republic (the negative characteristics after "Ciudad de luto" and the repetition of the preposition "sin").

After this point the tone begins to change gradually as the poet recalls his life in the city and unleashes his verbal fury at the Nationalists. At first he includes himself among Madrid's (Republican) inhabitants and he later distances himself somewhat as he recognizes that he is no longer in the capital. Yet a personified Madrid stands united in its resistance to the Falangist attacks:

> Sol pobre, sangre nuestra
> perdida, corazón terrible
> sacudido y llorando. Lágrimas como pesadas balas
> han caído en tu oscura tierra haciendo sonido
> de palomas que caen, mano que cierra
> la muerte para siempre, sangre de cada día
> y cada noche y cada semana y cada
> mes. Sin hablar de vosotros, héroes dormidos
> y despiertos, sin hablar de vosotros que hacéis temblar el agua
> y la tierra con vuestra voluntad insigne,
> en esta hora escucho el tiempo en una calle,
> alguien me habla, el invierno
> llega de nuevo a los hoteles
> en que he vivido,
> todo es ciudad lo que escucho y distancia
> rodeada por el fuego como por una espuma
> de víboras, asaltada por una
> agua de infierno.
> Hace ya más de un año

que los enmascarados tocan tu humana orilla
y mueren al contacto de tu eléctrica sangre:
sacos de moros, sacos de traidores,
han rodado a tus pies de piedra: ni el humo ni la muerte
han conquistado tus muros ardiendo. (67)

[Poor sun, our lost
blood, terrible heart
shaken and mourned. Tears like heavy bullets
have fallen on your dark earth sounding
like falling doves, a hand that death
closes forever, blood of each day
and each night and each week and each
month. Without speaking of you, heroes asleep
and awake, without speaking of you who make the water
and the earth
tremble with your glorious purpose,
at this hour I listen to the weather on a street,
someone speaks to me, winter
comes again to the hotels
where I have lived,
everything is city that I listen to and distance
surrounded by fire as if by a spume
of vipers assaulted by a
water from hell.
For more than a year now
the masked ones have been touching your human shore
and dying at the contact of your electric blood:
sacks of Moors, sacks of Traitors
have rolled at your feet of stone: neither smoke nor death
have conquered your burning walls.]

The first seven lines present the reader with a series of relatively abstract, symbolic images which need to be deciphered. In this context we encounter a dismembered body ("sangre," "corazón," "mano," "lágrimas" [blood, heart, hand, tears]) representing metaphorically the status of the Republican cause at this historical juncture. The parts of the body are present, but they do not seem to interact or associate with one another. In other words, like the real historical circumstances in Madrid in 1937, which Neruda describes, the form in these verses reflects the schism that has taken place in the content. By employing the passive voice Neruda heightens this sense of disarray as human suffering seems to be omnipresent, impersonal, and senseless. Furthermore, in naming the various physiological features or functions, these nouns are not accompanied—as they should be in the Spanish language—by articles designating possession. There is no room for individual(ist) suffering here; it is, discursively *collective* in nature. The same is true of the historical agent or protagonist, the sun, which makes sense as a metaphor that collaborates with such other images as light, sky, moon (of soldiers), and, most importantly, hope. The aspirations of the Republican cause—which are the vehicle of the poor (thus "pobre" [poor])—have been shaken ("sacudido" [shaken]) by the Nationalists. Once again the speaker identifies himself with the Republican cause in general ("*nuestra* sangre" [our blood]) because Neruda too was threatened by the Nationalists' attack on Madrid, but he distinguishes himself from the soldiers ("*vosotros,* héroes dormidos" [you, heroes asleep]) who actually engaged in a military confrontation with the Nationalists.

What makes these first seven verses rather dense is their disorder and disconnectedness. Logic tells us that bullets ("balas") cause bloodshed ("sangre nuestra perdida"), hence, suffering and mourning ("llorando," "Lágrimas" [crying, tears]). But the syntax here complicates our reading because we confront these confused and overlapping verses as though facing the chaos of emotional despair in a bellicose situation. The form here shapes and distorts content. It requires some energy on the reader's part to reconstruct and make sense of the scene Neruda describes. The structural and discursive disorder mirrors the chaos of war, a chaos that seems to him to be never ending (hence the repetition of temporal clauses).

After line seven, Neruda turns to the "héroes dormidos y despiertos" (heroes asleep and awake) who have defended the Republican cause, whose hardships exceed those of the civilian population. However, these heroic soldiers come off as the very embodiment of courage and strong will. Again, as in the case of the posters dedicated to the Republican effort and in the tradition of the epic, they are somewhat enigmatically unified in their will to defeat fascism. This recalls the fifth verse in the poem, "existen / más allá de la tierra, pero en la tierra" (they exist / beyond the earth, but on the earth). Read from a moral realist perspective, these lines appear to argue that the Republican soldiers' goal is more lofty than the Nationalists' because they are defending the sovereignty of the majority of Spanish citizens and, by extension, of humanity itself.

However, as noted above, Neruda is in Paris at this time living in a cheap hotel. So the lines from "En esta hora . . ." (At this hour) to the end of the section of the poem cited here are almost strictly autobiographical. In the first of these stanzas, the reader moves—without a break—from an account of the civil population's suffering, to the heroic stature of the Republican soldiers, to the poet's frustration at living in urban Paris at a distance from the civil war. Neruda wants to put his senses to work, but he is confined to waiting for news from Spain. Much to his dismay, "todo es ciudad lo que escucho" (everything I listen to is city). No longer living in a Madrid under constant attack by the Nationalists, Neruda changes the point of view. He calls attention to the Moroccan troops' assaults on the Spanish capital

5/NERUDA'S MORAL REALISM IN *ESPAÑA EN EL CORAZÓN*

and refers to Spain (the Republic) in the second person, underlining the distance between the exiled poet and the history he wishes to document. This might explain why the remainder of the poem is more abstract yet still denunciatory:

> Entonces,
> qué hay, entonces? Sí, son los del exterminio,
> son los devoradores: te acechan, ciudad blanca,
> el obispo de turbio testuz, los señoritos
> fecales y feudales, el general en cuya mano
> suenan treinta dineros: están contra tus muros
> un cinturón de lluviosas beatas,
> un escuadrón de embajadores pútridos
> y un triste hipo de perros militares.
> Loor de ti, loor en nube, en rayo,
> en salud, en espadas,
> frente sangrante cuyo hilo de sangre
> reverbera en la piedras malheridas,
> deslizamiento de dulzura dura,
> clara cuna en relámpagos armada,
> material ciudadela, aire de sangre
> del que nacen abejas.
> Hoy tú que vives, Juan,
> hoy tú que miras, Pedro, concibes, duermes, comes:
> hoy en la noche sin luz vigilando sin sueño y sin reposo,
> solos en el cemento, por la tierra cortada,
> desde los enlutados alambres, al Sur, en medio, en torno,
> sin cielo, sin misterio,
> hombre como un collar de cordones defienden
> la ciudad rodeada por las llamas: Madrid endurecida
> por golpe astral, por conmoción del fuego:
> tierra y vigila en el alto silencio
> de la victoria: sacudida
> como una rosa rota: rodeada
> de laurel infinito! (67–68)

> [Then,
> what's happening, then? Yes, they are the exterminators,
> they are the devourers: they spy on you, white city,
> the bishop of turbid scruff, the fecal and feudal
> young masters, the general in whose hand
> jingle thirty coins: against your walls are
> a circle of women, dripping and devout,
> a squadron of putrid ambassadors,
> and a sad vomit of military dogs.
> Praise to you, praise in cloud, in sunray,

in health, in swords,
bleeding front whose thread of blood
echoes on the deeply wounded stones,
a slipping away of harsh sweetness,
bright cradle armed with lightning,
fortress substance, air of blood
from which bees are born.
Today you who live, Juan,
today you who watch, Pedro, who conceive, sleep, eat:
today in the lightless night on guard without sleep
 and without rest,
alone on the cement, across the gashed earth,
from the blackened wire, to the South, in the middle, all around,
without sky, without mystery,
men like a collar of cordons defend
the city surrounded by flames: Madrid hardened
by an astral blow, by the shock of fire:
earth and vigil in the deep silence
of victory: shaken
like a broken rose, surrounded
by infinite laurel.]

The tone in the last three stanzas of "Madrid 1937" reflects the course of the civil war at this moment. While the Republicans carried out successful offensives against Aragón and Teruel in the fall and winter, by October 21, the Nationalists had managed to occupy the remaining Republican territories in the North: Asturias, Cantabria, and the Basque country. By this stage of the war, the Nationalists held approximately 60 percent of the national territory and, in spite of certain setbacks, held the momentum of the war in their hands as well. But the civil war was still far from over.[54]

In describing the brutal conditions in Madrid, and, in the first of the stanzas, portraying the Nationalists unfavorably, Neruda faces a difficult reality—that the Nationalists have gained the upper hand. This is tacitly acknowledged at the beginning of stanza one: "Entonces, / qué hay, entonces?" (Then, / what's happening, then?). The depopulated and ruined capital, like Spain itself Neruda suggests here, is in danger of letting the church, the military, and the neofeudalist bourgeoisie take power definitively.[55] Funded by German and Italian fascists, these institutions are willing to sell Spain to the highest bidder ("el general en cuya mano / suenan treinta dineros" [the general in whose hand / thirty coins jingle]). The tone of this stanza, with its emotional denunciation of the Nationalists, bears witness to the impotence that Neruda feels living in France and not participating directly in the defense of the Republic. The poet is revolted by the prospect of these institutional forces seizing power because they represent the interest of neofeudalist capitalism and an emerging fascism.

Seen from this vantage point, the last two stanzas reaffirm the poet's certainty that the Republican war effort is just. The first stanza, in particular, negotiates its way between a realistic depiction of the defense of Madrid and an epic (and therefore hyperbolic) characterization of the Republican soldiers. The Republicans represent a noble cause, incarnated in light ("rayo," "clara cuna," "relámpago" [sunray, bright cradle, lightning]), which struggles against the destructive tendencies of the Nationalists who appear only indirectly as causal agents. However, it is important to draw upon the discursive role of these terms throughout "España en el corazón" and the historical denotations of these descriptive adjectives. Otherwise, these terms might seem shallow or abstract. In other poems these types of concepts refer to the hope that fascism can be defeated and humankind advanced (with the Spanish Republic in the lead) to achieve a less alienated and thus more fulfilling life. These definitions are fortified in the last lines of the poem by references to the infinite and the stars ("golpe astral" [astral blow]), which allude to the abstract notion of harmony with nature and the universe. In sum, Neruda considers the multi-class Popular Front (the Second Republic) to be beneficial to the great majority of the Spanish population, whereas the Nationalist plan for Spain is conceived as unnatural, stagnating, and protective of the elite—the landholding oligarchies, the monarchy, and the church.

These two stanzas, and "Madrid 1937" taken as a whole, depict a historical dialectic whose ebbs and flows are skillfully sketched out by Neruda, grounding his moral/political stances in a sociohistorical reality. This sociohistorical framework gives more weight and plausibility to Neruda's subjective reactions to the atrocities of war in general, and the illegitimacy and barbarism of the Nationalists in particular. His sense of moral outrage is undergirded and substantiated by the sociohistorical and political events during the civil war. In both its formal and thematic features, this poetic version of history is sobering. Neruda's worldview here is history as tragedy, as the similes at the end of the poem underline succinctly: Madrid and the Republic are like "una rosa rota: rodeada / de laurel infinito!" (a broken rose, surrounded / by infinite laurel).

Conclusion

Although there are definite continuities between "España en el corazón" and the *Residencias* (and the first parts of *Tercera residencia*), the differences are what stand out most starkly. If the speaker's struggle with social and existential alienation is the focal point of the first sections of *Tercera residencia,* there is a clear progression out of that entrapment: the sociohistorical forces bearing down on the protagonist begin to reveal themselves as he becomes more conscious of his unfulfilling life and begins to depict it as he works toward liberating himself from the prison of language and isolation. Long-lasting friendships with leftist intellectuals, the outbreak of the civil war (which almost literally comes to his doorstep), his return to a Spanish-speaking country, and social life in Madrid prior to the war all contribute to erasing the corrosive effects of alienation on him. As a product of this period, "España en el corazón"—included in the 1947 edition of *Tercera residencia*—shows a humble yet indignant Neruda attempting to come to grips with his historical situation. This struggle and his reflections on it are inscribed in his poetry—little material can be salvaged outside of the poems of this period—which becomes more realist in its form and content.

Contrary to the received interpretations by Robin Warner, Alfred J. McAdam, René de Costa, and Enrico Mario Santí of "España en el corazón" and *Tercera residencia* more generally, I have maintained that this moment represents a distinctive and positive transformation in Neruda's political and moral consciousness and poetic method, leading him to attain a more comprehensive understanding of the social forces which formerly appeared hostile to him. If the Neruda of the *Residencias* perceived society, as Lukács puts it in another context, "as [an] incomprehensible, mythical power, whose fatalistic objectivity, devoid of any humanity, threatens the individual," the Neruda in "España en el corazón" is able to transcend that irrationalism, curing himself of alienation and immersing himself in the class struggles of the 1930s in Spain.[56]

The critical work of Alain Sicard, Jaime Concha, and Hernán Loyola argues compellingly that, even though Neruda is encumbered by his disaffection during the *Residencias* and this fact impairs his vision of the social totality, he manages in a remarkable dialectical turn to objectify his alienation in his realist and yet spontaneous portrayal. Indeed, against the canonical interpretations up to 1972 (including his own early interpretations),[57] Concha maintained that there is "Ningún tiempo menos metafísico que el de *Residencia en la tierra*" (no time less metaphysical than the one in *Residence on Earth*).[58] Sicard puts it this way:

> Es como si la reflexión poética sobre el tiempo evidenciara cada vez más la objetividad de la realidad por la que discurre, y como si, más allá de la destrucción temporal, el poeta descubriera en esta objetividad el secreto de una permanencia.[59]
>
> [It is as though his poetic reflections about time made evident ever more the objectivity of the reality through which it flows, and as though, beyond the destruction of time, the poet discovered in that objectivity the secret about permanence.]

Despite the alienation that confounded the poet from 1925–35, Sicard, Concha, and Loyola assert that Neruda was able to furnish a spontaneously developed realist view of his personal circumstances and the social environment that surrounded him.

My analysis in chapters 2 and 3 comes to similar conclusions; however, in chapter 4 and this chapter I have attempted to demonstrate that in *Tercera residencia* realist method and increasing moral and political consciousness become more complex. By "España en el corazón," with the weight of history on his shoulders and the working people's deepest tragedies fresh in his mind, Neruda tests his own feelings against the actual sociohistorical reality that he and millions of Spaniards lived during the war and thereby becomes more class conscious, more aware of the economic, sociohistorical, and political factors. Neruda's principle achievement at this stage is that he begins to understand class struggle as central to the development of history. While this level of awareness both as regards politics and poetic method far exceeds the heights reached in *Residencia en la tierra*, it is a nascent understanding in comparison with the dialectical complexity elaborated in the last section of *Tercera residencia* and, especially, *Canto general*.

6
Blood and Letters: Neruda and Antifascism

ON AUGUST 16, 1940, NERUDA ARRIVED IN MEXICO CITY AS THE Chilean consul and once again immediately stepped into a political environment that was brewing. Although little mention is made of this fact in his memoirs or in Volodia Teitelboim's biography of Neruda, he went to Mexico four days before the assassination of Leon Trotsky. The international conflict between the Popular Front and Nazi Germany (with its advance on Eastern Europe) found its home also on Mexican soil. But the Mexican political scenario both reflected and differed from these international developments. With the progressive Lázaro Cárdenas regime in power, the whole political spectrum shifted to the left. Moreover, the government took some significant symbolic stances, such as allowing the Mexican Communist Party (PCM) to operate freely and openly, and, at the behest of leftist painter Diego Rivera, providing Trotsky with asylum. However, Neruda arrived in Mexico at the tail end of the Cárdenas regime, when the government was backing off on its radical gestures and policies.

The PCM was also undergoing a metamorphosis. Pressures were being brought to bear upon it from the Communist International to take a more steadfast stance against fascist elements and their "collaborators" (among others, the Trotskyists). The PCM's reluctance to cooperate with Soviet plans to eliminate Trotsky and the Comintern's preoccupation with the PCM's uncritical and increasingly ineffectual relations with the government of Lázaro Cárdenas were coming to a head. The party needed to act swiftly and decisively to erase this reputation and avoid losing international support.[1] Domestically the PCM had collaborated with and battled the reigning PRM (Partido Revolucionario Mexicano) (Revolutionary Mexican Party), later to become the PRI.

The development of the "PCM's response to cardenismo involved a strange zigzag between uncompromising hostility toward the regime at the beginning and an uncritical acceptance of its revolutionary credentials after the imposition of the 'Unity at all Cost' slogan in the middle of 1937."[2] It was this oscillation that finally led to a crisis in the leadership and then to decisive and abrupt expulsions of some members in the party leadership in 1940.[3] For a time, these removals weakened the PCM considerably and almost irreparably as it lost a good deal of its membership due to disillusionment or anger. As the party aligned itself more closely with the Soviet Union and the antifascist cause and as it adopted as its own a policy of "National Unity" and began to affirm its patriotic sentiments and convictions, it looked to condemn all the more vigorously the "Trotskyists, chambistas, and dishonest elements."[4]

Neruda stepped right into the political fire. He joined the Committee for Aid to Russia in Times of War (Comité de Ayuda a Rusia en Guerra), was attacked by Nazis, and became friends with the most renowned left-wing writers and painters in Mexico. There were two particular friendships that seemed to have had the most impact on Neruda. On the one hand, he befriended the muralist David Alfaro Siqueiros, Communist Party leader and would-be assassin of Trotsky; and, on the other hand, he became a companion of and then an enemy of the future Nobel Prize-winning poet, Octavio Paz. This comraderie cast Neruda into the very heart of the left-wing political struggle in Mexico. Having already committed himself to the Republican cause in Spain and made close friends with several Communists there—including Delia del Carril, his partner—and having become a fellow traveler and an antifascist, Neruda's associations and friendships followed similar lines in Mexico. Siqueiros had already received recognition as a labor organizer, Communist militant, and muralist. In May 1940, after having returned from the Spanish civil war as part of the International Brigades, he plotted the attack on Trotsky's "military barracks" with other Communist soldiers, which according to Siqueiros's dubious account housed military firepower and posed a threat as a "counter-revolutionary" headquarters.[5]

According to historian Barry Carr, while most of the Mexican Communist Party refrained from attacking Trotsky and was supportive of the Soviet Union, Siqueiros apparently represented a sector of the PCM that believed that Trotsky should not have been given asylum in Mexico. This minority affirmed that Trotsky's stay in Mexico had tarnished the country's name in international, progressive circles, provided a base for "counter-revolutionary" activity right when the fight against fascism needed to take center stage, and challenged the legitimacy of the "Soviet government presided by Stalin."[6] Following in the wake of the "social fascist" period, Siqueiros and other members held that "Socialists and anarchists counted indirectly on the sympathy of the Mexican people in order to attack the Soviet Union."[7] They claimed that a critical view of the Soviet Union and ideological vacillation played into the hands of Nazi Germany, much as the German Social Democratic Party made alliances with the bourgeoisie and even collaborated with the Fascists.[8] In sum, Communists like Siqueiros questioned the sincerity of Cárdenas, the Socialists, and the anarchists.

According to Siqueiros, his serious doubts about Trotsky and Trotskyism were well founded. They began during the Spanish civil war, when there were tensions and military confrontations between the anarchists and POUM (Partido Obrero de Unificación Marxista [The Worker's Party for Marxist Unification]) and the Communist Party. The latter accused the former of having Fascist informers in their midst and, by inciting inner conflict among the Republican forces, tacitly supporting the Fascist cause. The POUM charged the PCE (Partido Comunista Español) (Spanish Communist Party) with abandoning social revolution. Siqueiros believed that Trotsky, from his home-in-exile in Mexico, had instigated a POUM rebellion against the Republican forces which took place in Barcelona in 1937. Young members of POUM and anarchists clashed there with primarily Communist military contingents, leaving tens of hundreds dead on the streets of Barcelona. Siqueiros concluded from this episode that:

> Los anarquistas españoles, en su tremenda confusión teórica, representando el único remanente de importancia que había subsistido en el mundo, después de la derrota teórica del prudonismo por el marxismo, en el campo obrero, estaban dispuestos a impedir la victoria de los comunistas, aunque fuera a costa de la victoria del nazifascismo.[9]

> [In their terrible theoretical confusion, the Spanish anarchists, representing the only important remnant that had subsisted in the world among the working-class after the theoretical defeat of Proudhonism by Marxism, were willing to impede the Communists' victory, even at the cost of Nazi fascism's victory.]

Following Siqueiros's logic, since Trotsky orchestrated the anarchist and POUM uprising, supposedly ordering the confrontation with Republican troops, the Russian revolutionary became an unwitting Nazi collaborator and counter-revolutionary whose stay in Mexico perpetuated these aims. Before attempting to assassinate Trotsky, Siqueiros sought to resolve things through peaceful means—he tried to convince President Lázaro Cárdenas to expel Trotsky from Mexico. Once that failed, Siqueiros and some of his comrades resorted to an armed assault on Trotsky's house. From the very beginning, Siqueiros asserts, they only intended to seize documentation, not spill any blood.

Siqueiros seems to have made an important impression on Neruda. During the Spanish civil war Neruda had already written a letter denouncing POUM as counter-revolutionary and Trotskyist, and he had aligned himself with members of the PCE (Partido Comunista Español [Spanish Communist Party]).[10] So the groundwork was already laid for his friendship with Siqueiros and other Mexican Communists. Indeed, Siqueiros's name comes up several times in Neruda's memoirs and Teitelboim's biography. Neruda befriended Siqueiros in jail, and frequently went out on the town with him since the jailer, because of Siqueiros's fame, often allowed him to go out for the night.[11] Neruda was such a good friend of Siqueiros, that as the

Chilean consul he arranged a visa to get the Mexican painter out of the country and onto Chilean soil. Unsurprisingly, this scandalous or courageous act—depending on one's political persuasions at the time—is mentioned in Neruda's memoirs and in Teitelboim's biography, but the whole Trotsky incident and the political implications surrounding it are left out.

Neruda's brief comments on this episode and on Siqueiros's character are rather strange. Neruda was led to believe that Siqueiros had been put up to the attack on Trotsky's house because at heart he was a "pacifist." Yet, in retelling some anecdotes, Neruda recalls going to a restaurant with David Alfaro and Jesús Siqueiros and seeing an attaché case full of pistols.[12] From this we could conclude that Neruda agreed that Trotsky was inadvertently aiding the Fascist cause or that he simply excused his friend Siqueiros because of his sentimental attachment to him.

Neruda's defense of Siqueiros was alarming to Trotskyists and independent left-wingers like Octavio Paz. Paz was also involved in the Spanish civil war and was influenced by Spanish Communists. However, as time went on during World War II, Paz began to have doubts "no dudas acerca de la justicia de nuestra causa sino de la moralidad de los métodos con los que se pretendía defenderla" (not doubts about whether our cause was just, but about the morality of the methods with which we attempted to defend it). He began to become disillusioned with the PCE's contradictory positions during the civil war:

> mis dudas no me cerraron los ojos ante la terrible grandeza de aquellos días, mezcla de heroísmo y crueldad, ingenuidad y lucidez trágica, obtuso fanatismo y generosidad. Los comunistas fueron el más claro y acabado ejemplo de esa dualidad. Para ellos la fraternidad entre los militantes era el valor supremo, aunque supeditada a la disciplina. Sus batallones y sus milicias eran un modelo de organización y en sus acciones mostraron que sabían unir la decisión más valerosa a la inteligencia táctica. Hicieron de la eficacia su dios—un dios que exigía el sacrificio de cada conciencia.[13]

> [my doubts did not blind me to the terrible grandeur of those days, a mixture of heroism and cruelty, innocence and tragic lucidity, obtuse fanatacism and generosity. The Communists were the clearest and most formidable example of that duality. For them fraternity among militants was of supreme importance, although subordinated to discipline. Its battalions and its militias were a model of organization and in their actions they showed that they knew how to combine the most valuable decision with tactical intelligence. They made efficiency into a god—a god that demanded sacrifice from all conscience.]

Since Paz harbored doubts about communist morality and the sacrifices it required, and since he refused to believe that Trotsky was indirectly collaborating with fascism by not attacking it head-on, he was considered to be a Trotskyist.[14] Paz had sided with the Republicans during the civil war and thought that the "cuestión del día era ganar la guerra y derrotar a los fascistas" (question of the day was to win the war and defeat the fascists), but after his disillusionment with the PCE, he became convinced of Trotskyism's virtues. However, during the civil war Paz disagreed with POUM's almost futile tactical insistence on revolution.[15] Consequently, his position was not unlike André Gide's. Indeed, although Gide had backed the Republican cause initially, his criticism of and disappointment with the Soviet Union in *Retour de l'URSS* led Communists to believe he was a traitor.[16]

Like many fellow travelers and actual party members, Paz had to deal with some controversial and uncomfortable political and moral questions in the party line. In 1939 he was asked to write an editorial with Mexican writer José Revueltas denouncing Trotsky as a Nazi collaborator. Shortly thereafter, the Soviet Union signed a non-aggression pact with Germany since the Allied forces chose to not align themselves with the USSR. Paz believed that the PCM and the Communist parties internationally had worked for a common front against fascism and that their ideal was undermined when the USSR signed the pact with Nazi Germany.[17] This is when Paz broke his ties with the Communists. For protesting the German-Soviet Pact he was admonished by close friends like Neruda and other Communists. When Siqueiros and his group tried to assassinate Trotsky, Paz ended his "doubts and vacillations." "Era imposible continuar colaborando con los estalinistas y sus amigos; al mismo tiempo, ¿qué hacer? Me sentí inerme intelectual y moralmente. Estaba solo. La lesión afectiva no fue menos profunda: tuve que romper con varios amigos queridos" (It was impossible to continue collaborating with the Stalinists and their friends; at the same time, what was one to do? I felt defenseless intellectually and morally. I was alone. The affective wound was no less profound: I had to break with several dear friends).[18]

From the Spanish civil war on, Paz's relationship with the Communists was tenuous. In his memoirs, *Itinerario* (Itinerary), he expresses his ambiguity toward the Communists and the USSR as an "adhesión ferviente y una reserva invencible" (fervent adherence and invincible reservations). In the end his reservations and criticisms accumulated and led Paz to break with the Communists for good. He made his parting official when he became alarmed about the existence of labor camps in the USSR and published an article in the Argentine magazine *Sur*, in 1951, denouncing them. Paz thus placed the blame squarely on Stalin's regime and became aligned with Trotskyism.[19]

It is worth observing that since the opening of the secret Soviet police archives in 1993, much more is known about the labor camps in the Soviet Union. Paz calls them "concentration camps" and ends up equating them with the horrors committed by the Third Reich during World War II. Recent records, however, make that comparison untenable. As Michael Parenti notes:

There was no systematic extermination of inmates, no gas chambers or crematoria to dispose of millions of bodies. Despite harsh conditions, the great majority of gulag inmates survived and eventually returned to society when granted amnesty or when their terms were finished. In any given year, 20 to 40% of the inmates were released, according to archive records.[20]

To be sure, many victims during the great purges included party officials, military officers, former Bolsheviks, managers, and other ostensibly threatening individuals or groups who were put in the labor camps created in the late 1930s. And knowledge of this policy was enough to make Paz break ranks with the communists.

As I show elsewhere, after singling out Stalin's regime for these crimes, Paz held out hope that socialism along the lines advocated by Trotsky would triumph.[21] However he soon became disenchanted with the Left opposition and Trotsky's "seguridad arrogante" (arrogant confidence) with regards to the victory of the non- and anti-Stalinist left and Trotsky's failure to denounce the USRR's "política expansionista" (expansionist policy), which the poet compares with the czarist empire. From there Paz navigated between liberal anti-communism and libertarian anti-capitalism.

Unlike Paz, Neruda sided with Siqueiros and, as a recent party member, was not aware of the purges in the Soviet Union.[22] In the name of antifascism Neruda supported the pact with Nazi Germany on the grounds that Stalin's regime had no choice given France's and England's unwillingness to form an alliance with the USSR. A fellow traveler of the Communists in the early 1940s, Neruda later became a Communist and remained in the party until his death in 1973.

This background on Siqueiros and Paz sheds some light on the cultural and political climate in Mexico at the time of the writing of the last nine poems in *Tercera residencia*. It helps to better understand Neruda's political and moral stance in the early 1940s, as his focus widened from antifascism to an open defense of the Soviet Union as it faced the invasion of the German Wehrmacht. His political declarations became more bold, more forthright, and perhaps for that very reason, his oeuvre and his moral stances became all the more difficult to understand, much less justify, unless we as readers are privy to the general cultural history in Mexico and Chile at the time and the history of World War II.

THE POPULAR FRONT IN CHILE

Prior to his arrival in Mexico, Neruda had worked assiduously for the Popular Front in Chile in 1938. The Popular Front was a center-left coalition consisting of Communist, Socialist, and Radical (members of the Radical

Party) adherents, which held on to political power in Chile from 1938 to 1952. By the elections in 1938 the Radical Party had become an anticapitalist party that believed in the electoral process. Espousing progressive politics enabled the Radicals to attract the bulk of voters to their cause, and, with the help of the Socialists and Communists, they won the election against "reactionaries and fascism."[23] The Popular Front program, notes Julio Faúndez:

> called for several economic and political reforms to modernise the system of production, broaden the size of the national market and achieve a more equitable distribution of income. More specifically, the Programme called for the establishment of a system of national planning, a revision of the tax structure and for the introduction of strict controls on the activities of foreign enterprises. The Programme also made a vague call for agrarian reform by demanding more state aid to medium and small landowners and legislation to improve working conditions among agricultural workers.[24]

As in Mexico, the objective for both Communists and Socialists in Chile was to defeat fascism on the international front while, on the domestic front, fighting for the social wages, benefits, and compensation as well as nationalization of vital national industries through an electoral framework. Revolution having been tabled, Communists worked on national unity, social reforms, and the development of the "bourgeois democratic" state. This tactic would ostensibly attract a greater mass of people and put a progressive government in power at a moment in which fascism was gaining force in Europe and, to a lesser extent, Latin America. Moreover, following Stalin's plan of "socialism in one country," the USSR could be more forthrightly defended in its building of socialism.

As a result, a moderate like the wealthy landowner Pedro Aguirre Cerda was elected on the Popular Front ticket. Neruda worked tirelessly to get Aguirre elected, thinking, as biographer Teitelboim put it, that "si triunfaba el Frente Popular en Chile, se podía ayudar a los republicanos españoles en peligro de muerte" (if the Popular Front triumphed in Chile, Spanish Republicans in danger of being killed could be helped).[25] Indeed, once Aguirre took office Neruda sought governmental help to aid Spanish Republicans seeking asylum in Chile. Upon receiving the aid, Neruda returned to France to organize the venture of loading hundreds of Spanish exiles onto the "Winnipeg," a boat provided by the Spanish Republic's government in exile.[26]

By the time Neruda arrived in Mexico, then, he had strengthened his ties with Popular Front politics and the Chilean Communist Party, and he had labored against the rise of fascism in Chile. (Chilean Nazis, in fact, passed out a flyer in which they denounced Neruda as a Jew paid by "international Judaism" who could not be a Chilean citizen.)[27] Once in Mexico Neruda's politics became more explicitly marxist as he associated himself with Communist Party members, was attacked by Mexican Nazis in Cuernavaca, and was repudiated for his acceptance of the Nazi-Soviet Non-Agression Pact of 1939 by leftists like Octavio Paz.

THE CANTOS TO STALINGRAD

The previous section, then, furnishes some background to the writing of the "Canto a Stalingrado" and "Nuevo canto a Stalingrado" and the remaining five poems at the end of *Tercera residencia*. In this segment we find moral/political positions resembling those Neruda took in Spain. The sense of indignation, desperation, and anger resonate in these verses as well, but the poetic analysis gains in depth as Neruda becomes more radicalized.

In choosing Stalingrad and the defense of the Soviet Union, Neruda deepened his commitment to both antifascism and socialism. We can see a visible progression and continuation of this commitment in the last part of *Tercera residencia*. The Soviet Union becomes the site of another "just war" in which the sides have been clearly delineated. Historian and journalist Alexander Werth captures the sentiments and thoughts that Neruda most likely had of the German invasion of the USSR:

> I never lost the feeling that this was a genuine People's War; first a war waged by a people fighting for their life against terrible odds, and later a war fought by a fundamentally unaggressive people, now raised by anger and determined to demonstrate their own military superiority.[28]

From Neruda's point of view, in this case as in Spain, the issue at hand was a "People's War," and the poet's duty to provide a literary rendering of it. If he was politically committed to left-wing or "progressive" causes and not indulged in self-absorption, he felt an urgency to address the paramount political matters of the day. To concentrate on divergent topics other than the defeat of fascism would be tantamount to avoiding one's duty as a poet. Thus, before Neruda left Mexico in 1943, he accused Mexican poets (among them Octavio Paz) of being concerned only with the cultivation of poetic form.[29] He firmly believed that the moment Germany invaded the USSR all force, strength, and ideas should have been used to support the People's War.

Neruda decided to take his own stance, to put poetry on the line, precisely at the pivotal "politico-psychological turning point" of the war: the attack on Stalingrad.[30] By July 8, the Germans began bragging that the "war in Russia was 'practically' won," so the intensity of the conflict for those living abroad became more acute as uncertainty reigned.[31] The invasion itself, and the Stalingrad attack in particular, heightened nationalistic fervor under the USSR's national leader, Joseph Stalin. During the battle for Moscow, Stalin had remained in the Kremlin, and this fact, according to biographer Issac Deutscher, had a "salutory effect" on Moscovites who "saw in it evidence that the will to victory, personified in Stalin, was unshaken. His presence in the Kremlin at this late hour was indeed a challenge to fate."[32] Russian troops had repulsed the Germans twice in Moscow before the deadly winter set in. Stalin was astute enough to recognize that his own fate and the USSR's destiny were at stake in the city named after him, so he patiently depended upon the wisdom of his generals and studied the war tactics in detail waiting for the moment in which the German troops would overextend themselves in Hitler's eagerness to take Stalingrad.[33]

In his first song to Stalingrad, published in 1942, Neruda, as René de Costa remarks, relies upon the tradition of the Spanish ballad—as he did in *España en el corazón*—to set up the conflict.[34] The poem is populated with references to heroic acts, honor, pride, sorrow, and tenacity. These psychological profiles are met by the moral tone that dominates the poem. Like the Spain poems, this one is filled with indignation, anger, fear, and persuasive appeals to the readership. The audience represents a relatively broad sector since the poem was first read to workers and then made into a poster and plastered on the walls.[35] Neruda clearly attempted to reach not only those who had joined the anti-fascist cause, but also liberals and progressives who had not yet committed themselves politically to the Popular Front. In this regard, this song to Stalingrad differs little from the Spanish civil war poems.

In stanzas four and five Neruda shows the continuity between the political issues of the Spanish civil war and the antifascist movement. Neruda provides the political and ethical transition from the defense of the Spanish Republic during the civil war to anti-fascism (the defense of Russia):

> Y el español recuerda Madrid y dice: hermana,
> resiste, capital de la gloria, resiste:
> del suelo se alza toda la sangre derramada
> de España, y por España se levanta de nuevo,
> y el español pregunta junto al muro
> de los fusilamientos, si Stalingrado vive:
> y hay en la cárcel una cadena de ojos negros
> que horadan las paredes con tu nombre,
> y España se sacude con tu sangre y tus muertos,
> porque tú le tendiste, Stalingrado, el alma
> cuando España paría héroes como los tuyos.[36]
>
> [And the Spaniard remembers Madrid and says: sister,
> resist, capital of glory, resist:

> from the soil rises all the spilt blood
> of Spain, and throughout Spain it is rising again,
> and the Spaniard asks, next to the
> firing-squad wall, if Stalingrad lives:
> and there is in prison a chain of black eyes
> that riddle the walls with your name,
> and Spain shakes herself with your blood and your dead,
> because you, Stalingrad, held out to her your heart
> when Spain was giving birth to heroes like yours.][37]

At first glance Stalingrad might be considered the "capital of glory" because it, like Republican Madrid, is fighting a just war and acting in self-defense. Just as Franco's nationalist war on the Republic violated the interests of the majority of the populace and consequently, international sympathy lay with the Republicans, so the fate of humanity (of the progressive advance of humanity) rests with Stalingrad. In the desperation of the moment, which intensifies as we read on, the poet has Republican Spaniards implore the Russian soldiers in Stalingrad to resist at a time in which ultra-nationalist forces have triumphed on the Iberian peninsula. (The ties that bind the Spanish Republic to socialist Russia are reinforced through the use of the familiar "tú" [you].) The Spanish Republic, and those who spilled their blood for the cause, "arise again" and dry themselves off with Stalingrad's blood and dead. In the poem, as in the real events of World War II, Stalingrad stands as synecdoche for the whole of Russia, with its "heroes" and "glory." However, like their Republican counterparts, the Russian heroes seem to be involved in a tragic and disastrous war; there is no optimistic note about the outcome.

Indeed, Neruda was writing at a time when the Second Front had yet to be formed. By 1942 it appeared that Russia would have to rely on its own fortuitous weather conditions, its superior organizational skills, and its determined and strategic military power to defeat the invading German forces. In stanza six Neruda expresses his sense of desperation and anger due to the failure of the Second Front:

> Hoy ya conoces eso, recia virgen,
> hoy ya conoces, Rusia, la soledad y el frío.
> Cuando miles de obuses tu corazón destrozan,
> cuando los escorpiones con crimen y veneno,
> Stalingrado, acuden a morder tus entrañas,
> Nueva York baila, Londres medita, y yo digo "merde",
> porque mi corazón no puede más y nuestros
> corazones
> no pueden más, no pueden
> en un mundo que deja morir solos sus héroes. (77)

[Today you know that, sturdy virgin,
today you know, Russia, loneliness and cold.
When thousands of howitzers shatter your heart,
when scorpions with crime and venom,
Stalingrad, rush to pierce your heart,
New York dances, London meditates, and I say "merde,"
because my heart can stand no more and our
hearts
can stand no more, cannot live
in a world that lets its heroes die alone.]

Like the Nationalists in *España en el corazón* the Germans are portrayed as animals, as scorpions who spread their "crime and venom" and unite to bite Russia's entrails. The first five lines contrast sharply with the future allies who have not committed themselves yet to the antifascist cause (the United States, England, and, indirectly, France). In New York, symbol of the U.S., people seem oblivious, even festive, as the Germans assault Stalingrad.

Although the question is open to debate, several historians, including Eric Hobsbawm, substantiate Neruda's claim that the U.S. preferred to observe as Nazi Germany and socialist Russia destroyed themselves in war. From the American political and military point of view, argues Hobsbawm, fascism was perhaps a better alternative to possible social revolutions (begun in the 1920s throughout Western Europe) and Bolshevism.[38] The U.S. maintained this position even though Stalin, well after the Nazi-Soviet Pact of 1939 and in the throes of the German invasion, had abandoned the Communist International and its call for proletarian revolution in the hopes of attracting the support of the U.S., France, and England.[39] Stalin's domestic and foreign policies (with potential allies) had a very similar orientation. Domestically, his objective was to unify the country under the banner of patriotism; the war against Germany was to be a "national patriotic war." So fervent was Stalin's desire to unify the nation that he granted freedom of religion, and, consequently, allowed the Russian Orthodox Church to regain its lands and its possessions.[40]

Neruda clearly believes that the vacillations of the potential allies are scandalous and he sides squarely with Russia. We can see this connection as he associates Stalingrad's destroyed "heart" with his own and those of millions of other supporters of Russia ("nuestros corazones" [our hearts]). In this time of crisis Neruda later confronts and appeals to those who would rather not take sides by warning them of the consequences:

Los dejáis solos? Ya vendrán por vosotros!
Los dejáis solos?
Queréis que la vida
huya a la tumba, y la sonrisa de los hombres

6/BLOOD AND LETTERS: NERUDA AND ANTIFASCISM

> sea borrada por la letrina y el calavario?
> Por qué no respondéis? (76–77)

> [You leave them alone? They will come for you!
> You leave them alone?
> Do you want life
> to flee to the tomb, and the smiles of men
> to be erased by cesspools and Calvary?
> Why do you not answer?]

The alarm and furor of these verses match the tone in "Explico algunas cosas" in *España en el corazón*. Neruda warns that if France, England, and the United States do not form an alliance with Russia, then fascism (death) will triumph:

> Queréis más muertos en el frente del Este
> hasta que llenen totalmente el cielo vuestro?
> Pero entonces no os va a quedar sino el infierno.
> El mundo está cansándose de pequeñas hazañas,
> de que en Madagascar los generales
> maten con heroísmo cincuenta y cinco monos
> El mundo está cansado de otoñales reuniones
> presididas aún por un paraguas. (77)

> [Do you want more dead on the Eastern Front
> until they totally fill your sky?
> But then you will have nothing left but hell.
> The world is getting bored with little deeds,
> bored that in Madagascar the generals
> heroically kill fifty-five monkeys.
> The world is bored with autumnal meetings
> still presided over by an umbrella.]

Neruda provides the answer to his own question in stanza seven: The French, Americans, and British do not respond because they are busy with "small feats" and "fall meetings" as Russia is desperately defending its national territory. From this point on the poem's tone begins to change significantly. His initial despair and anger turn to increased resoluteness and conviction:

> Ciudad, Stalingrado, no podemos
> llegar a tus murallas, estamos lejos.
> Somos los mexicanos, somos los araucanos,
> somos los patagones, somos los guaraníes,
> somos los uruguayos, somos los chilenos,

somos millones de hombres.
Ya tenemos por suerte deudos en la familia,
pero aún no llegamos a defenderte, madre.
Ciudad, ciudad de fuego, resiste hasta que un día
lleguemos, indios náufragos, a tocar tus murallas
con un beso de hijos que esperaban llegar.
Stalingrado, aún no hay Segundo Frente,
pero no caerás aunque el hierro y el fuego
te muerdan día y noche.
Aunque mueras, no mueres! (77)

[City, Stalingrad, we cannot
reach your walls, we are far away.
We are the Mexicans, we are the Araucanians,
we are the Patagonians, we are the Guaranis,
we are the Uruguayans, we are the Chileans,
we are millions of men.
We now luckily have relatives in the family,
but we still do not come to defend you, mother.
City, city of fire, resist until one day
we come, shipwrecked Indians, to touch your walls
like a kiss from sons who were eager to arrive.
Stalingrad, there is not yet a Second Front,
but you will not fall, even though iron and fire
pierce you day and night.
Even though you die, you do not die!]

In reaffirming a commitment to antifascism and the defense of Russia, he returns to the idea of a "people's war" and a Popular Front. Latin Americans *en masse* identify with the indigenous past and are ostensibly united in their support for Stalingrad. Neruda's position here parallels the official view promoted almost unilaterally by Communist parties in Latin America. As the home of socialism, the USSR is portrayed as the mother to all other countries and peoples who look to her for inspiration. Political analyst Michael Löwy shows how this organizational structure is set up following the Comintern's two overarching premises: "[que] l'URSS était la patrie du socialisme, dont la défense était un impératif primordial et . . . que la révolution democratico-nationale ouvrirait le chemin vers le but final du mouvement ouvrier: le socialisme" ([that] the USSR was the home of socialism, whose defense was a primordial imperative and . . . that the national-democratic revolution would open the road towards the final goal of the workers' movement: socialism.)[41] The USSR was to be the nucleus around which the Latin American "electrons" would move, as each country developed its own antifascist alliance:

Le tournant mondiale vers le front populaire—c' est-à-dire vers une alliance antifasciste entre des partis communistes, socialistes et bourgeois démocratiques— esquissée dès 1934 va etre officiellement sanctionné par le VIIe Congres des Komintern en juillet 1935. A partir de ce moment chaque parti communiste latino-américain essaie d'appliquer la nouvelle orientation, en chercent les parteniers pour un front populaire local. Dans la plupart des pays du continent, en l'absence de partis sociaux-démocrates, les alliance se feront directement avec des forces bourgeoises, considérés libérales ou nationalistes ou simplement non fascistes.[42]

[The turn worldwide toward the Popular Front—that is, toward an anti-fascist alliance among the Communist, Socialist and bourgeois Democratic parties— sketched out since 1934 will be officially sanctioned by the Comintern's Seventh Congress in July 1935. From that moment on each Latin American Communist Party tries to apply this new orientation, searching for partners for a local Popular Front. In most of the countries in the continent, given the absence of Social Democratic parties, the alliances were made directly with bourgeois forces, considered liberal or nationalists or simply non-fascists.]

Neruda, then, not only reaches out to those who might be sympathetic to the Communist Party's antifascist alliance, but also assumes that there is broad-based support for the cause. In Mexico, the political circumstances would have easily led Neruda to believe that antifascism received widespread popular and even governmental support.[43] Popular Front policy in the 1930s and 1940s gained its greatest political support and was most successful in Brazil, Chile, and Mexico.[44] Consequently, Neruda is expressing a popularly held opinion advocated by the Mexican Communist Party and its program.

While Neruda's poetic language and thematic concerns are very similar to those used in *España en el corazón,* the principal difference between these two periods consists of his insistence on class as the governing social category. In the transition from his genuine and inspired support of the Republic to his more mature comprehension of and participation in antifascist politics, Neruda begins to incorporate his understanding of class politics and the labor theory of value into his texts. This process begins in "Canto a Stalingrado" and reaches a fuller realization in "Alturas de Macchu Picchu" in *Canto general* (1950). I have purposely omitted the first three stanzas of "Canto" from the analysis so far in order to highlight this fundamental issue. We can now turn to the very significant first stanza:

> En la noche un labriego duerme, despierta y hunde
> su mano en las tinieblas preguntando a la aurora:
> alba, sol de mañana, luz del día que viene,
> dime si aún las manos más puras de los hombres

defienden el castillo del honor, dime aurora,
si el acero en tu frente rompe su poderío,
si el hombre está en su sitio, si el trueno está en su sitio,
dime dice el labriego, si no escucha la tierra
cómo cae la sangre de los enrojecidos
héroes, en la grandeza de la noche terrestre,
dime si sobre el árbol todavía está el cielo,
dime si aún la pólvora suena en Stalingrado. (75)

[At night the peasant sleeps, awakes, and sinks
his hand into the darkness asking the dawn:
daybreak, morning sun, light of the coming day,
tell me if the purest hands of men still
defend the castle of honor, tell me, dawn,
if the steel on your brow breaks its might,
if man is in his place, if thunder is in its place,
tell me, says the peasant, if earth does not listen
to how the blood falls from the reddened
heroes in the vastness of earthly night,
tell me if the sky is still above the tree,
tell me if gunpowder still sounds in Stalingrad.]

In "Canto a las madres de los milicianos muertos" (Song for the Mothers of Slain Militiamen) and "Como era España" (What Spain Was Like), from *España en el corazón,* Neruda made reference to the working class and the peasantry but within the broader framework of the united front against Spanish Nationalists. Here the worker is the focal point for the entire poem. The working class's hopes ("aurora") and livelihood depend on the outcome of this war against the invading Germans, just as the fate of the Soviet Union itself rides on the resilience and fortitude of the working class.

Neruda depicts the fortune of the working class and the effects of the war by showing the stark contrast between light and gloomy images. The light of the day, dawn, the morning sun, the Soviets' pure hands, and the sky converge in this stanza around the "castle of honor" (Stalingrad) and the laborers who defend it. However, given the questions the laborer poses to the dawn (to the future, to socialism), it is clear that these are probably not Soviet workers, but rather workers the world over. If that were not the case the worker would not implore the dawn this way: "Dime si aún las manos más puras de los hombres / defienden el castillo de honor" (tell me if the purest hands of men still / defend the castle of honor). The proletariat's destiny as a whole is being played out solemnly in Stalingrad. If the Germans take Stalingrad and the USSR, Neruda reasons, the advances of the working class and socialism will be erased. However, if the dark forces of fascism are defeated, the dawning of a new future for the world's toiling masses awaits.

The light images resurface in the second and third stanzas as well:

> Y el marinero en medio del mar terrible mira
> buscando entre las húmedas constelaciones
> una, la roja estrella de la ciudad ardiente,
> y halla en su corazón esa estrella que quema,
> esa estrella de orgullo quieren tocar sus manos,
> esa estrella de llanto la construyen sus ojos.
> Ciudad, estrella roja, dicen el mar y el hombre,
> ciudad, cierra tus rayos, cierra tus puertas duras,
> cierra, ciudad, tu ilustre laurel ensangrentado,
> y que la noche tiemble con el brillo sombrío
> de tus ojos detrás de un planeta de espadas. (75)
>
> [And the sailor in the midst of the terrible sea looks,
> seeking amid the watery constellations
> one, the red star of the flaming city,
> and he finds in his heart that burning star,
> his hands seek to touch that star of pride,
> his eyes are building that star of tears.
> City, red star, say sea and man,
> city, close your thunderbolts, close your hard doors,
> close, city, your glorious bloodied laurel
> and let night tremble with the dark luster
> of your eyes behind a planet of swords.]

The laborer image evolves into the seamen on the "mar terrible" (the war) in search of the "roja estrella" (red star), the beacon of socialist hope. In this stanza it is more evident that he is not a Soviet seaman, but rather a proletarian in search of class worthiness, pride, and sense of purpose. Neruda seems to suggest here that the seaman's social class and his moral consciousness should lead him to identify with and seek out the red star of the USSR. In the red star the worker finds the guiding light of socialism in part because the future of his class depends on it and because his own objective interests lie with it, but, of equal import, because he is convinced ethically that it is the right cause. This idea is encapsulated in the verse "halla en su corazón esa estrella que quema" (he finds in his heart that burning star). The mariner bequeaths his individual identity and moral consciousness to Stalingrad because the hopes for his class rest with the Soviet city. The mariner then joins the unafflicted sea—formerly polluted by the war—to ask Stalingrad to enclose itself like a castle to defeat the darkness ("y que la noche tiemble con el brillo sombrío / de tus ojos detrás de un planeta de espadas" [and let night tremble with the dark luster / of your eyes behind a planet of swords]).

The concept of a "just war" appears to motivate the verses and the ethical stance in the poem. Personified, the war is conceived of as an unnatural phenomenon that makes the sea "terrible" and unnecessarily spills the blood of the Soviet people. As was the case with the Spanish civil war, the Nazi invasion of the USSR is construed as tragic, as is Stalingrad's defense. The moral weight of these verses falls on the dialectical image of "brillo sombrío" (dark luster), which implies that the innocent people who defend Stalingrad must make use of war (sombrío) to maintain and sustain the socialist future (brillo).

My analysis of "Canto a Stalingrado" differs considerably from the view held by the canonical critics. Rodríguez Monegal, for example, considers that this poem and the rest of the poems at the end of *Tercera residencia* are "de tal acento proselitista que tiende a resonar apenas en el círculo predispuesto de los correligionarios del poeta" (so accented by proselitizing that it tends to resonate barely with a predisposed circle of the poet's fellow converts). Writing in 1966, Rodríguez Monegal states that, seen with the benefit of hindsight, Neruda presents a "deformed and tendentious" view of World War II. He ridicules Neruda's hyperbolic portrayal of the "glorioso pueblo ruso, del glorioso Ejército Rojo, del glorioso José Stalin" (the glorious Russian people, the glorious Red Army, the glorious Joseph Stalin) because he leaves out millions of people who participated in the anti-fascist struggle.[45] In so doing Rodríguez Monegal disregards Neruda's poetic license to focus on whatever aspect he might deem appropriate and central during World War II and he forgets the other poems Neruda dedicates to the anti-fascist cause in *Tercera residencia,* such as "Canto a los ríos de Alemania" (Song to the Rivers of Germany).

More importantly, Neruda is not alone in thinking that the battle of Stalingrad represented a pivotal triumph over Nazi military forces that led to the final defeat of fascism in Germany. In his *Russia at War: 1941–1945* journalist Alexander Werth declares that "for historical and geographical reasons . . . the Russians bore the main brunt of the fighting against Nazi Germany, and . . . it was thanks to this that millions of British and American lives were saved."[46] British historian Eric Hobsbawm puts it this way: "From Stalingrad on everyone knew that the defeat of Germany was only a question of time."[47]

In his commentary on "Canto a Stalingrado" René de Costa first points out the formal aspects of the poem and notes that this ballad has an "elegant simplicity" to it. Costa claims that were it not for the controversy this poem stirred as a poster in Mexico City, it "would perhaps be scarcely remembered." He adds that the "tender lyricism accorded to Stalin's namesake persuaded few and provoked many, and Neruda was forced to leave Mexico."[48] Besides the Mexican Nazis that attacked Neruda, there was some other opposition to his stance in "Canto a Stalingrado." As noted in the beginning of this chapter, Octavio Paz broke with Neruda over the latter's

6/BLOOD AND LETTERS: NERUDA AND ANTIFASCISM

stance on the Soviet Union and Trotsky. Though Paz was a fellow antifascist, he was very critical of the Stalin regime. Consequently, Neruda's poem, as well as his support for David Siqueiros, put him at odds with Paz. However, these were progressive years of the Lázaro Cárdenas regime in Mexico, so the opposition to Neruda's poem generally could not have been terribly strong. A member of the Comité de Ayuda a Rusia en Guerra (The committe on aid to Russia at war), Neruda read the poem first at a union hall in Mexico City. Later it was pasted as a poster on the city streets.[49] Nonetheless, Neruda was not obliged to leave Mexico because of the poem, but rather because he wanted to give Siqueiros—who attempted to assassinate Trotsky—asylum in Chile.

Nuevo canto a Stalingrado

"Nuevo canto a Stalingrado" (A New Song to Stalingrad) differs from the first canto because of the transformation in the poet's method and because of the hopeful developments in Stalingrad. As far as poetic objective is concerned this poem recalls "Explico algunas cosas" (I Explain a Few Things) in *España en el corazón,* where he defends his decision to put his melancholic and "metaphysical" *Residencia en la tierra* verses to rest. However, the immediacy of the political situation—the Madrid bombings in particular and the civil war in general—flooded and directed the course of "Explico" such that, save the first stanza, the poem focuses on Neruda's personal life right before and after the bombings (see chapter 4). By contrast, in "Nuevo canto" he creates a structural tension between his *Residencia en la tierra* poetry and his new poetry, finally negating the former in favor of the latter.

> Yo escribí sobre el tiempo y sobre el agua,
> describí el luto y su metal morado,
> yo escribí sobre el cielo y la manzana,
> ahora escribo sobre Stalingrado.
> Ya la novia guardó con su pañuelo
> el rayo de mi amor enamorado,
> ahora mi corazón está en el suelo,
> en el humo y la luz de Stalingrado.
> Yo toqué con mis manos la camisa
> del crepúsculo azul y derrotado:
> ahora toco el alba de la vida
> naciendo con el sol de Stalingrado.
>
> Yo sé que el viejo joven transitorio
> de pluma, como un cisne encuadernado,
> desencuaderna su dolor notorio

> por mi grito de amor a Stalingrado.
> Yo pongo el alma mía donde quiero.
> Y no me nutro de papel cansado,
> adobado de tinta y de tintero.
> Nací para cantar a Stalingrado.[50]

> [I wrote about the weather and about the water,
> I described mourning and its purple character,
> I wrote about the sky and the apple,
> now I write about Stalingrad.
> The bride already tucked away with her handkerchief
> the thunderbolt of my loving love,
> now my heart is on the ground,
> in the smoke and light of Stalingrad.
> I touched with my hands the shirt
> of the blue and defeated dusk:
> now I touch the dawn of life
> being born with the sun of Stalingrad.
> I know that the old transitory scribbling
> youth, like a leather-bound swan,
> unbinds his proverbial grief
> because of my love cry for Stalingrad.
> I put my heart where I choose.
> I do not feed upon weary paper
> dressed in ink and inkwell.
> I was born to sing to Stalingrad.][51]

Neruda does not disown his previous writing outright, but rather uses it as the force against which he can create his new poetry. The burning love he felt for his loved one—probably a reference to either the women of *Veinte poemas de amor y una canción desesperada* (Twenty Love Poems and One Desperate Song) or Josie Bliss from *Residencia en la tierra*—leaves the individual realm to find its home in collective love. While his feelings and desires diverge from his passion for his loved one, his commitment to Stalingrad clearly represents a sublimation of that love.

Likewise the alienating topics which dominated his *Residencia en la tierra* poetry—the primacy of time, his mourning, pessimism, and pain—have been transformed into a vital cry for Stalingrad and hope for socialism's future. Neruda's evaluation of his former and newly transformed poetry is summed up succinctly and beautifully in the "elderly youth" figure. By his own reckoning, the Neruda of the *Residencias* stage had become prematurely old because he was filled with anguish and pessimism and because his verse was created by a sea of books. Consequently, the poet became an advocate of metapoetry, a *modernista,* a "bound swan."

By issuing his call for politically committed poetry Neruda denounces his alienating circumstances. His previous stance up to and after the Spanish civil war gives way in the fifth stanza as the poet reverses the order of the verses. Whereas in the first four stanzas the poetry to 1936 took precedence structurally, in the fifth stanza he sets a different tone by declaring, "Yo pongo el alma mía donde quiero" (I put my heart where I choose), a line that seems to echo Rubén Darío's own "si hay un alma sincera, ésa es la mía" (If there is a sincere soul, it is mine).[52] As in "Explico algunas cosas," Neruda begins this manifesto-like declaration on the place of the poet and then moves on to the specificity of the Battle of Stalingrad.

In the next four stanzas he shifts the focus from the role of Neruda's poetry until 1936 to the key transformation in the first song to Stalingrad:

>Mi voz estuvo con tus grandes muertos
>contra tus propios muros machacados,
>mi voz sonó como campana y viento
>mirándote morir, Stalingrado.
>Ahora americanos combatientes
>blancos y oscuros como los granados,
>matan en el desierto a la serpiente.
>Ya no estás sola, Stalingrado.
>Francia vuelve a las viejas barricadas
>con pabellón de furia enarbolado
>sobre las lágrimas recién secadas.
>Ya no estás sola, Stalingrado.
>Y los grandes leones de Inglaterra
>volando sobre el mar huracanado
>clavan las garras en la parda tierra.
>Ya no estás sola, Stalingrado. (80)

>[My voice was with your great dead
>smashed to bits against your own walls,
>my voice sounded like bell and wind
>watching you die, Stalingrad.
>Now American fighters
>white and dark as pomegranates
>kill the serpent in the desert.
>You are alone no more, Stalingrad.
>France returns to the old barricades
>with a banner of fury raised
>above freshly dried tears.
>You are alone no more, Stalingrad.
>And the great lions of England
>flying over the stormy sea
>dig their claws into the brown earth.
>You are alone no more, Stalingrad.]

In the first of these stanzas Neruda reasserts his passionate commitment to the USSR as it attempts to repel the invading Nazi military forces. He refers to his public denunciation of that invasion in "Canto a Stalingrado": "Mi voz estuvo" (My voice was there); "mi voz sonó" (my voice sounded). But at the time of writing, the second front had not yet been formed and the USSR's fate appeared sealed. However, the past tense in the first stanza contrasts with the present tense in the following three stanzas, initiated with the invocation "Ahora" (Now). By this stage in the war the allies had joined the fight against fascism yet the second front had not been fully consolidated—nor was it until 1943. (I will return to this point below.) By this juncture the United States had launched its attack on Morocco and Algeria (November 8, 1942): "matan en el desierto a la serpiente" (kill the serpent in the desert). Although half of France was still occupied by the Germans, Neruda makes mention of the "pabellón de furia enarbolado" (banner of fury raised), a reference to the *Résistance*. Britain's "grandes leones" (great lions) which fly over the sea, were brought into the picture, most likely to remember the "1000-Bomber raid" of Germany in April 1942. This information is contrasted with and enhanced by the one-line chorus repeated at the end of these stanzas: "Ya no estás sola, Stalingrado" (You are alone no more, Stalingrad.)

Although the allied forces had joined the Soviet Union in its battle against Nazi Germany, the second front did not manifest itself until 1943. Historians Peter Calvocoressi and Guy Wint state that the "Western European democracies had shunned the USSR because in a number of ways their rulers preferred Hitler to communism"; consequently, it was not until 1943 that the "German armies [were] so mauled by the Russians that the western allies might hope to put their own great armies onto the continent without intolerable losses."[53] By contrast, Stalin had taken drastic measures to ensure the cooperation of the allies, such as discouraging sectarianism, dissolving the Comintern, and encouraging collaboration with all antifascists.[54]

In the tenth and eleventh stanzas the poem moves on chronologically to the beginning of the defeat of Nazi Germany. In these stanzas Neruda uses a familiar technique with the opposite purpose in mind. In *España en el corazón,* and later in *Canto general,* he isolates human body parts and then reunites them in a socially symbolic whole (e.g., the Spanish Republic). In this poetic composition the human body is never recomposed. This technique, together with the use of familiar possessive adjectives (tu, tus, tuyos [your]) and the verbs in the preterite tense, aid in showing the defeat of the Nazis in Stalingrad.

> Hoy bajo tus montañas de escarmiento
> no sólo están los tuyos enterrados:
> temblando está la carne de los muertos
> que tocaron tu frente, Stalingrado.

> Deshechas van las invasoras manos,
> triturados los ojos del soldado,
> están llenos de sangre los zapatos
> que pisaron tu puerta, Stalingrado. (80)

> [Today under your mountains of punishment
> your dead are not buried alone:
> trembling is the flesh of the dead
> who touched your brow, Stalingrad.
> Smashed are the invading hands,
> shattered the soldier's eyes,
> filled with blood are the shoes
> that trampled your door, Stalingrad.]

The anonymity of the dead contrasts sharply with the personification of Stalingrad. As agents of an unpardonable and cruel invasion, the Nazis are not even granted their humanity in the formal and thematic framework. By contrast, the rest of the poem focuses exclusively on a humanized Stalingrad. In this way Neruda objectifies the axis powers and exacts his revenge in his poetic denunciation.

Stanzas twelve through eighteen shift the focus from the effort to drive the Nazis back to the USSR. In this part of the poem Neruda employs a remarkable technique in the remaining stanzas: he distinguishes between intimacy incarnated in the possessive adjectives and the externalized force needed to confront the enemy, illustrated in the definite articles. The possessive adjectives are set off against the enemy forces. Neruda depicts the Soviet Union as a moral and social example for the rest of the world. Thus he speaks of "Tu acero azul de orgullo construido," "tu baluarte de panes divididos," and "tu Patria de martillos y laureles" (Your blue steel built of pride, / your bulwark of shared loaves, / Your fatherland of hammers and laurels). Then he fuses a personified USSR with nature: "el pecho traspasado de la tierra," "la sal profunda que de nuevo traes," "la rama de rojos capitanes," and, significantly, "La esperanza que rompe en los jardines" (the pierced breast / of the earth; The deep salt that you bring again [my translation]; the branch of red captains; The hope that breaks out in gardens) (80–81). Thus, Neruda's moral descriptions depend on his defense of the socialist economic system and of the "just war" that the USSR is fighting against Nazi Germany. Even though Neruda's assertions are historically and economically accurate, he depends on moral appeal to persuade the reader. Considering socialism's validity requires a belief in equality ("the free development of each is the condition for the free development of all" as Marx and Engels put it in *Manifesto of the Communist Party*) and the actual existence of it in the USSR.[55] By invoking the phrase "panes divididos" (shared loaves) Neruda indicates that in 1943 the Soviet Union had achieved a relative equality for all citizens. While that may have been generally true, Neruda decided to overlook some of the social and human costs that that meant to the Soviet population (such as the purges). Given the political situation at the time of writing, convincing readers or listeners of his poem that the USSR was involved in a "just war" would have been a relatively easy moral and political argument to make. After all, many liberals and most radicals felt, as the allied cause makes clear, that the Nazis had violated the Soviet Union's sovereignty by engaging in an imperialist war. Hence, in defending the Soviet Union the allied countries explicitly made it known that the invasion was wrong.

Neruda addresses the issue of sovereignty and of the "just war" by personifying the national territory and associating it directly with nature. So Nazi Germany's invasion of the USSR is perceived as unnatural, whereas Soviet citizens are seen as defending what is naturally theirs. Moreover, Neruda portrays these citizens as one body suffering from the war's ills and beating back the Nazi intruders.

In these same stanzas Neruda returns to the issue of his political and aesthetic commitment. In stanza sixteen the speaker unites nature, Stalingrad, and the writer's role:

> La esperanza que rompe en los jardines
> como la flor del árbol esperado,
> la página grabada de fusiles,
> las letras de la luz, Stalingrado. (81)
>
> [The hope that breaks out in the gardens
> like the flower of the hoped-for tree,
> the page engraved with guns,
> the letters of light, Stalingrad.]

Writing is here bound to the hope that bursts forth with the guns on the battlefield. However, the writers are the soldiers who metaphorically and literally write or make history. So the poem itself implicitly addresses the issue of its own use. It is judged to be inseparable from the struggle against fascism.

To sum up the phases of "Nuevo canto a Stalingrado": Neruda negates his old poetic self and advocates poetry of commitment in the first section; then he describes the optimistic outlook as the allies join the Soviet Union in the antifascist cause in the second section; and in the third section he focuses solely on the USSR's achievements, sorrows, and determination.

In the ensuing section Neruda puts pride and tragedy aside to concentrate once again on revenge. Robbed of its sovereignty—although it certainly did not provoke Nazi Germany into invading its territory—the Soviet Union has been wronged. Indeed, as observed above, Neruda would most likely have agreed with historians who claim that the Soviet Union went out of its way to appease Germany so as to assure the former's security and socioeconomic development. Historian Eric Hobsbawm, for instance, believes that is why the USSR signed the 1939 pact with Nazi Germany. Alexander Werth notes that France's and England's foreign policies followed the road of appeasement with Nazi Germany years before the 1939 pact and that the USSR feared that a united front could be formed against it or that it could perish at the hands of Nazi Germany as England and France looked on.[56] Neruda's two poems on Stalingrad seem to assume that that is the case because they express his feelings of outrage and indignation at the invasion of the USSR. In the first song to Stalingrad he showed less ire toward Germany's forces per se—since that was to be expected—than toward the future allies, who had yet to commit themselves to the antifascist cause. By the time he wrote the second song, the allies had joined the struggle. Therefore, the poem's focus shifts to exacting revenge on the Nazis for their violation of the USSR's (and therefore socialism's) sovereignty.

While it might appear that Neruda is so driven by fury that he has subordinated his analytical faculties to subjective factors, in the two poems to Stalingrad and in the poems in the last part of *Tercera residencia* his moral/political stances find their justification and meaning in the historical circumstances of World War II. They are, in other words, more than subjective impressions, more than "dogma." There is a logic and consistency that we can follow as Neruda stakes out a position against fascism and in defense of the USSR, however controversial the latter position might have been. From Neruda's memoirs we know that he could not believe the revelations about the purges in the Soviet Union; that he tacitly supported Stalin's policies in favor of socialism in one country, and that he actively upheld the goals and achievements of the Popular Front (he himself winning the senatorial elections under the Front's banner in Chile in 1945). However those accounts are not enough to indict Neruda as a "dogmatist" or as a "convert" to Marxism. To claim this, as several critics have, does not explain his complex, contradictory thoughts; it merely allows the reader to come to hasty conclusions about Neruda's Marxism without really delving into it.

In "Vision and Conversion" Enrico Mario Santí argues that the *Tercera residencia* poems are "dramatizations of the reading act itself, as they repeatedly expose the limits of the visionary speaker and his capacity for self-delusion." According to Santí, "the speaker ultimately loses control over the writing project and lapses into the fictions of reification and nostalgia as havens from the experience of time" thus producing a schism in the self.[57] We are thus left with the speaker (Neruda's mask) before and after the "conversion" who was unable to establish a viable link between these two phases and, consequently, failed to write conversion poems "because his penchant for historical immediacy invariably interferes with the attempt to establish an adequate retrospection." To Santí's mind, not enough space is accorded to introspection and retrospection because Neruda focuses only on the Allied victory in Europe. In other words, history invades the poem and takes away its capacity to be a conversion text, that is, to prove that an individual, poetic, and political transformation has taken place convincingly.[58]

Setting aside the question of a loaded term like "conversion," I agree with Santí if he means that once Neruda broke with the *Residencias* stage he entered a transitional moment when he reworked his poetic method and tried to find another poetic voice (the voice of political commitment). In my view Neruda became more conscious of his abilities as a social poet and of sociopolitical issues in poems like "Nuevo canto a Stalingrado," but, as was stressed above, the critical realism and the intuitive dialectic we perceive here does not fully blossom until *Canto general*.

However, the pivotal terms Santí employs place too much of a restriction on his analytical skills. "Conversion" immediately conjures up images of a religious experience that does not fit the Neruda case. To refer to the speaker's "active prophetic voice" in the later poems in *Tercera residencia* versus the "passive predecessor" (in *Residencia en la tierra*), obliges Santí to state that he sees no progress from one phase to the next, no final distancing from the passive predecessor. Although Santí makes reference to a dialectical solution, there is no operating dialectic in his conception of the former and contemporary selves. A dialectical move would imply the survival and growth of the Neruda of the *Residencias* in *Tercera residencia*. The alienated poet would then be negated (and partly affirmed) when he joined the historical forces of the Republican cause in Spain and the antifascist movement in Mexico. Indeed, it is the negated history and alienation in *Residencia en la tierra* that return and allow the poet to become more conscious in *Tercera residencia*.

In his insightful essay, Jaime Alazraki studies "Canto a Stalingrado" according to Jurif Lotman's theory "recodificación interna" (internal recodification), showing how Neruda developed a self-criticism of his worldview in his writing. Thus, he demonstrates that there is a thread of continuity holding Neruda's books together. As his self-criticism evolved it enabled him to craft his dialectical poetic method and make it even more nuanced. Comparing "Nuevo a Stalingrado" with Darío's classic poem "Yo soy aquel" (I am he) and citing from the first five stanzas, Alazraki shows how the speaker, and by extension (mutatis mutandis) Neruda, evokes images from his earlier books and then criticizes them for their limitations. In so doing Neruda "resolvió el problema de presentar y explicar su nueva voz poética no anulando la presencia de la otra voz sino haciéndola ingresar en pareja con su nuevo lenguaje" (resolved the problem of presenting and explaining his new poetic voice not by annihilating his other voice but rather by having it join together with his new language). At first Alazraki sees it as a binary opposition, but later he speaks of "interdependencia" (interdependence) and, shortly thereafter, of Neruda's insistence on his "dialectical rhythm." By analyzing several of Neruda's poems from 1925 to the end of his life, Alazraki shows how a distancing process takes effect toward the young Neruda. By the *Estravagario* (1958) stage, his former self becomes a "caricatura" (comic version); by the three books of odes it has become a parody and it leads to a total break with the young Neruda. Yet, as Alazraki correctly points out, the rejection goes hand in hand with "reconciliación y aceptación" (reconciliation and acceptance), thus fleshing out the dialectic in its mature stage.[59] This view complements my analysis of the Stalingrad poems in particular and the role *Tercera residencia* plays in Neruda's work in general.

From Antifascism to Socialism

The reader would expect Neruda, a fellow traveler of the Communist Party, to take moral and political stances in two of his most ardent political poems in *Tercera residencia*. Yet, one would not necessarily anticipate a poem like "Canto a los ríos de Alemania" (Song to the Rivers of Germany) unless one acknowledges that Neruda's socialist ideas were subtle and complex. From a Marxist point of view, Neruda's distinction between the German people and culture on the one hand and the Third Reich on the other makes perfect sense. He refuses to take German fascism as a representation of the people's political volition and he upholds the heroic examples of anti-fascists fighting in Germany. Granted, the particular position Neruda takes here does not dovetail with traditional Marxist class analysis, but it does not negate it either. In this poem Neruda expresses the stance of the United Front (against fascism) based on the principle of a cross-class alliance against fascism:

> Sobre el Rhin, en la noche, lleva el agua una boca
> y la boca una voz y la voz una lágrima
> y una lágrima corre por todo el Rhin dorado
> donde ya la dulzura de Loreley no vive,
> una lágrima empapa las cepas cenicientas
> para que el vino tenga también sabor de lágrimas.
> Sobre el Rhin, en la noche, lleva el agua una lágrima,
> una voz, una boca que lo llena de sal
> Toda la primavera se ha mojado de llanto
> porque el río la cubre de saladas raíces
> y las lágrimas suben al árbol lentamente
> hasta brillar encima como flores de hielo:

pasa la madre y mira su lágrima en la altura,
pasa el hombre y su largo silencio ha florecido:
y el prisionero desde su martirio conoce
lo que la primavera le dice desde el aire.[60]

[Upon the Rhine, in the night, the water bears a mouth
and the mouth a voice and the voice a tear
and a tear flows all along the golden Rhine
where Lorelei's sweetness no longer lives,
a tear soaks the ashen roots
so that the wine woo may have a taste of tears.
Upon the Rhine, in the night, the water bears a tear,
a voice, a mouth that fills it with salt.
Spring has become all wet with tears
because the river covers it with salty roots
and tears climb the tree slowly
until they shine on top like flowers of ice:
the mother passes and looks at her tear on high,
the man passes and his long silence has blossomed:
and the prisoner from his martyrdom knows
what spring says to him from the air.][61]

The beginning of the poem focuses on the rivers that cross the German national territory like veins carrying the life-blood of the German people who suffer under the Third Reich. As in the case in "Heights of Macchu Picchu" (in *Canto general*), the Rhine river carries its own untold story of the war through the river's mouth and voice ("lleva el agua una boca / y la boca una voz" [the water bears a mouth / the mouth a voice]). Marked by four references to tears in the first stanza alone, this tragic tale has stained the river and the wine growing region. The legendary nymph Lorelei, who served as the muse of the Rhine river, enticing the sailors with her sweetness, is contrasted with the salty "taste of tears" filling the river with the mouth and the voice of this sorrowful song (the "canto").

Neruda then links the tears to crying because the very roots of German culture have been eaten away by salt ("saladas raíces" [salty roots]). The tears then "climb the tree" and shine on top as ice flowers ("flores de hielo" [flowers of ice]), which represent the long silence and paralysis to which German culture has had to submit under the Nazis. In a clear allegory, springtime has been halted by the freezing; all that has flowered is the man's painfully ironic and long silence and the prisoner's martyrdom. And yet, as the next line and the rest of the poem show, the personified spring still has something to say through its rivers and the martyrs who have laid down their lives in the fight against fascism. This latent negation of the negation is found in the next two stanzas:

> El Elba ha recorrido toda tu fría tierra:
> algo quiere decirte su lengua congelada,
> calla bajo los puentes de la ciudad extrema
> y habla en los campos, solo, sin decir su mensaje,
> errante y vacilante como un niño perdido.
> Pero el Oder no tiene transparencia ni canto,
> el Oder lleva sangre que no canta ni brilla,
> sangre secreta llevan sus aguas hacia el norte
> y el Océano espera su sangre cada día:
> el viejo río tiembla su testimonio y corre
> para que no se pierda nuestra sangre en la tierra. (92–93)
>
> [The Elbe has flowed through all your frozen earth:
> its icy tongue tries to tell you something,
> it goes silent under the bridges at the city's edge
> and it talks in the fields, alone, without telling its message,
> wandering and hesitant as a lost child.
> But the Oder has no transparency, no song,
> the Oder bears blood that does not sing or shine,
> secret blood its waters bear toward the north
> and Ocean awaits its blood each day:
> the old river trembles like a new artery,
> it gathers from martyrdom its testimony and flows
> so that our blood will not be lost upon the earth.]

The personified Elbe river has also been silenced though it wishes to talk ("algo quiere decirte con su lengua congelada" [its icy tongue tries to tell you something]). In the open fields it "talks" like the flow of its currents without communicating its message. The Elbe river, then, stands for the sector of the German population that opposes and yet is stunned by the brutality of the Third Reich ("errante y vacilante como un niño perdido" [wandering and hesitant as a lost child]).

In contrast, the Oder river no longer carries a song in its current because this was one of the most ferociously defended areas when Soviet troops invaded Germany in 1945.[62] The Oder, then, becomes an artery carrying blood to the ocean, and yet, though it has no song, it gathers the testimonies of fallen Soviet martyrs so that they are not forgotten. And, in the final verse of the stanza, Neruda invokes the first person possessive adjective ("nuestra" [our]) to show his open solidarity and identification with the German resistance to fascism and with the Russian troops.

The following two stanzas mark a break in the poem. The tree that was emblematic in the second stanza is transformed from the tree of tragedy to the tree of the victorious struggle against the Nazis. Likewise, the rivers no longer carry a "pétalo de frío" (petal of cold) (from the "flowers of ice"); now they transport a "sanguinaria rosa" (bloody rose):

> Ya no llevan los ríos un pétalo de frío
> sino la sanguinaria rosa de los verdugos
> y la ilustre semilla del árbol de mañana:
> árbol extraño, mezcla de látigo y laurel.
> Bajo la tierra el agua de la venganza crece
> y la victoria pone los frutos de su parto
> sobre las viejas venas azules de la tierra,
> para que así se lave junto al agua sangrienta
> el corazón del hombre cuando nazca de nuevo. (93)
>
> [The rivers no longer bear a petal of cold
> but the bloody rose of the hangmen
> and the illustrious seed of the tree of tomorrow:
> a strange tree, mixture of scourge and laurel.
> Beneath the earth the water of vengeance swells
> and victory places the fruits of her labor
> upon the old blue veins of the earth,
> so that thus may be washed next to the bloody water
> the heart of man when he is born anew.]

The bloody rose, the blood shed by the fascists, becomes the point of origin for vengeance and victory. The rose becomes an "ilustre semilla del árbol de mañana"(illustrious seed of the tree of tomorrow); that is, a metaphor for the terrible past that needs to be negated but not forgotten to give way to a just future. As in the case of "España en el corazón," Neruda recognizes the tragedy of the circumstance and feels that it can only be overcome by exacting revenge. So, for instance, the tree is represented dialectically as "látigo y laurel" (whip and laurel). Meanwhile, the fruits of victory are to be placed in the river beds so that they, like human beings themselves, can be purified or absolved.

The following stanza can be seen as the heart of the poem. Using an apostrophe to refer to a free Germany, Neruda cries out for retaliation in a stanza of questions justifying such an act given the atrocities committed by the Nazis:

> Alemania Libre, quién dice
> que no luchas? Tus muertos hablan bajo la tierra.
> Alemania, quién dice que sólo eres la cólera
> del asesino? Y con quién comenzó el asesino?
> No amarraron tus puras manos de piedra un día
> para quemarlas? No levantó el verdugo
> sus primeros incendios
> sobre tu pura frente de música y de frío?
> No rompieron el pétalo más profundo de Europa
> sacándolo con sangre de tu corazón rojo?

Quién es el combatiente que se atreve
a tocar tu linaje de dolores? (93)

[Free Germany, who says
you are not struggling? Your dead speak beneath the earth.
Germany, who says that you are only the assassin's
anger? And with whom did the assassin begin?
Did they not tie your pure hands of stone one day
to burn them? Did the hangman not start
his first fires
upon your pure brow of music and frost?
Did they not crush the deepest petal of Europe
drawing it all bleeding from your red heart?
Who is the fighter who dares
to touch your lineage of sorrows?]

As in "Heights of Macchu Picchu," the buried talk, give testimony and encourage their compatriots to rise up against the fascists. The lines then describe the tortures to which a personified Germany was subjected by the Nazis. The free Germans' purity is contrasted with the assassins' rage as they tie the "pure hands" to burn them, as they burn the "pure forehead" and they rip the red heart (the rose). While Neruda describes graphically here the widespread repression against the German populace as a whole, and specifically against Jews, he also alludes to the open suppression and executions of Communists.

This reference is based on the Nazis' attempt to completely exterminate members of the German Communist Party (the KPD). It is worth exploring this question and a brief history of the KPD in order to better understand the specific German political situation at the time that Neruda was writing.

German Fascism and the Crushing of the KPD

By 1933 the Socialists and the Communists had both gone underground after having suffered mass arrests that had practically eliminated the KPD. Historian Eric D. Weitz sums up the period this way:

> The establishment of the Nazi regime at the end of January 1933 resulted in the immediate and massive repression of German communism. Within weeks the terror exercised by the SA, SS, and regular police rendered any kind of aboveground politics impossible. Individual communists suffered appallingly from the Nazis' systematic application of political violence. By the end of 1933, somewhere between sixty and one hundred thousand communists had been interned by the regime. By 1945, fully half of the three hundred thousand party

members in 1932 had endured Nazi jails and concentration camps. About twenty thousand communists were killed by the Nazis, some under the most brutal circumstances.[63]

To be sure, the Nazis' naked attack on the Communists was to be expected for ideological and practical political reasons. And yet, the National Socialists were able to capitalize on mistakes that the KPD made to first gain power and later crush the Communists.

According to the Comintern, in 1930 the KPD occupied a "foremost place among the Comintern sections of capitalist countries." The report continued: "It is one of the best organized Communist Parties, the largest numerically, with deep roots in the working class, and the leader of the broad masses."[64] With the largest and best-organized Communist Party in Europe Germany was considered a likely place for the beginning of a series of revolutions on the European continent. But several mistakes prevented this from happening and, at least indirectly, contributed to the Nazis taking power in 1933. Dimitrov, the head of the Comintern, in a report to this body after the fact admitted that the KPD had underestimated the danger of fascism. Moreover, ostensibly driven by sectarianism, the party had attacked the Weimar Republic when the "fascists were organizing and arming hundreds of storm-troopers against the working class." However, the KPD's most crucial mistake, which Dimitrov decided to pass over, was the party's sectarianism in accusing the Social Democrats of being "social fascists." Significantly and ironically, the KPD was the only Communist Party in Europe not to form a United Front against fascism.[65] The party only changed the course of its strategies months before Hitler came to power.[66]

But there is another version of these events, which presents a more critical assessment of the role of the Social Democrats. R. Palme Dutt maintains that dating as far back as 1918–19, the Social Democrats sought to "save Germany from Bolshevism," and, consequently, were unwilling to side with the Communists in the fight against fascism.[67] Following the policy of "lesser evil," the Social Democrats collaborated with the bourgeoisie under the Weimar Republic and, in so doing, helped "wipe out the remainder of the social gains of the revolution, in respect to social legislation, hours and wages, which had constituted the main basis of influence of Social Democracy."[68] In 1925, insisting on the pacifist line and their theory of "lesser evil," the Social Democrats threw their support behind the conservative monarchist Hindeberg against Hitler's candidacy and refused to join the Communists in their opposition to both right-wing tendencies. Indeed, they blamed the Communists for lending help to the fascists by running their own candidate, Ernest Thälmann.[69] Thrust from power in 1930, the Social Democrats were even willing to support the Brüning dictatorship that took their place. Dutt comments that:

Had Social Democracy been prepared to join forces with Communism in resisting the Brüning dictatorship and the hunger offensive, there is no question that the heavy capitalist attack need not have weakened the working-class front and played into the hands of Fascism, but would have on the contrary intensified the class struggle and strengthened the working-class front and the widest mobilisation on this basis, leaving no room for Fascism to win a hold.[70]

Following the confusion surrounding the 1939 Soviet-Nazi pact, the KPD remained isolated from the Allied coalition set up in 1941. According to Weitz, the party's general direction did not adjust to the Popular Front stage, but instead advocated no cooperation with bourgeois antifascists and called for a revolution to "topple capitalism and the establishment of the KPD as the vanguard of the working class."[71] Ernst Thälmann, party chairman of the KPD, argued forcefully for this position. Fernando Claudín notes that in this kind of circumstance "to call for the dictatorship of the proletariat, as an immediate issue, meant blocking the road to unity of action by the working class and hurling the middle classes into the arms of Fascism." Indeed, as early as 1930, Trotsky had called for the creation of a united front against fascism precisely to head off any possibility of the middle classes being frightened into allying with the Nazis.[72] But the KPD remained understandably hostile to alliances with the Social Democrats given their past record. The error of the "social fascism" stance even led the party to "participate, alongside the Nazis and the Stahlhelm, in the referendum of 9 August 1931, against the Social Democratic government of Prussia."[73] This, added to the 1939 pact, left the KPD in a very vulnerable situation and open to being crushed by the Nazis.

Antifascism and Socialism

This information about the KPD, then, serves as the backdrop for Neruda's denunciation of the repression against the Communists. Neruda had the advantage of time in reassessing the historical and political events. At the time of writing, 1943, a united front against fascism was unarguably the most dominant position on the left, so Neruda agreed with and represented broadly felt antifascist sentiments. And, as indicated at the beginning of this chapter, Neruda had been attacked publicly on at least two occasions for his openly antifascist and pro-Soviet stances.

In the following stanzas of "Canto a los ríos de Alemania," Neruda begins to represent the resistance to a Germany violated and seized by the Nazis. The poet thus considers the sociopolitical situation dialectically: a free, developing Germany, like the Spanish Republic prior to the civil war, has been subjected to barbarism, yet the forces of freedom and resistance arise from this bleak situation in nature stymied and polluted by the fascists and later nourished by the blood of the antifascist martyrs. Born after the defeat of fascism, the new Germany will not be a return to the Germany of old (capitalist Germany); rather it will be a new socialist society that will build on and supersede the previous system.

In the seventh stanza Neruda addresses Germans as a whole and assumes that they have joined the united front against the fascist "wolves":

> Brigadas
> de alemanes hermanos:
> atravesasteis todo el silencio del mundo
> para poner el ancho pecho junto a nosotros,
> vuestras prisiones eran como un río de noche
> que hacia España llevaban vuestra secreta voz,
> porque ésa era la grave patria que defendimos
> de los hambrientos lobos que os mordían el alma.[74]

> [Brigades
> of German brothers:
> you crossed all the silence of the world
> to put your great heart next to us,
> your prisons were like a night river
> that carried toward Spain your secret voice,
> for that was the noble country that we defended
> from the ravenous wolves that were eating away your soul.][75]

In this poem, as in a plethora of other later poems, Neruda makes a deliberate effort to show the reader the political link that he has made between antifranquismo and antifascism. He thus demonstrates how he became more politically (and class) conscious and how his thought advanced from a progressive defense of the Spanish Republic to embracing socialism. This move, in turn, reminds us that *Tercera residencia*'s objective is to serve as interlaced personal, poetic, and political stages that show Neruda's greater awareness in all three realms as we read this book. He does this by appealing to the German antifascist brigades and including himself ("junto a nosotros" [next to us]) among those who fought against reactionary forces in Spain ("que defendimos de los hambrientos lobos" [that we defended / from the ravenous wolves]). He unites the Spanish and German causes by returning to the river image; in this case, a nocturnal river laden with prisoners and the bodies of the dead which, nonetheless, carries their silent message. Silent because their words pale and lose force before the starkness of reality, as they paradoxically communicate their suffering. Neruda also establishes a link between Spain and Germany by referring to that same pernicious enemy: fascism rearing its head and biting the German citizens' souls ("os mordían el alma" [eating away your soul]).

In the eighth stanza the focus becomes pre-Nazi, humanist culture, the essential voices of the people carrying the river current along:

> La voz de Einstein era una voz de ríos.
> La voz de Heine cantaba como el agua en nosotros.
> La voz de Mendelssohn, de las viejas montañas
> bajaba, a refrescar nuestras secas gargantas. (94)

> [The voice of Einstein was a voice of rivers.
> The voice of Heine sang like water in us.
> The voice of Mendelssohn down from the old mountains
> came to cool our parched throats.]

In this context Einstein, Heine, and Mendelssohn become representatives of universal culture, of the substance of humanity without which "we" cannot live. Likewise, in the next stanza, Thälmann (the secretary general of the KPD)—is described as a "río enterrado" (buried river) who guides the struggle of man and all the other voices of the resistance in an "inmensa catarata fluvial" (immense fluvial waterfall).

The poem approaches its denouement in the ninth stanza, when all the personified rivers are united in Germany as they fight for liberation:

> Todos los ríos hablan de lo que precipitas.
> Sordas venas de sangre tu territorio cruzan
> y el alma encadenada se sacude en tu tierra. (94)

> [All the rivers speak of what you hasten.
> Mute veins of blood cross your domains
> and the chained soul is shaken in your earth.]

The "secret voice" from the seventh stanza and the heroic voices from the subsequent stanzas become rivers that speak of what is "precipitated," which I assume denotes the hastening decline of fascism in Germany. The rivers have transformed themselves into "sordas venas" (mute veins), implying, in a dialectical move, that they carry a message in their current but it is ignored, much as the soul is enchained but shakes the earth. This dialectical relation then gives way to its sublation in the final stanza.

> Libre Alemania, madre de este río secreto
> que desde el hacha brota, desde la cárcel llega
> refrescando los pasos del soldado invisible:
> en la noche, en la niebla se oye tu voz ahogada
> crecer, unirse, hacerse, repartirse y correr
> y cantar con tu voz antigua el viejo canto.
> Un nuevo río corre profundo y poderoso

desde tu torturado corazón, Alemania,
y desde la desdicha sus aguas se levantan.
La voz secreta crece junto a las rojas márgenes
y el hombre sumergido se levanta y camina. (94)

[Free Germany, mother of this secret river
that gushes from the torch, from the prison comes
refreshing steps of the invisible soldier:
in the night, in the fog your muffled voice is heard
growing, uniting, shaping, spreading, flowing
and singing with your ancient voice the old song.
A new river flows deep and powerful
from your tortured heart, Germany,
and from misfortune its waters rise.
The secret voice grows next to the red banks
and the sunken man rises up and walks.][76]

Here Neruda begins with an apostrophe and inverts the order of the adjective and noun to underscore a condition that does not exist in Germany ("Libre Alemania" [Free Germany]) but whose potential to be realized is ever-present. The clandestine resistance to fascism is symbolized by the "río secreto" (secret river) and combines with the "secreta voz" (secret voice) and the "soldado invisible" (invisible soldier) to become the promise to defeat the Nazis ("desde el hacha brota" [from the ax blooms (my translation)]). Although the Nazis had not yet been defeated, Neruda refers realistically to the collective "voz ahogada" (muffled voice) then bellowed throughout the land. An ancient voice sings the old song, presumably of national unity before the rise of the Nazis.

But what, then, could be the reference point for the "nuevo río"(new river)? The answer to that question lies in the last two verses of the poem. Rising concurrently with the "secret voice" are the "rojas márgenes" (red banks), an allusion to the impact of the Soviet troops and Communist partisans on Nazi Germany. By association the "hombre sumergido" (sunken man) appears to be the same one in this stanza whose drowning voice is heard. The submerged man is a symbolic representative of the liberation of Germany ("Libre Alemania") whose freedom implies dismantling the Third Reich with the help of the Red army.

However, what should replace fascism—bourgeois democratic capitalism or socialism? There are at least two major readings here describing the transition from the old to the new. It could be argued that Neruda is advocating a return to bourgeois democracy after the horrors of the Third Reich. In that case the "hombre sumergido" who "se levanta y camina" (rises up and walks) would stand for restoration. However, it could also be maintained that the "hombre sumergido" is oppressed, not only in political terms (Nazi repression), but also in an economic sense. Significantly, he joins hands with the red margins and then he arises and walks. This reading would indicate that he is the German working class who rises up, takes over, and makes its own future. The old bourgeois society, which is esteemed insofar as it created volcanic voices like Einstein, Heine, and Mendelssohn, makes way for the new passage to socialism.

To my knowledge René de Costa is the only critic who has analyzed this poem. He did so because he deems it one of the "more moving war-poems." However, in concert with his judgments about *Tercera residencia* as a whole, he notes that the poem's message is "simple, even simplistic" even though the literary form "is powerful and persuasive." Following Costa's reading, then, Neruda has mastered the form and has reached the reader in a moving way, but the poem's content has been diluted. "Rather than continue to labor toward the perfection of a style so uniquely personal that his phrases literally drip with himself," comments Costa, "as he once said of the first *Residencia,* Neruda now is more concerned that his poetry be effective, that it reach his reader in the most direct way possible."[77] Yet it is still puzzling that Neruda is able to succeed in reaching the reader yet is incapable of truly persuading him. Because if the content is "simple" or "simplistic" it will only convince those who are satisfied with that elementary message. True, the premise of the poem—that Germany can rise up against the fascists and liberate itself—is direct and readily understood. However, as my analysis above indicated, the sociohistorical events connected to this premise and the poem's development of those nodal points in history are complex.

Conclusion

As readers we can observe continuities and discontinuities with the rest of the book. On the one hand, Neruda's political awareness and commitment become more radical and defined; on the other hand, the poet's moral positions in the 1940s resonate with the stances he took during the Spanish civil war. As regards the first issue, Neruda was shaken and moved by the historical moment in which he was living and could not help but express this fundamental transformation in his poetry.

From the moment he began living in Mexico he met key political actors on the left and became embroiled in national and international politics. Given his anarchist leanings as an adolescent and later his rapproachment with the defense of the Republic in Spain it is not surprising that he became even more politically aware during the 1940s, joined the Chilean Communist Party, and ran for the senate under the Party banner in 1945. In Mexico he associated with artists on the left, but was more drawn to Communists such as Siqueiros and was thus persuaded that the formation of the United Front and the defense of the USSR were paramount. Although there are similarities between his political consciousness in Spain during the civil war and the 1940s in Mexico, the difference is significant. While Neruda's position was consonant with the Spanish Communist Party's defense of the Republic, condemnation of economic backwardness, exploitation and its denunciation of Falangist barbarism, in the Mexican context he allied himself closely with the fate of the Soviet Union and, consequently, in his eyes, the destiny of socialism. As I will argue in the conclusion to this book, we can notice a further progression and refinement in his class consciousness in *Canto general* and *Odas elementales*. In those books Neruda stresses history from the point of view of the laborer and the theory of surplus value. His recognition of the importance of these socioeconomic matters and the class struggle as central to the understanding of capitalism and socialism led him to create poetry based on his dialectical realism and anchored in the objectivity of the external world and history. In short, Neruda's poetry strove increasingly toward the approximate comprehension of the totality of reality via the mediation of language.

By contrast, Neruda's moral positions during World War II are virtually the same ones he took during the Spanish civil war, but his understanding of the historical situation make them more intricate. The German assault on the Soviet Union is perceived as an unjust war organized by a government whose intent is to bring about the destruction of civilization. If Nazi Germany triumphs, Neruda believes barbarism will reign supreme and humanity will have retreated to the Middle Ages. Neruda feels that the Third Reich has broken all pacts, all civilized agreements, and has set as its task the conquering of the USSR at any cost. So the Soviets are forced into self-preservation, defending themselves from extinction and, consequently, are fighting a just war. The moral declarations all hinge upon and are rooted in this premise. Anger, fear, and indignation arise because of the inhuman destruction wrought by the Nazis and they lead ultimately to the unification of the Soviet people against the enemy. Once the people have unified in Stalingrad they regain their pride and honor and fight for universal human flourishing because the downfall of the Soviet Union could very well contribute to the spreading of fascism worldwide. In this poetic context pride and honor, for instance, come charged with historical connotations that give them an authority and explanatory potential that may not be immediately obvious to the reader. Neruda's moral affirmations, then, depend on his comprehension of the class wars between the fascists and the progressive and Communist forces in Spain in particular and Europe in general (World War II) and those ethical positions are reinforced and defended by those sociohistorical situations.

Therefore, the last part of *Tercera residencia* transcends both the moral phrases and political observations in "España en el corazón" while sharing clear affinities deriving from the political commonalities between the Spanish civil war and World War II (specifically the German invasion of the Soviet Union). In this section, as in this poetic text as a whole, Neruda's intent is precisely to show how his political consciousness and poetic form developed over a span of twenty years. The different stages are here represented and interlocked with each other to reveal the progression that occurs in these domains, an advancement that continues well into *Canto general* and *Odas elementales*.

Conclusion:
Neruda's Work During the Cold War

IF THERE IS CONTINUITY AND PROGRESS IN NERUDA'S POETIC METHOD AND political/moral consciousness from approximately 1925 to 1945, then these changes must be present in his works after *Tercera residencia* as well. The refinement of Neruda's method, his "guided spontaneity," must stand out in his later poetry in a way that is unmatched in *Residencia en la tierra* and *Tercera residencia*. To Neruda a dialectical realist, Neruda's critical imagination had to have developed in his method and capacity to capture in poetic form the unfolding contradictions in capitalism and the possibilities of superseding them in socialism (and finally, communism). In *Residencia en la tierra* the mimetic representation of the brutal consequences of modernization both in Chile and Asia came about despite the avant-gardist form. In that sense, Neruda's poetry of these years is akin to Oswaldo de Andrade's work in that, as Roberto Schwarz astutely notes, realism remains despite the avant-gardist techniques: "in spite of the mobility of the perspective and the compressed composition, both of which push the poem in a constructivist direction, the poet does not abandon his mimetic gift, something which he possessed to an extraordinary degree."[1] Jaime Concha and Alain Sicard take this stance one step further in arguing that what appear to be chaotic images willfully controlled by Neruda are actually the result of the poet's lack of control of the sociohistorical circumstances in which he is engrossed. Nonetheless, as Concha puts it, in his early poetry up through *Residencia en la tierra,* Neruda attempts to represent that "internalized exteriority" in a nascent dialectic that has its ties to the mature dialectic in works such as *Canto general*.[2] In chapters 3, 4, 5, and 6, I argued along similar lines that Neruda's poetic method advanced from a species of realism, to critical realism, to dialectical realism in *Tercera residencia*. In chapter 2, I analyzed poems from *Canto general* and *Odas elementales* to demonstrate how Neruda's "guided spontaneity" works and to show that it is intimately tied to his greater political and moral understanding of his times. However, to show the steady yet nonlinear development of the poet's method that thesis needs to be corroborated with more evidence in his poetry after *Tercera residencia*.

Canto general (1950) and *Odas elementales* (1954) are two books of poetry that show an elaborate understanding of the dialectic in history, politics, and nature, and, as such, mark a qualitative leap in Neruda's class-consciousness and maturity as a poet. Significantly, the political and historical context during the late 1940s and early 1950s and Neruda's passionate commitment to left-wing politics contribute significantly to his further understanding of Marxism and to the further refinement of his poetic method. After the defeat of the Nazis in Germany at the hands of the Allies, he became an official member of the Chilean Communist Party and won a seat in the senate the very same year after campaigning vigorously for the Popular Front presidential candidate Gabriel González Videla. These are years of intense political activism for Neruda until 1948, when the Chilean Communist Party was outlawed, ironically, by the González Videla government. To appreciate Neruda's specific political dispositions during these years it is worth examining the political and economic factors that gave rise to *Canto general* and *Odas elementales*.

IN THE HEAT OF THE COLD WAR

The post-World War II political and economic climate in Chile changed drastically after the Popular Front political alliance during the war. Although the United States put political and economic pressure on Latin American countries during the war to support the Allies, it was generally too busy fighting fascism in Europe to pursue, as it had in the past, an interventionist policy. Consequently, in Chile the Popular Front was able to create a robust working class and middle class and to establish a successful welfare state. Its left-wing populism triumphed through the electoral system and carried out many social reforms that benefited its broad constituency.[3] Despite these gains and because it considered the Communist Party "antinational, antidemocratic, and insufficiently antifascist," in 1941 the Socialist Party abandoned the Popular Front but remained in the government. The Chilean Socialists backed the United States and argued that "democratic imperialism" was preferable to "totalitarian imperialism." They thus inadvertently laid the groundwork for the Cold War policy that came about at the end of World War II by favoring US capitalism over Soviet socialism.[4]

From 1941 to 1944, sectors of the Chilean Communist Party embraced Earl Browder's ideas—then secretary general of the Communist Party of the United States—that peaceful collaboration between socialism and capitalism could be achieved because they had joined forces during the war to defeat fascism. While Browderism influenced a sector of the PCCh, according to Julio Faúndez, it did not become Party policy.[5] As in the 1930s, the Communist Party in the 1940s considered that a "bourgeois democratic revolution" (a revolutionizing of the means of production) had to be spearheaded by the working class in collaboration with the middle class and the "enlightened" bourgeoisie. This road, the party argued, would lead to a socialist revolution.[6] Given the onslaught of fascism in Europe and the shift in the developed and developing economies toward the war effort, the focus in Europe in general and countries like Chile in particular was on defeating fascism. However, as mentioned above, the PCCh aligned itself more clearly with the Soviet Union, whereas the Socialist Party looked for ties with the United States in its pursuit of a "third path" between socialism and capitalism.

In the aftermath of World War II, the Chilean economy fell into a recession and most emphatically so by 1947. Given the Marshall Plan's focus on rebuilding Europe and the end of exportations to the Old World, the Chilean economy began to falter. The United States made its presence felt like never before with capital influx and loans and, as is its custom, with the pressure it put on Chile to turn its back on the economic gains during the Popular Front (i.e., import substitution, protectionist tariffs, and nationalizations). In the end, the United States generally got what it wanted both economically and politically because the attack on modest, populist economic achievements during the Popular Front led to the demise of that political alliance.[7]

Thus, although Gabriel González Videla, of the Alianza Democrática (Democratic Alliance), became president with the strong support of the Communist Party and the labor movement, he did so with the backing of the Liberal Party as well. Significantly, he had only won a plurality of the vote, which meant that Congress had the right to choose the next president: either González Videla or the Conservative candidate, Eduardo Cruz-Coke, who won thirty percent of the vote. González Videla was chosen, but he owed an immediate political debt to the liberals, so his political and economic agenda swung slowly to the right.[8] The Communists, who had supported González Videla initially, split unofficially into two different camps: the moderates and the militants. However, during the transition from 1945 to 1946 the majority of the party members came out firmly against Browderism's abjuration of class struggle.[9] As the Party became more radical, tensions developed both internally (with liberals and the right-wing) and externally (with Washington). A huge national coal strike in 1947 led by the Communists pushed things over the edge and González Videla dismissed Communists from his cabinet, banned rural unions, and later repressed the coal strike. Despite this move, the United States did not relinquish its pressure on the government. President Truman became increasingly concerned about communism in the hemisphere and sought to apply even more pressure on Chile via economic bribery. Julio Faúndez describes the situation this way: "to secure a complete break between the government and the Communist Party, the United States maintained the informal embargo on credits to Chile, which had been in effect since González took office in November 1946." Furthermore, once González Videla carried out his repression of the coal strike, outlawed *El siglo* (the Communist newspaper), and broke off diplomatic ties with the USSR, Faúndez notes, "the United States supported Chile's application for World Bank loans and supplied an Exim-Bank credit for twenty-three million dollars." For the next year González Videla repressed strikes and cracked down on working class organizations and then, in 1948, predictably outlawed the Communist Party.[10] For the next ten years—1948 to 1958—the Communist Party went underground, including its most renowned poet, Neruda.[11]

During these years Neruda became very active in party politics, was elected to the Senate, and wrote *Canto general*. The more committed he became to left-wing politics, the more his poetic method and aesthetic inclinations changed. Likewise, the more embroiled he became in politics, the more knowledgeable and class-conscious he became and the more convinced that sophisticated realism—what I have called "dialectical realism"— was consonant with his Marxist worldview.

A Question of Method

Chapter 2 outlined Neruda's method of "guided spontaneity" and likened it to dialectical realism. It was also noted that, on the surface, Neruda's commentaries on realism and literature appear to be contradictory: at times it seems as though he is assailing modernism; at others it appears he is taking realism to task. In essence, Neruda objects to realism when it is formulaic, when it sets up pre-established guidelines to follow or it pretends to näively mimic reality. But, as his works after *Residencia en la tierra* demonstrate very well, Neruda depended on realist epistemology and crafted a type of realist poetry from his understanding of geography, geology, oceanography, history, politics, economics, as well as "personal experience, in which time, reality and dreams all play parts."[12] His work, then, is anchored in philosophical realism, or what philosopher Roy Bhaskar calls a "dialecticized transcendental realism and critical naturalism," meaning that dreams and thoughts, as temporary referential detachments, can lead to greater insights into our understanding of objective reality.[13]

In the final analysis, of course, all literature is realist. Epistemologically, as Lukács argues, "realism is not one style among others, it is the basis of literature; all styles (even those seemingly most opposed to realism) originate in it or are significantly related to it."[14] Hence, the personal experiences and dreams to which Neruda refers do not, in principle, contradict realism. Indeed, they might provide the spark of imagination to see beyond the appearance of reality. It seems to me that that is what Neruda means when, in writing to Alfredo Cardona Peña, he associates "revolutionary Romanticism" with realism:

> Debo advertir que si salen muchos nombres propios, así como reseñas de actos importantes e insignificantes, esto se debe a que por una parte he querido dar la sensación de nuestras luchas continentales a través de un romanticismo revolucionario que no está en desacuerdo con el realismo a que aspira a tener el libro.[15]

> [I should forewarn you that if there are many proper names, as well as summaries of insignificant and important events [in *Canto general*], this is due, on the one hand, to my wanting to give the sense of our continental struggles through a revolutionary Romanticism, which is not in disagreement with the realism that the book aspires to have.]

It is likely that Neruda was aware of the aesthetic pronouncements in the 1920s and 1930s by RAPP (Russian Association of Proletarian Writers) regarding the matter of "revolutionary Romanticism" and that he was taking a stance on that debatable position. Indeed, Dmitri Pisarev contrasted "escapist dreams" that led the people astray politically to dreams that "had the effect of a vision, supporting and strengthening morale." Valeri Kirpotin also argued that the artist had the right to idealize certain aspects of reality as long as his work "fulfills the demand for the faithful description of life, of socialist realism."[16] However, as opponents of socialist realism—among them Georg Lukács—were quick to point out, this represented an inconsistency with historical materialism and with the theory of literary realism. According to Lukács, writing three decades later, "revolutionary romanticism" in socialist realism is equivalent to "economic subjectivism" because it "confuses what is subjectively desirable with what is objectively there. It reduces perspective . . . to the level of practical day-to-day exigency. Life is thus robbed of its poetry." In the end, like modernism, revolutionary romanticism tends to eschew literary method and it succumbs to a description of immediacy. Although his argument is more clearly stated in his essays in *Writer and Critic and Other Essays,* in this context Lukács states that "the laws of existence are more complex than thought can easily express, and the realization of these laws a process so involved as to elude prediction." Understandably, Lukács' fear is that this romanticism can lead potentially to idealist conclusions, which have little or nothing to do with the political, economic, and social reality. That is why he turns to Marx's famous remarks in *The Eighteenth Brumaire of Louis Bonaparte* on the importance of a self-criticism in the proletarian revolution "bordering on cruelty." The revolution must always return to this framework if it is not to drift into the seas of idealism.

However, this does not mean Lukács rules out dreaming from literary representation *tout court.* Indeed, he does find a place for dreaming in Lenin's thought:

Lenin's "dreaming" is simply that profound, passionate vision of a future which it is in the power of realistic revolutionary measures to construct. This "dreaming" adds a new dimension to every revolutionary act, however insignificant. But only if that act is based on a correct understanding of objective reality, taking into account the complexity, the "slyness" of reality.[17]

Once again Lukács turns to the question of realist method as the necessary foundation for dreams that reveal their potential in the development of socioeconomic, political, individual factors and class-consciousness. Dreaming, then, as I understand it, would be a mapping of possible futures based on the dialectical analysis of concrete conditions and events.

That explanation comes closest to representing Neruda's aesthetic stance regarding revolutionary romanticism's compatibility with dialectical realism. Consequently, Neruda refuses to accept the status quo politically and economically, although realist appearances might indicate that such injustices are forever part of the human condition. By fervently condemning social injustices in *Canto general* based on a deep, realistic understanding of the sociohistorical and political possibilities and limitations during the 1940s, Neruda cast himself as a "revolutionary Romantic" who called for a radical transformation of socioeconomic and political inequalities under capitalism. As a dialectical and moral realist, Neruda describes those sociopolitical injustices in a realist manner, but he also denounces them and suggests alternatives to those social conditions.

Neruda's dialectical realist method presents the great challenge of expressing the complexity of the socio-historical, political, economic, and psychological realities of Latin America circa 1948 in accessible language. As the poet states on another occasion regarding *Canto general,* "Me propongo ser más sencillo, cada día, en mis nuevos cantos. Me propuse también abarcar nuestra inmensidad americana sin tener la fulguración de los héroes ni pasar por alto los crímenes que nos han ensangrentado" (I set out to be more simple, every day, in my new cantos. I also set out to encompass our American immensity without the flashing of our heroes nor avoiding the crimes which have left us bloody).[18] He develops a more palatable poetic language and dialectical method that depicts critically and fruitfully the existing social totality. As such, as he declares in another context, he fulfills his passionate duty as a chronicler of his times:

El poeta debe ser, parcialmente, el CRONISTA de su época. La crónica no debe ser quintaesencia, ni refinada, ni cultivista. Debe ser pedregosa, polvorienta, lluviosa y cotidiana. Debe tener la huella miserable de los días inútiles y las execraciones y lamentaciones del hombre.[19]

[Poets should be, partially, the CHRONICLERS of their times. The chronicles should not be quintessence, nor refined, nor elitist. They must be stony, dusty, rainy and quotidian. They should have the miserable imprints of the useless days and the abhorrence and the laments of man.]

As a chronicler the poet is a participant/observer who not only describes the very immediacy of what he is observing, but also the deeper undercurrent of unified yet contradictory sociohistorical, political, and individual events. Neruda's direct participation in the antifascist movement and the political campaign in the saltpeter mines in northern Chile or his empathy with the Incan laborers when he visited Macchu Picchu gave him the ardor and commitment to be a chronicler of his times. That passionate commitment is evident, for instance, when he remarks that in Machu Picchu "Sentí que mis propias manos habían trabajado allí en alguna etapa lejana, cavando surcos, alisando peñascos" (I felt that my own hands had worked there at some distant stage, digging furrows, smoothing boulders).[20] It is that inner drive and his identification with the working man that pushed him to investigate reality further.

But the most enthusiastic commitment, in and of itself, cannot compensate for the extraordinary ability to *understand* the dynamics of social and natural forces and the dramatic conflicts within the individual and between his fellow human beings and himself, and, more importantly, to then *portray* these issues accurately in the medium of a particular genre. Many writers are committed to narrating these matters in their work, but few have the *vision* and the *method* to do so. A great poet, like Neruda, is dedicated to the betterment of humanity when he participates in the class struggle and gains in his concrete perception of the social world as he does so. What makes his work classical is his tremendous talent for seeing the dialectical interplay and unity of the dehumanization of social relations under capitalism and the degradation and exploitation caused by the drive for profit. Neruda perceives the manner in which this seemingly insurmountable alienation can be overcome through close and painstaking analysis and the transformation of the social reality. That is what Neruda achieves by the time he writes *Canto general* and he refines that poetic method even more in *Odas elementales*.

Three Poems with Guided Spontaneity

As noted in chapter 1, several critics have taken *Canto general* to task for its "simplistic" or "black and white" version of history and thus asserted that Neruda's worldview is manichean.[21] In the following analysis of "La cabeza en el palo" (Head on a Spear) and "Homenaje a Balboa" (Homage to Balboa), I do not want to suggest, of course, that Neruda's method in *Canto general* is beyond reproach. These poems, together with "Alturas de Machu Picchu" and "El oro" are representative of *Canto general,* but, it should be noted, Neruda's dialectical realism cannot be appreciated equally throughout the book. Inevitably, there are inspiring poems more profound in their grasp of the place of the individual in the grid of the sociohistorical and political events, as there are poems which insufficiently describe these same events or which fail to provide richness in detail. In the main, though, *Canto general* is chock full of all-encompassing portraits of the geography, history, class politics, human dramas, and everyday tragedies.

Taken together "Head on a Spear" and "Homage to Balboa" provide a moving tragic and dialectical portrayal of Balboa the individual and a categorical statement regarding Neruda's analysis of the conquest. The conquistador is depicted as an individual corrupted by the brutal dehumanization of Spain's mission in the continent even though he demonstrated genuine curiosity and intelligence.

Neruda begins "La cabeza en el palo" by focusing on the ferocious alienation that drove Balboa to murder and enslave the Native Americans in Darien and in the South Sea:

> Balboa, muerte y garra
> llevaste a los rincones de la dulce
> tierra central, y entre los perros
> cazadores, el tuyo era tu alma:
> Leoncico de belfo sangriento
> recogió al esclavo que huía,
> hundió colmillos españoles
> en las gargantas palpitantes,
> y de las uñas de los perros
> salía la carne del martirio
> y la alhaja caía en la bolsa.[22]

> [Balboa, you brought death and claw
> to the corners of the sweet central land,
> and among the manhunting dogs,
> yours was your soul:
> bloody thick-lipped little Leo
> brought to bay the fleeing slave,
> sank Spanish fangs
> into the pulsating throats,
> and from the dogs' claws
> the flesh went off to martyrdom,
> and the treasure fell into the purse.][23]

Neruda associates Balboa with his constant companion, his dog Leoncico, who helped the conquistador track down and kill fleeing slaves and secure gold for his master. Balboa has become so dehumanized that his heart has become like a manhunting dog and has governed his actions with irrational impunity. Like a starved hound that finally smells food, Balboa hunts down Native Americans in search of treasures to rob:

Malditos sean perro y hombre,
el aullido infame en la selva
original, el acechante
paso del hierro y del bandido.
Maldito sea la espinosa
corona de la zarza agreste
que no saltó como un erizo
a defender la cuna invadida. (54)

[Accursed dog and man,
the infamous howl in the primal
jungle, the prowling
step of iron and bandit.
Accursed the thorny
crown of wild brambles
that didn't bristle like a sea urchin
to defend the invaded homeland.]

Dog and man are now one being living out the most lowly type of existence. They let out a "howl" and they have a "prowling" step as they hunt down ("iron") things to steal ("bandit").

This portrait of Balboa is in keeping with historical accounts of his exploits. According to historian J. H. Parry, once he founded the city of Darien, Balboa "achieved ascendancy over the Indians of the isthmus by a combination of force, terror, conciliation and diplomacy; he collected from them great quantities of food and gold."[24] Historian F. A. Kirkpatrick cites from a letter Balboa wrote to the king in 1513 bragging about the enormous amount of "marvellous riches" that could be found in the region and adding that there was so much "gold and wealth with which great part of the world can be conquered."[25] Moreover, although Balboa was conciliatory with tribes he encountered on his way to the South Sea, he did hunt down runaway slaves and demand that cannibals be burnt at the stake. It is for that reason that Neruda begins by likening Balboa's heart to a manhunting dog. Eventually, though, Balboa was stopped by his fellow conquistadors' equal or greater lust for power and wealth:

Pero entre los capitanes
sanguinarios se alzó en la sombra
la justicia de los puñales,
la acerba rama de la envidia.
Y al regreso estaba en medio
de tu camino el apellido
de Pedrarias como una soga.
Te juzgaron entre ladridos
de perros matadores de indios.

> Ahora que mueres, oyes
> el silencio puro, partido
> por tus lebreles azuzados?
> Ahora que mueres en las manos
> de los torvos adelantados,
> sientes el aroma dorado
> del dulce reino destruido? (54)

> [But among the bloodthirsty
> captains, the justice of daggers,
> the bitter branch of envy
> rose out of the shadows.
> And when you returned, the name
> of Pedrarias stood in the middle
> of your road like a noose.
> You were tried amid the barks
> of Indian-killing dogs.
> Now, as you die, do you hear
> the pure silence, shattered
> by your incited greyhounds?
> Now, as you die at the hands
> of the fierce captains-general,
> do you smell the golden aroma
> of the sweet ravaged kingdom?]

Undoubtedly, envy was the factor that drove Pedrarias. Nicknamed "furor domini," he was the governor of Darien and, incredibly, Balboa's father-in-law. Pedrarias had a then little known but perhaps more alienated Francisco Pizarro arrest Balboa, and then had him executed. As a conquistador who felt slighted by the Spanish Crown and in competition with his own father-in-law, Balboa certainly adhered to the same "justice of daggers" that finally did him in.[26] Like starved and mistreated dogs, the "bloodthirsty captains" turned on each other in their despairing estrangement. With an ironic note, Neruda seems to say that Balboa was tried by Pizarro before he even reached Darien (he was tried "amid the barks of Indian-killing dogs"). His fate was sealed by trumped up charges of treason before he set foot in the city he helped found.

In the penultimate stanza, Neruda appears to ask himself if at the moment of his execution, as his terrible feats echoed in his ears, Balboa realized the horror of what he had done. Did Balboa become aware of his own destructiveness? Did he perceive himself as something other than a man-hunting dog? According to the last stanza, the answer is negative:

> Cuando cortaron la cabeza
> de Balboa, quedó ensartada

> en un palo. Sus ojos muertos
> descompusieron su relámpago
> y descendieron por la lanza
> en un goterón de inmundicia
> que desapareció en la tierra. (54–55)

> [When they cut off Balboa's
> head, it was left impaled
> on a spear. His lifeless eyes
> released their lightning
> and ran down the shaft
> in a great drop of filth
> that vanished into the earth.]

In the end, no redemption is at hand for Balboa, who did not have slightest awareness that he had become entrapped in his own tragedy.

In "Homage to Balboa" Neruda shows similarly how Balboa's virtues were corrupted by the social environment and by the conquistador's "arrogant aurora." He became alienated because of the pressures of the social conditions, but, as Neruda sees it, Balboa refused to confront and prevail over his own disaffection:

> Descubridor, el ancho mar, mi espuma,
> latitud de la luna, imperio del agua,
> después de siglos te habla por boca mía.
> Tu plenitud llegó antes de la muerte.
> Elevaste hasta el cielo la fatiga,
> y de la dura noche de los árboles
> te condujo el sudor hasta la orilla
> de la suma del mar, del gran océano.
> En tu mirada se hizo el matrimonio
> de la luz extendida y del pequeño
> corazón del hombre, se llenó una copa
> antes no levantada, una semilla
> de relámpagos llegó contigo
> y un trueno torrencial llenó la tierra.
> Balboa, capitán, qué diminuta
> tu mano en la visera, misterioso
> muñeco de la sal descubridora,
> novio de la oceánica dulzura,
> hijo del nuevo útero del mundo. (55)

> [Discoverer, centuries later, the vast sea—
> my foam, lunar latitude, empire of the water—
> speaks to you through my mouth.
> Your plenitude came before your death.

> You raised fatigue to the sky,
> and from the trees' hard night
> toil led you to the sum
> of the seashore, the great ocean.
> In your gaze the marriage of diffused
> light and the little heart of man
> was consummated, a chalice never
> raised before was filled,
> a seed
> of lightning bolts accompanied you,
> and a torrential thunder filled the earth.
> Balboa, captain—how diminutive
> your hand on your visor—mysterious
> marionette of the discovering salt,
> groom of the oceanic sweetness,
> son of the world's new uterus.][27]

In this first stanza Neruda extols Balboa's human virtues. He considers Balboa to be a man of the Renaissance because of the insatiable curiosity and determination that led him to find the Pacific Ocean. From this vantage point, Balboa represents the best side of humanity: he sees inspiration and hope in the "heart of man" (in contrast to his own manhunting heart in the previous poem). Neruda depicts the conquistador as the "child of the world's new uterus," as a pioneer of a new epoch that could have struggled for the dawning of a different Latin American civilization, not the one that triumphed. This is the Balboa who deserves the homage Neruda pays him; the individual who, like the poet, ceaselessly sought out the mysteries of the natural world and who did not do so out of avarice, but out of burning curiosity and a concern for the common good.

This portrayal of Balboa also mirrors historical accounts on the conquistador and the early sixteenth century. Kirkpatrick describes Balboa as a "man of about thirty-five years, tall, well-built, strong, intelligent, impatient of repose and idleness, strong in the endurance of fatigue and labor. His energy, capacity and local knowledge ... brought him to the front."[28] But like Kirkpatrick, Neruda also underlines the tragic descent of Balboa, who then let himself be overtaken, possessed by his own inflated self-worth and turned against the enlightened side of his personality:

> Por tus ojos entró como un galope
> de azahares el olor oscuro
> de la robada majestad marina,
> cayó en tu sangre una aurora arrogante
> hasta poblarte el alma, poseído!
> Cuando volviste a las hurañas tierras,
> sonámbulo del mar, capitán verde

eras un muerto que esperaba
la tierra para recibir tus huesos.
Novio mortal, la traición cumplía.
No en balde por la historia
entraba el crimen pisoteando, el halcón devoraba
su nido, y se reunían las serpientes
atacándose con lenguas de oro.
Entraste en el crepúsculo frenético
y los pasos perdidos que llevabas,
aún empapado por las profundidades,
vestido de fulgor y desposado
por la mayor espuma, te traían
a las orillas de otro mar: la muerte. (55–56)

[The obscure odor of the ravished
marine mystery entered your eyes
like galloping orange blossoms,
an arrogant aurora fell into your blood
until it filled your soul, possessed man!
When you returned to the taciturn lands,
sleepwalker of the sea, green captain,
The earth awaited your corpse,
eager to embrace your bones.
Mortal bridegroom, betrayal was requited.
Not in vain throughout history
crime has trampled in, the falcon has devoured
its nest, and the serpents have assembled,
striking one another with tongues of gold.
You entered the frenetic twilight
and the lost steps that you took,
still drenched by the depths,
dressed in splendor and wed
by the greatest foam, brought you
to the shores of another sea: death.]

Neither a medieval nor a renaissance man, Balboa wanted to possess the beauty of the sea that enveloped him; he wanted to seize its majestic wonders ("marine majesty") for the Spanish majesty and for his own gluttonous satisfaction. Profit from the commodification of nature, Neruda seems to say, became his primary concern. By commodifying the natural elements Balboa became more alienated from them, and by seeking personal gain at the expense of the indigenous people and even of other conquistadors, he grew alienated from his fellow human beings and himself. The "bridegroom" who, in the first stanza, had in his look the "marriage of diffused / light and the little heart of man," and who was associated with the "oceanic sweetness," later betrayed his betrothed (nature), the indigenous people and even his fellow conquistadors ("the servants have gathered, / striking one another with tongues of gold").

In the last stanza Neruda sums up the resolution of this interpenetration of opposites wonderfully. While Balboa is driven frenetically like a possessed man by his individualism which carries him uncontrollably ("lost steps") to his death ("twilight"), he is still married to enlightened progress and the common good ("still drenched by the depths, / dressed in splendor and wed / by the greatest foam"). Wed to the sea, his treason now carries him to the "shores of another sea: death." A type of Faustian figure, Balboa embodies both "civilization" and barbarism. On the one hand, he furnishes creativity and adventurous inquisitiveness; on the other hand, he displays the self-absorption, greed, and inhuman cruelty that figure prominently as features of nascent capitalism and its imperial mission. Neruda describes Balboa as a unique and conflictive individual who is, simultaneously, a representative of his social class and his time. As Mariano Picón Salas argues, the conquistadors are neither "hombres de la Edad Media—como tan frecuentemente se ha dicho—ni son enteramente del Renacimiento. Son hombres de la frontera, que ejemplarizan para España el paso de una a otra edad histórica" (men of the Middle Ages—as it has been so frequently affirmed—nor are they entirely of the Renaissance. They are men on the edge, who exemplify for Spain the transition from one historical period to another).[29]

Neruda's homage to Balboa then has all the makings of a classic tragedy, in which he depicts Balboa's individual vicissitudes and the sociohistorical conditions which impinged upon him and which, to some degree, he helped to shape. Historian Arthur Helps maintains that we can envision Balboa "growing more and more indifferent to the destruction of life—the life of animals, of his adversaries, of his companions, even his own—retaining the adroitness and sagacity of man and becoming fell, reckless, and rapacious as the fiercest brute of the forest."[30] Having lived through a situation that was somewhat analogous, having suffered from alienation in Asia, Neruda does not allow Balboa to escape responsibility for his actions. For Neruda, Balboa is both a man of his conflictive epoch and a unique individual who, unlike Bartolomé de las Casas, becomes a willing instrument of the Spanish Conquest. However, since Neruda takes so much care to describe concretely the salient merits and the contradictory and finally destructive characteristics of Balboa, this conquistador is cast as a representative of the conquest, but he is not a superficial allegory for it.

Canto general is full of dialectical portraits of history that, in their approximation to the sociohistorical and moral issues of that period and later epochs, give the reader multiple vantage points to understand meaningfully the conquest as tragedy. "Duerme un soldado" (A Soldier Sleeps), poem "XXIV" (about Magellan), "A pesar de la ira" (XXV) (Despite the Fury),

"Ercilla," "Fray Bartolomé de Las Casas" (Brother Bartolomé de Las Casas), are some of the other poems which succeed in portraying the complexity and calamity of the conquest. There are, as well, numerous penetrating poetic renderings of Latin America from the Incas to 1949, among them his masterful poems,"Heights of Macchu Picchu" and "Que despierte el leñador" (Let the Woodcutter Awaken). The two poems examined here are typical of Neruda's finest depictions in *Canto general* and they show his poetic method at its best.

ODAS ELEMENTALES AND THE COLD WAR

The development and enhancement of Neruda's poetic method can be appreciated from a different yet compatible angle several years later with the publication of *Odas elementales* (1954) (Odes to Common Things). From 1948 to 1952 Neruda spent most of his time traveling around the world. In 1948, after the González Videla government outlawed the Communist Party, Neruda gave a speech condemning the government's actions against the party and was thereby sought by the police. With the aid of comrades he lived a clandestine life and then was able to leave the country. During this time Neruda finished writing *Canto general*. By February 1949 he was able to cross the Andes mountains on horseback and settle briefly in Argentina. In April of that same year he traveled to Paris for the World Congress of Peace Supporters and became a member of the World Council for Peace. In June he traveled to the Soviet Union for the first time, and, a month later, to Poland and Hungary. In August he went to Mexico with Paul Eluard and he remained there until the end of the year due to his ill health. However, by January 1950 Neruda continued with his dizzying schedule of trips: Guatemala, Prague, Paris, Rome, New Delhi (to interview Nehru), Warsaw (for the Second World Congress of Peace Supporters), and Czechoslovakia. In 1951 he began traveling again: first to Italy, Paris, Moscow, Prague, East Berlin, Mongolia, and then China. Finally, in 1952 Neruda settled down in Capri for six months, but by July he traveled with Matilde Urrutia to Berlin and then Denmark. He then returned to Santiago where he was given a warm and celebrated welcome. By December, he was off to the USSR to be a member of the jury for the International Peace Prize. At that point he began writing *Odas elementales*. With the exception of a trip to the USSR in January 1953, Neruda spent the next two years in Chile and, in 1954, published *Odas elementales*.[31]

Since Neruda spent two years—1948 to 1950—almost constantly on the road, traveling primarily in artistic and Communist circles in different countries, in large measure his ideas were based on the international issues and debates of his day. Neruda was an especially active Communist militant and poet during the Cold War years, in many ways sharing the major positions of Cominform, but also developing his own stances that his verses best reveal.

He became committed to peace after World War II for both national and international reasons. As noted above, the economic recession in Chile in the immediate post-war period led to the downfall of the Popular Front strategy and the crackdown on the Communist Party as the González Videla government felt heavy financial pressure from the United States. During the "Underground" period (1948–58), the party split into two tendencies: those who favored armed struggle (led by Luis Reinoso) and those who fundamentally wanted to depose the González Videla government in the long run and in the short term carry out clandestine party organizing (Galo González, Volodia Teitelboim, Luis Corvalán, and others).[32] A minority within the party, the former group was eventually expelled; the latter consisted of most of the party leadership.

Given Neruda's close friendship with Teitelboim, it is safe to say that the poet agreed with the majority opinion. By the time all this was happening, of course, Neruda was out of the country and therefore all the more dependent on second-hand accounts of the events. During this period the party turned to its struggle for a "bourgeois democratic revolution." This meant radical change led by the working class and the "enlightened" bourgeoisie, further industrialization of the country, and paving the way for socialism.

This policy, in turn, went along with the prevailing ideas of the Cominform after the War. While the United States came out of the war as, arguably, the strongest economic power due to the destruction of the European economies, the war had been catastrophic in the Soviet Union. The United States had benefited financially from the war and it was anxious to secure a sphere of economic and political influence in the former Allied and Axis nations. According to historian Walter LaFeber, the Truman government insisted that to preserve "personal freedom" the United States "had to rebuild the areas west of the Iron Curtain before these lands collapsed into anarchy, radical governments, or even communism."[33] The Truman Doctrine created the ideological scare for this war on communism, while the Marshall Plan provided the economic planning to rebuild these countries. Any major political problems that arose on the other side of the "iron curtain" were considered, henceforth, as "Communist inspired," allowing the United States to reap the financial benefits of the restoration of Western Europe. LaFeber sums up the impetus behind the Marshall Plan this way:

> [A] rejuvenated Europe could offer many advantages to the United States: eradicate the threat of continued nationalization and socialism by releasing and stimulating the investment of private capital, maintain demand for American exports, encourage Europeans to produce strategic goods which the United States could

buy and stockpile, preserve European and American control over the Middle Eastern oil supplies from militant nationalism which might endanger the weakened European holdings, and free Europeans from economic problems so they could help the United States militarily.[34]

The United States was thus positioned economically and militarily—given that it was the only nation at the time with the atom and hydrogen bombs—to fulfill its role as the new empire.

By contrast, the USSR had lost approximately twenty million people in the war and was suffering as much as it was during the war. A horrific drought had brought famine to millions in 1946, the infrastructure was largely destroyed, the country was in dire need of financial aid, and the USSR could hardly contemplate the possibility of being a military threat.[35] Historian Eric Hobsbawm summarizes the Soviet Union's postwar tragedy thus:

> On any rational assessment, the USSR presented no immediate danger to anyone outside the reach of the Red Army's occupation forces. It emerged from war in ruins, drained and exhausted, its peacetime economy in shreds, its government distrustful of a population much of which, outside Great Russia, had shown a distinct and understandable lack of commitment to the regime. On its western fringe, it continued to have trouble with Ukranian and other nationalist guerrillas for some years. It was ruled by a dictator who had demonstrated that he was as risk-averse outside the territory he controlled directly as he was ruthless within it: J.V. Stalin . . . It needed all the economic aid it could get, and, therefore, had no short-term interest in antagonising the only power that could give it, the USA.[36]

From the USSR's point of view "peaceful coexistence" was a survival mechanism until it could rebuild the infrastructure and ignite the economy. The USSR, then, presented no economic or political threat to U.S.'s aims at hegemony in the post-World War II era. At an immense human expense, during the Stalin years the USSR industrialized, attained the goals set during the Five-Year Plan in 1946, and improved education significantly for the masses.[37] As Issac Deutscher put it, "None of the great nations of the West has carried out its industrial revolution in so short a time and under such crippling handicaps."[38]

As regards foreign affairs, with very few exceptions in the immediate postwar period, the Soviet Union was content to support "bourgeois democratic revolutions" in developing countries. Indeed, Hobsbawm argues that the Soviet Union planned on "not building states on the model of the USSR, but mixed economies under multi-party parliamentary democracies, which were specifically distinguished from the 'dictatorship of the proletariat', and 'still more' of a single party."[39] However, Stalin's government firmly opposed U.S. imperialism and increasing encroachment on the world financial market. In that sense, the objectives of the Chilean Communist Party dovetailed with those of the Soviet Union. However, during the underground years and even through 1973, the party remained committed to the peaceful road to socialism.[40]

Neruda, naturally, was involved in domestic and international affairs on the left, and especially so in the case of the Communist Party. While traveling through the Soviet Union in particular and the socialist countries in general from 1948 to 1950 he gave poetry recitals at factories, attended writers' conferences, and gathered with friends he had in those countries, such as Ilya Ehrenburg in the USSR. Once he was back in Chile he threw himself into political activity, working tirelessly for Salvador Allende—the 1952 presidential candidate of the People's Front—organizing the Continental Cultural Congress in early 1953, and going to the Second Soviet Writers Congress in the USSR in December of that same year.

His political work, both domestically and abroad, and his traveling had a noteworthy impact on his poetic method and his poetry after *Canto general*. In his prologue to the publication of *Poesía política* (Political Poetry), written in 1952, Neruda conceived of his writing this way:

> Es esta relación entre la tierra, el tiempo y el hombre la que necesita riego y fulgor, es decir, poesía, para resplandecer y frutificar, para que la dicha universal sea nuestro reino común . . .
> El camino de la poesía sale hacia afuera, por calles y fábricas, escucha en todas las puertas de los explotados, corre y advierte, susurra y congrega, amenaza con la voz pesada de todo el porvenir, está en todos los sitios de las luchas humanas, en todos los combates, en todas las campanas que anuncian el mundo que nace, porque con fuerza, con esperanza, con ternura y con dureza lo haremos nacer.[41]

> [It is this relationship between the earth, time and man that needs irrigation and flash, that is, poetry, in order to shine and be fruitful, so that the universal word will be our common kingdom . . .
> The road of poetry goes outwards through the streets and the factories, it listens at the doors of the exploited, it runs and warns, it whispers and unites, it threatens with the heavy voice of the future, it is everywhere there are human struggles, in all battles, in all the bells announcing the world being born, because with strength, with hope, with tenderness and with firmness we will make it come about.]

As this manifiesto indicates, Neruda provides transparent literary form so that the lives of the exploited and their struggles for social justice become an integral part of his poetry.

An Ode to the Dialectic

Neruda's poetry during these years, which includes *Odas elementales* (Odes to Common Things), *Las uvas y el viento* (The Grapes and the Wind), and *Los versos del capitán* (The Captain's Verses), seeks to be a dialectical description of the depth of social conflicts and innermost tragedies during the Cold War years and a catalytic force for those involved in the struggles. Dialectical realism unites these works to be sure, but each takes on a unique focus. *Las uvas y el viento* could be seen as a sequel to *Canto general* because it is rich in its openly historical and political references about the socialist countries; *Los versos del capitán* is an ardently written book of love poems primarily, although the complexity of the relationship is often entangled with sociopolitical concerns; and *Odas elementales,* as indicated in chapters 1 and 2, is a dialectical meditation on noncommodified nature in the matrix of material and historical relations. In all three works, but perhaps more significantly in *Odas,* Neruda's poetic method is at least as elaborate as it is in *Canto general* if not superior. The apparent simplicity of the form, which relies on a conversational tone and register and seems to deal with objects of everyday use from the point of view of common sense, is deceptive. These short verses and long poems, written in a very accessible language, give the impression that Neruda is merely praising these natural objects as things in themselves, or as objects whose commodification is accepted. However, that interpretation is only possible if the reader is caught up in the dominant ideology and perceives no exit from the drive for profit in capitalist society. Any attentive reader will readily note that that interpretation only holds on the level of appearance. For these odes cut much deeper into the object's different layers of social and natural relations so that, as Jaime Concha astutely points out, "Todo objeto, toda forma singular equivale a una sinécdoque del cosmos, en la medida en que participa de las fuerzas solidarias de la realidad" (every object, every singular form is the equivalent of a synecdoche of the cosmos, to the degree that it participates in the forces of solidarity in reality).[42] In that way the common sense view of the object and the accepted ideological denigration of the object as a commodity are rendered inadequate, inexpressive of the deeper dialectical forces at work in the poems.

Take, for instance, the case of "Oda a la cebolla" (Ode to the Onion), an apparently pleasant but innocuous celebration of the onion (whose companion, as in the typical Chilean salads, is the "Oda al tomate" [Ode to the Tomato]):

> Cebolla,
> luminosa redoma,
> pétalo a pétalo
> se formó tu hermosura,
> escamas de cristal te acrecentaron
> y en el secreto de la tierra oscura
> se redondeó tu vientre de rocío.
> Bajo la tierra

fue el milagro
y cuando apareció
tu torpe tallo verde,
y nacieron
tus hojas como espadas en el huerto,
la tierra acumuló su poderío
mostrando tu desnuda transparencia,
y como en Afrodita el mar remoto
duplicó la magnolia
levantando sus senos,
la tierra
así te hizo,
cebolla,
clara como un planeta,
y destinada
a relucir
constelación constante,
redonda rosa de agua,
sobre
la mesa
de las pobres gentes.[43]

[Onion,
shining flask,
your beauty assembled
petal by petal,
They affixed your crystal scales to you
and your belly of dew grew round
in the secret of the dark earth.
The miracle took place
underground,
and when your lazy green stalk
appeared
and your leaves were born
like swords in the garden,
the earth gathered its strength
showing your naked transparency,
and just as the distant sea
copied the magnolia in Aphrodite
raising up her breasts,
so the earth
made you,
as bright as a planet
and fated
to shine,
constant constellation,
round rose of water,

> on poor people's
> dining tables.]⁴⁴

Neruda praises the onion's physical beauty for its translucent shape, purity, fragrance, inviting taste and its role as an aphrodisiac. Following the mythological traces of Aphrodite he describes the onion as both celestial and earthly, a shining wonder embedded in the dark richness of the earth. Neruda compares it to a planet, "fated / to shine," and a constellation set against the immensity of the black night. Later he calls it a star and, in a dialectical move, a "celestial seed," thus drawing a comparison between the earth and the pitch-dark nighttime sky. The onion attains its luminous, heavenly qualities in its contrast to the darkness, but also for what it bequeaths the families and friends who share its delectable wonder.

While Neruda judges it to be a preciously beautiful and celestial sphere, its presence makes itself felt at the most humble of abodes: "on poor people's / dining tables." Matched with a magnolia and a "round rose of water" (and later a "snowy anemone"), the onion's purity and magnificence lie in its sensorial hypnosis on those who eat it and its egalitarian disposition; its being "within the people's / reach." In Marjorie Agosín's words, the onion is "almost sublime" because of its beauty and it is "the essential food of the poor." She argues that "Neruda's technique consists of announcing the object through a series of ennobling characteristics—the transparency of its skins and the gentle curves of its form—and then adding to these virtues the sustaining and nutritive power of the object in the practical realm."⁴⁵ Neruda develops the underlying essence behind the splendor of appearance in the following verses:

> También recordaré como fecunda
> tu influencia el amor a la ensalada
> y parece que el cielo contribuye
> dándote fina forma de granizo
> a celebrar tu claridad picada
> sobre los hemisferios de un tomate.
> Pero al alcance
> de las manos del pueblo,
> regada con aceite,
> espolvoreada
> con un poco de sal,
> matas el hambre
> del jornalero en el duro camino.
> Estrella de los pobres,
> hada madrina
> envuelta
> en delicado
> papel, sales del suelo,

eterna, intacta, pura
como semilla de astro,
y al cortarte
el cuchillo en la cocina
sube la única lágrima
sin pena.
Nos hiciste llorar sin afligirnos.
Yo cuanto existe celebré, cebolla,
pero para mí eres
más hermosa que un ave
de plumas cegadoras,
eres para mis ojos
globo celeste, copa de platino,
baile inmóvil
de anémona nevada
y vive la fragancia de la tierra
en tu naturaleza cristalina. (94)

[I shall also proclaim how your influence
livens the salad's love,
and the sky seems to contribute
giving you the fine shape of hail
praising your chopped brightness
upon the halves of the tomato.
But within the people's
reach,
showered with oil,
dusted
with a pinch of salt,
you satisfy the worker's hunger
along the hard road home.
Poor people's star,
fairy godmother
wrapped
in fancy paper,
you rise from the soil,
eternal, intact, as pure
as a celestial seed,
and when the kitchen knife
cuts you
the only painless tear
is shed.
You made us weep without suffering.
I have celebrated every living thing, onion,
but for me you are
more beautiful that a bird
of blinding plumage;

> to my eyes you are
> a heavenly balloon, platinum cup,
> the snowy anemone's
> motionless dance
> and the fragrance of earth is alive
> in your crystalline nature.]

In these verses Neruda begins with the onion's stimulation as an aphrodisiac; like the Greek goddess it induces love and comes from the heavens to live among mere mortals. Despite its fine and exquisite natural architecture, it is "within the people's / reach" and it satisfies "the worker's hunger / along the hard road home." So much insistence on the onion being at the table of the poor invites the reader to examine it allegorically perhaps as hope for a more egalitarian society. It is a "Poor people's star," it makes its fans "weep without suffering," and it fills the earth with its fragrance in its "crystalline nature."

Robert Pring-Mill deals with the intimate connection between Neruda's poetic method and his political stance by demonstrating that in the initial version of the poem Neruda was already conscious of the political vantage point behind his praise for the onion. Pring-Mill affirms that Neruda decided to put greater emphasis on the onion's natural beauty first and then tie it to the "campesino" (farmer). Thus, Neruda underscores the earth's labor in creating this magnificent onion.[46] And this admiration for the onion's beauty is revisited in the last lines of the poem. It is likened to the snowy anemone, found all around Isla Negra seasonally, and referred to as an "estrellamar" (seastar), a flower whose permanence is celebrated by lovers in Chile. The anemone's dialectical "motionless dance" is like the eternal love shared among lovers, friends, and family around the table as they share the onion's fragrance. In essence, "motionless dance" sums up Neruda's somewhat humorous and complex rendering of the onion. Apparently immobile, because of its very nature, it mobilizes a series of social relations as a catalyst or as a "dance," a dance to hope for the future.

In his analysis of the odes in general and "Ode to the Onion" in particular René de Costa correctly writes of a "philosophic speaker" in the odes whose transparent medium belies the complexity of his message. However, in noting that Neruda conceives of the poem as an "intellectual creation," Costa believes that the poet now rejects realism and "social realism" in favor of "his own reality."[47] But this conclusion appears to contradict Costa's previous observations in his chapter about the odes:

> In *Odas elementales* . . . the poem is designed to involve us in the process of intellection, hence the importance of the pattern of enunciation, transformation, and ratiocination. The poem is designed as a didactic artifice, helping us to see, to witness, and to speculate on the marvelous significance of the world in which

we live, all of us. For this reason, the elementary ode almost always ends sententiously, with a kind of philosophic maxim summarizing the lesson, an epiphenomenon to help the reader grasp the poem's practical import.[48]

Costa's comments here rightly tie the philosophical eye of the poet to the reality that informs that mode of thought. As Marjorie Agosín notes, Neruda is not just a philosopher per se who contemplates objects phenomenologically or observes nature's transcendent splendor in his isolation. Rather, he is a "poet-philosopher" who adheres to a "sensual and earthy materialism" anchored in his "Marxist ideology."[49] Hence, Agosín helps define the type of philosophy underlying Neruda's political stance. Neruda is not just a philosopher per se, but rather a Marxist thinker and poet. Hence the division between organic and inorganic objects in the odes: nature's creative and indispensable work is compared to the work of the proletariat. When Neruda marvels at all commodities in "Oda a las cosas" (Ode to Things) he does so because of their use value and congealed labor. In his view "Lo que se hizo por la mano del hombre, toda cosa" (All that man made with his hands, all things) are beautiful and worthy of praise, and even more so, objects made without the exploitation of man.[50]

Conclusion

"Ode to the Onion" shows Neruda's dialectical imagination at work in the internal relations in the poem itself and its interplay with factors pointing beyond the isolation of the text or even its intertextuality in *Odas elementales* and in other books by Neruda. This poem illustrates how an object can never be a thing-in-itself since it is always located at the heart of natural and social relations. Only a multifaceted appreciation of an object like the onion can account satisfactorily but not fully for its complexity. But the various points of view, in and of themselves, must be prioritized and given more or less emphasis according to Neruda's dialectical method. Neruda moves from the general to the concrete and back, he appreciates the internal contradictions in nature and class society, he underscores the development and transformation of all things and beings, he shows affinities between nature and society, and he finally selects a definitive vantage point on which this poem's message rests.

"The Onion," then, like much of Neruda's poetry after *Tercera residencia,* is representative of his mastery of dialectical realism. Indeed, that same method can be appreciated in a host of brilliant poems in *Canto general, Odas elementales*—such masterpieces as "Que despierte el leñador" or "Oda al tiempo"—*Estravagario, Cien sonetos de amor* (One Hundred Love Sonnets), and *Plenos poderes* (Full Powers). They show that over the years

Neruda's grasp of the dialectic as the motorforce of his poetic method and political thought became almost second nature to him and enabled him to expose the breadth and variety of individual, social, and political experiences in a way that, arguably, no poet of the twentieth century did. Despite the horrors and grand struggles of his century, Neruda found hope still in his own poetic labor and worldview thanks in no small measure to his involvement in egalitarian struggles against injustice. Like Brecht, who in "The Learner" noted that "The scars were painful / Now it is cold. But I often said: only the grave / Will have nothing more to teach me," Neruda could not quench his thirst for life.[51] In what could be seen as comparable, late in *Memorial de Isla Negra* (Isla Negra Memorial, 1964) the Chilean wrote these lines in "La verdad" (The Truth): "No me cierren los ojos / aun después de muerto, / los necesitaré aún para aprender, / para mirar y comprender mi muerte" (Do not close my eyes / even after my death, / I will need them still to learn, / to gaze at and understand my own death).[52] However, as in Brecht's case, this individual quest and expectation combined with Neruda's belief in the collective betterment of humankind. As much as these words spoke to readers then, in the late years of his life, they speak to the millions who work to bring about a more just world at the beginning of the twenty-first century:

> Hoy es hoy. Ha llegado este mañana
> preparado por mucha oscuridad:
> no sabemos si es claro todavía
> este mundo recién inaugurado:
> lo aclararemos, lo oscureceremos
> hasta que sea dorado y quemado
> como los granos duros del maíz.[53]

> [Today is today. This tomorrow has arrived
> prepared by much darkness:
> we do not know if this recently inaugurated
> world is clear as yet:
> we will clear it up, we will darken it
> until it is golden and burnt
> like corn's hard grains.]

Notes

INTRODUCTION: LIGHT AGAINST THE DARKNESS

1. Cited on the cover of *Pablo Neruda: Selected Poems,* ed. and with a foreword by Nathaniel Tarn (Boston: Houghton Mifflin / Seymour Lawrence, 1990).
2. See Parenti's superb *Blackshirts & Reds: Rational Fascism and the Overthrow of Communism* (San Francisco: City Lights Books, 1997), 74. On this topic see esp. chapters 3 and 4.
3. Hugo Achugar, "The Book of Poems as a Social Act: Notes Toward an Interpretation of Contemporary Hispanic American Poetry," in *Marxism and the Interpretation of Culture,* ed. and with an introduction by Cary Nelson and Lawrence Grossberg (Urbana: University of Illinois Press, 1988), 654.
4. See Renato Poggioli's "The Concept of a Movement," particularly his section on antagonism in *The Theory of the Avant-Garde* (Cambridge, MA: Harvard University Press, 1968), 42–59.
5. Georg Lukács, *Writer and Critic and Other Essays* (New York: Universal Library, 1971), 83.
6. Volodia Teitelboim, *Neruda,* 5th ed. (Santiago: Ediciones Bat, 1991), 153.
7. See Alan Gilbert, "Marx's Moral Realism: Eudaimonism and Moral Progress," in *After Marx,* eds. James Farr and Terence Ball (Cambridge University Press, 1984), 155. See also Gilbert's fuller development of this argument in *Democratic Individuality* (Cambridge: Cambridge University Press, 1990).
8. See chapter 2 in Gilbert, *Democratic Individuality.* Gilbert argues that our "human capacities for moral personality" are an "ethical fact about humans" (106).
9. Pablo Neruda, *Confieso que he vivido,* 11th ed. (Buenos Aires: Editorial Losada, 1992), 268.
10. Neruda, *Confieso,* 189.
11. Ibid.

CHAPTER 1. CRITICISM AND IDEOLOGY: NERUDA AND THE COLD WAR

1. See Stonor Saunders book (New York: The New Press, 1999), 344–58.
2. David Schidlowsky, *Las furias y las penas: Pablo Neruda y su tiempo* (Berlin: Wissenschaftlicher Verlag, 2003), 11.
3. Ibid., 19.
4. Ibid., 12.
5. Ibid., 15.
6. Ibid., 17.
7. Gene Bell-Villada, *Art for Art's Sake and Literary Life: How Politics and Markets*

Helped Shape the Ideology and Culture of Aestheticism, 1790–1990 (Lincoln and London: University of Nebraska Press, 1996), 3.

8. See Ahmad's chapter "Literary Theory and 'Third World' Literature" in *In Theory: Classes, Nations, Literatures* (London: Verso, 1993) and Terry Eagleton's *Literary Theory: An Introduction* (Minneapolis: University of Minnesota Press, 1983), esp. "The Rise of English."

9. Pablo Neruda, *Canto general,* 4th ed. by Enrico Mario Santí (Madrid: Cátedra, 1997), 19.

10. Jean Franco, *The Decline & Fall of the Lettered City: Latin America in the Cold War* (Cambridge, MA: Harvard University Press, 2002).

11. Ibid., 48.

12. Emir Rodríguez Monegal, *Borges por él mismo* (Caracas: Monte Avila, 1980). Hereafter pages are cited in the text.

13. See "Conclusion: Political Criticism" in Eagleton, *Literary Theory: An Introduction,* 199.

14. See his "Introduction: Literature Among the Signs of Our Times," *In Theory: Classes, Nations, Literatures:* "[Poststructuralism] suppresses the very conditions of intelligibility within which the fundamental facts of our time can be theorized; and in privileging the figure of the reader, the critic, the theorist, as the guardian of the texts of this world, where everything becomes a text, it recoups the main cultural tropes of bourgeois humanism—especially in its Romantic variants, since the dismissal of class and nation as so many 'essentialisms' logically leads towards an ethic of non-attachment as the necessary condition of true understanding, and because breaking away from collective socialities of that kind inevitably leaves only the 'individual'—in the most abstract sense epistemologically, but in the shape of the critic/theorist concretely—as the locus of experience and meaning, while the well-known poststructuralist scepticism about the possibility of rational knowledge impels that same 'individual' to maintain only an ironic relation with the world and its intelligibility" (36).

15. Emir Rodríguez Monegal, *Viajero inmóvil: Introducción a Pablo Neruda* (Buenos Aires: Losada, 1966). Hereafter pages are cited in the text.

16. E. P. Thompson, *Witness against the Beast: William Blake and the Moral Law* (New York: The New Press, 1993), xvii.

17. Pablo Neruda, *Canto general,* 2d ed. (Barcelona: Editorial Seix Barral, 1982), 49. Hereafter pages are cited in the text.

18. Rubén Darío, *Azul . . . Cantos de vida y esperanza,* José María Martínez ed. (Madrid: Cátedra, 1995), 340. Hereafter pages are cited in the text.

19. See "El caracol y la sirena" in Paz's *Cuadrivio,* 3d ed. (Mexico: Joaquín Mortiz, 1972), 20.

20. Quoted in David Harvey, *Justice, Nature & the Geography of Difference* (Oxford: Blackwell Publishers, 1996), 439.

21. Enrico Mario Santí, *El acto de las palabras: Estudios y diálogos con Octavio Paz* (Mxico: Fondo de cultura económica, 1997), 12. Hereafter pages are cited in the text.

22. Octavio Paz, *El laberinto de la soledad* (Mexico: Fondo de cultura económica, 1981[1950]), 106–34.

23. Enrico Mario Santí, *Pablo Neruda: The Poetics of Prophecy* (Ithaca: Cornell University Press, 1982), 14. Hereafter pages are cited in the text.

24. Harold Bloom, *The Anxiety of Influence: A Theory of Poetry* (Oxford: Oxford University Press, 1973).

25. See Ahmad, *In Theory,* 54.

26. I am referring to Richard Boyd's term in "Metaphor and Theory Change: What is 'Metaphor' a metaphor for?" in Andrew Ortony ed., *Metaphor and Thought* (Cambridge: Cambridge University Press, 1979), 356–408. See also his "How to be a Moral Realist" in

Geoffrey Sayre-Cord, ed., *Essays on Moral Realism* (Ithaca: Cornell University Press, 1988), 181–228.

27. "Gold" in Pablo Neruda, *Canto General*, Jack Schmitt trans. (Berkeley: University of California Press, 1993), 295.

28. Pablo Neruda, "El oro" in *Canto general*, 2d ed. (Barcelona: Seix Barral, 1982 [1950]), 353–54.

29. In re-reading Alain Sicard's *El pensamiento poético de Pablo Neruda* (Madrid: Editorial Gredos, 1981), I came across his analysis of "El oro," which is very similar to my discussion of the poem. See 275–77.

30. Karl Marx, *Capital*, vol. 1 (New York: Vintage Books, 1977), 283.

31. Ibid., 128

32. Ibid., 188

33. René de Costa, *The Poetry of Pablo Neruda* (Oxford: Oxford University Press, 1979), ix.

34. René de Costa, *Vicente Huidobro: The Careers of a Poet* (Oxford: Oxford University Press, 1984), 108–9.

35. Ibid., 83.

36. Ibid., 1.

37. Eagleton, *Literary Theory: An Introduction*, 51.

38. Costa, *The Poetry of Pablo Neruda*, 64. Hereafter pages are cited in the text.

39. See, for instance, George Lakoff and Mark Turner, *More than Cool Reason: A Field Guide to Poetic Metaphor* (Chicago: The University of Chicago Press, 1989). The authors say the following: "Great poets can speak to us because they use the modes of thought we all possess. Using the capacities we all share, poets can illuminate our experience, explore the consequences of our beliefs, challenge the ways we think, and criticize our ideologies" (xi). Later on in the book Lakoff and Turner sum up the poet's intent wonderfully, "Poetry has the power to instruct us in what to notice, how to understand, and how to conduct our lives" (160).

40. Costa refers to Hernán Loyola's *Ser y morir en Pablo Neruda* (Being and Death in Pablo Neruda) (Santiago: Editorial Santiago, 1967), 92–94.

41. Mike González and David Treece, *The Gathering of the Voices: The Twentieth-Century Poetry of Latin America* (London: Verso, 1992), 202–3.

42. Pablo Neruda, *Confieso que he vivido*, 11th ed. (Buenos Aires: Losada, 1992), 446.

43. Pablo Neruda, *Tercera residencia*, 3d ed. (Barcelona: Editorial Seix Barral, 1983 [1947]), 17–18.

44. Saúl Yurkievich, "Mito e historia: Dos generadores del 'Canto general'" (Myth and History: Two Generators of 'General Song') in Emir Rodríguez Monegal and Enrico Mario Santí, eds., *Pablo Neruda* (Madrid: Taurus Ediciones, 1980), 199. Hereafter pages are cited in the text.

45. Bertell Ollman, *Dialectical Investigations* (New York: Routledge, 1993), 23.

46. Ibid., 65.

47. Manuel Durán and Margery Safir, *Earth Tones: The Poetry of Pablo Neruda* (Bloomington: University of Indiana Press, 1991), 57. Hereafter pages are cited in the text.

48. Volodia Teitelboim, *Neruda*, 5th ed. (Santiago: Editorial Bat, 1992), 176–80.

49. Jaime Concha, *Neruda: 1904–1936* (Santiago: Editorial Universitaria, 1972). Hereafter cited in the text.

50. Alain Sicard, *El pensamiento poético de Pablo Neruda* (Madrid: Gredos, 1981), 338.

51. Hereafter cited in the text.

52. See Teitelboim, *Neruda*, esp. 152–55. See also Hernán Loyola, "Las dos residencias" (The Two Residences) in Loyola ed., *Residencia en la tierra* (Madrid: Ediciones Cátedra, 1987), 13–60.

53. For a condensed version of his argument, excerpted from *Poesía y estilo de Pablo Neruda* (Poetry and Style in Pablo Neruda), see "Angustia y desintegración" [Anguish and Disintegration] in Emir Rodríguez Monegal and Enrico Santí eds., *Pablo Neruda* (Madrid: Taurus Ediciones, 1980), 119–33.
54. Pablo Neruda, *Nuevas odas elementales,* 3d ed. (Buenos Aires: Losada, 1971), 84.
55. Ibid., 84–85.
56. Sicard made this comment to me in a conversation we had in Poitiers, France, in the fall of 1994.

Chapter 2. Realism, Surrealism, Socialist Realism, and Neruda's "Guided Spontaneity"

1. With regards to the affinity between the works of García Lorca, Alberti, Aleixandre and Cernuda, see Anthony L. Geist's "Las mariposas en la barba: una lectura de Poeta en Nueva York," *Cuadernos hispanoamericanos,* no. 433–46 (July–October 1986): 547–65. Geist argues, correctly in my opinion, that the poets from the generation of 1927 go through personal crises around the time of economic crash of 1929 and turn to avant-gardist form to express themselves in their work. As far as the publication of García Lorca's *Poeta en Nueva York,* see Eutimio Martín's introduction in *Poeta en Nueva York y Tierra luna* (Barcelona: Ariel, 1981), 18–19.
2. See Forster's "Pablo Neruda and the Avant-garde," *Symposium* (Fall 1978): 208–20.
3. The dates vary according to the critic. Regarding the European avant-garde, in *The Theory of the Avant Garde* (Cambridge, MA: Harvard University Press, 1968), Renato Poggioli marks the end of its third phase with the end of Dadaism (1922), but he argues that it informed modern art well into the 1960s (229–30). Miklós Szabolscsi, "La 'vanguardia' literaria y artística como fenómeno internacional," *Casa de las Américas* 74 (September–October 1972), maintains that the second phase of the avant-garde lasts until 1938 (5). There is no consensus regarding periodization in the Latin American context either. In "Literatura de postguerra: Renovación y Vanguardia," *Texto Crítico* 24–25 (January–December 1982) and "Para una caracterización histórica del vanguardismo literario hispanoamericano,"*Revista iberoamericana* 114–15 (January–June 1981), Nelson Osorio establishes 1918–30 as the dates corresponding to Latin American vanguardismo (116; 254). Hugo Verani, in his introduction to *Las vanguardias literarias en Hispanoamérica (manifiestos, proclamas y otros escritos)* (Rome: Bulzoni Editore, 1986), establishes the following limits to the avant-garde: 1916–35 (11). Like Szabolscsi, Federico Schopf considers that the avant-garde meets its fate at the end of Spanish civil war (1939) in "El vanguardismo poético en Hispanoamérica," a chapter in his recent book, *Del vanguardismo a la antipoesía: ensayos sobre la poesía en Chile* (Santiago: LOM, 2000), 27.
4. The accusation that Neruda was a socialist realist can be found, for example, in Emir Rodríguez Monegal, *El viajero inmóvil: Introducción a Pablo Neruda* (Buenos Aires: Losada, 1966). After warning readers that they must not consider *Canto general* an assignment by the Communist Party, Monegal says that "A pesar de su explícita adhesión a las huestes del realismo socialista y de la poesía edificante, el *Canto general* no está todo en la línea simple y simplificadora" (235, 251–52). Manuel Durán and Margery Safir in their *Earth Tones: The Poetry of Pablo Neruda* (Bloomington: University of Indiana Press, 1981) do not accuse Neruda of being a socialist realist openly, but rather claim that he was a "strict Soviet-style Communist" when they refer to his political ideas in *Canto general.* Needless to say, at no moment do they explain what that description means. Enrico Mario Santí's introduction to Pablo Neruda, *Canto general* (Madrid: Ediciones Cátedra, 1997) does not baldly call Neruda a socialist realist but Santí does allege that Neruda falls for a "sectari-

anismo apasionado" (76) and "una interpretación apocalíptica del marxismo" (92). In another passage and not without reason, Santí associates Neruda with the tragedies in the Soviet Union under Stalin's regime: "Años después de los infames Juicios de Moscú, y en días en que ya se tenía conocimiento de la existencia de campos de concentración en la Unión Soviética y de la destrucción por el régimen de Stalin de la clase campesina, el libro [*Canto general*] hace caso omiso de todos estos acontecimientos, aún cuando dedica buena parte de una sección a elogiar la dirigencia del país" (77). For a full discussion of this context, see my chapter 5; for an analysis of Nerudian criticism and political reductionism, see chapter 2.

5. Pablo Neruda, *Confieso que he vivido*, 11th ed. (Buenos Aires: Losada, 1992), 362.

6. Ibid., 426.

7. Although I try to capture Neruda's poetic method as it develops naturally in his work, I rely on Roy Bhaskar's understanding of the dialectic in *Dialectic: The Pulse of Freedom* (London: Verso, 1993) and, especially, Bertell Ollman's analysis of the dialectical method in *Dialectical Investigations* (London: Routledge, 1993). I also depend on Georg Lukács' explication of the connection between critical and self-critical realism and the social world (see my discussion below). Basically I observe the general categories of the dialectic in Neruda's poetry: quantitative changes leading to qualitative transformations and vice versa, the interpenetration of opposites, and the negation of the negation. These are three of the cornerstones of the dialectic found in Neruda's method and at work in his poetry. From 1936 on, as I contend in this chapter, Neruda elaborates the dialectic and employs it to understand sociopolitical, economic, and aesthetic issues better and he renders that in his own mediated way in his verse.

8. See Concha's *Neruda 1904–1936* (Santiago: Editorial Universitaria, 1972) and Sicard's *El pensamiento poético de Pablo Neruda* (Madrid: Gredos, 1981). As indicated in the introduction and chapter 1, these are indispensable studies on Neruda's poetry and politics.

9. A. Zhadanov, *Problems of Soviet Literature: Reports and Speeches of the First Soviet Writer's Congress* (Moscow-Leningrad: Cooperative Publishing Society of Foreign Workers in the USSR, 1935), 15. Hereafter the citations appear in the text.

10. As regards this historical period see, for instance, "Against the Common Enemy" in Eric Hobsbawm, *The Age of Extremes: A History of the World, 1914–1991* (New York: Pantheon, 1994), 142–77.

11. See Cristian Delporte's *Intellectuels et Politique* (Firenze: Casterman-Giunti, 1995), 54–69. In Spain the question of commitment or of "impure poetry"—a phrase that Neruda himself coins—revolves around the journal *Octubre*, which took a revolutionary stance and advocated social poetry. See Juan Cano Ballesta, *La poesía española entre pureza y revolución* (Madrid: Gredos, 1972), 201–27.

12. Both poems, which I analyze in chapter 5, are in *Tercera residencia*.

13. Mark Polizzotti, *Revolution of the Mind: The Life of André Breton* (New York: Farrar, Strauss, and Giroux, 1995), 246.

14. André Breton and Louis Aragon, *Surrealismo frente a realismo socialista*, ed. Oscar Tusquets (Barcelona: Tusquets, 1973), 32. Hereafter the pages appear in the text.

15. Georg Lukács, *Essays on Realism,* ed. Rodney Livingstone (Cambridge, MA: The MIT Press, 1980), 36–37.

16. Georg Lukács, *Realism in Our Time* (New York and Evanston: Harper & Row, 1962). See especially "Critical Realism and Socialist Realism," 93–135.

17. For recent information on the forces behind the purges, see J. Arch Getty and Oleg V. Naumov, *The Road to Terror: Stalin and the Self-Destruction of the Bolsheviks, 1932–1939* (New Haven, CT: Yale University Press, 1999).

18. André Breton / Louis Aragon, *Surrealismo frente a realismo socialista,* ed. Oscar Tusquets (Barcelona: Tusquets, 1973), 54. Hereafter the pages are cited in the text.

19. As far as I have been able to ascertain, no critic accuses him of this directly. However,

there are several that allege that Neruda was influenced by the Party's "propaganda." Besides the aforementioned criticism (Enrico Mario Santí and Emir Rodríguez Monegal) see, for example, Cedomil Goic's "'Alturas de Macchu Picchu': La torre y el abismo" in *Pablo Neruda,* eds. Santí and Monegal (Madrid: Taurus Ediciones, 1980), 219–44. In the same book see also Saúl Yurkievich's "Mito e historia: Dos generadores del *'Canto general',"* 198–218. It is worth quoting from Yurkievich's essay to underline the critic's subjectivist political position:

> Neruda se autocensura, se autocercena. Abandona el ritual, el verbo oracular, el ámbito sacralizado para intentar una poesía utiliaria, herramienta o arma de la revolución, una poesía proletaria. Los problemas que ella plantea siguen vigentes: ¿puede una poesía juzgarse en términos de lucha de clases? ¿La función estética debe subordinarse a la ideología o viceversa? ¿Cuál es el valor cognoscitivo de una poesía que renuncia a su función estética en aras de la referencial? ¿Vale la pena ampliar la audiencia en detrimento de la especificidad poética? ¿Optar por un nivel popular de lectura significa llegar al pueblo? ¿Cuál es la eficacia práctica de la poesía política? ¿Qué es lo decible y lo indecible poéticos? ¿Cómo decir poéticamente lo político? (216)

> [Neruda censors himself, he curtails himself. He abandons the ritual, the oracular verb, the sacred zone to attempt a utilitarian poetry, tool or arm of the revolution, a proletarian poetry. The problems it poses continue in force: Can poetry be judged in terms of the class struggle? Should the aesthetic function be subordinated to the ideological or vice versa? What is the cognitive value of poetry that renounces its aesthetic function for the sake of referential poetry? Is it worth broadening the readership to the detriment of poetic specificity? Does opting for a popular level of readership mean reaching out to the people? What is the practical efficiency of political poetry? What is expressible or inexpressible in poetry? How should one express politically the poetic?]

Yurkievich adheres to a dualist view of art and politics: he either assumes that the two can exist independently or believes, presumably in the case of left-wing politics, that politics impinges itself on poetry. The cases of Neruda, César Vallejo, and Miguel Hernández, to name a few renowned committed, left-wing poets, should leave no doubt that the elaboration and cultivation of form can take place in tandem with the deepening of content. Poetry cannot escape ideology nor can evade it the class struggle since the latter indirectly or more directly informs the poet's political and artistic consciousness. For a lengthier discussion of this issue, see my chapter 2.

20. Ariane Chebel d'Appollonia, *Histoire politique des intellectuels en France (1944–1954)* (Bruxelles: Editions Complexe, 1991), 16–17.

21. Mary Ann Caws, *The Poetry of Dada and Surrealism: Aragon, Breton, Tzara, Eluard and Desnos* (Princeton: Princeton University Press, 1970), 38–39.

22. Enrico Mario Santí, *El acto de las palabras: Estudios y diálogos con Octavio Paz* (Mexico: Fondo de cultura económica, 1997), 12, 37–38.

23. Quoted in ibid., 99–100.

24. Octavio Paz, *Itinerario* (Mexico: Fondo de cultura económica, 1993), 63–65. For more on the POUM, see my chapter 4.

25. Ibid., 64.

26. Santí, *El acto de las palabras,* 51.

27. For a full account of Paz's politics see his *Itinerario* (cited above).

28. Paz, *Itinerario,* 88.

29. Santí, *El acto de las palabras,* 70.

30. Ibid., 100.

31. See Octavio Paz, *Los hijos del limo,* primera edición en Biblioteca de Bolsillo (Barcelona: Editorial Seix Barral, 1987), 194–96, 206–10.

32. Ibid., 208–10.

33. Neruda, *Confieso,* 395.

34. As regards criticism about *Residencia en la tierra,* the works that seem most inno-

vative and essential are the following: Jaime Concha, *Neruda (1904–1936)* (Santiago: Editorial Universitaria, 1972); Alain Sicard, *El pensamiento poético de Pablo Neruda* (Madrid: Gredos, 1981); Hernán Loyola, "Las dos *Residencias*," the introduction to *Residencia en la tierra* (Madrid: Ediciones Cátedra, 1987).

35. Neruda, *Confieso*, 205.
36. Pablo Neruda, *Canto general*, 2d ed. (Barcelona: Seix Barral, 1982), 32.
37. See Neruda's *Confieso*, in particular, the emotional poetry readings he did for the Carriers Union of la Vega in Chile (346–47) and the reading before 10,000 miners in the Plaza de Lota (349–50). As biographer Volodia Teitelboim notes in *Neruda*, 5th ed. (Santiago de Chile: Ediciones BAT, 1991), 281–84, in running his campaign for the Senate, Neruda often read poems to hundreds of miners in northern Chile rather than giving political speeches.
38. Neruda, *Confieso*, 361.
39. Ibid., 377.
40. See in particular Lukács' "Art and Objective Truth" in *Writer and Critic and Other Essays* (New York: Universal Library, 1971), 32; and *Realism in Our Time: Literature and Class Struggle* (New York and Evanston: Harper & Row, 1962), 93–135.
41. Neruda, *Confieso*, 269.
42. Ibid., 271.
43. Bertolt Brecht, "Against Georg Lukács" in *Aesthetics and Politics,* second printing (London: Verso, 1986), 82.
44. Pablo Neruda, *Para nacer he nacido* (Barcelona: Planeta, 1989), 94.
45. Ibid., 95.
46. See "The PCCh in the Period 1912–1948" in Carmelo Furci's *The Chilean Communist Party and the Road to Socialism* (London: Zed Books, 1984). In particular Furci says "The PCCh's leadership basically refused to accept the directives of the Communist International, and this refusal meant political suicide, in view of the mood prevailing within the International under Stalin" (31).
47. Neruda, *Canto general,* 29.
48. Neruda, *Canto general,* Jack Schmitt trans. (Berkeley: University of California Press, 1993), 29.
49. On the impact of Eliot on Neruda, consult any of the following: Majorie Agosín, "The *Residence* Cycle" in *Pablo Neruda* (Boston: Twayne Publishers, 1986), 36–57; Manuel Durán and Marjorie Safir, *Earth Tones: The Poetry of Pablo Neruda* (Bloomington: Indiana University Press, 1981), 43–54; Emir Rodríguez Monegal, *El viajero inmóvil: Introducción a Pablo Neruda* (Buenos Aires: Losada, 1966), 202–28.
50. See Frank Lentricchia, *Modernist Quartet* (Cambridge: Cambridge University Press, 1994), 239–86. Eliot's bourgeois and, paradoxically, anticapitalist sentiments made rightwing positions more palatable to him as Lentricchia notes:

> stands against humanitarianism and the enthusiasm that all men are worthy of a promiscuous sympathy and benevolence; against the belief in the kingdom of man through the interventions of science (the religion of "progress"), against the rule of impulse ("one impulse from a vernal wood"); against the "inordinate exaltation of the individual," the democratic spirit, the "pedantry of individualism," and the "free play of one's individual faculties." He stands for discipline, constraint, and the ideals of community; for tradition and classical literary values that stress impersonality and the universal life (as opposed, in Eliot's dark imagery from Dante and Bradley, to the prison of self); for the muses of memory over those of inspiration and genius. (255)

Gene Bell-Villada's *Art for Art's Sake and Literary Life: How Politics and Markets Helped Shape the Ideology & Culture of Aestheticism, 1790–1990* (Lincoln: University of Nebraska Press, 1996) provides critical information about Eliot's interest in the French monarchist Charles Maurras and in fascism. See 224–39.

51. Neruda made it clear in a short essay that "El comienzo [de "Alturas de Macchu Picchu"] es una serie de recuerdos autobiográficos" (The beginning [of the poem] is a series of autobiographical memories). See Hernán Loyola's "Poema-síntesis" in Angel Flores ed., *Aproximaciones a Pablo Neruda* (Barcelona: Llibres de Sinera, 1974), 190.

52. Pablo Neruda, *Canto general,* segunda edición (Barcelona: Editorial Seix Barral, 1982): 30–31. Hereafter the pages refer to this edition and are present in the text.

53. See Loyola's essay in footnote 46, page 192.

54. Neruda, *Canto general,* Jack Schmitt trans., 34.

55. Hugo Montes, "'Alturas de Macchu Picchu'": El viaje" in Flores, *Aproximaciones a Pablo Neruda,* 186.

56. Lewis S. Feuer, *Marx and Engels: Basic Writings on Politics and Philosophy* (Garden City, NY: Anchor Books, 1959), 29.

57. Neruda, *Canto general,* Jack Schmitt trans., 35.

58. The works of Alain Sicard, Jaime Concha, and Hernán Loyola argue along similar lines.

59. Federico Kauffman Doig, in *Perú antiguo: El incario: Una nueva perspectiva* (Lima: Kompaktos Editores, 1990) states the following:

> Juicios valorativos aparte, sin la presencia de una aristocracia gobernante como la de los Incas, que ordenaba a las multitudes lo que debía hacerse, no se habrían podido construir las grandes obras públicas destinadas a acelerar la producción de los alimentos, como los canales de riego, ni cumplido con la meta de recolectar para distribuir equitativamente los productos; tampoco tendríamos Machu Picchu (160).

> [Value judgments aside, without the presence of a governing aristocracy like the one the Incas had, which organized the multitudes for what need to be done, it would not have been possible to construct all the public work projects aimed at accelerating the production of food, like the irrigation canals, nor to accomplish the goal of harvesting and distributing the products equally; neither would we have Machu Picchu.]

J. Alden Mason, in *The Ancient Civilizations of Peru* (New York: Pelican, 1975) puts it this way:

> The Inca state was a queer blend of theocracy, monarchy, socialism, and communism, its categorization in one system or another depending mainly on definition. It has often been termed a socialistic empire, for it was an aristocratic and autocratic socialism, not a democratic one. (180)

Mason adds that there was a "large class of nobles and priests, supported by the masses" (180). In his *The History of the Incas* (New York: Schocken Books, 1970), Alfred Métraux makes a similar commentary as regards the Incan empire:

> the Inca empire combined absolute despotism with respect for the social and political forms of the subject peoples. The Inca reigned as absolute monarch, but his will reached the common man only through the local chiefs, whose authority and privileges were maintained, if not reinforced. Centralization of power was combined, after a fashion, with the exercise of indirect rule, if such an anachronistic phrase may be allowed. (93)

60. Neruda, *Canto general,* Jack Schmitt trans., 40–41.

61. Ibid., 41–42.

62. Karl Marx, *Capital,* vol. 1 (New York: Vintage Books, 1977), 342. In "Economic and Philosophical Manuscripts" in *Karl Marx: Early Writings* (New York: Vintage Books, 1975), Marx puts it even more precisely:

> The fact simply means that the object that labour produces, its product, stands opposed to it as *something alien,* as a *power independent* of the producer. The product of labour is labour embodied and

made material in an object, it is the *objectification* of labour. The realization of labour is its objectification. In the sphere of political economy this realization of labour appears as a loss of reality for the worker, objectification as loss of and bondage to the object, and appropriation as estrangement, as alienation [entäusserung]. (324)

63. I am contending here that Neruda was a moral realist: that his moral positions are intimately tied to approximate human knowledge about social and physical reality. Alan Gilbert suggests the following definition of moral realism: it "recognizes progress in morality and advance in moral theory through successive approximations to the truth about human potentials for cooperation and freedom. Further, progress in moral theory rests heavily on progress in social theory" (155). See his "Marx's Moral Realism: Eudaimonism and Moral Progress" in *After Marx,* ed. James Farr and Terence Ball (Cambridge: Cambridge University Press, 1984). For more on moral realism see Gilbert, *Democratic Individuality* (Cambridge: Cambridge University Press, 1993) and Geoffrey Sayre-McCord, ed., *Essays on Moral Realism* (Ithaca: Cornell University Press, 1988), especially Richard Boyd's "How to be a Moral Realist," 181–228.

64. Emir Rodríguez Monegal, *El viajero inmóvil: Introducción a Pablo Neruda* (Buenos Aires: Losada, 1966), 236–38.

65. Enrico Mario Santí, *Pablo Neruda: The Poetics of Prophecy* (Ithaca: Cornell University Press, 1982), 17.

66. See Goic's "'Alturas de Macchu Picchu': La torre y el abismo" in *Pablo Neruda,* ed. Emir Rodríguez Monegal and Enrico Mario Santí, 220 (Madrid: Taurus, 1980).

67. See my commentary on Yurkievich's analysis of *Canto general* in chapter 1.

68. In a similar vein, Juan Loveluck makes the case for a phenomenological reading of "Alturas de Macchu Picchu." His interpretation is so centered on an abstract human condition that he misses the sociohistorical references to the exploitation of the Incas at the beginning of part 3. See "Alturas de Macchu Picchu: Cantos I–IV" in *Revista Iberoamericana* 82 (1973): 175–88.

69. Pablo Neruda, *Odas elementales,* ed. Jaime Concha, 8th ed. (Madrid: Ediciones Cátedra, 1999), 42.

70. Although Gómez Paz underlines Neruda's realist impulse in the odes, she never moves beyond a realist description of bourgeois reality. Unlike Neruda, she is unwilling to enter the post-capitalist and Marxist poetic framework that the poet has put in place. See her "Odas elementales (1954)" in *Aproximaciones a Pablo Neruda,* ed. Angel Flores (Barcelona: Llibres de Sinera, 1974), 223–26.

71. Jaime Concha, "Neruda, desde 1952: 'No entendí nunca la lucha sino para que ésta termine' en *Coliloquio Internacional sobre Pablo Neruda (La obra posterior al* Canto general) (Poitiers: Publications du Centre de Recherche Latino-Américaines de l'Université de Poitiers, 1979), 61.

72. Cited in Jaime Concha's excellent introduction to Neruda, *Odas elementales,* 39.

73. See R. D. F. Pring-Mill, "El Neruda de las *Odas elementales*" in *Coliloquio internacional sobre Pablo Neruda (La obra posterior a* Canto general) (Poitiers: Centre du Recherche Latino-américaines, 1979), 261–300.

74. Neruda, *Odas elementales,* 141.

75. Ibid. See note 68. Hereafter the page numbers for "El hombre invisible" appear in the text.

76. My translation. See the previously cited essay by Pring-Mill, 273.

77. See Georg Lukács, "Art and Objective Truth" in *Writer and Critic and Other Essays* (New York: Universal Library, 1971). In *Realism in Our Time* Lukács says that in Kafka's work—despite its virtues—the "reflection of a distortion becomes a distorted reflection" (New York: Harper & Row, 1962), 53.

78. See Concha's previously cited introduction to *Odas elementales,* 30.

79. See René de Costa's *The Poetry of Pablo Neruda* (Cambridge, MA: Harvard University Press, 1979), 163.

80. In "Naciendo en los bosques," found in *Tercera residencia,* 3rd ed. (Barcelona: Seix Barral, 1983), Neruda expresses it this way: "porque para nacer he nacido, para encerrar el paso / de cuanto se aproxima, de cuanto mi pecho golpea como un / nuevo / corazón tembloroso" (because I was born to be born, to cut off at the pass / all that comes close, all that in my breast beats like a / new / trembling heart) (18).

CHAPTER 3. REALISM AND THE BATTLE WITH LANGUAGE IN THE *RESIDENCIAS*

1. Pierre Bourdieu, *The Field of Cultural Production,* ed. Randall Johnson (New York: Columbia University Press, 1993). See "The Field of Cultural Production, or: The Economic World Reversed," 29–73.

2. Ibid., 68.

3. Jaime Concha, *Vicente Huidobro* (Madrid: Ediciones Jacar, 1980), 101.

4. Pierre Bourdieu, *In Other Words: Essays Towards a Reflexive Sociology,* trans. Matthew Adamson (Stanford: Stanford University Press, 1990), 108–9.

5. See René de Costa's sharp analysis of "Altazor" in *Huidobro: Careers of a Poet* (Oxford: Oxford University Press, 1984), 137–61. To be a leader of the avant-garde was to be modern, to join the latest developments in aesthetics in the developing countries, and, in so doing, to leave "provincialism" behind. See Enrique Lihn's "El lugar de Huidobro," in René de Costa, ed., *Vicente Huidobro y el creacionismo* (Madrid: Taurus, 1975).

6. René de Costa, "Sobre Huidobro y Neruda" *Revista iberoamericana* 45, no. 106–7 (1979): 379–86.

7. By "referential detachment" Bhaskar does not mean to imply what post-structuralists commonly do assert: the undecidability or obfuscation of the referent. Referential detachment is the prerequisite to any understanding of the world existing apart from our individuality; we need to refer to something other than ourselves (*Dialectic* 40). It is then a question of attempting to engage that reality that exists outside and inside us via knowledge—which is an approximately true, yet fallibilist, understanding of the world and its laws. It follows from this that if we attempt to maximize our explanatory potential of these phenomena, we will have a better and more accurate understanding of them. (*Dialectic* and *Plato Etc.* passim.)

8. Pablo Neruda, *Para nacer he nacido,* ed. Matilde Neruda and Miguel Otero Silva (Barcelona: Planeta, 1989), 62.

9. Ibid., 61.

10. Amado Alonso, "Angustia y desintegración," in *Pablo Neruda,* ed. Emir Rodríguez Monegal and Enrico Mario Santí, 126 (Madrid: Taurus Ediciones, 1980).

11. Juan Larrea, *Del surrealismo a Macchu Picchu* (México: Editorial Joaquín Mortiz, 1967). See especially pages 82–100. The contention that Neruda was a surrealist has been persuasive to many literary critics. Durán and Safir, Costa, Rodríguez Monegal, Alonso, and Agosín all argue that *Residencia en la tierra* is indebted to surrealism.

12. I am indebted to George Lakoff and Mark Turner's terminology in *More Than Cool Reason: A Field Guide to Poetic Metaphor* (Chicago: University of Chicago Press, 1988) in Chapter 2: "The Power of Poetic Metaphor," 57–139.

13. Pablo Neruda, *Tercera residencia,* 3rd ed. (Madrid: Seix Barral, 1983) and *Residencia en la tierra* (volumes 1 and 2), 4th ed. (Buenos Aires: Losada, 1958).

14. Pablo Neruda, *Confieso que he vivido,* 11th ed. (Buenos Aires: Losada, 1992), 116–17.

15. Ibid., 119.

16. Hernán Loyola, "Las dos residencias," introduction to *Residencia en la tierra,* by Pablo Neruda, ed. Hernán Loyola (Madrid: Ediciones Cátedra, 1987), 24.
17. Ibid; see also the poem "Comunicaciones desmentidas" in vol. 2 of *Residencia en la tierra.*
18. Alain Sicard, *El pensamiento poético de Pablo Neruda* (Madrid: Gredos, 1981); Jaime Concha, *Neruda: 1904–1936* (Santiago: Editorial Universitaria, 1972); Volodia Teitelboim, *Neruda,* 5th ed. (Santiago: Ediciones Bat, 1991); and Hernán Loyola, *Ser y morir en Pablo Neruda* (Santiago: Editorial Santiago, 1967) as well as "Las dos residencias" in his edition of *Residencia en la tierra* (Madrid: Ediciones Cátedra, 1987).
19. Joseph L. Scarpaci, "Chile" in *Latin American Urbanization: Historical Profiles of Major Cities,* ed. Gerald Michael Greenfield (Westport, CT: Greenwood Press, 1994), 116–17.
20. See Fernando Pérez Oyarzún and José Rosa Vera, "Cities Within the City: Urban and Arquitectural Transfers in Santiago de Chile" in *Planning Latin America's Capital Cities, 1850–1950,* ed. Arturo Almandoz (London: Routledge, 2002), 128, and Scarpaci, "Chile," 117.
21. Julio Faúndez, *Marxism and Democracy in Chile: From 1932 to the Fall of Allende* (New Haven: Yale University Press, 1988), 6–11. I have also relied on Tulio Halperín Donghi's *Historia contemporánea de América Latina,* 13th ed. (Madrid: Alianza Editorial, 1990), 343–47; and Charles Bergquist's *Labor in Latin America: Comparative Essays on Chile, Argentina, Venezuela and Colombia* (Palo Alto, CA: Stanford University Press, 1986), 59–70.
22. See Jaime Concha's discussion of Neruda during the Alessandri and Ibáñez years in *Pablo Neruda 1904–1936* (Santiago: Editorial Universitaria, 1972), 230–35.
23. Amado Alonso, "Angustia y desintegración" in *Pablo Neruda,* ed. Emir Rodríguez Monegal and Enrico Mario Santí (Madrid: Taurus, 1980), 119–33.
24. Ibid., 119.
25. See, for instance, "Two Choruses from 'The Rock'" in T. S. Eliot, *The Waste Land and Other Poems* (New York: Harcourt Brace Jovanovich, 1962), 86.
26. Margarita Aguirre, *Pablo Neruda / Héctor Eandi: Correspondencia durante "Residencia en la tierra"* (Buenos Aires: Editorial Sudamericana, 1980), 34.
27. Loyola, "Las dos residencias," 14.
28. See Costa's reading of "Galope muerto" in *The Poetry of Pablo Neruda* (Cambridge, MA: Harvard University Press, 1979), 61–65.
29. In Agosín's chapter 3, "The Residence Cycle: Neruda and the Avant-Garde" in *Pablo Neruda* (Boston: Twayne Publishers, 1986), 36–57, esp. 40–42.
30. Enrico Mario Santí, *Pablo Neruda: The Prophetics of Prophecy* (Ithaca: Cornell University Press, 1982), 29–37.
31. See Schopf's introduction to *Residencia en la tierra* (Santiago: Editorial Universitaria, 1992), 13–32, esp. 17–20.
32. Concha, *Pablo Neruda 1904–1936,* 264. His interpretation of "Galope muerto" covers pages 247–64.
33. Hernán Loyola, *Ser y morir en Pablo Neruda: 1918–1945* (Santiago de Chile: Editora Santiago, 1967), 86.
34. Pablo Neruda, *Residencia en la tierra,* 4th ed. (Buenos Aires: Losada, 1958), 9. Hereafter the pages cited in the text refer to this edition and book.
35. "Dead Gallop" in Pablo Neruda, *Residence on Earth,* Donald D. Walsh trans. (New York: New Directions, 1973), 3, 5.
36. See Concha, *Neruda 1904–1936* and Alain Sicard, *El pensamiento poético de Pablo Neruda* (Madrid: Gredos, 1981).
37. See for instance René de Costa's comments on the language in "Galope muerto" in *The Poetry of Pablo Neruda,* 61–65, and Enrico Mario Santí's analysis in *Pablo Neruda,* esp. 31–36.

38. In "La objetivación del fenómeno en la génesis de la noción de la materia" *Revista iberoamericana* 82–83 (January–June 1973): 99–110, Sicard argues persuasively that Neruda is confronted with astonishing "exceso de realidad" (reality's excess) in the world and his own limits as a poet. "Es objetivándose cómo el tiempo revela en él una contradicción esencial: simultáneamente, desintegración y realización (aumento, crecimiento), destrucción y permanencia, fragmentación y acumulación" (110).

39. Neruda, *Residencia,* 17.

40. Neruda, *Residence on Earth,* Donald D. Walsh, trans., 15.

41. Jaime Concha, "Observaciones sobre algunas imágenes de *Residencia en la tierra*" in *Simposio Pablo Neruda: Actas,* ed. Issac Jack Lévy and Juan Loveluck, 109–22 (Madrid: University of South Carolina Las Américas, 1978). See pages 116 and 121.

42. Santí, *Pablo Neruda,* 58–60.

43. Neruda, *Residence on Earth,* Donald D. Walsh trans., 53.

44. As regards alienation I follow Marx's study in the "Economic and Philosophical Manuscripts (1844)" in *Early Writings,* ed. Lucio Colleti, trans. Rodney Livingstone and Gregor Benton (New York: Vintage Books, 1975), 279–400. The idea of using one's alienation against itself stems in part from Roy Bhaskar's notion of "absenting absences" (or, negating negations). At this stage Neruda is conducting a "transformative negation"—in Bhaskar's terms—and not a "radical negation." Neruda has consciously begun to work toward identifying and eradicting his social alienation, so this juncture is tranformative. His radical negation individually and politically emerges in "España en el corazón." See Bhaskar's *Dialectic* (previously cited), 5–6.

45. See Pablo Neruda, *Estravagario* (Buenos Aires: Losada, 1958), 10. The translation is mine.

46. Rodríguez Monegal, *El viajero inmóvil,* 32–38.

47. Concha, *Pablo Neruda 1904–1936,* 236.

48. Costa, *The Poetry of Pablo Neruda,* 79–89.

49. Rodríguez Monegal, *El viajero inmóvil,* 202–12.

50. Jaime Concha, "Interpretación de *Residencia en la tierra*" in *Tres ensayos sobre Pablo Neruda* (Palma de Mallorca: Mossèn Alcovar, 1974), 31–84. I come to the conclusion that Concha uses a "metafísica materialista" in a Hegelian way given his many references to the German philosopher in this essay and his insistence on Neruda's dialectical method. This would be in keeping with, for example, W. H. Walsh's description of the nature of metaphysics in the *Encyclopedia of Philosophy,* vols. 5 and 6 (New York: MacMillan Press, 1967), 300–307.

51. Concha, "Interpretación," 57, 64.

52. See Loyola's *Ser y morir en Pablo Neruda 1918–1945* (Santiago de Chile: Editora Santiago, 1967), 122.

53. Loyola, "Las dos residencias," 15.

54. Pablo Neruda, *Residencia en la tierra,* 4th ed. (Buenos Aires: Editorial Losada, 1958), 109. Hereafter the pages appear in the text.

55. Pablo Neruda, *Residence on Earth,* Donald D. Walsh trans., 155, 157.

56. Marx, *Early Writings,* 325. See the "Economic and Philosophical Manuscripts."

57. Ibid., 328.

58. Jaime Concha, *Neruda: 1904–1936* (Santiago: Editorial Universitaria, 1972), 198.

59. See Thomas E. Skidmore and Peter H. Smith, *Modern Latin America,* 5th ed. (Oxford: Oxford University Press, 2001), 74.

60. Charles S. Sargent, "Argentina" in *Latin American Urbanization: Historical Profiles of Major Cities* (Westport, CT: Greenwood Press, 1994), 22.

61. Ramón Gutiérrez, "Buenos Aires, A Great European City" in *Planning Latin America's Capital Cities,* 66–67.

62. Neruda, *Residencia en la tierra,* 85. Hereafter the pages appear in the text.

63. Pablo Neruda, *Residence on Earth,* Donald D. Walsh trans., 119, 121.
64. See Benjamin's "On Some Motifs in Baudelaire" in *Illuminations,* ed. Hannah Arendt (New York: Shocken Books, 1969), 172.
65. Pablo Neruda, *Residence on Earth,* Donald D. Walsh trans. My translations differ from Donald D. Walsh's regarding "con un golpe de oreja" and "cuchillo verde." The former is better translated as "with a blow on the ear," thus emphasizing the punitive measures taken in the schools and/or the church's turning a deaf ear to social problems; the latter should be a "green knife," thus underscoring the color as a symbol of nature.
66. Loyola, "Las dos residencias," 43.
67. Benjamín, "On Some Motifs," 174.
68. Santí, *Pablo Neruda,* 70–74.
69. Marjorie Agosín, *Pablo Neruda* (Boston: Twayne Publishers, 1986), 40–41.
70. Manuel Durán and Margery Safir, *Earth Tones: The Poetry of Pablo Neruda* (Bloomington: Indiana University Press, 1991). See esp. Chapter 2, "The Nature Poet" (33–73). For more information on *Earth Tones* see my commentary in chapter 1. Hereafter pages cited in text.
71. Federico García Lorca, *Poeta en Nueva York / Tierra luna* (Barcelona: Editorial Ariel, 1983).
72. See Teitelboim's *Neruda,* 132 and 144 respectively.
73. Neruda talks about his love for Albertina in a letter on February 11, 1930 and notes that she is the subject of that early book of poetry. See Margarita Aguirre, ed., *Pablo Neruda / Héctor Eandi: correspondencia durante "Residencia en la tierra"* (Buenos Aires: Editorial Sudamericana, 1980), 77–78.
74. Loyola, "Las dos residencias," 31.
75. Pablo Neruda, *Veinte poemas de amor y una canción desesperada,* 8th ed. (Madrid: Alianza Editorial, 1995), 29–30.
76. *Pablo Neruda: Selected Poems,* Nathaniel Tarn ed. (Boston: Houghton Mifflin, 1990), 17.
77. See Hernán Loyola, "Las dos residencias," 44–45.
78. Neruda, *Residencia en la tierra,* 106.
79. Pablo Neruda, *Residence on Earth,* Donald D. Walsh, 151, 153.
80. *Residencia en la tierra,* 101–2.
81. Pablo Neruda, *Residence on Earth,* Donald D. Walsh, 143, 145.
82. Hernán Loyola, "Las dos residencias." See pp. 26 to 33 and esp. p. 27.
83. Pablo Neruda, *Confieso que he vivido,* 11th ed. (Buenos Aires: Editorial Losada, 1992), 120.
84. Neruda, *Residencia en la tierra,* 30–31.
85. Pablo Neruda, *Residence on Earth,* Donald D. Walsh, 33, 35.
86. Neruda, *Confieso,* 121.
87. See Concha's discussion of the hero in *Pablo Neruda 1904–1936,* 262–66.
88. Neruda, *Residencia en la tierra,* 52.
89. Neruda, *Para nacer he nacido,* 140.

Chapter 4. The Struggle against Alienation in *Tercera residencia*

1. See *Pablo Neruda: Antología poética,* ed. and with a prologue by Rafael Alberti (Madrid: Espasa-Calpe, 1983); and *Pablo Neruda: Antología esencial,* ed. and with a prologue by Hernán Loyola (Buenos Aires: Editorial Losada, 1971).
2. *Pablo Neruda: Five Decades: A Selection* (1925–1970), ed. and trans. Ben Belitt

(New York: Grove Press, 1974); and *Pablo Neruda: Selected Poems,* ed. and with a foreword by Nathaniel Tarn (Boston: Houghton Mifflin/Seymour Lawrence, 1970).

3. Neruda, *Confieso que he vivido,* 11th ed. (Buenos Aires: Editorial Losada, 1992), 124.

4. Antonio Gramsci, *Selections from the Prison Notebooks* (London: Lawrence and Wishart, 1971), 87.

5. Pablo Neruda, *Tercera residencia,* 3rd ed. (Barcelona: Seix Barral, 1983), 12–13.

6. Pablo Neruda, *Residence on Earth,* Donald D. Walsh trans. (New York: New Directions, 1973), 219.

7. Pablo Neruda, *Canto general,* 2d ed. (Barcelona: Seix Barral, 1982), 32.

8. Pablo Neruda, *Odas elementales,* 6th ed. (Barcelona: Editorial Bruguera, 1986), 279.

9. Pablo Neruda, *Residencia en la tierra,* 4th ed. (Buenos Aires: Editorial Losada, 1971): 11–12.

10. Pablo Neruda, *Residence on Earth,* Donald D. Walsh trans., 7.

11. Andrew Marvell, "To His Coy Mistress," in *The Norton Anthology of Poetry,* 3rd ed., ed. Alexander W. Allison et. al. (New York: W. W. Norton, 1983).

12. Enrico Mario Santí, *Pablo Neruda: The Prophetics of Prophecy* (Ithaca: Cornell University Press, 1982), 50–52.

13. Neruda, *Tercera residencia,* 3rd ed., 10–11. Hereafter references to this poem appear in parenthesis in the text.

14. Neruda, *Residence on Earth,* 215, 217.

15. For a condensed version of his argument see Alonso's "Angustia y desintegración" in *Pablo Neruda,* ed. Emir Rodríguez Monegal and Enrico Mario Santí (Madrid: Taurus Ediciones, 1980), 119–33. The quote from Alonso is on p. 132.

16. Emir Rodríguez Monegal, "El sistema del poeta" in Rodríguez Monegal and Santí. See note 8.

17. Neruda, *Tercera residencia,* 17. Hereafter the page references appear in the text.

18. Neruda, *Residence on Earth,* 227, 229.

19. Pablo Neruda, *Para nacer he nacido* (Barcelona: Planeta, 1989).

20. I am referring to Baudelaire's "Parfum exotique" (Exotic Perfume) in *The Flowers of Evil,* trans. James McGowan (Oxford: Oxford University Press, 1993), 48.

21. Alain Sicard's analysis in *El pensamiento poético de Pablo Neruda* (Madrid: Editorial Gredos, 1981), 223.

22. Ibid., 500–506.

23. Neruda, *Residencia,* 63–64.

24. See Alan Gilbert's introduction to *Democratic Individuality* (Cambridge: Cambridge University Press, 1990), 1–18.

25. Florence L. Yudin, "The Dialectical Failure in Neruda's 'Las furias y las penas'," in *Pablo Neruda,* ed. Harold Bloom (New York: Chelsea House Publishers, 1989), 280.

26. Neruda, *Tercera residencia,* 25. Hereafter the page references appear in the text.

27. Neruda, *Residence on Earth,* 231–43.

28. See Pablo Neruda, *Los versos del capitán,* 4th ed. (Buenos Aires: Editorial Losada, 1968), 43–44.

29. "Tango del viudo" in *Residencia,* 63–64,

30. Pablo Neruda, *Veinte poemas de amor y una canción desesperada,* 8th ed. (Madrid: Alianza Editorial, 1995), 108. For the full poem see 107–9.

31. See Yudin, "Dialectical Failure," 277–90.

32. Sicard, *El pensamiento poético de Pablo Neruda,* 501, 504.

33. I have relied on Bertell Ollman's analysis of Marx's dialectical method. It stands to reason that there would be cross-resonances between his organization of thought and Neruda's since the latter considered himself to be a Marxist. I demonstrate that Neruda's

poetic thought resembles Marx's modus operandi to a large degree. See Ollman's *Dialectical Investigations,* "Putting Dialectics to Work: The Process of Abstraction in Marx's Method" (London/New York: Routledge, 1993), 23–83.

34. See Neruda, *Confieso,* 162–64, and Volodia Teitelboim, *Neruda,* 5th ed. (Santiago de Chile: Bat Ediciones, 1992), 192–97.

35. Neruda, *Confieso,* 474.

36. Hernán Loyola, ed., "Las dos residencias," *Pablo Neruda: Residencia en la tierra* (Madrid: Ediciones Cátedra, 1987), 53.

37. Loyola, Concha, and Sicard demonstrate persuasively that Neruda's interest in radical politics began early in his life. In his youth he was attracted to anarchist ideas; by 1937 he was a fellow traveler of the Communist Party. In his memoirs, Neruda declares that "aunque el carnet militante lo recibí mucho más tarde en Chile, cuando ingresé oficialmente al partido, creo haberme definido ante mí mismo como un comunista durante la guerra de España" (although I received by member's card much later, when I officially joined the party, I believe I defined myself to myself as a Communist during the war over Spain), *Confieso,* 187.

38. Ronald Fraser, *The Blood of Spain: An Oral History of the Spanish Civil War* (New York: Pantheon, 1986), 550. Hereafter cited in text.

39. Hugh Thomas, *The Spanish Civil War* (New York: Touchstone, 1986), 143.

40. Teitelboim, *Neruda,* 178.

41. Neruda, *Confieso,* 187, 441.

42. See Alastair Reid's introduction to *Neruda: Selected Poems* (Boston: Houghton Mifflin / Seymour Lawrence, 1990).

43. Neruda, *Residence on Earth,* 245, 247.

44. Neruda, *Tercera residencia,* 35. Hereafter the page references appear in the text.

45. Loyola, "Las dos residencias," 33–41, and Teitelboim, *Neruda,* 144–52.

46. José Miguel Velloso, *Conversaciones con Rafael Alberti* (Madrid: Ediciones Sedmay, 1977), 137.

47. Neruda, *Confieso,* 474–77.

48. Gene Bell-Villada, *Art For Art's Sake and Literary Life: How Politics and Markets Helped Shape the Ideology and Culture of Aestheticism 1790–1990* (Lincoln: University of Nebraska Press, 1998), 145.

49. Neruda, *Confieso,* 133.

50. Mario Rodríguez Fernández, "'Reunión bajo las nuevas banderas' o de la conversión poética de Pablo Neruda" in *Aproximaciones a Pablo Neruda,* ed. Angel Flores (Barcelona: Llibres de Sinera, 1974), 151–64.

51. Pierre Bourdieu, *The Field of Cultural Production* (New York: Columbia University Press, 1993), 264–65.

52. Emir Rodríguez Monegal, "El sistema del poeta" in Rodríguez Monegal and Santí, 63–91.

53. See Bourdieu's "The Historical Genesis of the Pure Aesthetic," in *The Field of Cultural Production,* 254–66.

Chapter 5. Neruda's Moral Realism in España en el Corazón

1. Pablo Neruda, *Tercera residencia,* 3rd ed. (Barcelona: Seix Barral, 1983), 42.

2. Pablo Neruda, *Residence on Earth,* Donald D. Walsh trans. (New York: New Directions, 1973), 253.

3. Alfred J. McAdam, "Neruda's *España en el corazón:* Genre and Historical Moment," in *Pablo Neruda,* ed. Harold Bloom (New York: Chelsea House Publishers, 1989), 291–99.

4. Robin Warner, "The Politics of Pablo Neruda's *España en el corazón,*" in Bloom, 233–41.

5. René de Costa, *The Poetry of Pablo Neruda* (Cambridge, MA: Harvard University Press, 1979), 89–104. See esp. pp. 90 and 92.

6. Alan Gilbert, *Democratic Individuality* (Cambridge: Cambridge University Press, 1990), 8.

7. Richard Boyd, "How to be a Moral Realist," in *Essays on Moral Realism,* ed. Geoffrey Sayre-McCord (Ithaca, NY: Cornell University Press, 1988), 182–85. There are several types of moral realism—see Peter Railton's summary of those positions in "Moral Realism" in his book *Facts, Values, and Norms: Essays toward a Morality of Consequence* (Cambridge: Cambridge University Press, 2003), 3–42. I have relied on the version that recognizes an affinity between historical materialism and moral realism. Besides the Boyd article, see Alan Gilbert's book cited above and Roy Bhaskar, *Dialectic: The Pulse of Freedom* (London: Verso, 1993).

8. César Vallejo, *Obra poética completa,* ed. and with an introduction by Enrique Ballón Aguirre, 2d ed. (Caracas: Biblioteca Ayacucho, 1985), lxviii.

9. Ibid., 195–216. Miguel Hernández, *Viento del pueblo: Poesía en la guerra,* 2d ed. (Buenos Aires: Editorial Lautaro, [1937] 1956). One should also take into consideration the impact of Rafael Alberti's *El poeta en la calle (1931–1936).* See *Poesía, 1924–1937* (Madrid: Editorial Signo, 1938).

10. See Volodia Teitelboim, *Neruda,* 5th ed. (Santiago: Ediciones Bat, 1991), 167–238, and Pablo Neruda, *Confieso que he vivido,* 11th ed. (Buenos Aires: Losada, 1992), 151–90.

11. See chapter 2 for a discussion of moral realism. The basis for my argument comes from Gilbert, *Democratic Individuality,* and Bhaskar, *Dialectic,* as well as *Plato Etc.: The Problems of Philosophy and their Resolution* (London: Verso, 1994).

12. Neruda, *Tercera residencia,* 39. Hereafter the pages are cited in the text.

13. Neruda, *Residence on Earth,* 249.

14. Bertell Ollman, *Dialectical Investigations* (New York: Routledge, 1993). See especially, "Putting Dialectics to Work: The Process of Abstraction in Marx's Method," 23–83. Ollman argues convincingly for a philosophy of internal relations, which consists of three main components: the level of generality, extension, and vantage point. The first deals with ways of examining the "boundaries for thinking the part and the whole"; the second looks at time and space within each abstraction; and the third identifies the "place within a relation from which to view, reconsider other components of the relation" (39–40). When I speak of abstraction here I am referring to Ollman's theory of abstractions adapted as I see fit in the case of Neruda. The levels of generality include, but not exhaustively, the person or situation, what is general to people (e.g., capitalism), capitalism as such, class society, human society (the species), the animal world, and qualities that are a part of nature. Vantage point takes into account the angle of different social classes involved in the relations of production, the general dispositions that would lead them to make presuppositions or judgments based on class position, the "objective" point of view of the different elements pertaining to the forces of production (e.g., from the point of view of accumulation, surplus value), and so on. Extension "brings the various organic and historical movements together under the same rubric, making how things happen a part of what they are, but it is [Marx's] abstraction of vantage point that enables him (and us) to actually catch sight of them as a single tendency" (77–78). See esp. 55–78.

15. Neruda, *Residence on Earth,* 249, 251.

16. Robin Warner, "The Politics of Pablo Neruda's *España en el corazón,*" 238–39.

17. Alan Gilbert speaks of a "mutual regard" of all citizens and Roy Bhaskar of "mutual respect" as the fundamental core of any egalitarian society.

18. Hugh Thomas, *The Spanish Civil War*, 4th ed. (New York: Touchstone, 1986), 219.
19. Ibid., 208–9.
20. Ibid., 227–31.
21. Neruda, *Residence on Earth*, 251, 253.
22. "An immediate consequence of man's estrangement from the product of his labour, his life activity, his species-being, is *the estrangement of man from man*." Karl Marx, *Early Writings*, ed. Quintin Hoore, 329–30 (New York: Vintage Books, 1975).
23. Ronald Fraser, *Blood of Spain: An Oral History of the Spanish Civil War* (New York: Pantheon, 1986), 513.
24. I disagree with Donald D. Walsh's translation of "pobredumbre" as "putrefaction"; an "abundance of poverty" would be best.
25. The original edition was published in the Montserrat Monastery in Catalonia. Republican soldiers put it together and printed it during wartime. See Teitelboim, *Neruda*, 220–21 and Neruda, *Confieso*, 170–71.
26. Jaime Alazraki, "Punto de vista y recodificación en los poemas de autoexégesis de Pablo Neruda," *Symposium* (1978): 184–97; esp. p. 188.
27. Neruda, *Residence on Earth*, 254–61.
28. Here again this poem acts as a type of diary. We have little other detailed information about his life in Madrid other than this testimony. But see also Teitelboim, *Neruda*, 210–14.
29. Costa, *The Poetry of Pablo Neruda*, 94–95.
30. Gilbert, *Democratic Individuality*, 32–44.
31. Pablo Neruda, *Canto general*, 2d ed. (Barcelona: 1982 [1950]), 305–8).
32. Thomas, *The Spanish Civil Wary*, 982–84.
33. Ibid., 486–87.
34. Pablo Neruda, *Tercera residencia*, 3rd ed. (Barcelona: Seix Barral, 1983), 51–52. Hereafter the page references appear in the text.
35. Neruda, *Residence on Earth*, 271, 273.
36. Thomas, *The Spanish Civil War*, 486.
37. Thomas considers these casualty figures, cited by R. Salas Larrazábal, to be too low, 487.
38. Neruda, *Tercera residencia*, 57.
39. In his chapter, "Putting Dialectics to Work: The Process of Abstraction in Marx's Method," Bertell Ollman points to Marx's ability to abstract a part of the social totality under capitalism, examine it, and then see how it functions in its interaction with the whole. "Abstract" comes from the Latin "abstrahere," which means "to pull from." As a dialectical thinker, Neruda often uses the same method. One need only think of those wonderful odes to the tomato, the onion, wine, and so on. See Ollman's *Dialectical Investigations*, 23–83.
40. Neruda, *Tercera residencia*, 60–61. Hereafter page references appear in the text.
41. Neruda, *Residence on Earth*, 286–91.
42. Marx, *Early Writings*, 328.
43. Ibid., 329.
44. Fraser, *Blood of Spain*, 455.
45. Helen Graham, *The Spanish Republic at War 1936–1939* (Cambridge: Cambridge University Press, 2002), 189.
46. In my view "harina" would be better translated as "flour."
47. Georg Lukács, *Essays on Realism* (Cambridge, MA: The MIT Press, 1980), 37.
48. Neruda, *Confieso*, 170–82, and Teitelboim, *Neruda*, 216–36. For publication information see the chronology at the end of *Confieso*, 475.
49. "Almería," written in reaction to the Nationalist bombing of that Spanish town, had to have been composed after May 31, 1937. It is probable that they were written between

June 1 and October 28—the date in which the Republican government was moved from Valencia to Barcelona, signaling the beginning of the end of the civil war (Thomas, *The Spanish Civil War,* 773).
    50. Neruda, *Tercera residencia,* 66–67. Hereafter page references appear in the text.
    51. Neruda, *Residence on Earth,* 296–303.
    52. Thomas, *The Spanish Civil War,* 732–33.
    53. Ibid., 770.
    54. Ibid., 710–33. Sixty percent is my estimate based on the map on 732.
    55. Ibid., 936–37.
    56. Lukács, *Essays on Realism,* 129.
    57. See Concha's "Interpretación de *Residencia en la tierra*" in *Tres ensayos sobre Pablo Neruda* (Palma de Mallorca: Mosén Alcover, 1974), 31–84. Originally published in 1963 in *Mapocho.*
    58. Jaime Concha, *Neruda 1904–1936* (Santiago de Chile: Editorial Universitaria, 1972), 220.
    59. See Sicard's *El pensamiento poético de Pablo Neruda* (Madrid: Gredos, 1981), 105.

Chapter 6. Blood and Letters: Neruda and Antifascism

    1. Barry Carr, *Marxism and Communism in Twentieth-Century Mexico* (Lincoln: University of Nebraska Press, 1992), 50.
    2. Ibid., 48.
    3. Ibid., 69.
    4. Ibid., 71.
    5. David Siqueiros, *Me llamaban el coronelazo: Memorias* (Mexico: Editorial Grijalbo, 1977), 360. All translations are mine.
    6. Ibid., 356.
    7. Ibid., 357.
    8. For more on the relationship between the KPD (the German Communist Party), the Social Democratic Party, and the National Socialists in Germany in the 1920s and 1930s, see R. Palme Dutt, *Fascism and Social Revolution* (New York: International Publishers, 1934), 107–32; and Fernando Claudín, *The Communist Movement: From Comintern to Cominform* (New York and London: Monthly Review Press, 1975), 145–66. These are very different accounts of these years just prior to the rise of fascism in Germany. Dutt lays most of the blame on the Social Democrats for believing in the pacifist road to socialism even as the National Socialists were gaining strength. With its policy to "save Germany from Bolshevism" and to support "the lesser evil," Dutt argues, Social Democracy played into the hands of the fascists. By contrast, Claudín contends that by following the Comintern's dictates regarding "social fascism," and thus attacking both Social Democracy and the National Socialists, the KPD made a grave mistake that led to the rise of fascism. He does not defend Social Democracy directly, but rather argues, like Trotsky, for the need for a united front against fascism. Neruda unquestionably sided with the line advanced by Dutt.
    9. Siqueiros, *Memorias,* 359.
    10. I would like to thank the Fundación Pablo Neruda for allowing me to see the unedited letters on file, and especially for this letter written on August 3, 1937, from Paris.
    11. Pablo Neruda, *Confieso que he vivido: Memorias,* 11th ed. (Buenos Aires: Losada, 1992), 214–15.
    12. Ibid., 214.
    13. Octavio Paz, *Itinerario* (Mexico: Fondo de Cultura Económica, 1993), 59
    14. Ibid., 62–63.

15. Ibid.
16. Ibid., 63.
17. Ibid., 69–70.
18. Ibid., 73.
19. Current historical research indicates that the repression in the late 1930s in the USSR was due to factions in the Stalin regime and to peasants who carried out revenge for personal or economic reasons. See J. Arch Getty's "The Politics of Repression Revisited" in *Stalinist Terror: New Perspectives*, ed. J. Arch Getty and Roberta T. Manning (Cambridge: Cambridge University Press, 1993); and Moshe Lewin's *The Making of the Soviet System* (New York: The New Press, 1995).
20. Michael Parenti, *Blackshirts and Reds: Rational Fascism and the Overthrow of Communism* (San Francisco: City Lights Books, 1997), 79.
21. See my essay, "Octavio Paz: El camino hacia la desilusión" in *Octavio Paz: La dimensión estética del ensayo*, ed. Héctor Jaimes (Mexico: Siglo XXI Editores 2004), 133–48.
22. Neruda, *Confieso*, 293.
23. Volodia Teitelboim, *Neruda*, 5th ed. (Santiago: Ediciones Bat, 1992), 243.
24. Julio Faúndez, *Marxism and Socialism in Chile* (New Haven, CT: Yale University Press, 1988), 42.
25. Teitelboim, *Neruda*, 243.
26. Ibid., 245–57 and Neruda, 200–204.
27. I found an account of these events in the Neruda library collection at the Biblioteca Central at the Universidad de Chile, in Santiago, in *Aurora de Chile* (December 3, 1938).
28. Alexander Werth, *Russia at War: 1941–1945* (New York: Carroll & Graf, 1964), xvi.
29. Teitelboim, *Neruda*, 213.
30. Werth, xv.
31. Ibid., 144.
32. Issac Deutscher, *Stalin: A Political Biography* (New York: Oxford University Press, 1969), 469.
33. Ibid., 470–72.
34. René de Costa, *The Poetry of Pablo Neruda* (Cambridge, MA: Harvard University Press, 1979), 99.
35. Teitelboim, *Neruda*, 210.
36. Pablo Neruda, *Tercera residencia*, 3rd ed. (Barcelona: Seix Barral, 1983), 76. Hereafter the page references are cited in the text.
37. Pablo Neruda, *Residence on Earth*, Donald D. Walsh trans., 308–13.
38. Hobsbawm, *The Age of Extremes: A History of the World, 1914–1991* (New York: Pantheon, 1994), 156.
39. See Deutscher, *Stalin*, 474, and Hobsbawm, *Age of Extremes*, 168–69.
40. Werth, *Russia at War*, 430–36.
41. Michael Löwy, *Le Marxisme en Amerique Latine de 1909 à nos jours: anthologie* (Paris: F. Maspero, 1980), 32.
42. Ibid., 33.
43. See Ruth Berins Collier's "Labor Politics and Regime Change: Internal Trajectories Versus External Influences" in *Latin America in the 1940s: War and Postwar Transitions*, ed. David Rock (Berkeley: University of California Press, 1994), 59–88.
44. Thomas E. Skidmore and Peter H. Smith, *Modern Latin America* (Oxford: Oxford University Press, 1992), 122–26, 160–70, 234–37.
45. See Emir Rodríguez Monegal, *El viajero inmóvil: Introducción a Pablo Neruda* (Buenos Aires: Losada, 1966), 235.
46. Werth, *Russia at War*, xiv.
47. Hobsbawm, *Age of Extremes*, 40.
48. Costa, *The Poetry of Pablo Neruda*, 99–100.

49. Teitelboim, *Neruda*, 260.
50. Neruda, *Tercera residencia*, 79. Hereafter the page references appear in the text.
51. Neruda, *Residence on Earth*, 315–23.
52. Jorge Campos, ed., *Rubén Darío: Poesía*, 2d ed. (Madrid: Alianza Editorial, 1980), 70.
53. Peter Calvocoressi and Guy Wint, *Total War: The Story of World War II* (New York: Pantheon, 1972), 314–15.
54. Ibid., 315–16.
55. Karl Marx and Frederich Engels, "Manifesto of the Communist Party" in *Marx & Engels: Basic Writings on Politics & Philosophy*, ed. Lewis S. Feuer 29 (New York: Doubleday Anchor, 1959).
56. See Hobsbawm, *Age of Extremes*, 147–56, and Werth, *Russia at War*, 5–6.
57. Enrico Mario Santí, *Pablo Neruda: The Prophetics of Prophecy* (Ithaca: Cornell University Press, 1982), 66–67.
58. Ibid., 102–103.
59. Jaime Alazraki, "Punto de vista y recodificación en los poemas de autoexégesis de Pablo Neruda, *"Symposium"* (1978), 184–97.
60. Neruda, *Tercera residencia*, 92. Hereafter the page references appear in the text.
61. Neruda, *Residence on Earth*, 339–43.
62. See Werth, *Russia at War*, 766.
63. Eric D. Weitz, *Creating German Communism, 1890–1990: From Popular Protests to Socialist State* (Princeton: Princeton University Press, 1997), 280.
64. Claudín, *Communist Movement*, 127.
65. Weitz, *Creating*, 295–96.
66. Claudín, *Communist Movement*, 129.
67. Dutt, *Fascism*, 112.
68. Ibid., 117–23.
69. William L. Shirer, in his classic *The Rise and Fall of the Third Reich* (New York: Fawcett Crest, 1960), defends the Social Democratic line: "The Communists, shouting that the Social Democrats were 'betraying the workers' by supporting Hindenburg, ran their own candidate, Ernst Thaelmann, the party's leader. It was not the first time, nor the last, that the Communists, on orders of Moscow, risked playing into Nazi hands" (221). Yet, as Dutt argues, the Social Democrats did betray the workers and, as such, much of their own constituency. Indeed, they lost a half a million votes during the elections of 1930, most likely due to this stance. Even so, as Claudín points out, by 1931, only 4 per cent of the factory committees in Germany were led by the Communists, whereas the Social Democrats controlled an overwhelming 84 percent (160).
70. Dutt, *Fascism*, 118.
71. Weitz, *Creating*, 305–06.
72. Claudín, *Communist Movement*, 161–63.
73. Ibid., 163.
74. Neruda, *Tercera residencia*, 94. Hereafter the page references appear in the text.
75. Neruda, *Residence on Earth*, 341.
76. My translation differs from Walsh's in this case: "desde el hacha brota" should be "that blossoms from the ax."
77. Costa, *The Poetry of Pablo Neruda*, 100–103.

Conclusion: Neruda's Work During the Cold War

1. See Roberto Schwarz's "The Cart, the Tram and the Modernist Poet" in his book *Misplaced Ideas: Essays on Brazilian Culture* (London: Verso, 1992), 115.

2. Jamie Concha, *Neruda: 1904–1934* (Santiago: Editorial Universitaria, 1972), 13.

3. Paul W. Drake, "International Crises and Popular Movements in Latin America: Chile and Peru from the Great Depression to the Cold War" in *Latin America in the 1940s: War and Postwar Transitions*, ed. David Rock (Berkeley: University of California Press, 1994), 115.

4. Ibid., 121.

5. Julio Faúndez, *Marxism and Democracy in Chile: From 1932 to the Fall of Allende* (New Haven: Yale University Press, 1988), 95.

6. Ibid., 91.

7. Drake, "International Crisis," 124–25.

8. Faúndez, *Marxism,* 72–73.

9. Drake, "International Crisis," 126.

10. Faúndez, *Marxism,* 74–75.

11. Carmelo Furci, *The Chilean Communist Party and the Road to Socialism* (London: Zed Books, 1984), 43–62. During this period the party was divided between those who sought a more rapid route to socialist revolution (led by Luis Reinoso) and those who believed in a more long-term objective to achieving socialist revolution (led by Galo González, Volodia Teitelboim, and Luis Corvalán).

12. Rita Guibert, *Seven Voices: Seven Latin American Writers Talk to Rita Guibert* (New York: Alfred E. Knopf, 1973), 54.

13. This is my rewording of Bhaskar's position on transcendental realism in *Dialectic: The Pulse of Freedom* (London: Verso, 1993), 405.

14. Georg Lukács, *Realism in Our Time: Literature and the Class Struggle* (New York: Harper & Row, 1962), 48.

15. Quoted in Pablo Neruda, *Canto general,* ed. Enrico Mario Santí, 17–18 (Madrid: Cátedra, 1997). The translations are mine.

16. See James Murphy's discussion of "revolutionary romanticism" in *The Proletarian Moment: The Controversy over Leftism in Literature* (Urbana & Chicago: University of Illinois Press, 1991), 101–4.

17. Lukács, *Realism,* 125–26. For the reference in Marx, see *The Eighteenth Brumaire of Louis Bonaparte* (New York: International Publishers, 1990), 19.

18. Santí, Enrico, Mario ed. of Pablo Neruda, *Canto general* (Madrid: Cátedra, 1997), 19.

19. Ibid., 25.

20. Pablo Neruda, *Confieso que he vivido,* 11th ed. (Buenos Aires: Losada, 1974).

21. See chapter 1. Manuel Durán and Margery Safir in *Earth Tones: The Poetry of Pablo Neruda* (Bloomington: Indiana University Press, 1981), 81–105, argue along those lines, as does Emir Rodríguez Monegal in *El viajero inmóvil: Introducción a Pablo Neruda* (Losada: Buenos Aires, 1966), 235–54.

22. Pablo Neruda, *Canto general,* 2d ed. (Barcelona: Editorial Seix Barral, 1982), 53–54. Hereafter the page references appear in the text.

23. Pablo Neruda, *Canto general,* Jack Schmitt trans. (Berkeley: University of California Press, 1993), 49–50.

24. J. H. Parry, *The Spanish Seaborne Empire* (New York: Alfred A. Knopf, 1966), 52.

25. See F. A. Kirkpatrick, *The Spanish Conquistadors,* 3rd ed. (London: Adam & Charles Black, 1963), 52.

26. Ibid., 47–59.

27. Neruda, *Canto general,* 50–51.

28. Ibid., 49.

29. Mariano Picón Salas, *De la conquista a la independencia: tres siglos de historia cultural hispanoamericana* (Mexico: Fondo de Cultura Económica, 1985), 61.

30. Quoted in Kirkpatrick, *Spanish Conquistadors,* 53.

31. The clearest way to follow Neruda's itinerary, I have found, is to consult *Confieso que he vivido: Memorias,* 11th ed. (Buenos Aires: Losada, 1992), 471–85.

32. Furci, *Chilean Communist Party,* 43–62.
33. Walter LaFeber, *America, Russia, and the Cold War, 1945–1980,* 4th ed. (New York: John Wiley & Sons, 1980), 56.
34. Ibid., 62.
35. Issac Deutscher, *Stalin: A Political Biography,* 2d ed. (New York: Oxford University Press, 1969), 572–76; and LaFeber, *America,* 50–51.
36. Eric Hobsbawm, *The Age of Extremes: A History of the World, 1914–1991* (New York: Pantheon, 1994), 232.
37. Deutscher, *Stalin,* 572–75.
38. Issac Deutscher, *Russia After Stalin* (Indianapolis, New York: The Bobbs-Merrill Company, 1968), 55. See especially chapter 4, "The Legacy of Stalinism: Domestic Affairs," 53–73.
39. Hobsbawm, *Age of Extremes,* 232.
40. Furci, *Chilean Communist Party,* 57.
41. Quoted in Jaime Concha's critical introduction to Pablo Neruda, *Odas elementales* (Madrid: Cátedra, 1999), 50–51.
42. Ibid., 45.
43. Neruda, *Odas elementales,* 92–94. Hereafter the page references appear in the text.
44. Pablo Neruda, *Ode to Common Things,* Ken Krabbenhoff trans. (Boston: Bullfinch Press Book, 1999), 135–139.
45. See Agosín's discussion of "Ode to the Onion" in her book, *Neruda* (Boston: Twayne Publishers, 1986), 99–105.
46. See "La elaboración de la cebolla" by Robert Pring-Mill in *Aproximaciones a Pablo Neruda,* ed. Angel Flores (Barcelona: Ed. Llibres de Sinera, 1974), 234, 239.
47. See Costa's analysis of *Odas elementales* in *The Poetry of Pablo Neruda* (Cambridge, MA: Harvard University Press, 1979), 144–74.
48. Ibid., 159.
49. Agosín, *Neruda,* 96.
50. Pablo Neruda, *Odes to Common Things* (Boston: A Bullfinch Press Book, 1999), 12. I am quoting from the Spanish original.
51. Bertolt Brecht, *Poems 1913–1956* (New York: Routledge, 1987), 257.
52. Hernán Loyola, ed., *Pablo Neruda: obras completas II: De "Odas elementales" a "Memorial de Isla Negra" 1954–1964* (Barcelona: Galaxia Gutenberg, 1999), 1327.
53. Hernán Loyola ed., *Pablo Neruda: obra completas III: De "Arte de pájaros" a "El mar y las campanas" 1966–1973* (Barcelona: Galaxia Gutenberg, 1999), 752.

Bibliography

Achugar, Hugo. "The Book of Poems as a Social Act: Notes Toward an Interpretation of Contemporary Hispanic American Poetry." In *Marxism and the Interpretation of Culture*, edited by Cary Nelson and Lawrence Grossberg, 651–62. Urbana: University of Illinois Press, 1988.

Agosín, Marjorie. *Pablo Neruda*. Boston: Twayne Publishers, 1986.

Ahmad, Aijaz. *In Theory: Classes, Nations, Literatures*. London: Verso, 1993.

Alazraki, Jaime. "Punto de vista y recodificación en los poemas de autoexégesis de Pablo Neruda." *Symposium* (1978): 184–97.

Alberti, Rafael. *Poesía, 1924–1937*. Madrid: Editorial Signo, 1938.

Allison, Alexander W., et. al., eds. *The Norton Anthology of Poetry*, 3rd ed. New York: W. W. Norton, 1983.

Almandoz, Arturo, ed. *Planning Latin America's Capital Cities, 1850–1950*. London: Routledge, 2002.

Alonso, Amado. "Angustia y desintegración." In *Pablo Neruda*, edited by Emir Rodríguez Monegal and Enrico Mario Santí. Madrid: Taurus Ediciones, 1980.

———. *Poesía y estilo en Pablo Neruda*. Madrid: Editorial Gredos, 1997.

Baudelaire, Charles. *The Flowers of Evil*. Translated by James McGowan. Oxford: Oxford University Press, 1993.

Bell-Villada, Gene H. *Art for Art's Sake and Literary Life: How Politics and Markets Helped Shape the Ideology and Culture of Aestheticism, 1790–1990*. Lincoln: University of Nebraska Press, 1996.

Benjamin, Walter. *Illuminations*. Edited by Hannah Arendt. Translated by Harry Zohn. New York: Shocken Books, 1969.

Bergquist, Charles. *Labor in Latin America: Comparative Essays on Chile, Argentina, Venezuela and Colombia*. Palo Alto, CA: Stanford University Press, 1986.

Bhaskar, Roy. *Dialectic: The Pulse of Freedom*. London: Verso, 1993.

———. *Plato Etc*. London: Verso, 1994.

Bloom, Harold. *The Anxiety of Influence: A Theory of Poetry*. Oxford: Oxford University Press, 1973.

———, ed. *Pablo Neruda*. New York: Chelsea House Publishers, 1989.

Bourdieu, Pierre. *In Other Words: Essays Towards a Reflexive Sociology*. Translated by Matthew Adamson. Stanford: Stanford University Press, 1990.

———. *The Field of Cultural Production*. Edited by Randall Johnson. New York: Columbia University Press, 1993.

Boyd, Richard. "Metaphor and Theory Change: What is 'Metaphor' a metaphor for?" In *Metaphor and Thought*, edited by Andrew Ortony, 356–408. Cambridge: Cambridge University Press, 1979.

———. "How to be a Moral Realist." In *Essays in Moral Realism,* edited by Geoffrey Sayre-Cord, 181–229. Ithaca, NY: Cornell University Press, 1988.

Brecht, Bertolt. "Against Georg Lukács." In *Aesthetics and Politics,* edited by Ronald Taylor, 68–85. London: Verso, 1986.

———. *Poems: 1913–1956.* Edited by John Willett and Ralph Manheim. New York: Routledge, 1987.

Breton, André / Louis Aragon. *Surrealismo frente a realismo socialista.* Edited by Oscar Tusquets. Barcelona: Tusquets, 1973.

Calvocoressi, Peter and Guy Wint. *Total War: The Story of World War II.* New York: Pantheon, 1972.

Cano Ballesta, Juan. *La poesía española entre pureza y revolución.* Madrid: Gredos, 1972.

Carr, Barry. *Marxism and Communism in Twentieth-Century Mexico.* Lincoln: University of Nebraska Press, 1992.

Chebel d'Appollonia, Ariane. *Histoire Politique des intellectuels en France 1944–1954,* vol. 2. Bruxelles: Editions Complexe, 1991.

Claudín, Fernando. *The Communist Movement: From Comintern to Cominform,* 2 vols. New York and London: Monthly Review Press, 1975.

Collier, Ruth Berins. "Labor Politics and Regime Change: Internal Trajectories Versus External Influences." In Rock, *Latin America in the 1940s,* 59–88.

Concha, Jaime. *Neruda 1904–1936.* Santiago: Editorial Universitaria, 1972.

———. "Introducción." In *Odas elementales.* Madrid: Ediciones Cátedra, 1999.

———. "Neruda, desde 1952: 'No entendí nunca la lucha sino para que ésta termine.'" In *Coliloquio Internacional sobre Pablo Neruda (La obra posterior al Canto general),* edited by Alain Sicard, 47–78. Poitiers: Publications du Centre de Recherche Latino-Américaines de l'Université de Poitiers, 1979.

———. "Observaciones sobre algunas imágenes de *Residencia de la tierra.*" In *Simposio Pablo Neruda: Actas,* edited by Issac Jack Lévy and Juan Loveluck, 109–22. Madrid: University of South Carolina / Las Américas, 1978.

———. *Tres ensayos sobre Pablo Neruda.* Palma de Mallorca: University of South Carolina, 1974.

———. *Vicente Huidobro.* Madrid: Ediciones Júcar, 1980.

Costa, René de. "Sobre Huidobro y Neruda." *Revista iberoamericana* 45, (no. 106–7 (1979): 379–86.

———. *The Poetry of Pablo Neruda.* Cambridge, MA: Harvard University Press, 1979.

———. *Vicente Huidobro: The Careers of a Poet.* Oxford: Oxford University Press, 1984.

———, ed. *Vicente Huidobro y el creacionismo.* Madrid: Taurus, 1975.

Darío, Rubén. *Azul... Cantos de vida y esperanza.* Edited by José María Martínez. Madrid: Cátedra, 1995.

———. *Rubén Darío: Poesía,* 2d ed. Edited by Jorge Campos. Madrid: Alianza Editorial, 1980.

Dawes, Greg. "Octavio Paz: El camino hacia la desilusión." In *Octavio Paz: La dimensión estética del ensayo,* edited by Héctor Jaimes, 133–48. Mexico: Siglo XXI Editores, 2004.

Delporte, Cristian. *Intellectuels et Politique.* Firenze: Casterman-Giunti, 1995.

Deutscher, Issac. *Stalin: A Political Biography.* New York: Oxford University Press, 1969.

———. *Russia After Stalin.* Indianapolis, New York: The Bobbs-Merrill Company, 1968.

Drake, Paul W. "International Crises and Popular Movements in Latin America: Chile and

Peru from the Great Depression to the Cold War." In Rock, *Latin America in the 1940s,* 109–40.

Durán, Manuel and Margery Safir. *Earth Tones: The Poetry of Pablo Neruda.* Bloomington: University of Indiana Press, 1981.

Eagleton, Terry. *Literary Theory: An Introduction.* Minneapolis: University of Minnesota Press, 1983.

Edwards, Paul, ed. *Encyclopedia of Philosophy.* Vols. 5–6. New York: MacMillan Press, 1967.

Eliot, T. S. *The Wasteland and Other Poems.* New York: Harcourt Brace Jovanovich, 1962.

Faúndez, Julio. *Marxism and Democracy in Chile: From 1932 to the Fall of Allende.* New Haven, CT: Yale University Press, 1988.

Feuer, Lewis S. *Marx and Engels: Basic Writings on Politics and Philosophy.* Garden City, NJ: Anchor Books, 1959.

Flores, Angel, ed. *Aproximaciones a Pablo Neruda.* Barcelona: Llibres de Sinera, 1974.

Forster, Merlin H. "Pablo Neruda and the Avant-garde." *Symposium* (Fall 1978): 208–20.

Franco, Jean. *The Decline and Fall of the Lettered City: Latin America and the Cold War.* Cambridge, MA: Harvard University Press, 2002.

Fraser, Ronald. *The Blood of Spain: An Oral History of the Spanish Civil War.* New York: Pantheon, 1986.

Furci, Carmelo. *The Chilean Communist Party and the Road to Socialism.* London: Zed Books, 1984.

García Lorca, Federico. *Poeta en Nueva York / Tierra luna.* Edited by Eutimio Martín. Barcelona: Editorial Ariel, 1983.

Geist, Anthony L. "Las mariposas en la barba: una lectura de *Poeta en Nueva York.*" *Cuadernos hispanoamericanos,* no. 433–46 (July–October 1986): 547–65.

Getty, J. Arch, and Roberta T. Manning. *Stalinist Terror: New Perspectives.* Cambridge: Cambridge University Press, 1993.

——— and Oleg V. Naumov. *The Road to Terror: Stalin and the Self-Destruction of the Bolsheviks, 1932–1939.* New Haven, CT: Yale University Press, 1999.

Gilbert, Alan. *Democratic Individuality.* Cambridge: Cambridge University Press, 1990.

———. "Marx's Moral Realism: Eudaimonism and Moral Progress." In *After Marx,* edited by James Farr and Terence Ball, 154–83. Cambridge: Cambridge University Press, 1984.

Goic, Cedomil. "'Alturas de Macchu Picchu': La torre y el abismo." In Rodríguez Monegal and Santí, *Pablo Neruda,* 219–44.

Gómez Paz, Julieta. "*Odas elementales* (1954)." In Flores, *Aproximaciones a Pablo Neruda,* 223–26

González, Mike and David Treece. *Gathering of the Voices: The Twentieth Century Poetry of Latin America.* London: Verso, 1992.

Graham, Helen. *The Spanish Republic at War, 1936–1939.* Cambridge: Cambridge University Press, 2002.

Gramsci, Antonio. *Selections From the Prison Notebooks.* London: Lawrence and Wishart, 1971.

Greenfield, Gerald Michael, ed. *Latin American Urbanization: Historical Profiles of Major Cities.* Westport, CT: Greenwood Press, 1994.

Guibert, Rita. *Seven Voices: Seven Latin American Writers Talk to Rita Guibert.* New York: Alfred E. Knopf, 1973.

Gutiérrez, Ramón. "Buenos Aires, A Great European City." In Almandoz, *Planning,* 45–74.

Halperín Donghi, Tulio. *Historia contemporánea de América Latina,* 13th ed. Madrid: Alianza Editorial, 1990.

Harvey, David. *Justice, Nature & the Geography of Difference.* Oxford: Blackwell Publishers, 1996.

Hernández, Miguel. *Viento del pueblo: Poesía en la guerra,* 2d ed. Buenos Aires: Editorial Lautaro, 1956.

Hobsbawm, Eric. *The Age of Extremes: A History of the World, 1914–1991.* New York: Pantheon, 1994.

Kauffman Doig, Federico. *Perú antiguo. El incario: Una nueva perspectiva.* Lima: Kompaktos Editores, 1990.

Kirkpatrick, F. A. *The Spanish Conquistadors,* 3rd ed. London: Adam & Charles Black, 1963.

LaFeber, Walter. *America, Russia, and the Cold War: 1945–1980,* 4th ed. New York: John Wiley and Sons, 1980.

Lakoff, George, and Mark Turner. *More Than Cool Reason: A Field Guide to Poetic Metaphor.* Chicago: The University of Chicago Press, 1989.

Larrea, Juan. *Del surrealismo a Macchu Picchu.* Mexico: Editorial Joaquín Mortiz, 1967.

Lentricchia, Frank. *Modernist Quartet.* Cambridge: Cambridge University Press, 1994.

Loveluck, Juan. "Alturas de Macchu Picchu: Cantos I–IV." *Revista iberoamericana* 82 (1973): 175–88.

Löwy, Michael. *Le Marxisme en Amerique Latine de 1909 à nos jours: Anthologie.* Paris: F. Maspero, 1980.

Loyola, Hernán. "Las dos residencias." In Neruda, *Residencia en la tierra,* 13–80.

———. *Ser y morir en Pablo Neruda: 1918–1945.* Santiago: Editora Santiago, 1967.

———. "Poema-síntesis." In Flores, *Aproximaciones a Pablo Neruda,* 190–99.

Lukács, Georg. *Essays on Realism.* Edited by Rodney Livingstone. Cambridge, MA: The MIT Press, 1980.

———. *Realism in Our Time.* New York: Harper & Row, 1962.

———. *Writer and Critic and Other Essays.* New York: Universal Library, 1971.

Martín, Eutimio. "La entidad proteica de 'Poeta en Nueva York'." In García Lorca, *Poeta en Nueva York,* 11–60.

Marvell, Andrew. "To His Coy Mistress." In Allison et al., *Norton Anthology,* 178–79.

Mason, J. Alden. *The Ancient Civilizations of Peru.* New York: Pelican, 1975.

Marx, Karl. *Capital,* vol. 1. Translated by Ben Fowkes. New York: Vintage Books, 1977.

———. *Early Writings.* Edited by Lucio Colleti. Translated by Rodney Livingstone and Gregor Benton. New York: Vintage Books, 1975.

———. *The Eighteenth Brumaire of Louis Bonaparte.* Translated by C. P. Dutt. New York: International Publishers, 1990.

McAdam, Alfred J. "Neruda's *España en el corazón:* Genre and Historical Moment." In Bloom, *Pablo Neruda,* 291–99.

Métraux, Alfred. *The History of the Incas.* New York: Schocken Books, 1970.

Murphy, James. *The Proletarian Moment: The Controversy Over Leftism in Literature.* Urbana: University of Illinois Press, 1991.

Neruda, Pablo. *Canto general,* 2d ed. Barcelona: Seix Barral Editores, 1982.

———. *Canto general,* translated by Jack Schmitt. Berkeley: University of California Press, 1993.
———. *Confieso que he vivido,* 11th ed. Buenos Aires: Editorial Losada, 1992.
———. *Los versos del capitán,* 5th ed. Buenos Aires: Losada, 1968.
———. *Nuevas odas elementales,* 3rd ed. Buenos Aires: Losada, 1971.
———. *Obras completas.* Vols. 1–5. Edited by Hernán Loyola. Barcelona: Galaxia Gutenberg, 1999.
———. *Odas elementales,* 6th ed. Barcelona: Bruguera, 1986.
———. *Ode to Common Things.* Translated by Ken Krabbenhoft. Boston: A Bulfinch Press Book, 1999.
———. *Para nacer he nacido.* Barcelona: Planeta, 1989.
———. *Residencia en la tierra.* Edited by Hernán Loyola. Madrid: Ediciones Cátedra, 1987.
———. *Residence on Earth,* translated by Donald D. Walsh. New York: New Directions, 1973.
———. *Tercera residencia,* 3rd ed. Barcelona: Editorial Seix Barral, 1983.
———. *Veinte poemas de amor y una canción desesperada,* 8th ed. Madrid: Alianza Editorial, 1995.
Ollman, Bertell. *Dialectical Investigations.* New York: Routledge, 1993.
Osorio Tejada, Nelson. "Literatura de posguerra: Renovación y Vanguardia." *Texto crítico* 24–25 (January–December 1982): 113–33.
———. "Para una caracterización histórica del vanguardismo literario hispanoamericano." *Revista iberoamericana,* no. 114–15 (January–June 1981): 227–54.
Palme Dutt, E. *Fascism and Social Revolution.* New York: International Publishers, 1934.
Parenti, Michael. *Blackshirts & Reds: Rational Fascism and the Overthrow of Communism.* San Francisco: City Lights Books, 1997.
Parry, J. H. *The Spanish Seaborne Empire.* New York: Alfred A. Knopf, 1966.
Paz, Octavio. *Cuadrivio,* 3rd ed. Mexico: Joaquín Mortiz, 1972.
———. *Itinerario.* Mexico: Fondo de Cultura Económica, 1993.
———. *Los hijos del limo.* Barcelona: Editorial Seix Barral, 1987.
Pérez Oyarzún, Fernando, and José Rosa Vera. "Cities Within the City: Urban and Arquitectural Transfers in Santiago de Chile." In Almandoz, *Planning,* 109–38.
Picón Salas, Mariano. *De la conquista a la independencia: tres siglos de historia cultural hispanoamericana,* 9th ed. Mexico: Fondo de Cultura Económica, 1985.
Poggioli, Renato. *The Theory of the Avant-Garde.* Cambridge, MA: Harvard University Press, 1968.
Polizzotti, Mark. *Revolution of the Mind: The Life of André Breton.* New York: Farrar, Strauss, and Giroux, 1995.
Pring-Mill, Robert. "El Neruda de las *Odas elementales.*" In *Coliloquio Internacional sobre Pablo Neruda (La obra posterior al Canto general),* edited by Alain Sicard, 261–300. Poitiers: Publications du Centre de Recherche Latino-Américaines de l'Université de Poitiers, 1979.
———. "La elaboración de la 'Oda a la cebolla'." In Flores, *Aproximaciones a Pablo Neruda,* 29–41.
Railton, Peter. *Facts, Values and Norms: Essays Toward a Morality of Consequence.* Cambridge: Cambridge University Press, 2003.

Rock, David, ed. *Latin America in the 1940s: War and Postwar Transitions.* Berkeley: University of California Press, 1994.

Rodríguez Fernández, Mario. "'Reunión bajo las nuevas banderas' o de la conversión poética de Pablo Neruda." In Flores, *Aproximaciones a Pablo Neruda,* 151–64.

Rodríguez Monegal, Emir. *Borges por él mismo.* Caracas: Monte Avila, 1980.

———. *El viajero inmóvil: Introducción a Pablo Neruda.* Buenos Aires: Losada, 1966.

——— and Enrico Mario Santí, eds. *Pablo Neruda.* Madrid: Taurus Ediciones, 1980.

Santí, Enrico Mario. *El acto de las palabras: Estudios y diálogos con Octavio Paz.* Mexico: Fondo de Cultura Económica, 1997.

———. Introduction to *Canto general,* by Pablo Neruda, 4th ed. Edited by Enrico Mario Santí. Madrid: Ediciones Cátedra, 1997.

———. *Pablo Neruda: The Poetics of Prophecy.* Ithaca, NY: Cornell University Press, 1982.

Sargent, Charles S. "Argentina." In Greenfield, *Latin American Urbanization,* 1–38.

Scarpaci, Joseph L. "Chile." In Greenfield, *Latin American Urbanization,* 116–17.

Schidlowsky, David. *Las furias y las penas: Pablo Neruda y su tiempo.* Berlin: Wissenschaftlicher Verlag, 2003.

Schopf, Federico. *Del vanguardismo a la antipoesía: ensayos sobre la poesía en Chile.* Santiago: LOM, 2000.

Schwarz, Roberto. *Misplaced Ideas: Essays on Brazilian Culture.* London: Verso, 1992.

Shirer, William L. *The Rise and Fall of the Third Reich.* New York: Fawcett Crest, 1960.

Sicard, Alain. *El pensamiento poético de Pablo Neruda.* Madrid: Editorial Gredos, 1981.

———. "La objetivación del fenómeno en la génesis de la noción de la materia." *Revista iberoamericana,* no. 82–83 (January–June 1973): 99–110.

Siqueiros, David. *Me llamaban el coronelazo: Memorias.* Mexico: Editorial Grijalbo, 1977.

Skidmore, Thomas E., and Peter H. Smith. *Modern Latin America,* 5th ed. Oxford: Oxford University Press, 2001.

Stonor Saunders, Frances. *The Cultural Cold War: The CIA and the World of Arts and Letters.* New York: The New Press, 1999.

Szabolscsi, Miklós. "La 'vanguardia' literaria y artística como fenómeno internacional." *Casa de las Américas* 74 (September–October 1972): 4–17.

Tarn, Nathaniel, ed. *Pablo Neruda: Selected Poems.* Boston: Houghton/Mifflin / Seymour Lawrence, 1990.

Teitelboim, Volodia. *Neruda,* 5th ed. Santiago: Ediciones BAT, 1991.

Thomas, Hugh. *The Spanish Civil War.* New York: Touchstone, 1986.

Thompson, E. P. *Witness Against the Beast: William Blake and the Moral Law.* New York: The New Press, 1993.

Vallejo, César. *Obra poética completa,* 2d ed. Edited and with an introduction by Enrique Ballón Aguirre. Caracas: Biblioteca Ayacucho, 1985.

Velloso, José Miguel. *Conversaciones con Rafael Alberti.* Madrid: Ediciones Sedmay, 1977.

Walsh, W. H. "Metaphysics." In Edwards, *Encyclopedia of Philosophy,* 300–07.

Warner, Robin. "The Politics of Pablo Neruda's *España en el corazón.*" In Bloom, *Pablo Neruda,* 233–41.

Weitz, Eric D. *Creating German Communism, 1890–1990: From Popular Protests to Socialist State.* Princeton, NJ: Princeton University Press, 1997.

Werth, Alexander. *Russia at War: 1941–1945.* New York: Carroll & Graf, 1964.

Yudin, Florence L. "The Dialectical Failure in Neruda's 'Las furias y las penas'." In Bloom, *Pablo Neruda*, 277–90.

Yurkievich, Saúl. "Mito e historia: dos generadores del 'Canto general.'" In Rodríguez Monegal and Santí, *Pablo Neruda*, 198–218.

Zhadanov, A. *Problems of Soviet Literature: Reports and Speeches of the First Soviet Writers' Congress*. Moscow-Leningrad: Cooperative Publishing Society of Foreign Workers in the USSR, 1935.

Index

Achugar, Hugo, 15
Adorno, Theodore, 25
Andrade, Oswaldo de, 266
Agosín, Marjorie, 112, 135–36, 286, 289
Aguirre Cerda, Pedro, 234
Ahmad, Aijaz, 24, 29, 38, 292 n. 14
Alazraki, Jaime, 196, 252–53
Alberti, Rafael, 51, 65–66, 68, 148, 169–71, 174, 195, 198
Aleixandre, Vicente, 65, 169
Alessandri, Arturo, 111
Alianza Democrática, 268
Allende, Salvador, 283
Alonso, Amado, 14, 24, 55, 59, 106, 111, 113, 158, 174
Altolaguirre, Manuel, 169
Aphrodite, 285–86
Aragon, Louis, 16–17, 68, 74–75
Asturias, Miguel Angel, 25
Asturias uprising, 169–71, 213, 224. *See also* Spanish civil war
Avant-garde (avant-gardist), 16, 42, 65–68, 70–72, 74, 76–79, 83–84, 87, 89, 95–96, 101, 103–5, 107, 112, 135, 149, 160, 172, 175–76 179–81, 266, 294 n. 3

Baudelaire, Charles, 81, 130, 162
Bécquer, Adolfo, 142
Belitt, Ben, 148
Bell-Villada, Gene, 24, 175, 297 n. 50
Benedetti, Mario, 77
Benjamin, Walter, 25, 130, 134
Bergamín, José, 169
Bhaskar, Roy, 269, 295 n. 7, 300 n. 7. *See also* Neruda, Pablo: moral realism
Blake, William, 14, 30–31, 161, 169
Bliss, Josie, 18, 38, 85, 110, 142–46, 155, 157, 162–66, 168–69, 171, 173, 246
Bloom, Harold, 37–38, 43, 49
Bourdieu, Pierre, 104, 179

Boyd, Richard, 292 n. 26. *See also* Neruda, Pablo: moral realism
Brecht, Bertolt, 80–81, 209, 290
Breton, André, 68–69, 74, 77. *See also* surrealism
Browder, Earl (Browderism), 267

Caballero, Largo, 204
Calvocoressi, Peter, and Guy Wint, 248
Camus, Albert, 77
Cardenal, Ernesto, 77
Cárdenas, Lázaro, 228–30, 245
Cardona Peña, Alfredo, 270
Carpentier, Alejo, 25
Carr, Barry, 229
Carril, Delia del, 23, 157, 169–71, 229, 234. 268
Caws, Mary Ann, 75
Cernuda, Luis, 65, 169
Chebel d'Appollonia, Ariane, 75
Chilean Communist Party (PCCH), 17, 23, 31, 42, 55, 63, 82, 104, 148,172, 267, 282. *See also* Neruda, Pablo: Chilean Communist Party
Chilean Socialist Party (PS), 234, 267–68
Claudín, Fernando, 259, 308 n. 8, 310 n. 69
Cold War, 13–14, 64, 266–90
Comintern (Communist Internacional), 82, 203, 228, 238, 240–41, 248, 258
Cominform (Communist Information Bureau), 281
Concha, Jaime, 15–16, 21, 25, 52–57, 64, 66, 94, 98, 107, 110–11, 113–15, 119, 123–24, 127, 145–47, 158, 226–27, 266, 284, 300 n. 50. *See also* Neruda, Pablo: marxist critics
Confederación Española de Derechos Autónomos (CEDA), 170
Conferación General de Trabajadores (CGT), 171

Conferación Nacional del Trabajo (CNT), 170–71, 192
Congress for Cultural Freedom, 22, 26
Corvalán, Luis, 281
Costa, René de: 14, 24, 42–47, 49–52, 98–99, 112, 124, 182–83, 201, 226, 236, 244, 263, 288–89; on Vicente Huidobro, 42–44; on Pablo Neruda, 43–47. *See also* Neruda, Pablo: liberal critics
Cruz-Coke, Eduardo, 268

Darío, Rubén, 30, 33–34, 164, 247, 252
DeMan, Paul, 37
Deutscher, Issac, 236, 282
Dialectical realism (dialectical method): 17, 32, 46, 52, 57–62, 66, 70, 71, 77–102, 158, 168, 178, 180–81, 202, 206, 209–17, 226–27, 244, 252–53, 256, 259, 261, 264, 266–67, 269, 271–90. *See also* Marx, Karl; Neruda, Pablo: espontaneidad dirigida, moral realism, marxism; Ollman, Bertell
Dimitrov, Georgi, 258
Durán, Manuel, 14, 24, 50–52. *See also* Neruda, Pablo: liberal critics

Eandi, Héctor, 112
Eagleton, Terry, 24, 29, 43
Ehrenburg, Ilya, 283
Einstein, Albert, 261, 263
Eliot, T. S., 43, 85, 112, 114
Eluard, Paul, 68, 79, 280

Faúndez, Julio, 111, 234, 267–69
Formalism, 24, 42–43. *See also* Neruda, Pablo: liberal critics
Forster, Merlin H., 65
Franco, Francisco, 171, 181, 189, 204, 237. *See also* Spanish Nationalists
Franco, Jean, 26
Fraser, Ronald, 193, 214
French Communist Party (PCF), 16, 69, 75, 104
Freud, Sigmund, 37
Furci, Carmelo, 297 n. 46, 311 n. 11

García Lorca, Federico, 51, 65, 68, 125, 136, 169, 198
García Márquez, Gabriel, 13
Gelman, Juan, 77

German Communist Party (KPD), 252, 257–61
German Social Democratic Party (SPD), 229, 241, 258–59
German Socialist Party (SP), 257–58
Gide, André, 232
Gilbert, Alan, 19, 164, 182. *See also* Neruda, Pablo: moral realism
God that Failed, The, 44
Goic, Cedomil, 92, 295–96 n. 18
Gómez Paz, Ana, 299 n. 70
González, Mike and David Treece, 46
González Tuñón, Raúl, 198
González Videla, Gabriel, 267–69, 280–81
Gorky, Maxim, 73
Graham, Helen, 214
Gramsci, Antonio, 149
Guillén, Nicolás, 25, 195

Hagenaar, María Antonieta (Maruca), 23, 132, 139
Heine, Heinrich, 261, 263
Helps, Arthur, 279
Hernández, Miguel, 25, 68, 169, 186, 195, 198
Hitler, Adolf, 22, 236, 248, 258. *See also* Nazi Germany
Hobsbawm, Eric, 238, 244, 251, 282
Huidobro, Vicente, 25, 42–44, 65, 104

Ibáñez, Carlos, 111
Italian Communist Party, 22–23

Jiménez, Juan Ramón, 30

Kauffman Doig, Federico, 298 n. 59
Kirkpatrick, F. A., 274, 277
Kirpotin, Valeri, 270
Korsch, Karl, 25

LaFaber, Walter, 281
Lakoff, George and Mark Turner, 293 n. 39
Larrea, Juan, 107
Las Casas, Bartolomé de, 279–80
Le Corbusier, 129
Lenin, V. I., 67, 70, 73, 215, 271–72
Lentricchia, Frank, 297 n. 50
Lezama Lima, José, 77
Loveluck, Juan, 299 n. 68

Lowell, Robert, 22
Löwy, Michael, 240
Loyola, Hernán, 15–16, 25, 57, 64, 85, 107, 110, 114, 124–25, 134, 137, 142, 148, 158, 169–70, 226–27. *See also* Neruda, Pablo: marxist critics
Lukács, Georg, 17–18, 25, 29, 70–74, 77, 79–80, 82, 97, 217, 226, 269–71. *See also* dialectical realism; Neruda, Pablo: realism; socialist realism

Marcuse, Herbert 156
Mariátegui, José Carlos, 25
Marshall Plan, 268, 281
Marvell, Andrew, 153
Marx, Karl, 37, 39, 41, 71, 91, 126, 211, 217, 298 n. 60, 302 n. 44, 307 n. 22 and Frederick Engels, 87, 249. *See also* dialectical realism; Neruda, Pablo: marxism
Mason, J. Alden, 298 n. 59
Mayakovsky, Vladimir, 81–82
McAdam, Alfred J., 182–84, 226
Mendelssohn, Felix, 261, 263
Molina, Enrique, 77
Montes, Hugo, 86
Mexican Communist Party (PCM), 36, 76, 228–34, 241
Mexican socialists, 229

Nazi Germany (Third Reich), 23, 203, 228–29, 232–33, 238, 244, 248–51, 253–55, 262, 264. *See also* Hitler, Adolf
Nazi invasion (of the USSR), 21, 244
Neruda, Pablo, alienation (solitude, disaffection, estrangement), 17–18, 38, 55–57, 59, 78, 84–85, 101, 105, 107–11, 119–21, 123, 125–26, 129, 132–35, 137, 141, 143, 147–49, 152, 155, 157–58, 161, 163, 169, 173–76, 178, 180, 182, 185, 195, 212, 225–27, 272–73, 275–76, 279; Asia (the Orient), 17–18, 30, 38, 55–57, 59, 78, 85, 102, 105–10, 114, 118, 126, 129, 136–37, 146–47, 149, 169, 172–73, 178, 180, 186, 188, 208, 217, 266, 279; anti-fascism, 21, 68, 105, 186, 204, 228–65, 267; Chilean Communist Party, 23–24, 31, 42, 55, 66, 82, 91, 234, 267–69, 280, 283, 305 n. 37 (*see also* Chilean Communist Party);

Comité de ayuda a Rusia en Guerra, 229, 245; Continental Cultural Congress, 283; criticism, 13–14, 22–64, 148; espontaneidad dirigida (guided spontaneity), 17, 65–103, 146, 209–17, 226–27, 266, 269, 272 (*see also* dialectical realism); Grupo hispanoamericano de ayuda a España, 217; liberal critics on, 14, 16, 18–19, 24, 26–52, 91–92, 158, 183–85, 191, 193–94, 200, 202, 208 (*see also* Costa, René; Durán, Manuel; Rodríguez Monegal, Emir; Safir, Marjory; Santí, Mario Enrico; Yurkievich, Saúl); Marxist critics on, 19, 52–64 (*see also* Concha, Jaime; Loyola, Hernán; Sicard, Alain); Marxism, 13–14, 18–19, 24–26, 29, 31–32, 34–35, 38–39, 42–46, 50–52, 55, 59, 64, 83, 91–92, 107, 168, 183, 185, 202, 230, 234, 251, 253, 267, 269, 289 (*see also* Marx, Karl); moral realism, 19–21, 56, 91, 105, 107, 161, 164, 168–71, 179–227, 231, 233, 235–36, 243–44, 249–51, 253, 263–64, 266, 271, 279, 299 n. 63 (*see also* Boyd, Richard; dialectical realism; Gilbert, Alan); realism, 18, 53–56, 58, 65–66, 70, 74–75, 77–79, 81–82, 93, 95, 104, 124, 135–37, 149, 158, 170, 180–81, 252, 266, 269–70, 288; Second Soviet Writers' Congress, 283; World Congress of Peace Supporters, 280; World Council for Peace, 280
—Works of: "A pesar de la ira," 279; "Agua sexual," 139–42; "Alianza (Sonata)," 152, 153, 157; "Almería," 307–8 n. 49; "Alturas de Macchu Picchu," 38–39, 42, 52, 74, 78, 82–93, 98, 100–102, 127–28, 152, 241, 254, 257, 272, 280; "Bartolomé de las Casas," 280; "Bombardeo/maldición," 189–92, 198; *Caballo verde para la poesía*, 146, 169; "La cabeza en el palo," 272–76; "Canto a las madres de los milicianos muertos," 242; "Canto a los ríos de Alemania," 44, 244, 253–57; "Canto a Stalingrado," 68, 235–44, 248, 252; *Canto general*, 21, 25, 30–33, 38–42, 45, 47–49, 51–52, 63, 66, 75, 82–83, 91–94, 107, 110, 115, 124, 126–28, 136, 149, 152, 180, 185, 188,

202, 209–10, 227, 241, 248, 252, 254, 264–67, 269–73, 279–80, 283–84, 289; "Canto sobre unas ruinas," 210–17; *Cien sonetos de amor,* 14, 143, 289; "Cómo era España," 242; *Confieso que he vivido,* 46; "El corazón magallánico," 279; "Duerme un soldado, 279; "Ercilla," 280; "Entrada a la madera," 123–29; *La espada escendida,* 38; *España en el corazón,* 18, 52, 78–79, 103, 149, 170, 172, 179–83, 187–88, 196, 217, 236, 238–39, 241–42, 245, 248; "España en el corazón" (in *Tercera residencia*), 105, 136, 146, 183, 186, 188, 217, 225–27, 256, 264; "España pobre por culpa de los ricos," 192, 202; *Estravagario,* 35, 46, 121, 158, 253, 289; "Explico algunas cosas," 195–202, 205, 239, 245, 247; "Las furias y las penas," 105, 162–64, 166–69, 172;"Galope muerto," 112–14, 118–20, 132, 145; "El hombre invisible," 62, 74, 82, 95–102; "Homenaje a Balboa," 272–73, 276–79; "Invocación," 187–88; "El joven monarca," 145; "Juntos nosotros," 145; "Llegada a Madrid de la brigada internacional," 203–10; "Madrid, 1937," 217–25; *Memorial de Isla Negra,* 290; "Naciendo en los bosques," 47, 100, 149, 158–63, 169, 300 n. 80; "Nuevo canto a Stalingrado," 68, 235, 245–53; "Oda al tomate," 284; "Oda a la cebolla," 284–89; "Oda a las cosas," 289; "Oda a la lavandera nocturna," 60–62; "Oda al tiempo," 289; "Oda a la vida," 152; "Oda con un lamento," 139, 141–42; *Odas elementales,* 16, 21, 45–46, 51, 60, 83, 93–102, 152, 264–65, 266–67, 272, 280, 283–84, 289–90; "El oro," 39–42, 272; "Paisaje después de una batalla," 216; *Para nacer he nacido,* 77; "Pido silencio," 121; *Plenos poderes,* 289; "Poema 1," 137–39; "Poema 20," 166–67; *Poesía política,* 283; "Que despierte el leñador," 202–3; 280; *Residencia en la tierra,* 16–18, 21, 23–24, 30, 38, 43, 55–59, 65–66, 78, 83–85, 87, 93, 96, 102–8, 110–13, 115, 118–21, 124, 126–29, 132, 134–37, 139, 141–43, 145–49, 152, 156, 158–59, 162, 165, 169–70, 172–75, 177–81, 184–86, 226–27, 245–46, 252, 266, 269; "Reunión bajo las nuevas banderas," 105, 149, 172–75, 179; "Sonata y destrucciones," 119, 122, 132, 151; "Tango del viudo," 146, 164–65, 167; *Tercera residencia,* 16–17, 21, 23–24, 44, 46–47, 63, 66, 82–83, 100, 102–5, 107–8, 119, 147–49, 152–53, 158, 163–64, 179–87, 202, 205, 210, 217, 225–27, 233, 235, 244, 251–53, 260, 263–64, 266, 289; "El tigre," 165; *uvas y el viento, Las,* 46, 46, 283–84; "Vals," 149–52; *Veinte poemas de amor y una canción desesperada,* 14, 16, 50, 78, 98, 124, 137–38, 140–41, 159–60, 178, 246; *Los versos del capitán,* 14, 16, 143, 284; "Walking around," 78, 85, 116, 129–37, 154, 156, 303 n. 65
Nietzsche, Friedrich, 37

Ollman, Bertell, 50, 295 n. 7, 304–5 n. 33, 306 n. 14, 307 n. 39. *See also* dialectical realism; Marx, Karl

Palme Dutt, E., 258, 308 n. 8, 310 n. 69
Parenti, Michael, 13–14, 232
Parra, Nicanor, 77
Parry, J.H., 274
Partido Radical (Chile), 233–34
Partido Revolucionario Mexicano (PRM or Partido Revolucionario Institucional, PRI), 228
Paz, Octavio, 16, 33, 34–37, 42, 229, 231–33, 235, 244–45; avant-garde, 65–66, 75–77; left-wing politics, 65–66, 75–77, 230–33; Santí on, 34–37. *See also* avant-garde; Mexican Communist Party; Spanish civil war; surrealism; Trotsky.
Pedrarias Dávila (Pedro Arias de Avila), 274–75
Perse, Saint John, 30
Picón Salas, Mariano, 279
Pisarev, Dmitri, 270
Pizarro, Francisco, 275
Polizzotti, Mark, 68
POUM (Partido obrero de unificación marxista), 76, 230, 232
Popular Front, 21, 171–72, 191, 193, 196, 225, 228, 233–34, 236, 240–41, 251, 259

"postino, Il" (The Postman), 22
Pring-Mill, Robert, 94, 96, 288

Quevedo, Francisco, 169

RAPP (Russian Association of Proletarian Writers), 270
Radek, Karl, 67–68, 74–75
Reinoso, Luis, 281
Reverdy, Pierre, 77
Revueltas, José, 232
Rimbaud, Arthur, 14, 30
Rivera, Diego, 228
Rodríguez, Mario, 179
Rodríguez Monegal, Emir, 14, 24, 26–34, 44, 46–47, 49–51, 55, 91, 122, 124, 158, 180, 182, 244; on Jorge Luis Borges, 26–29, 34; on Pablo Neruda, 26–34; on Soviet Union, 27–28. *See also* Neruda, Pablo: liberal critics
Rojas, Gonzalo, 42
Rosa, Albertina, 138
Rosales, Luis, 94
Rousseau, Henri, 37, 191

Sabines, Jaime, 77
Safir, Margery, 14, 24, 50–52. *See also* Neruda, Pablo: liberal critics
Santí, Enrico Mario, 14, 24, 34–39, 42–44, 46–47, 49–50, 76, 92, 110, 112–13, 119, 135, 153, 180, 226, 251–52; on Octavio Paz, 34–37, 42; on Pablo Neruda, 35–42
Santos González Vera, José, 109
Sargent, Charles S., 129
Schidlowsky, David, 23–24
Schopf, Federico, 113–14
Schwarz, Roberto, 266
Shirer, William L., 310 n. 69
Sicard, Alain, 15, 21, 25, 56–64, 66, 107, 110, 115, 118, 124, 146–47, 158, 163–64, 168, 226–27, 266, 293 n. 29, 302 n. 38
Siqueiros, David Alfaro, 229–33, 245, 263
Skidmore, Thomas E. and Peter H. Smith, 129
Skármeta, Antonio, 22
Socialist countries, 13, 283–84
Socialist realism, 16, 65–81, 83, 100, 180, 270, 294 n. 4. *See also* Zhdanov, Andrei
Soviet Union, 13–14, 16, 19–20, 25, 36, 66, 67, 69–71, 73–76, 80, 81–83, 181, 229, 232–36, 240, 242–45, 248–51, 264–65, 268–69, 280–83, 309 n. 19; and the XXth Party Congress, 23, 46; First Soviet Writers Congress, 67. *See also* Stalin, Joseph; World War II
Spanish Civil War, 18, 35–36, 63, 65–66, 75–76, 78, 102, 105–6, 168–70, 172, 180–83, 185, 187–95, 202, 210–11, 217, 229–32, 236, 244, 247, 263–65
Spanish Communist Party (PCE), 20, 36, 76, 171, 193, 204, 230–32, 264
Spanish Nationalists (Falangists), 16, 18, 83, 181–85, 188, 191, 200–2, 204–5, 208–9, 213, 215, 217, 219–20, 222, 224–25, 238, 241–42
Spanish Republicans, 65, 75–76, 83, 105, 107, 149, 170, 183–85, 187–91, 193–94, 196, 200–5, 208–9, 213–17, 219–22, 224–25, 229–30, 232, 234, 237, 252
Spanish Socialist Party, 185, 193–94, 208
Stalin, Joseph, 66–69, 73–76, 80, 229, 232–34, 236, 238, 244–45, 248, 251, 282
Stalin Prize, 22, 46, 74
"Stalinism," 23, 66, 69, 76. *See also* Stalin, Joseph
Stonor Saunders, Frances, 22
Surrealism, 16–17, 65, 66, 68, 70–71, 74–79, 135–37, 140, 180. *See also* Breton, André

Tarn, Nathaniel, 148
Tavernier, René, 22
Teitelboim, Volodia, 18, 58, 110, 137, 228, 230–31, 234, 281
Thälmann, Ernest, 258–59, 261
Thomas, Hugh, 204, 219
Trotsky, Leon (Trotskyism), 36, 68–69, 76–77, 228–33, 245, 259

Unión General de Trabajadores (UGT), 171, 192
Urrutia, Matilde, 22, 137, 146, 164–65, 280

Valéry, Paul, 134
Vallejo, César, 25, 65, 68, 146, 185–86, 195, 217
Vargas Llosa, Mario, 23
Villamediana, Juan de Tarsis, 169

Warner, Robin, 183, 190, 226
Weitz, Eric D., 257, 259
Werth, Alexander, 235, 244, 251
Whitman, Walt, 81
World War II, 16, 21, 68, 77, 203, 231–33, 237, 244, 251, 264–65, 267–68, 281–82. *See also* Nazi Germany; Soviet Union

Yrigoyen, Hipólito, 129, 132
Yudin, Florence L., 164, 168, 180
Yurkievich, Saúl, 14, 47–51, 295–96 n. 18. *See also* Neruda, Pablo: liberal critics

Zhdanov, Andrei, 67, 75. *See also* socialist realism